A 3-level grammar embodiment project: visualizing grammar and writing practice

Level 3

Grammar ViSTA

DARAKWON

Grammar
ViSTA Level 3

지은이 김해자, 손의웅, 최현진
펴낸이 정규도
펴낸곳 (주)다락원

초판 1쇄 발행 2018년 4월 5일
초판 9쇄 발행 2024년 2월 20일

편집 이희경
디자인 조수정, 박은비, 김나경
일러스트 이경
영문 감수 Amy L. Redding, Michael A. Putlack

다락원 경기도 파주시 문발로 211
내용문의 (02)736-2031 내선 503
구입문의 (02)736-2031 내선 250~252
Fax (02)732-2037
출판등록 1977년 9월 16일 제 406-2008-000007호

ISBN 978-89-277-0827-8 54740
       978-89-277-0824-7 54740(set)

---

http://www.darakwon.co.kr
다락원 홈페이지를 방문하시면 상세한 출판정보와 함께
동영상강좌, MP3자료 등 다양한 어학 정보를 얻으실 수 있습니다.

A 3-level grammar embodiment project:
visualizing grammar and writing practice

Level 2

Grammar ViSTA

정답과 해설

DARAKWON

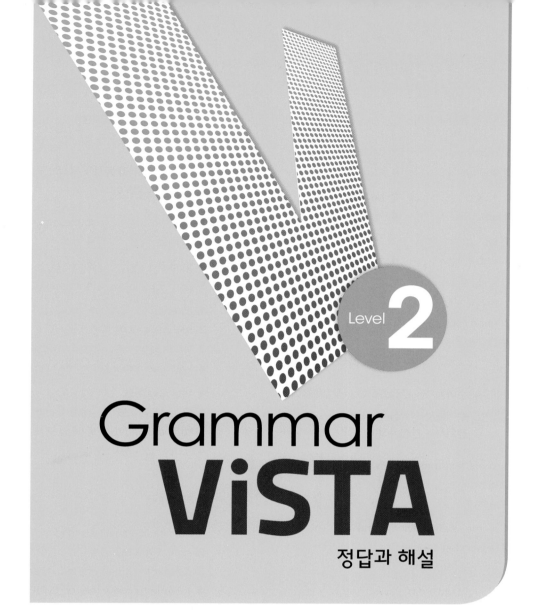

Grammar ViSTA

Level **2**

정답과 해설

- 본 교재
- workbook

Chapter 01 문장의 형태

GP Practice 01 동사 + 보어 　　　p. 13

A 　1 pretty 　　　2 became
　　3 sounds like 　4 cold

B 　1 looks 　　　　2 taste
　　3 smell like 　　4 feels

C 　1 look great 　　　2 smells sweet
　　3 turn yellow 　　4 sounded excited

D 　1 quiet / 명사·형용사
　　2 happy / 형용사
　　3 good / 형용사
　　4 O / 명사, ~처럼 보이다

GP Practice 02 수여동사 + 간접목적어 + 직접목적어
GP Practice 03 수여동사 + 직접목적어 + 전치사 + 간접목적어 　　　p. 15

A 　1 me a text message
　　2 gave 　　　3 for
　　4 ask 　　　　5 to

B 　1 some useful advice to me
　　2 a wooden seesaw for the children
　　3 his secret to me

C 　1 bought his mom a silver ring
　　2 teaches me Chinese
　　3 showed us a funny video clip

D 　1 O / ~에게 ~를, 간목 + 직목
　　2 to / ~를 ~에게, to
　　3 of / ~를 ~에게, of
　　4 for / ~를 ~에게, for

GP Practice 04 동사 + 목적어 + 목적격보어 　　　p. 17

A 　1 to sit 　　　　2 to believe
　　3 him a rich man 　4 happy

B 　1 Ⓑ 　2 Ⓐ 　3 Ⓒ 　4 Ⓓ

C 　1 told me to keep the change
　　2 call this stone Alien
　　3 allow me to skip breakfast
　　4 keeps the baby's head warm

D 　1 excited / 형용사
　　2 to get / to + 동사원형
　　3 healthy / 형용사
　　4 to repeat / to + 동사원형

GP Practice 05 사역·지각 동사 + 목적어 + 목적격보어 　　　p. 19

A 　1 keep 　　　　2 playing
　　3 to rest 　　　4 ride

B 　1 think 　　　　2 drive
　　3 burn (burning) 　4 to arrive

C 　1 listened to Judy talk (talking)
　　2 had me pay back
　　3 let us join
　　4 watched a monkey climb (climbing)

D 　1 feel / 동사원형
　　2 O, cut / 동사원형, 동사원형 + -ing
　　3 to find, find / to + 동사원형, 동사원형
　　4 to fix / to + 동사원형

Grammar & Writing 　　　p. 20

A 　1 sounds like an amazing idea
　　2 makes me relaxed
　　3 bought his grandmother a bracelet
　　4 told me to chew the food well
　　5 cooked a nice dinner for her guest
　　6 made me wash my sneakers

B 　1 calls me a princess
　　2 smells delicious
　　3 lent Mike my bicycle
　　4 asked him to set up
　　5 saw two boys leave (leaving)
　　6 gave me three tickets
　　7 made the boy feel

C 　1 dance (dancing) on the stage
　　2 to read her blog
　　3 shake (shaking) suddenly
　　4 wear his new hat

D 　1 make your trip exciting
　　2 give you some tips
　　3 send it to me
　　4 help you to travel

Actual Test p. 22

1 ④ 2 ① 3 ④ 4 ⑤ 5 ① 6 ②,⑤ 7 ①,③
8 ③ 9 ① 10 ② 11 ④ 12 ④ 13 ③ 14 ④
15 ③ 16 to 17 walking 18 set 19 to solve
20 ④ 21 ⑤ 22 ③ 23 read (reading) 24 to
follow 25 advised us to save energy 26 found
paper-folding very fun 27 let 28 talking → to talk,
to + 동사원형 29 to → for, 3형식, for 30 This novel
makes me think about nature

1 sound는 주격보어로 형용사를 사용함.

2 [show + 직접목적어 + to + 간접목적어]

3 expect는 목적격보어로 [to + 동사원형]을 사용함.

4 [buy + 직접목적어 + for + 간접목적어]

5 [make + 목적어 + 동사원형]: 목적어를 ~하도록 만들다

6 see는 목적격보어로 동사원형과 [동사원형 + -ing]를 사용함.

7 [teach + 간접목적어 + 직접목적어] = [teach + 직접목적어 + to + 간접목적어]

8 [bring + 간접목적어 + 직접목적어] = [bring + 직접목적어 + to + 간접목적어]

9 감각동사 look, taste는 주격보어로 형용사를 사용함.

10 want는 목적격보어로 [to + 동사원형]을 사용하고 make는 목적격보어로 형용사를 씀.

11 ①, ②, ③, ⑤ 5형식 문장 [주어 + 동사 + 목적어 + 목적격보어], ④ 4형식 문장 [주어 + 동사 + 간접목적어 + 직접목적어]

12 look like 뒤에는 명사가 와야 함.

13 tell, ask, get, want는 목적격보어로 [to + 동사원형]을 사용하고, have는 목적격보어로 동사원형을 사용함.

14 [give, send, hand, offer + 직접목적어 + to + 간접목적어], [make + 직접목적어 + for + 간접목적어]

15 advise는 목적격보어로 [to + 동사원형]을 사용하고 have, make, help, watch는 목적격보어로 동사원형을 사용함.

16 [lend + 간접목적어 + 직접목적어] = [lend + 직접목적어 + to + 간접목적어]

17 지각동사 see는 목적격보어로 동사원형과 [동사원형 + -ing] 둘 다 사용 가능함.

18 [get + 목적어 + to + 동사원형] = [have + 목적어 + 동사원형]

19 help는 목적격보어로 동사원형과 [to + 동사원형] 둘 다 사용 가능함.

20 make는 목적격보어로 동사원형을 사용하므로 feel을 써야 함.

21 allow는 목적격보어로 [to + 동사원형]을 사용하므로 to enter를 써야 함.

22 ⓑ의 get은 목적격보어로 [to + 동사원형]을 사용하므로 to carry를 써야 하고, [tell + 직접목적어 + to + 간접목적어]이므로 ⓓ의 for는 to로 바꿔야 함.

23 지각동사 see는 목적격보어로 동사원형과 [동사원형 + -ing]

24 tell은 목적격보어로 [to + 동사원형]을 사용함.

25 advise는 목적격보어로 [to + 동사원형]을 사용함.

26 find는 목적격보어로 형용사를 사용함.

27 let은 '~가 ~하도록 허락하다'라는 의미이며 목적격보어로 동사원형을 사용함.

28 5형식 동사 want의 목적격보어는 [to + 동사원형]이다.

29 3형식 동사로 쓰인 cook 뒤의 어순은 [직접목적어 + for + 간접목적어]이다.

30 make는 목적격보어로 동사원형을 사용함.

Grammar Mapping p. 26

① 주격보어 ② They became friends. ③ 간접목적어
④ 직접목적어 ⑤ He made me a cake. ⑥ 직접목적어
⑦ 전치사 ⑧ 간접목적어 ⑨ He made a cake for me.
⑩ 목적격보어 ⑪ She keeps her room clean.

Chapter 02 시제

GP Practice 06 현재완료
GP Practice 07 과거와 현재완료 p. 29

A 1 lost   2 eaten
  3 has been to 4 in
  5 have you

B 1 has been   2 has gone to
  3 has forgotten

C 1 Have you tried the recipe
  2 enjoyed the magic show
  3 has not gotten enough sleep

D 1 met / 과거, 과거
  2 has met / has
  3 have not come / have + not + p.p.
  4 O / Have + 주어

GP Practice 08 현재완료 용법 p. 31

A 1 have seen   2 since
  3 yet   4 been

B 1 have learned 2 has worked
  3 have, lived   4 has, won

3

C
1 has been busy since last week
2 have just finished dinner
3 has erupted many times
4 hasn't saved enough money

D
1 O / 방금 막 끝냈다, has + just + p.p.
2 have worked / ~해 왔다, 완료
3 has gone / ~로 가버렸다, gone
4 for / ~ 동안 계속, for, 기간

Grammar & Writing

p. 32

A
1 has never touched my pet snake
2 has had the symptom for two months
3 have moved four times since 2015
4 How long has she studied
5 painted *The Starry Night* in
6 have never been to Tokyo

B
1 have tracked the lion since
2 hasn't opened his birthday gifts
3 has sponsored poor children since
4 has changed diapers for her baby nine times
5 broke her promise yesterday
6 Why have people left

C
1 played, has played
2 arrived, has, arrived
3 lived, has lived
4 ran, has run

D
1 visited Spain
2 he hasn't
3 has visited
4 has been to, two times (twice)

Actual Test

p. 34

1 ⑤ **2** ③ **3** ③ **4** ⑤ **5** ④ **6** ① **7** ⑤ **8** ⑤
9 ② **10** ⑤ **11** ① **12** ⑤ **13** ① **14** has eaten
15 has gone to **16** ③ **17** ② **18** ④ **19** been
20 have not (haven't) named, yet **21** played
22 has played the piano for **23** have deleted the files by mistake **24** Have you ever ridden in
25 haven't **26** has collected figurines for three years **27** have been to the zoo many times
28 have died → died, 과거, 과거 **29** not has →

has not, has + not + p.p., 아직 ~안 했다 **30** This company has built seventeen buildings since last year

1 과거부터 시작된 일이 현재에 영향을 미칠 때 현재완료시제를 씀.
2 '~전에'란 의미의 과거부사 ago는 과거시제와 사용함.
3 현재완료 의문문 [Have / Has + 주어 + p.p. ~?]
4 '~해 봤다'라는 뜻으로 과거부터 현재까지의 경험을 나타내므로 현재완료시제를 씀.
5 과거부터 현재까지 계속된 일은 현재완료시제를 씀.
(since: ~부터 지금까지 계속)
6 ②의 yet은 '아직'이란 의미로 부정문과 사용하고 ③은 현재까지 계속해 온 것이므로 현재완료 [have + p.p.]를 쓰고 ④는 have를 써야 하고 ⑤의 when은 과거의 시점이므로 과거시제를 씀.
7 과거부터 현재까지 계속된 일은 현재완료시제를 씀.
(for + 기간: 과거부터 지금까지 ~ 동안)
8 과거부사인 [in + 년도]는 과거시제와 함께 쓰고, [since + 시점]은 과거시점부터 지금까지 계속되는 것이므로 현재완료와 함께 씀.
9 과거부터 지금까지 계속되는 일을 묻는 현재완료 의문문은 [의문사 + have + you + p.p. ~?]이다.
10 3인칭 단수주어의 완료시제 의문문 [Has + she + p.p. ~?]
11 [have gone to ~]는 '~에 가버리고 여기 없다'란 의미이므로 1인칭 주어와 사용할 수 없음.
12 '어젯밤'은 과거부사이므로 과거시제와 사용함.
13 [since + 과거시점]은 '~ 이래로 지금까지'의 뜻으로 현재까지 계속해 온 일을 나타냄.
14 과거부터의 일이 현재에 완료된 것은 [have / has + p.p.]이다.
15 '~로 가버리고 여기에 없다'는 '결과'를 나타내는 현재완료를 씀.
16 보기와 ③은 경험, ①과 ②는 완료, ④는 계속적 용법, ⑤는 '가버리고 없다'란 의미로 '결과'를 나타냄.
17 보기와 ②는 과거부터 현재까지 계속해 온 일, ①은 여러 번 해 본 경험, ③은 해 본 적 없는 경험, ④는 한 번 가 본 경험, ⑤는 막 끝낸 완료를 나타냄.
18 3인칭 주어의 완료시제는 [has + p.p.], '~에 가 본 적 있다'는 [have been to + 장소 명사], since(~이후로)는 현재완료시제와 함께 사용함.
19 [has been at]은 '지금까지 계속 ~에 있어 왔다'(계속)을 뜻하고, [has been to]는 '지금까지 ~에 가 본 적 있다'(완료)를 의미함.
20 '아직 ~하지 않았다'는 [주어 + have / has + not + p.p. + yet]이다.
21 과거부사 then은 과거시제와 사용함.
22 과거부터 현재까지 '~ 동안 계속해 오다'는 [has + p.p. + for + 기간]이다.

(21–22) 해석

우리 엄마는 1988년에 피아노를 배우기 시작하셨다. 엄마는 그때 거의 매일 피아노를 치셨다. 이제, 약 30년 동안 피아노를 연주해 오셨다.

23 과거부터의 일이 현재에 완료되는 것은 [have + p.p.]이다.

24 경험을 묻는 현재완료 의문문 [Have / Has + 주어 + ever + p.p. ~?]

25 완료시제 의문문에 대한 부정 대답은 [No, 주어 + haven't (hasn't)]이다.

26 과거부터 현재까지 '~ 동안 계속해 오다'는 [have / has + p.p. + for + 기간]이다.

27 '~에 가 본 적이 있다'는 [have been to + 장소]이다.

28 ago는 과거를 의미하는 부사여서 과거시제와 사용함.

29 현재완료 부정문의 어순은 [has + not + p.p.]이고 의미는 '아직 ~ 안 했다'이다.

30 [since + 과거시점]은 '~ 이래로 지금까지'를 뜻하므로 과거부터 현재까지 계속해 온 일을 나타냄.

Grammar Mapping p. 38

① 있는 ② 없는 ③ have / has + p.p. ④ not ⑤ just
⑥ 경험 ⑦ never ⑧ 계속 ⑨ ~에 갔다 왔다
⑩ have gone to ⑪ 기간 ⑫ 과거시점

Chapter 03 조동사

GP Practice 09 can, may, will p. 41

A			
1 May		**2** Would	
3 can		**4** turn	
5 might			

B			
1 may		**2** could	
3 Will			

C			
1 may be		**2** are able to dive	
3 Can you bring			

D			
1 May / 허락, May		**2** work / 동사원형	
3 would / 가능, would			
4 be able to / 불가능, be able to			

GP Practice 10 must, have to, should p. 43

A			
1 had to		**2** didn't have to	
3 should		**4** must	

B			
1 must		**2** didn't have to	
3 must not		**4** had to	

C		
1 Should I say sorry		
2 You must not swim		
3 don't have to feel		
4 must be the only child		

D		
1 should not / 조동사 + not		
2 have to / 불가능, have to로		
3 don't have to / ~할 필요 없다, don't		
4 must be busy / 동사원형, be + 형용사		

GP Practice 11 had better, used to, would like to p. 45

A			
1 had better		**2** to join	
3 used to		**4** had better not	

B			
1 had better		**2** used to	
3 would		**4** would like to	

C		
1 used to live on land		
2 had better not pop		
3 would, like to visit		
4 had better break		

D		
1 visit / 습관, 동사원형		
2 had / 충고, had		
3 had better not / 뒤, not		
4 to order / to + 동사원형		

Grammar & Writing p. 46

A	
1 your uncle used to be very cute	
2 had better not eat	
3 must not cut in line	
4 We will have to compete	
5 That may not be a dog	
6 doesn't have to thank	

B	
1 must be over 100 meters tall	
2 It may rain today	
3 will become a mother next year	
4 You should not make fun of	
5 cannot fill	
6 was able to move the table	
7 had better get some rest	

C			
1 has to		**2** used to	

3 Can   **4** had better

5 must

D
  1 You had better add some salt to it
  2 had better buy the ticket online
  3 You had better not wear the cap

Actual Test p. 48

1 ① **2** ④ **3** ⑤ **4** ④ **5** ② **6** ⑤ **7** ① **8** ⑤
9 ⑤ **10** ④ **11** ④ **12** ① **13** must **14** would
15 can't **16** ② **17** ④ **18** ⑤ **19** ④ **20** was
not (wasn't) able to write **21** is going to hold
22 You don't have to try on a bigger size
23 I had better recycle this gift box **24** ③
25 must **26** would like to **27** used to **28** will
popular → will be popular, be + 형용사 **29** can →
be able to, 불가능, be able to **30** don't had better
→ had better not, 뒤, not **31** You will have to
enter the correct password

1   must는 강한 추측을 나타내는 조동사로 '~임에 틀림없다'를 의미함.

2   [used to]는 '~하곤 했다'란 의미로, 현재와는 다른 과거의 상태나 행동을 의미함.

3   '~할 수 있을 것이다' 의미는 [will be able to]이다. 조동사 뒤에 바로 조동사가 올 수 없음.

4   [had better + 동사원형]: ~하는 것이 낫다

5   [would like to]: ~하고 싶다

6   '~할 필요가 없다'는 [doesn't have to]이고, [must not]은 '~하면 안 된다'를 의미함.

7   [would like to + 동사원형]: ~하고 싶다

8   [be going to]는 미래 표현으로 '~할 예정이다'를 의미함.

9   '~해야 한다'의 must는 [have (has, had) to]로 대체함.

10   can't: ~할 수 없다

11   [had better]: ~하는 것이 낫다(충고, 권유)

12   보기의 문장과 ①은 강한 추측(~임에 틀림없다)이고, 나머지 must는 의무를 나타냄.

13   must 용법 중 ⓐ는 '~해선 안 된다'(금지), ⓑ는 '~임에 틀림없다'(강한 추측)이다.

14   ⓐ의 [would you like to]는 '~하고 싶다'이고, ⓑ의 would는 '~하곤 했다'이다.

15   can의 용법 중 부정형으로 ⓐ는 '~하면 안 된다', ⓑ는 '~할 수 없다'이다.

16   ①, ③, ④, ⑤는 약한 추측(~일지도 모른다)이고, ②는 허락(~해도 된다)을 의미함.

17   [don't have to]는 '~할 필요 없다'로 '~하면 안 된다'와 의미가 다름.

18   상대에게 요청할 때 쓰는 조동사는 can (could), will (would)이고, [May I ~?]는 본인이 상대에게 허락을 구하는 표현임.

19   [used to]는 '~하곤 했다'로 현재와 다른 과거의 상태나 행동을 의미함.

20   [could not]은 [was not able to]와 같은 쓰임으로 '~할 수 없었다'를 의미함.

21   [will = be going to]: ~할 것이다

22   [don't have to + 동사원형]: ~할 필요 없다

23   [had better + 동사원형]: ~하는 것이 낫다

24   ⓑ는 [had better] '~하는 것이 낫다' ⓒ는 [조동사 + 동사원형]이므로 [should be careful] ⓓ는 [주어 + used to] '~하곤 했었다'가 필요함.

25   [must + 동사원형]: ~임에 틀림없다(강한 추측)

26   [would like to + 동사원형]: ~하고 싶다

27   [used to]는 '이전에는 ~이었다'로 현재와 다른 과거의 상태나 행동을 의미함.

28   조동사 뒤에는 동사원형이 오므로 [조동사 + be + 형용사] 어순이다.

29   [조동사 + 조동사]는 불가능하므로 will 뒤의 can은 [be able to]로 사용함.

30   [had better]의 부정형은 바로 뒤에 not을 붙임.

31   조동사 뒤에 조동사가 바로 올 수 없으므로 미래 조동사 will 뒤에 '~해야 한다'란 의미의 [have to]를 사용함.

Grammar Mapping p. 52

① 동사원형   ② 조동사 + not   ③ be able to
④ ~해 주시겠어요?   ⑤ 허락   ⑥ ~일지도 모른다
⑦ 강한 추측   ⑧ had to   ⑨ don't have to   ⑩ must not
⑪ had better not   ⑫ ~하곤 했다

Chapter 04   수동태

GP Practice 12   능동태와 수동태 p. 55

A
  1 bakes   **2** is spoken
  3 threw   **4** appeared
  5 was made

B
  1 is grown in many countries by
  2 was painted by
  3 was written by me

C **1** were destroyed by

2 is used   **3** was broken by

D **1** solved / 풀리는, be동사 + p.p.

2 is loved / 사랑받는, be동사 + p.p.

3 arrived / 도착하다, 불가능

4 were / are / were

GP Practice 13 수동태의 시제
GP Practice 14 수동태의 여러 형태 p. 57

A **1** wasn't   **2** are

3 be posted   **4** are being eaten

B **1** cannot be copied   **2** Was, returned

3 is being watched

C **1** When was, ordered

2 were not taken by

3 will be caught by

D **1** Was / Was + 주어 + p.p.

2 being / is being

3 be / be + p.p.

4 was not / be동사 + not

GP Practice 15 동사구 수동태
GP Practice 16 by 이외의 전치사를 쓰는 수동태 p. 59

A **1** with   **2** about

3 in   **4** to

B **1** was looked after   **2** will be carried out

3 were brought up

C **1** is known for   **2** was pleased with

3 are turned on

D **1** with / with   **2** at / at

3 was put off / put off

4 from / from

Grammar & Writing p. 60

A **1** was changed by this book

2 The cello was being played

3 You will be satisfied with

4 is the learning material uploaded

5 was laughed at by everyone

6 am tired of the same lunch menu

B **1** was not delivered

2 was the ninth planet discovered

3 is being built

4 can be collected

5 are satisfied with

6 was carried out by researchers

C **1** was made by Andrew

2 are caused by speeding

3 is being read by young women

4 was not (wasn't) seen by them

D **1** is covered with

2 is taught by

3 is disappointed with

4 is looked after by

Actual Test p. 62

1 ⑤ **2** ③ **3** ① **4** ④ **5** ③ **6** ④ **7** ① **8** ②
9 ③ **10** ⑤ **11** was laughed at by **12** was surprised at **13** ② **14** ① **15** ⑤ **16** are answered **17** was not (wasn't) seen **18** was taken care of **19** ⑤ **20** ④ **21** ① **22** was made by **23** be pulled **24** ③ **25** ⓐ wrote ⓑ written **26** must opened → must be opened, 열리다, be + p.p. **27** for → with, 느끼다, with **28** is known for its beautiful scenery **29** was built **30** visited

1 기계가 발명되는 것이므로 수동태 문장. 과거시제 수동태는 [was / were + p.p.]이다.

2 서점이 발견되는 것이므로 수동태 문장이다. 조동사가 있으므로 [조동사 + be + p.p.]이다.

3 [be interested in]: ~에 관심이 있다

4 시는 누군가에 의해 쓰여지는 것이므로 수동태 문장이다. 수동태의 부정형은 [be동사 + not + p.p.]이다.

5 동사구 look after의 수동태는 [be동사 + looked after + by 행위자]로 표현함.

6 의문사 없는 의문문의 수동태는 [Be동사 + 주어(능동태의 목적어) + p.p. + by 행위자(능동태의 주어) ~?]

7 현재시제 수동태 [주어(능동태의 목적어) + am / are / is + p.p. + by 행위자(능동태의 주어)]

8 사진이 찍혀지는 것이므로 수동태 [was + taken]의 형태가 돼야 함.

9 disappear(사라지다)는 자동사이므로 수동태 불가함.

10 현재진행시제 능동태 [주어(수동태의 by행위자) + am / are

7

/ is + 동사원형 + -ing + 목적어(수동태의 주어)]

11 [be laughed at by]: ~에게 비웃음을 당하다

12 [be surprised at]: ~에 놀라다

13 ⓐ는 '우리가 아이들을 구하는 것'이므로 능동태이고, ⓑ는 '아이들이 구해지는 것'이므로 수동태임.

14 ⓐ는 be satisfied with(~에 만족하다), ⓑ는 의문사 없는 의문문의 수동태이므로 [Be동사 + 주어 + p.p. ~?]이다.

15 who가 주어인 의문문의 수동태는 [By whom + be동사 + 주어 + p.p. ~?] '누구에 의해서 ~되었니?'이다.

16 주어로 쓰인 questions는 동사 answer(대답하다)의 대상이므로 수동태 [be동사 + p.p.]이다.

17 주어 sunrise는 동사 see(보다)의 대상이므로 수동태이고 수동태의 부정형은 [be동사 + not + p.p.]이다.

18 주어 sister는 동사구 [take care of]의 대상이므로 수동태로 [be동사 + taken care of]이다.

19 read의 과거분사는 read이다.

20 의문사가 있는 문장의 수동태는 [의문사 + be동사 + 주어 + p.p. ~?]

21 수동태에서 행위자가 일반인이거나 내용상 불분명하고 중요하지 않은 경우에는 [by + 행위자] 생략 가능함.

22 주어로 쓰인 This movie는 동사 make의 대상이므로 수동태이고 과거형은 [was / were + p.p.]이다.

23 주어로 쓰인 tooth는 동사 pull(뽑다)의 대상이고, 조동사의 수동태는 [조동사 + be + p.p.]이다.

24 ⓑ와 ⓒ가 맞는 표현이고, ⓐ는 주어가 복수이므로 수동태 [were + built], ⓓ는 현재진행시제 수동태로 [is being chased], ⓔ는 동사구 look after의 수동태로 [be동사 + looked after + by]이다.

25 ⓐ는 주어 who가 동사 write의 주체이므로 능동태이고, ⓑ는 《해리포터》라는 책이 write(쓰다)의 대상이므로 수동태임.

26 조동사가 있는 수동태는 [조동사 + be + p.p.]이다.

27 [be동사 + disappointed with]: ~에 실망하다

28 [be동사 + known for]: ~로 유명하다

29 Eiffel Tower가 과거에 지어진 것이므로 수동태 과거 [was + p.p.]이다.

30 주어(에펠타워)가 '여전히 방문된다'이므로 수동태 [is + p.p.]이다.

해석 (29~30)
파리의 에펠타워는 1889년에 지어졌다. 프랑스 사람들은 이것을 싫어했다. 일부는 이것이 '굴뚝'처럼 생겼다고 말했다. 하지만 이것은 요즈음 전 세계에서 오는 많은 관광객들에 의해 방문되어진다.

Grammar Mapping p. 66

① be동사 + p.p. ② not ③ Be동사 + 주어 ④ 조동사
⑤ was / were ⑥ will be ⑦ being ⑧ in, at, with

Chapter 05 to부정사

GP Practice 17 to부정사의 명사적 쓰임 p. 69

A	1 to have	2 to invite
	3 to keep	4 to hear
B	1 where to get off	2 how to pose
	3 It, to spend our vacation on the moon	
C	1 is to find	2 It, to read
	3 agreed to hold	
D	1 It / 가주어, It	2 to have / to부정사
	3 not / not, 앞	4 when / 언제, when

GP Practice 18 to부정사의 형용사적 쓰임 p. 71

A	1 to eat	2 to explain
	3 to feed	4 to succeed
B	1 in	2 about
	3 on	4 with
C	1 two books to return	
	2 nothing interesting to watch	
	3 the best way to release	
D	1 to break / 뒤, 동사원형	
	2 O / 명사 + to부정사	
	3 to live in / live in a house, in	
	4 nothing special / 명사 + 형용사	

GP Practice 19 to부정사의 부사적 쓰임 p. 73

A	1 ②, 눈을 보게 되어서
	2 ③, 먹기에
	3 ⑤, (결국) 가수가 되다
	4 ①, 게임을 이기기 위해
	5 ④, 비행기를 사는 것을 보니
B	1 ⑧ 2 ⓒ 3 ⓓ 4 ⓐ 5 ⑤
C	1 was sad to break up with
	2 lived to be
	3 is difficult to answer
D	1 happy / 감정형용사
	2 easy / 형용사
	3 to buy / to부정사
	4 to solve / to부정사

GP Practice 20 to부정사의 의미상의 주어
GP Practice 21 to부정사를 이용한 구문

p. 75

A 1 of 2 for
   3 too 4 strong enough
   5 her

B 1 strong enough to lift
   2 too short to reach
   3 so, that, could

C 1 wise of him to take
   2 for my English teacher to speak
   3 was hot enough to fry

D 1 for him / 없으면, for
   2 of her / 있으면, of
   3 old enough /~하기에 충분한, 형용사 + enough
   4 O / ~하기엔 너무 ~한, too + 형용사

Grammar & Writing

p. 76

A 1 decide to become an artist
   2 a partner to work with
   3 too small for us to sleep in
   4 how to throw a frisbee
   5 is to open next month
   6 time to make

B 1 His plan was to read
   2 silly of you to spend
   3 are to fill out
   4 when to turn off
   5 where to go
   6 for him to have
   7 so young that she couldn't remember

C 1 too late to watch
   2 of them to save
   3 to live in
   4 how to wrap
   5 to meet my Korean fans

D 1 boring, to listen to
   2 difficult, to solve
   3 fun, to ride

Actual Test

p. 78

1 ⑤ **2** ⑤ **3** ③ **4** ⑤ **5** ⑤ **6** ④ **7** ① **8** ③
9 ② **10** ④ **11** for me **12** to remember **13** ③
14 ④ **15** ① **16** ③ **17** to read **18** enough to
see **19** ③ **20** something important to tell
21 must be brilliant to understand **22** ⑤ **23**
not to wake the baby **24** for you to watch **25**
what to buy **26** too lazy to move **27** end →
to end, 목적어, to부정사 **28** enough kind → kind
enough, ~하기에 충분한, 형 + enough **29** for → of,
있으면, of **30** Ten minutes is too short to take a
break.

1 앞에 성품형용사가 없을 때 to appear를 행하는 주체는 [for + 목적격]의 형태임.

2 [where + to부정사]: 어디로 ~할지를

3 [가주어 it, 진주어 to부정사]

4 [형용사 / 부사 + enough + to부정사]: ~하기에 충분히 ~한

5 [명사 + to부정사 + 전치사]의 형태로 '같이 살 ~'을 의미함.

6 [too 형용사 + to부정사]: 너무 ~해서 ~할 수 없다

7 [-thing으로 끝나는 대명사 + 형용사 + to부정사]

8 to부정사의 형용사 용법 [명사 + to부정사 + (전치사)]

9 [의문사 + to부정사] 형태에서 의문사 why는 사용 불가함.

10 [forget + to부정사]는 명사적 용법으로 '~하는 것을 잊다'를 의미하고, 나머지는 부사적 용법의 '목적'으로 '~하기 위해'를 뜻함.

11 성품형용사가 없으면 to부정사의 의미상 주어는 [for + 목적격]이다.

12 [가주어 It, 진주어 to부정사]

13 성품형용사가 앞에 없을 때 to부정사의 의미상 주어는 [for + 목적격]이다.

14 [가주어 it, 진주어 to부정사]

15 성품형용사(nice)가 앞에 있을 때 to부정사를 행하는 의미상 주어는 [of + 목적격]이고, ②, ③, ④, ⑤와 같이 성품형용사가 없을 때는 [for + 목적격]이다.

16 형용사 용법은 ⓐ와 ⓓ, 부사적 용법은 ⓒ, 명사적 용법은 ⓑ와 ⓔ이다.

17 [be동사 + to부정사] 용법 중 '의무'로 '~해야 한다'를 의미함.

18 [형용사 / 부사 + enough to부정사]: ~하기에 충분히 ~한

19 [how + to부정사]: ~하는 방법

20 [대명사 ~thing + 형용사 + to부정사]

21 to부정사의 부사적 용법의 판단의 근거는 [(판단)동사 + to부정사]이다.

22 [명사 + to부정사 +전치사]의 형태로 [a chair to sit on]이 되어야 함.

23 to부정사의 부정은 [not + to부정사]의 형태로 '~하지 않기 위해'를 의미함.

24 to부정사를 행하는 의미상 주어는 [for + 목적격]이다.

25 [의문사 what + to부정사]의 형태로 '무엇을 ~할지'를 의미함.

26 [so + 형용사 + that + 주어 + can't ~] = [too + 형용사 + to부정사]

27 agree는 목적어로 to부정사를 가짐.

28 '~하기에 충분한'의 어순은 [형용사 + enough + to부정사]이다.

29 성품형용사가 있으면 의미상주어는 [of + 목적격]이다.

30 [too + 형용사 / 부사 + to부정사]: ~하기에 너무 ~한

Grammar Mapping
p. 82

① to + 동사원형 ② 명사 ③ 형용사 ④ 부사 ⑤ 주어
⑥ 목적어 ⑦ 의문사 ⑧ 명사 수식 ⑨ 목적 ⑩ 감정의 원인
⑪ 형용사 수식 ⑫ for ⑬ of ⑭ 충분히 ⑮ enough to
⑯ 너무 ⑰ to

Chapter 06 동명사

GP Practice 22 동명사의 명사적 쓰임
GP Practice 23 동명사의 관용적 쓰임
p. 85

A　**1** designing　**2** Cooking
　3 making　**4** playing
　5 watching

B　**1** taking a shower　**2** building ships
　3 making noise

C　**1** is busy collecting　**2** Raising three sons
　3 keeps changing

D　**1** Sleeping / 주어, 동명사
　2 singing / 동명사
　3 not / not, 앞
　4 building / 동명사

GP Practice 24 동명사와 to부정사
p. 87

A　**1** to call　**2** to ride, riding
　3 to study　**4** playing

B　**1** to see　**2** waiting
　3 to wear　**4** to take

C　**1** gave up moving　**2** expect to see
　3 started to snore　**4** stop bothering

D　**1** O, keeping / to부정사, 동명사
　2 to find / ~하려고 노력하다, to부정사
　3 worrying / ~하는 것을, 동명사
　4 O / ~했던 것을, 동명사

Grammar & Writing
p. 88

A　**1** keep looking at the clock
　2 stopped barking at me
　3 learned to ride a horse
　4 has difficulty remembering
　5 mind moving your foot
　6 spent three hours doing his homework

B　**1** wanted to do volunteer work
　2 is fond of raising reptiles
　3 enjoy watching bullfighting
　4 forgot borrowing a (one) dollar
　5 tried to find an exit
　6 expects to find out more

C　**1** calling　**2** Eating
　3 painting　**4** staying
　5 to invite　**6** buying

D　**1** Taking a sand bath
　2 building a sandcastle
　3 running along the beach

Actual Test
p. 90

1 ④ **2** ② **3** ① **4** ④ **5** ② **6** ④ **7** ② **8** ④
9 ③ **10** ④ **11** ③ **12** to say **13** ⑤ **14** ① **15** ③
16 making **17** seeing **18** walking **19** ③
20 eating **21** drawing **22** ⑤ **23** ⑤ **24** avoided
answering his call **25** gave up growing my hair
26 forgot counting **27** was afraid of hurting
28 speaking → to speak, 말할 것을, to부정사 **29** to
move → moving, ~하던 것을, 동명사 **30** We are
looking forward to meeting you next month

1 '~먹는 것'을 주어로 할 때 동명사 주어(동사원형 + -ing) 또는 to부정사 주어(to + 동사원형) 가능함.

2 expect는 목적어로 to부정사(to + 동사원형)를 취함.

3 전치사 for의 목적어로 동명사를 씀.

4 '~했던 것을 기억하다'의 remember는 목적어로 동명사를 취함.

5 '~하던 것을 멈추다'의 stop은 목적어로 동명사를 취함.

6 ①, ②, ③, ⑤는 동사 또는 전치사 뒤의 목적어로 쓰였고, ④는 보어로 쓰임.

7 [practice + 동명사]: ~하는 것을 연습하다

8 [enjoy + 동명사]: ~하는 것을 즐기다

9 ⓑ의 '~타는 것'은 동명사 또는 to부정사 주어가 와야 하고, ⓓ의 avoid는 동명사 목적어를 갖는 동사이다.

10 [remember + to부정사]: ~할 것을 기억하다
[forget + to부정사]: ~할 것을 잊다

11 [keep + 동명사]: 계속 ~하다
[hope + to부정사]: ~할 것을 희망하다

12 hate는 동명사와 to부정사 모두를, decide는 to부정사를 목적어로 갖는 동사이다.

13 plan은 목적어로 to부정사를 취함.

14 mind는 목적어로 동명사를 갖는 동사이다.

15 '설거지 하는 것'을 주어로 할 때 동명사 주어 또는 to부정사 주어가 가능함.

16 [stop + 동명사]: ~하는 것을 멈추다

17 [remember + 동명사]: ~했던 것을 기억하다

18 [enjoy + 동명사]: ~하는 것을 즐기다

19 [forget + to부정사]: ~할 것을 잊다
[forget + 동명사]: ~했던 것을 잊다

20 [try + not + to부정사]는 '~하지 않기 위해 노력하다'이고 [avoid + 동명사]는 '~하는 것을 피하다'이다.

21 [be good at + 동명사]: ~하는 것을 잘하다

22 '책들을 읽는 것'은 books가 주어가 아니라 동명사가 주어이므로 단수 취급하여 동사 is를 사용함.

23 [try + to부정사]는 '~하기 위해 노력하다'이다. to부정사를 부정할 때는 not, never를 바로 앞에 씀.

24 [avoid + 동명사]: ~하는 것을 피하다

25 [give up + 동명사]: ~하는 것을 포기하다

26 [forget + 동명사]: ~했던 것을 잊다

27 [be afraid of + 동명사]: ~하는 것을 두려워하다

28 [remember + to부정사]: ~할 것을 기억하다

29 [stop + 동명사]: ~하던 것을 멈추다

30 [look forward to + 동명사]: ~하는 것을 고대하다

Grammar Mapping

p. 94

① 동사원형 + -ing ② 주어 ③ 목적어 ④ 동사 ⑤ 전치사
⑥ 보어 ⑦ go -ing ⑧ be busy -ing ⑨ 동명사
⑩ finish, keep ⑪ to부정사 ⑫ expect, decide ⑬ 없는
⑭ hate, begin ⑮ 있는 ⑯ ~할 것을 ⑰ ~했던 것을
⑱ 노력하다 ⑲ ~해 보다

Chapter 07 분사

GP Practice 25 현재분사와 과거분사
GP Practice 26 분사의 형용사적 쓰임
p. 97

A	**1** used		**2** singing	
	3 boiled		**4** playing	
B	**1** sleeping		**2** made	
	3 running		**4** wounded	
C	**1** her lost necklace			
	2 wearing sunglasses			
	3 rolling stone			
	4 filled with			
D	**1** dancing / 진행, 현재			
	2 cooked / 수동, 과거			
	3 O / 완료, 과거			
	4 scarf made in Italy / 뒤			

GP Practice 27 감정을 나타내는 분사
GP Practice 28 현재분사와 동명사
p. 99

A	**1** satisfied		**2** surprising	
	3 excited		**4** shocking	
B	**1** 세탁기, 동명사		**2** 잠자는 미녀, 현재분사	
	3 수영하는 것, 동명사		**4** 지루하게 하는, 현재분사	
C	**1** waiting room		**2** driving test	
	3 was not shocked		**4** sounds interesting	
D	**1** boring / 느끼게 하는, 현재			
	2 surprised / 느낀, 과거			
	3 O / 느끼게 하는, 현재			
	4 running / 달리는 용도, 동명사			

GP Practice 29 분사구문
p. 101

A	**1** Waiting		**2** Buying	
	3 Hearing		**4** Not wanting	
B	**1** Wearing these glasses			
	2 Losing an arm			
	3 Being tired			
C	**1** After the boys took off			
	2 When he left the stage			
	3 Because she loved Eric			

D   **1** 삭제 / 주어, 함

     2 Hearing / 부사절, 동사원형 + -ing

     3 Not knowing / not, 앞

     4 O / 접속사

Grammar & Writing

p. 102

A   **1** Seeing a dragonfly

     2 a skirt worn by Scottish men

     3 She was surprised

     4 After heating glass

     5 feel exhausted

     6 Although being fast in water

B   **1** sleeping beauty

     2 Loving rap music

     3 was disappointed with my drawing

     4 While driving

     5 is very touching

     6 look worried

C   **1** 부사절   **2** 접속사

     3 접속사   **4** 주어

     5 동사원형

D   **1** Following our boat

     2 Opening a book

     3 Washing her jacket

Actual Test

p. 104

1 ⑤   **2** ⑤   **3** ③   **4** ⑤   **5** ④   **6** ④   **7** ①   **8** ①   **9** ④
10 ⑤   **11** ①   **12** ③   **13** singing   **14** shocking
15 Reading   **16** ③   **17** ⑤   **18** ②   **19** ①   **20** made
21 satisfied   **22** ③   **23** Being young   **24** Finishing
her meal   **25** Taking this shortcut   **26** sitting in
the first row   **27** written by the writer   **28** Feeling
frightened   **29** keeping → kept, 수동, 과거   **30** She
→ 생략, 주어

1 '흐르고 있는 물'이므로 진행 상태를 나타내는 현재분사를 씀.

2 '손을 흔드는 여성'이므로 진행 상태를 나타내는 현재분사를 씀.

3 '나무로 만들어진 장난감 말'이므로 수동 상태를 나타내는 과거분사를 씀.

4 축구 기술이 '놀라게 하는' 감정을 유발하므로 현재분사를 씀.

5 '샤워하면서'라는 의미로 시간을 나타내는 분사구문(= While he took)을 씀.

6 '웃고 있는 남자'는 진행 상태를 나타내는 현재분사를 씀.

7 계획이 '흥미롭게 하는' 감정을 유발하므로 현재분사를 씀.

8 '잘려진 케이크'이므로 수동 상태를 나타내는 과거분사 cut을 씀.

9 분사구문 만들 때, 부사절의 ① 접속사를 생략하고 ② 주절과 같은 주어를 생략하고 ③[동사원형 + -ing]의 형태로 바꿈.

10 분사구문의 부정형은 not을 분사구문 앞에 씀.

11 ①은 '안전벨트를 매서'이므로 이유를 나타내는 분사구문 ②는 '비록 아파도' ③은 '좌회전을 하면' ④는 '처음 보았을 때' ⑤는 '도착했을 때'를 의미함.

12 '~하는 동안'을 의미하는 분사구문이며, 부사절은 [While S + V ~]이다.

13 '노래방' 용도를 나타내는 동명사와 '노래하는 중인' 진행을 나타내는 현재분사를 씀.

14 '~ 충격을 주는' 감정을 유발하므로 현재분사를 씀.

15 '~ 읽으면서 (동시 동작)'을 나타내는 분사구문이므로 현재분사를 씀.

16 ③의 '기다리는 중'은 진행을 의미하는 현재분사이며, 나머지는 동명사로 ①은 '탈의실' ②는 '운전교육' ④는 '대기실' ⑤는 '세탁기'를 의미함.

17 ⑤는 be동사의 [동사원형 + -ing] 형태의 동명사로 '~가 되는 것'을 의미하며 나머지는 현재분사이다.

18 ⓑ의 '구입된 바지'는 과거분사이므로 [buying → bought] ⓒ에서 분사구문의 부정은 [not + 동사원형ing]이므로 [Don't having → Not having] ⓔ는 '먹어서'이므로 [Eat → Eating]이다.

19 '과녁을 맞힌다면'의 뜻으로 조건을 나타냄.

20 '~로 만들어진 신발'이므로 수동을 나타내는 과거분사를 씀.

21 '만족한 감정을 느낀' 것이므로 과거분사를 씀.

22 '실망을 시키는' 감정을 유발하는 것이므로 현재분사를 씀.

23 분사구문을 만들 때 부사절은 ① 접속사를 생략하고 ② 주절과 같은 주어를 생략하며 ③[동사원형 + -ing] 형태로 바꿈.

24 분사구문을 만들 때 부사절은 ① 접속사를 생략하고 ② 주절과 같은 주어를 생략하며 ③[동사원형 + -ing] 형태로 바꿈.

25 '만약 ~한다면'을 나타내는 분사구문이며, 부사절은 [If you take this shortcut]이다.

26 '앉아 있는'은 진행을 나타내므로 [현재분사 + 수식어구]가 명사를 뒤에서 수식함.

27 '쓰여진'은 수동을 나타내므로 [과거분사 + 수식어구]가 명사를 뒤에서 수식함.

28 '느낄 때'를 나타내는 현재분사를 씀. 부사절은 [When it feels ~]이다.

29 동물원에 '갇힌'은 수동의 의미이므로 과거분사를 씀.

30 분사구문에서 주절과 같은 부사절의 주어는 생략함.

Grammar Mapping

p. 108

① 동사원형 + -ing   ② ~하고 있는   ③ (감정을) 갖게 하는

④ 동사원형 + -ed ⑤ ～당하는 ⑥ (감정을) 느낀
⑦ 명사 수식 ⑧ 분사 ⑨ 분사 + 수식어구 ⑩ 주어
⑪ 목적어 ⑫ ～하는 용도의 ⑬ 부사절 ⑭ 접속사 ⑮ 주어
⑯ 동사원형 + -ing

Chapter 08 대명사

GP Practice 30 재귀대명사
p. 111

A
1 yourself 2 ourselves
3 herself 4 themselves

B
1 목적어, 불가 2 강조, 가능
3 목적어, 불가 4 강조, 가능

C
1 take care of yourself
2 enjoyed themselves
3 Help yourself to
4 wrote this thank-you letter herself

D
1 ourselves / 같음, 재귀대명사
2 me / 다름, 인칭대명사
3 o / 주어, 그녀가 직접
4 himself / 혼자서, himself

GP Practice 31 부정대명사 one, another, other
GP Practice 32 one, another, other(s)의 표현
p. 113

A
1 it 2 another
3 ones

B
1 the other 2 another
3 others 4 the others

C
1 one 2 One, the other
3 another, the other 4 Some, others

D
1 it / 같음, it
2 O / 다른, one
3 the other / the other
4 others / others

GP Practice 33 부정대명사 all, both
GP Practice 34 부정대명사 each, every
p. 115

A
1 Both 2 All

B
3 Each 4 Every

B
1 has 2 is
3 is 4 are

C
1 Each had 2 All the questions
3 Every journey 4 both of them live

D
1 is / 단수 2 O / 단수
3 All / all 4 has / 단수, 단수

Grammar & Writing
p. 116

A
1 all the dishes herself
2 Each of the girls is
3 ordered a new one
4 Some like K-pop, the others don't
5 did not read either of
6 was angry with herself

B
1 some visit, others go
2 neither of the two cars
3 everything about himself
4 Both of us have
5 Could you play some
6 is the other

C
1 another, the other
2 the other
3 Some, others

D
1 Some, The others, herself, Each, all, themselves

Actual Test
p. 118

1 ⑤ **2** ② **3** ① **4** ③ **5** ④ **6** ④ **7** ⑤ **8** ④
9 ② **10** ① **11** ⑤ **12** ④ **13** ③ **14** Each, each
15 themselves **16** Both **17** help **18** Every
19 by **20** ②, ⑤ **21** ③ **22** ④ **23** Each of them
is **24** usually talks to herself **25** another
26 The others **27** Each **28** other → the other,
the other **29** her → herself, 같음, 재귀대명사
30 Some are Koreans, and the others are
Canadians.

1 앞에 언급한 불특정한 명사를 지칭하는 부정대명사이다.
2 불특정 다수에서 몇몇은 [some ～], 다른 몇몇은 [others ～]이다.
3 [between ourselves]: 우리끼리 이야기지만

4 셋 중에 하나는 one, 다른 하나는 another, 나머지 하나는 the other이다.

5 Every student(모든 학생), every Sunday(일요일마다)

6 앞에 언급한 '스커트'와 같은 종류의 또 다른 하나는 another를 사용하여 [another + 단수명사]를 씀.

7 every 뒤에는 [of + 복수명사]를 쓸 수 없고 [every + 단수명사]를 씀.

8 재귀대명사가 주어를 강조할 때 주어 뒤 또는 문장 끝에 위치함.

9 [beside oneself]: 제정신이 아닌

10 ①은 [other + 복수명사] ②는 불특정한 연필이므로 one ③은 또 다른 한 조각을 의미하므로 another ④는 불특정한 다수에서 [some ~, others ~] ⑤는 셋 이상의 창문이므로 [all of them]이다.

11 Becky와 나는 '우리'이므로 재귀대명사는 ourselves이다.

12 재귀대명사는 주어(she)를 강조하고, 셋 이상의 '모두'는 all이다.

13 둘 중 하나는 one, 나머지는 the other, [Let's ~]의 생략된 주어는 we이므로 재귀대명사는 ourselves이다.

14 [each + of + 복수명사]와 [each + 단수명사]를 씀.

15 학생들을 강조하고 그들 자신을 나타내는 재귀대명사는 themselves이다.

16 [both + (of) + 복수명사]는 '둘 중에 둘 다'를 의미함.

17 [help oneself to]: 마음껏 먹다

18 [every + 단수명사]

19 alone(혼자서) = by oneself

20 enjoy yourself, hide himself, teach himself의 재귀대명사는 목적어 역할을 함.

21 ③은 강조 용법으로 쓰인 재귀대명사이므로 생략 가능함.

22 ④는 앞에서 언급한 불특정한 명사를 대신하는 대명사가 들어가야 하므로 one, 그 외에는 인칭대명사 it을 사용함.

23 [each of + 복수명사 + 단수동사]

24 [talk to oneself]: 혼잣말을 하다

25 셋 중 하나는 one, 다른 하나는 another, 나머지 하나는 the other이다.

26 셋 중 하나는 one, 나머지 모두는 the others이다.

27 [each + of + 복수명사 + 단수동사]

28 네 마리의 코알라 중 셋을 제외한 나머지는 the other이다.

29 주어와 목적어가 같으므로 재귀대명사를 사용함.

30 제한된 범위(10명) 중 몇몇은 some, 나머지는 the others이다.

Grammar Mapping
p. 122

① himself ② ourselves ③ yourselves
④ themselves ⑤ 재귀용법 ⑥ 목적어 ⑦ 불가 ⑧ 강조
⑨ 가능 ⑩ 홀로 ⑪ 스스로 ⑫ another ⑬ other
⑭ the other ⑮ 다른 하나는 ⑯ others

Chapter 09 비교표현

GP Practice 35 원급, 비교급, 최상급
p. 125

A	**1** worse	**2** most slowly
	3 smooth	**4** more popular
B	**1** smaller	**2** luckiest
	3 large	**4** important
C	**1** as healthy as	
	2 as light as a feather	
	3 earlier than me	
	4 the worst day	
D	**1** faster / 비교급 + than	
	2 poor / as + 원급 + as	
	3 O / better	
	4 the biggest / the + 최상급	

GP Practice 36 원급을 이용한 표현
GP Practice 37 비교급을 이용한 표현
GP Practice 38 최상급을 이용한 표현
p. 127

A	**1** hotter and hotter	**2** a lot
	3 The less	**4** girls
B	**1** as gently as	**2** as long as
	3 the funniest	**4** the more
C	**1** as carefully as possible	
	2 two times as heavy as	
	3 The faster, the earlier	
	4 the most delicious pizzas	
D	**1** much / 훨씬, much	
	2 O / the + 비교급	
	3 runners / 복수	
	4 twice as / 배수사 + as	

Grammar & Writing
p. 128

A	**1** not as crowded as
	2 much heavier than mine
	3 as often as possible
	4 the most fashionable person
	5 the best movie that I have ever seen
	6 The closer, the faster

B　　**1** as hard as

　　　　2 cleverer than cats

　　　　3 as soon as possible

　　　　4 The hotter, the more

　　　　5 the best painting he has ever painted

　　　　6 one of the most endangered animals

C　　**1** younger than

　　　　2 the oldest

　　　　3 heavy

　　　　4 the heaviest

　　　　5 three times as heavy

　　　　6 younger than

D　　**1** as old as　　　　　**2** later than

　　　　3 the cheapest　　　　**4** as much as

Actual Test

p. 130

1 ④ **2** ① **3** ② **4** ⑤ **5** ④ **6** ② **7** ① **8** ⑤
9 ④ **10** ④ **11** ⑤ **12** ② **13** ① **14** ⑤ **15** ①
16 ② **17** more **18** much **19** more and more
popular in Asia **20** were much bigger than
elephants' tusks **21** ① **22** ④ **23** two times
as long as **24** more important **25** the hardest
26 The more, the happier **27** better and better
28 worst → worse, 비교급 **29** game → games,
것들, 복수 **30** Brian is the most talkative student
in my class

1 [little – less - least]

2 [as + 원급 + as]: ~만큼 ~한

3 [비교급 + than] 형식이다. fast의 비교급은 faster이다.

4 [the + 최상급 + 명사 + (that) + 주어 have (has) ever
p.p.] 형식이다. -ful로 끝나는 형용사의 최상급은 [most + 원
급]이다.

5 [the + 최상급 + 명사 + 장소부사]: ~에서 가장 ~한

6 원급 비교 부정은 [not + as + 원급 + as]이다.

7 very는 원급을 강조하고 much, even, far, a lot은 비교급
을 강조함.

8 ⑤번을 제외하고 모두 Jin이 Robert보다 '작다'라는 표현임.

9 [a lot + 비교급 + than]: ~보다 훨씬 더 ~한

10 [the + 최상급 + 명사 + (that) + 주어 have / has ever p.p.]:
지금껏 ~한 것 중 가장 ~한

11 [as + 원급 + as + possible] 또는 [as + 원급 + as + 주어 +
can]: 가능한 ~한(하게)

12 [비교급 and 비교급]: 점점 더 ~한

[much + 비교급]: 훨씬 더 ~한

13 [the + 최상급 + 명사 + in 장소]: ~에서 가장 ~한
[one + of + the + 최상급 + 복수명사]: 가장 ~한 것들 중
하나

14 [A not as 원급 as B]: A는 B만큼 ~하지 않다

15 [as 원급 as 주어 + can (could)] 문장에서 동사 drove의 시
제가 과거이므로 could를 사용함.

16 ①은 as wise as ③은 the sweeter ④는 soon ⑤는
more interested가 올바른 표현임.

17 [the 비교급 ~ the 비교급]은 '~하면 할수록 더 ~하다' 의미
함. often의 비교급은 more often이다.

18 [much + 비교급]: 훨씬 더 ~한
[twice as much as]: ~의 두 배 많이

19 [비교급 + and + 비교급]: 점점 더 ~한

20 매머드의 상아와 코끼리의 상아는 같은 대상을 비교한 것이다.
[much + 비교급]: 훨씬 더 ~한

21 ② thinner → thinnest: [the 최상급 + of 명사]
③ scientist → scientists: [one of the 최상급 + 복수명사]
④ More → The more: [the 비교급, the 비교급]
⑤ very → much: 비교급 강조는 much(even, far, a lot)
이다.

22 '더 좋다'는 good의 비교급인 better를 사용함.

23 [배수사 + 비교급 + than] = [배수사 + as + 원급 + as]

24 [비교급 + than]: ~보다 더 ~하다

25 [the + 최상급]: 가장 ~한(하게)

26 [the 비교급 ~, the 비교급 ~]: ~하면 할수록 더 ~하다

27 [비교급 and 비교급]: 점점 더 ~하는

28 than 앞에는 bad의 비교급을 사용함.

29 [one of the 최상급 + 복수 명사]: 가장 ~한 것들 중 하나

30 [the + 최상급 + in + 장소]: ~에서 가장 ~한

Grammar Mapping

p. 134

① 배수사　② possible　③ 두 개　④ than　⑤ much
⑥ 비교급 and 비교급　⑦ the 비교급　⑧ 셋 이상　⑨ in / of
⑩ one　⑪ have / has ever p.p.

Chapter 10　접속사

GP Practice 39 시간 접속사

GP Practice 40 이유 접속사　　　p. 137

A　　**1** when　　　　　　**2** because

　　　　3 falls　　　　　　**4** before

B **1** While   **2** after
     3 since   **4** because

C **1** Because (As, Since) she is color-blind
     2 when you sneeze
     3 Since it was late
     4 until it turned into

D **1** until / 할 때까지, until
     2 after / 온 후에, after
     3 Because / 부드러워서, Because
     4 arrives / 부사절, 현재

GP Practice 41 조건 접속사
GP Practice 42 양보 접속사
GP Practice 43 명령문 and / or
p. 139

A **1** if   **2** Unless
     3 if   **4** though

B **1** Ⓑ **2** Ⓓ **3** Ⓐ **4** Ⓒ

C **1** if you don't eat it quickly
     2 (Al)though Evan doesn't know Korean
     3 and you can save trees
     4 Unless you are a member

D **1** Although / 나지만, Although,
     2 삭제 / if~not, 사용불가
     3 does / 부사절, 현재
     4 O / and S + V, 그러면

GP Practice 44 접속사 that
GP Practice 45 상관접속사
p. 141

A **1** That   **2** nor
     3 It   **4** both
     5 that

B **1** either, or   **2** as well as
     3 not only, but (also)

C **1** that he was rich
     2 Both, and
     3 It, that a beaver can cut down

D **1** It / It
     2 that / that + S + V
     3 nor / nor, 둘 모두 아닌
     4 talks / B

Grammar & Writing
p. 142

A **1** when he rides long distances
     2 before you use the machine
     3 unless I raise my voice
     4 Although it rained a lot
     5 Neither Emily nor Olivia
     6 or you will get wet

B **1** Though (Although) the teacher is not friendly
     2 before you click "Next"
     3 that bananas don't grow
     4 either go home, wait for me here
     5 because (as/since) it has
     6 Unless you wash your hands

C **1** If you buy this bike online
     2 while others are speaking
     3 Even though it is the rainy season
     4 My sister as well as I

D **1** – ① – ⓓ   **2** – ④ – ⓐ
     3 – ③ – ⓒ   **4** – ② – ⓑ

     1 because the Wi Fi doesn't work well
     2 until you came back
     3 if you buy this shampoo
     4 while he was listening to music

Actual Test
p. 144

1 ④ **2** ④ **3** ④ **4** ① **5** ③ **6** ③ **7** ① **8** ④
9 ⑤ **10** ② **11** ⑤ **12** or **13** As, as **14** ④
15 ⑤ **16** ⑤ **17** as well as **18** that
19 Although, Though, Even though **20** after
21 neither **22** ② **23** ④ **24** and the game will start **25** if it loses balance **26** either "Yes" or "No" **27** since there was a full moon
28 Neither Jim nor I am good at cooking
29 will come → comes, 시간, 현재 **30** doesn't wear → wears 또는 Unless → If, if ~ not, 사용 불가

1 while: ~하는 동안

2 although: 비록 ~이지만

3 unless: ~하지 않는다면

4 [both A and B]: A, B 둘 모두

5 [that S + V]가 명사절로 목적어 역할을 할 때 '주어가 ~하는 것' 의미함.

6 ③은 '~한 이래로'이고 나머지는 '~ 때문에'이다.

7 시간 부사절(~할 때까지)과 조건 부사절(~한다면)은 미래시제 대신 현재시제를 사용함.

8 ④는 because / as / since(이유 접속사)이고 나머지는 though / although(양보 접속사)이다.

9 ⑤는 As → (Al)though가 되어야 함.

10 ② will rain → rains: 시간과 조건 부사절에서는 미래시제 대신 현재시제를 사용함.

11 ⑤ are → am: 상관접속사 [B as well as A]가 주어로 쓰일 때 B에 동사를 일치시킴.

12 [either A or B]는 'A, B 둘 중 하나'이고 [명령문, or ~]는 '~해라, 아니면 ~할 것이다'이다.

13 as: ① (이유) ~ 때문에 ② (시간) ~할 때

14 ④는 의문사 '언제'이고 나머지는 접속사 '~할 때'이다.

15 ⑤는 '~ 때문에'이고 나머지는 '~할 때'이다.

16 '둘 모두를 부정' 할 때는 [neither A nor B]를 씀.

17 [B as well as A]: A뿐만 아니라 B도 역시

18 know의 목적어는 명사절 [that S + V]이다.

19 Although, Though, Even though가 답으로 가능함. 모두 '비록 ~이지만'을 의미함.

20 시간의 전후를 나타내는 접속사로 after(~한 후에), before(~하기 전에)를 씀.

21 [neither A nor B]: A도 B도 둘 다 아닌

22 [either A or B]: A와 B 둘 중 하나

23 ⓑ의 [both A and B]는 항상 복수이므로 (has → have), ⓒ의 목적어로 쓰인 명사절은 [that S + V]이므로 (that → that he), ⓓ의 양보를 나타내는 접속사는 (As → (Al)though)를 씀.

24 [명령문, and ~]: ~해라, 그러면 ~할 것이다

25 [if S + V]: 만약 ~한다면 (조건)

26 [either A or B]: A와 B 둘 중 하나

27 [since S + V]: ~하기 때문에

28 [neither A nor B]는 'A도 B도 둘 다 아닌'을 뜻하는데, 주어로 쓰이면 B에 동사를 일치시킴.

29 시간 부사절에서 미래시제 대신 현재시제를 사용함.

30 unless는 [if ~ not]의 의미여서 not과 동시에 사용 불가함.

Grammar Mapping

p. 148

① 접속사 ② 시간 ③ 이유 ④ 조건 ⑤ 양보 ⑥ 현재
⑦ 미래 ⑧ that ⑨ 주어 ⑩ 목적어 ⑪ both ⑫ either
⑬ nor ⑭ but also ⑮ as well as

Chapter 11 관계사

GP Practice 46 관계대명사의 역할과 종류
GP Practice 47 주격 관계대명사 who, which, that
GP Practice 48 목적격 관계대명사
who(m), which, that   p. 151

A	**1** which	**2** whom	
	3 who	**4** which	
B	**1** who(m) I like	**2** which was	
	3 which he lost		
C	**1** who (that) are always late		
	2 which (that) I send		
	3 which (that) has many pockets		
	4 whom (who, that) Jessica drew		
D	**1** which (that) / 사물, 주격		
	2 O / 사람, 목적격		
	3 삭제 / 주격, 삭제		
	4 삭제 / 목적격, 삭제		

GP Practice 49 소유격 관계대명사 whose
GP Practice 50 관계대명사 that   p. 153

A	**1** that	**2** whose	
	3 that	**4** which, that	
B	**1** whose fur is	**2** that understands	
	3 whose bottom is		
C	**1** whose hobby is		
	2 the only, that knows		
	3 the very, that Sandra wrote		
	4 whose battery lasts		
D	**1** whose / 소유격	**2** O / 사물, that	
	3 that / that	**4** 삭제 / 소유격, 삭제	

GP Practice 51 관계대명사 생략
GP Practice 52 관계대명사 what   p. 155

A	**1** O	**2** X	
	3 O	**4** O	
B	**1** what	**2** that	
	3 What		

C 1 What I want to drink
2 the hospital we visited
3 The man sitting by the window
4 what you heard about Hans

D 1 which (that) / which
2 O / 가능
3 what / what
4 O / 가능

GP Practice 53 관계부사
when, where, why, how
p. 157

A 1 why   2 when
3 where   4 the way, how

B 1 where she feels comfortable
2 why your parents love you
3 how he made Apple Computer

C 1 the date when Ann left Korea
2 how Eskimos greet
3 the place where I spend
4 the reason why earthquakes happen

D 1 when / 시간, when
2 삭제 / 방법, 없음
3 O / 이유, why
4 where / 장소, where

Grammar & Writing
p. 158

A 1 which has a big garden
2 who answered the question
3 which we visited last month
4 What I want to teach
5 whose pedal was broken
6 when you came back home

B 1 that arrived at the concert
2 which (that) I taught today
3 how cheesecake is made
4 why they canceled the festival
5 What TV shows us
6 which (that) are produced in Korea

C 1 whose tail is long
2 which is from Korea
3 when we throw out the garbage

D 1 why the accident happened here
2 where my parents studied
3 which will surprise him
4 how we can keep our bodies warm
5 whom many Koreans are proud of

Actual Test
p. 160

1 ④ 2 ③ 3 ② 4 ② 5 ③ 6 ④ 7 ⑤ 8 ① 9 ②
10 ① 11 ③ 12 ④ 13 ② 14 how 15 that
16 whose 17 what 18 where 19 ③ 20 ④
21 ③ 22 ⑤ 23 boys that are playing soccer
24 where my parents got married 25 which
sells recycled bags 26 what he is making
27 when the alarm clock goes off 28 it → 삭제,
목적격, 삭제 29 The way how → the way 또는
how, 쓸 수 없다 30 This is a picture that (which)
he took in the Arctic.

1 [사물 선행사 + 주격 관계대명사(which) + 동사]

2 선행사가 glasses이고 빈칸은 '안경의'라는 의미가 되어야 하므로 소유격 관계대명사 whose를 사용함.

3 [사람 선행사 + 목적격 관계대명사(whom) + 주어 + 동사]

4 선행사가 사람인 목적격 관계대명사 whom, who, that 가능, 목적격이므로 생략도 가능함.

5 선행사가 사물인 주격 관계대명사는 which, that이고, 선행사가 사람인 주격 관계대명사는 who, that이다.

6 선행사가 시간(the day, the time)을 나타낼 때 관계부사 when을 사용함.

7 선행사가 포함되어 있으므로 관계대명사 what을 사용함.

8 관계대명사는 선행사(the dress) 바로 뒤에 위치함.
→ The dress which she bought is for Halloween.

9 [주격 관계대명사 + be동사]는 생략 가능함.

10 선행사가 장소(a restaurant)를 나타낼 때 관계부사 where를 사용함. 밑줄 앞에 선행사가 없으므로 선행사를 포함하는 관계대명사 what을 사용함.

11 선행사가 이유(the reason)를 나타낼 때 관계부사 why를 씀. 선행사가 사람일 때 주격 관계대명사 who를 사용함.

12 ① whom → who / that ② whose → who / whom / that ② whom → which / that ⑤ who → whose

13 ②의 선행사가 이유(the reason)를 나타내므로 관계부사 why를 사용함.

14 방법을 나타내는 관계부사 how를 사용함.

15 선행사가 the very와 최상급을 포함할 때 관계대명사 that을 사용함.

16 선행사가 a king이고 빈칸에는 '왕의'라는 뜻이므로 소유격

관계대명사 whose를 사용함.

17 선행사가 없으므로 선행사를 포함하는 관계대명사 what을 사용함.

18 선행사가 장소 (the house)를 나타낼 때 관계부사 where를 사용함.

19 ① ② ④ ⑤의 who는 관계대명사이고 ③의 who는 의문사이다.

20 ④의 주격 관계대명사 who는 생략 불가함.

21 ③은 선행사가 없으므로 관계대명사 what을 사용함.

22 ① ~ ④는 which (that) ⑤는 선행사가 a book이고 빈칸에는 '책의' 라는 뜻이므로 소유격 관계대명사 whose를 씀.

23 [사람 선행사 + 주격 관계대명사 (that) + 동사]

24 선행사가 장소(the palce)를 나타낼 때 관계부사 where를 씀.

25 [사물 선행사 + 주격 관계대명사 (which) + 동사]

26 선행사 포함하는 what을 사용해서 두 문장을 연결함.

27 선행사가 시간(7 o'clock)을 나타낼 때 관계부사 when를 사용함.

28 목적격 관계대명사 뒤에는 선행사를 나타내는 목적어를 삭제함.

29 선행사 the way와 관계부사 how는 같이 쓸 수 없다.

30 선행사가 사물이고, 그가 찍었던 사진이므로 목적격 관계대명사 that (which)를 씀.

Grammar Mapping
p. 164

① 선행사 ② 사람 ③ V ④ which ⑤ 사람 / 사물 / 동물
⑥ S + V ⑦ whose ⑧ 명사 ⑨ ~하는 것 ⑩ 없다
⑪ 목적격 ⑫ 시간 ⑬ 장소 ⑭ 이유 ⑮ 방법 ⑯ 생략
⑰ 전치사

Chapter 12 가정법

GP Practice 54 가정법 과거
GP Practice 55 단순 조건문과 가정법 과거
p. 167

A
1 studied, 가정법   2 are, 조건문
3 will, 조건문   4 would, 가정법

B
1 had, could go
2 saw, could say
3 were not, could go

C
1 spoke, would understand
2 had, would visit
3 sang another song, would enjoy

D
1 bothered / 없는, 과거, would
2 take / 있는, 현재, will
3 were / 없는, were, could
4 O / 있는, 현재, will

GP Practice 56 I wish + 가정법 과거
GP Practice 57 as if + 가정법 과거
p. 169

A
1 weren't   2 were
3 were   4 traveled

B
1 were   2 carried
3 knew

C
1 as if he were
2 I wish I had
3 as if she were
4 I wish I remembered her name

D
1 were / 사실의 반대, 과거
2 O / 사실의 반대, 과거
3 didn't / 과거
4 opened / 과거

Grammar & Writing
p. 170

A
1 If my dog were, would take
2 pass, will treat
3 as if it were his first meal
4 wish the fine dust disappeared
5 If I learned, could join
6 as if I liked his food

B
1 miss this chance, will regret
2 were less scary, would enjoy
3 as if she understood
4 were not afraid of water, could see
5 I wish they could feel
6 as if she didn't know

C
1 would play badminton
2 could help sick people
3 had more money, I could buy

D
1 as if, agreed
2 I wish, weren't
3 I wish, were
4 had, could ask

1 ③ **2** ① **3** ④ **4** ⑤ **5** ④ **6** ② **7** ① **8** ② **9** ⑤ **10** ② **11** ④ **12** ④ **13** ① **14** ③ **15** were **16** had **17** if they could speak **18** as if she were a native speaker **19** were dressed up, could enter **20** as if they were **21** ② **22** ③ **23** had **24** lived **25** were **26** wish I had **27** were, would wait for **28** is → were, 사실의 반대, 과거 **29** will → would, 없는, would **30** I wish I had an older sister like Emily.

1 실현 가능성 없는 가정법 [If + S + 과거동사, S + would + 동사원형]

2 단순 조건문 [If + S + 현재동사, S + will + 동사원형]

3 실현 가능성 없는 가정법 [If + S + 과거동사, S + could + 동사원형]

4 현재 사실의 반대처럼 일 때 [as if + S + 과거동사]를 씀.

5 현재에 이루기 힘든 소망 [I wish + S + 과거동사]

6 '내가 너라면, 카메라를 사지 않을 텐데'라는 의미이므로 주절에 [would + not + 동사원형]을 씀.

7 실현 가능성 없는 가정법 [If + S + 과거동사, S + would + 동사원형]

8 ②는 [would → will], 단순조건문은 [If + S + 현재동사, S + will + 동사원형]이다.

9 ① [have → had] ② [are → were] ③ [won't → would not] ④ [will be → were]

10 현재 사실의 반대처럼 일 때 [as if + S + 과거동사]를 씀.

11 현재에 이루기 힘든 소망 [I wish + S + 과거동사]

12 실현 가능성 없는 가정법에서 주절이 먼저 나왔으므로 [S + could + 동사원형, if + S + 과거동사]를 씀.

13 실현 가능성 없는 가정법은 [If + S + 과거동사, [S + would + 동사원형] 사용, 현재에 이루기 힘든 소망은 [I wish + S + 과거동사]를 사용함.

14 ③은 현재 실현 가능성 있는 조건문이므로 [if + 주어 + 현재동사], 나머지는 현재 실현 가능성 없는 가정법이므로 [if + 주어 + 과거동사]를 씀.

15 as if 가정법 과거, I wish 가정법 과거에서 be동사는 were를 사용함.

16 현재에 이루기 힘든 소망은 [I wish + S + 과거동사]이므로 had, 실현 가능성 없는 가정법에서 주절이 먼저 나왔으므로 [S + would + 동사원형, if + S + 과거동사]이므로 had를 씀.

17 현재 실현 가능성 없는 가정법 [If + S + 과거동사, S + could + 동사원형]

18 현재 사실의 반대처럼 일 때 [as if + S + 과거동사]를 씀.

19 실현 가능성 없는 가정법 [If + S + 과거동사, S + could + 동사원형]

20 현재 사실의 반대처럼 일 때 [as if + S + 과거동사]를 씀.

21 가정법 과거는 직설법 현재시제로 전환함.

22 ⓐ 가정법에서는 조동사 과거이므로 [we could ~] ⓒ 만약 ~한다면 [if + 주어 + 동사과거형]이므로 were ⓔ 현재 사실의 반대를 희망하므로 [I wish I had ~]를 씀.

23 실현 가능성 없는 가정법 [If + S + 과거동사, S + would + 동사원형]

24 현재에 이루기 힘든 소망 [I wish + S + 과거동사]

25 현재 사실의 반대처럼 일 때 [as if + S + 과거동사]를 씀.

26 현재에 이루기 힘든 소망 [I wish + S + 과거동사]

27 실현 가능성 없는 가정법 [If + S + 과거동사, S + would + 동사원형]

28 현재 사실의 반대처럼 일 때 [as if + S + 과거동사]를 씀.

29 실현 가능성 없는 가정법 [If + S + 과거동사, S + would + 동사원형]

30 현재에 이루기 힘든 소망 [I wish + S + 과거동사]

Grammar Mapping p. 176

① 반대되는 ② 과거동사 ③ 조동사 과거 ④ 현재동사
⑤ 좋을 텐데 ⑥ 마치 ~인 것처럼

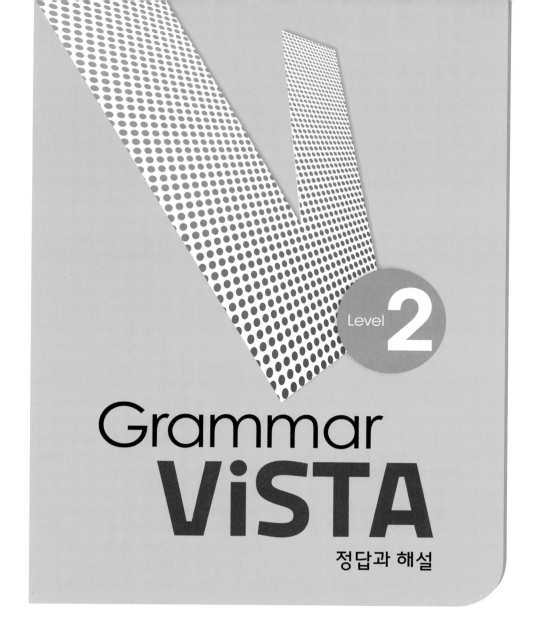

Grammar ViSTA
정답과 해설

Level **2**

● 본 교재   ● **workbook**

동사 + 보어

A　1 friendly　　　2 sweet
　　　3 bad　　　　　4 well
　　　5 gray　　　　　6 sleepy
　　　7 silent

B　1 smell　　　　2 look
　　　3 is getting　　4 felt
　　　5 walked

C　1 terrible　　　2 a singer
　　　3 nice　　　　4 tired

D　1 always looks energetic
　　　2 ran across the field
　　　3 the roads became slippery
　　　4 it went bad
　　　5 put a sticker on my notebook
　　　6 This soup tastes very bitter

E　1 smelled strange
　　　2 didn't taste sour
　　　3 looked like teachers
　　　4 His face turned pale
　　　5 always sounds scary
　　　6 She felt gloomy

수여동사 + 간접목적어+직접목적어
수여동사 + 직접목적어 + 전치사 + 간접목적어

A　1 to　　　　　2 to
　　　3 for　　　　4 for
　　　5 of　　　　6 to
　　　7 to

B　1 ~을·를, 3형식　　2 ~에게, 4형식
　　　3 ~에게, 4형식　　4 ~을·를, 3형식
　　　5 ~에게, 4형식　　6 ~을·를, 3형식

C　1 me the chilli sauce
　　　2 a baseball glove for his friend
　　　3 a lunchbox to me
　　　4 lemonade for my brother

D　1 sent pictures of Mars to the Earth
　　　2 handed her pupils colored paper
　　　3 asked me some private questions
　　　4 give the pianist a big hand
　　　5 built houses for poor people
　　　6 show the guard our ID cards

E　1 gave him my electronic dictionary
　　　2 wrote me a letter of apology
　　　3 taught his brother how to drive
　　　4 send yellow tulips to the patients
　　　5 bought robot toys for his children
　　　6 found us our lost puppy

동사 + 목적어 + 목적격보어

A　1 helpful　　　2 to water
　　　3 me　　　　　4 to bring
　　　5 him　　　　6 to sit
　　　7 to take off　8 strong

B　1 그, 멈추　　　2 우리, 일어나
　　　3 내, 콜라를 마시　4 나, 야채를 먹으

C　1 warm for me
　　　2 to eat less salt
　　　3 a walking dictionary
　　　4 to play in the sand
　　　5 fantastic

D　1 found the rumor false
　　　2 expect me to be perfect
　　　3 named his dog Superpower
　　　4 told the baby pigs to open the door
　　　5 wants me to buy clothes online
　　　6 make the students nervous

E　1 called Tom a bookworm
　　　2 make people less tired
　　　3 asked the police to help her
　　　4 found the box empty
　　　5 wanted dad to turn off the computer
　　　6 didn't allow me to use her pillow

사역·지각동사 + 목적어 + 목적격보어

A　1 feel　　　　2 wash

	3 boil	**4** knocking	
	5 go	**6** pick	
	7 to help		

B **1** fly (flying) **2** smile
    3 to be **4** pass (to pass)
    5 play (playing) **6** go
    7 stay

C **1** run around the house
    2 shaking a bit
    3 read an English newspaper
    4 cry (crying) in the street
    5 burning in the yard
    6 to clean up after the party

D **1** let me pay for lunch
    2 watched the train leaving the station
    3 made people stay at home
    4 heard the band play jazz music
    5 helped her to carry her luggage
    6 had me hang out the laundry

E **1** felt someone touch (touching)
    2 see a stranger stand (standing)
    3 had us believe his story
    4 heard my brother talk (talking)
    5 got us to take out
    6 let my friend stay

Error Correction   p. 16

1	삭제	명사
2	O	형용사, 명사
3	to	~를 ~에게, 직목 + to + 간목
4	for	~를 ~에게, 직목 + for + 간목
5	O	~에게 ~를, 간목 + 직목
6	him	목적격
7	clean	형용사
8	O	to + 동사원형
9	clean	동사원형
10	O	동사원형
11	watch	동사원형
12	draw, drawing	동사원형

13	O	동사원형 + -ing

Sentence Writing   p. 17
도전! 필수구문 156   p. 133

1 001	He became a sports hero.
2 002	Your bag looks fashionable.
3 003	Mr. Brown taught math to us.
4 004	Mary bought some cookies for her kids.
5 005	He asked his doctor two questions.
6 006	We elected him chairman of our club.
7 007	We must keep our room clean.
8 008	I want him to exercise every day.
9 009	She made him clean the bedroom.
10 010	I had my brother do his homework.
11 011	My mom didn't let me watch horror movies.
12 012	I saw her draw (drawing) a picture.
13 013	We heard a parrot say (saying) hello.

● ● ● ● ● ● ● ● ● ● ● ● ● ● ● ● ●

Chapter 02 | **시제**

Unit 05   p. 20
현재완료·과거와 현재완료

A **1** broke, 과거에만
    2 have passed, 현재까지
    3 did you go, 과거에만
    4 have never met, 현재까지
    5 moved, 과거에만
    6 Have, 현재까지

7 How long, 현재까지

8 learned, 과거에만

9 have read, 현재까지

10 got, 과거에만

B
1 broke

2 have never read

3 Have you been

4 have just eaten

5 met

6 Where have you been

7 has gone to

C
1 has just called me

2 cut his finger last night

3 has not slept since last night

4 How have you been

5 has already worn my new jacket

6 haven't finished playing yet

7 rode that cable car two months ago

D
1 have loved the idol group

2 made a TV program

3 have not watched the film

4 have just finished the group project

5 lasted for 116 years

6 won two gold medals

Unit 06   p. 22

현재완료 용법

A
1 has, graduated		**2** Have, seen	
3 has grown a lot		**4** has shopped	
5 have visited		**6** has been	
7 has, left		**8** has, called	

B
1 have studied, for		**2** has been sick	
3 has gone to		**4** have sold	
5 has been to			

C
1 have collected		**2** have, played	
3 have, seen		**4** has, taught	
5 has worked			

D
1 has broken two times

2 have worked on the puzzle for two

3 has lost his way

4 have already eaten five chocolate bars

5 has become colder since last week

6 Have you ever been to

7 has invented 437 items so far

E
1 Have you ever heard this word

2 have read the book three times

3 have known each other for 12 years

4 has studied Spanish since last October

5 How long have you stayed

6 has gone back to Canada

Error Correction   p. 24

1	has never seen	has + never + p.p.
2	O	Have + 주어
3	haven't	haven't
4	lost	과거, 과거
5	O	현재완료
6	come	방금 막 왔다, has + just + p.p.
7	traveled	p.p.
8	for	~ 동안 계속, for, 기간
9	has	잃어버리고 지금 없다, has
10	watched	본 적 있다, have + p.p.
11	have grown	해 왔다, 완료
12	O	~에 가 본 적이 있다, been
13	O	~으로 가버렸다, gone

Sentence Writing   p. 25

도전! 필수구문 156   p. 134

1 014	Oliver has never seen snow in Sydney.
2 015	Have you ever heard of moving stones?
3 016	No, I haven't.
4 017	He lost the key two days ago.
5 018	He has lost the key.
6 019	My sister has just come back home.
7 020	Have you ever traveled by ship?

8
021 He has lived in Paris for two years.

9
022 She has lost interest in music.

10
023 She has watched the movie ten times.

11
024 You have grown a lot since I last saw you.

12
025 She has been to London.

13
026 She has gone to London.

Chapter 03 | 조동사

Unit 07
p. 29

can, may, wil

A
1 catch
2 Will
3 would
4 may not
5 Can
6 Can he
7 make

B
1 ①
2 ③
3 ④
4 ②
5 ①

C
1 Can
2 may
3 Will
4 may not
5 Would

D
1 This bike may belong to Austin
2 can you hold your breath
3 Can I try on these sandals
4 Jane would pass the audition
5 may take your friends to my concert
6 Are you going to plant roses

E
1 may not know the answer
2 Would you stand in line
3 He was able to swim
4 may I have your attention
5 can cook Vietnamese dishes well
6 will not take long

Unit 08
p. 31

must, have to, should

A
1 have to
2 should
3 must be
4 have to
5 have to
6 must
7 save
8 has to

B
1 ④, 뛸 필요 없다
2 ③, 도와야 한다
3 ④, 설명할 필요가 없었다
4 ①, ~임에 틀림없다
5 ②, 낭비하면 안 된다

C
1 have to
2 must
3 should not
4 don't have to

D
1 We should not drive fast
2 The bakery must be popular
3 I didn't have to turn on
4 Does she have to write a report
5 will have to share a room
6 You must finish the test in

E
1 must be lonely in the cage
2 should tell the truth to your boss
3 don't have to go
4 had to melt chocolate
5 should not run around
6 Must drivers drive

Unit 09
p. 33

had better, used to, would like to

A
1 had
2 to join
3 used
4 had better not
5 to wear
6 be

B
1 follow
2 used to be
3 would you like to visit
4 used to
5 had better not
6 eat

C
1 had better walk
2 would like to meet
3 used to be
4 had better not believe

D 1 had better not   2 used to
    3 would like to   4 had better

E 1 used to have curly hair
    2 would eat heavy meals for breakfast
    3 What would you like to ride first
    4 had better not bring

F 1 used to be an old bookstore
    2 had better leave the puppy alone
    3 Would you like to drink more tea
    4 would go to the library

Error Correction   p. 35

1	read	동사원형
2	be able to	불가능, be able to
3	may	약한 추측, may
4	will	의지, will
5	must be false	be + 형용사
6	must not	조동사 + not
7	have to	불가능, have to
8	doesn't have to	~할 필요 없다, don't have to
9	had	충고, had
10	had better not	had better not
11	O	습관, 동사원형
12	used to	상태, used to
13	would like to	to + 동사원형

Sentence Writing   p. 36
도전! 필수구문 156   p. 135

1 027   She can read people's minds.

2 028   He will be able to find the answer.

3 029   The bird may look ugly, but it is very clever.

4 030   I will keep my promise.

5 031   The rumor must be false.

6 032   You must not tell the secret to anyone else.

7 033   You will have to hurry.

8 034   She doesn't have to get up early on Sundays.

9 035   You had better turn off your cell phone.

10 036   Jack had better not eat junk food.

11 037   My brother used to collect rocks.

12 038   The president used to be an actor.

13 039   I would like to travel to Europe.

Chapter 04 | 수동태

Unit 10   p. 40
능동태와 수동태

A 1 are cut   2 was hurt
    3 happened   4 was ordered
    5 carried   6 appeared
    7 are grown

B 1 was written, 쓰여졌다
    2 is played, 경기되다
    3 painted, 칠했다
    4 made, 만들었다
    5 was built, 지어졌다
    6 was brought up, 키워졌다

C 1 A victory is celebrated
    2 We were invited
    3 The baby was laid
    4 Korean culture is loved
    5 A package is delivered

D 1 Etiquette is taught in the home
    2 This great castle was built by slaves
    3 was injured in a motorcycle accident
    4 magazine is published by teenagers
    5 The trees are trimmed by my dad
    6 The bouquet was tossed into the air

E
1 are born
2 is advertised
3 are sent
4 The rat was placed
5 The picture was, photoshopped
6 Hot coffee was served

Unit 11 p. 42

수동태의 시제와 여러 형태

A
1 Was　　　　2 are being cut
3 By whom　　4 Does
5 were not mixed　6 be helped
7 not be added

B
1 Were, bought
2 were being changed
3 Can, be solved
4 By whom was, seen
5 is being read

C
1 Did, drop　　2 did not make
3 could solve　4 pulled
5 is collecting

D
1 Where will the next Olympics be held
2 could not be removed
3 When was the package delivered
4 is going to be hired next week
5 were being washed by the rain
6 What is this flower called

E
1 was not put
2 By whom was, edited
3 were being flown
4 Was the floor cleaned
5 money will be spent
6 is being questioned

Unit 12 p. 44

동사구 수동태 by 이외의 전치사를 쓰는 수동태

A
1 with　　2 after
3 in　　　4 at
5 at　　　6 for

B
1 are, tired of
2 is filled with

3 are worried about
4 is satisfied with
5 are pleased with
6 is known to
7 is, known for

C
1 was turned off
2 laughed at the plan
3 will be looked for
4 turn down the volume
5 are being taken care of

D
1 will be covered by the moon
2 is filled with cute pink clothes
3 The boat is being pushed away
4 She is worried about the pimples
5 was brought up by his uncle
6 is known for its beautiful beaches

E
1 am disappointed with her behavior
2 is not known to people
3 is interested in space exploration
4 was taken care of by Heungbu
5 was pleased with the pay raise
6 My wisdom tooth will be pulled out

Error Correction p. 46

1	is loved	사랑받다, be동사 + p.p.
2	by	by + 행위자
3	will be used	be + p.p.
4	being	being + p.p.
5	O	being + p.p.
6	was not written	be동사 + not
7	designed	Be동사 + 주어 + p.p.
8	When was Hangeul created	be동사 + 주어
9	followed	be + p.p.
10	was turned on	turned on
11	was taken care of	보살펴졌다, p.p.
12	with	with
13	O	to

1 040	The singer is loved by a lot of girls.
2 041	All her fans were invited by the actress.
3 042	This program will be used by college students.
4 043	My car is being washed by Sam.
5 044	Dinner was being prepared in the kitchen by my dad.
6 045	The book was not written by him.
7 046	Was the building designed by Fred?
8 047	When was Hangeul created by King Sejong?
9 048	The rules should be followed by people.
10 049	The music app was turned on by him.
11 050	The egg was taken care of by the mother eagle.
12 051	We are satisfied with the English class.
13 052	K-pop is known to most teenagers in Asia.

Chapter 05 | to부정사

to부정사의 명사적 쓰임

A
1 stand
2 It
3 is
4 how
5 not to
6 to move
7 be

B
1 It, to download the travel app
2 It, to understand baby talk
3 It, to take a break every hour
4 It, to buy the cheaper bike

C
1 what to bring
2 how to fold
3 where to stay
4 when to stop

D
1 not to talk back
2 when to talk, when to listen
3 learn how to swim
4 was not easy to solve the quiz
5 decided not to eat ice cream
6 expect to see my mom

E
1 to design school uniforms
2 tried to protect their country
3 forget to walk
4 patience to teach students
5 impossible to predict
6 how to spell your name

to부정사의 형용사적 쓰임

A
1 rules to follow
2 time to say
3 pictures to show
4 best season to read
5 many people to help
6 great to surprise

B
1 in, to live in
2 in, to sleep in
3 on, to write on
4 with, to play with

C
1 떠나야만 한다, ③
2 성공하고자 한다, ⑤
3 보여질 수 있다, ①
4 못 돌아올 운명이었다, ②
5 도착할 예정이다, ④

D
1 courage to travel around the world
2 no reason to get angry
3 a great hotel to stay at
4 many bedtime stories to tell
5 nothing to worry about
6 are to move to New York

E
1 many things to throw away
2 time to waste
3 the easiest way to please
4 a goal to achieve

5 to grab this chance

6 something amazing to tell

7 a partner to work with

Unit 15   p. 56

to부정사의 부사적 쓰임

A   **1** to learn   **2** to stay

     3 to come   **4** to repair

     5 to reach

B   **1** 신선한 공기를 얻기 위해, ①

     2 결국 댄서가 되다, ④

     3 소식을 듣게 되어서, ②

     4 풀기에, ③

     5 혼자 사는 것을 보니, ⑤

C   **1** ②   **2** ②   **3** ③   **4** ③   **5** ③

D   **1** worked out to build muscle

     2 be smart to understand

     3 Are you ready to make a speech

     4 was proud to show my painting

     5 return to the river to breed

     6 grew up to be the president

E   **1** difficult to learn

     2 sad to move

     3 only to find

     4 was very frightened to see

     5 the password not to forget

     6 rolled up my sleeve to give

Unit 16   p. 58

to부정사의 의미상 주어·to부정사를 이용한 구문

A   **1** 그녀, 돌보   **2** Nick, 보

     3 그, 요리   **4** 내, 가

B   **1** for me, 없음, for

     2 of her, 있음, of

     3 for us, 없음, for

     4 of them, 있음, of

     5 for him, 없음, for

     6 for you, 없음, for

C   **1** too hungry to sleep

     2 smart enough to answer

---

3 careless enough to lose

4 too difficult, to understand

5 kind enough to show

D   **1** too big for the kid to hold

     2 so full that he could not eat

     3 generous of you to donate

     4 important for teens to follow

     5 for him to learn

     6 interesting for adults to watch

E   **1** of you to take

     2 for us to protect

     3 too strict for me to follow

     4 small enough to hide

     5 so sick that he couldn't go

     6 so big that ten people can sleep

Error Correction   p. 60

1	It	가주어, It
2	to keep	to부정사
3	to study	to부정사
4	live in	live in a house, in
5	anything cold	명사 + 형용사
6	to stay	목적, to부정사
7	surprised	감정 원인, 감정형용사
8	to have	판단의 근거, to부정사
9	for	없으면, for
10	of	있으면, of
11	strong enough	~하기 충분한, 형용사 + enough
12	O	can
13	too tired	~하기엔 너무 ~한, too + 형용사

Sentence Writing   p. 61

도전! 필수구문 156   p. 137

1
053   It is my dream to invent a flying car.

2
054   My friends promised to keep my secret.

3
055   Please don't tell me when to study.

4
056 She bought a house to live in.

5
057 Do you have anything cold to drink?

6
058 I work out every day to stay healthy.

7
059 He was surprised to hear the news.

8
060 You must be popular to have so many fans.

9
061 It is hard for me to study all night.

10
062 It was brave of the firefighter to save the boy.

11
063 He is strong enough to lift the wooden box.

12
064 He is so strong that he can lift the wooden box.

13
065 Cathy was too tired to wake up at six.

Chapter 06 | 동명사

Unit 17 p. 64

동명사의 명사적·관용적 쓰임

A	1 Having	2 chasing
	3 finishing	4 watching
	5 playing	6 finding

B	1 먹는, ②	2 사는, ③
	3 지키는, ①	4 디자인하는, ④
	5 외식하는, ③	

C
1 collecting model trains
2 expressing her feelings
3 Meeting Tom at 2 p.m.
4 walking on a cloud

D
1 cleaner keeps moving
2 How about taking
3 Did you enjoy traveling
4 mind turning off your phone
5 Setting a goal is the first step
6 have difficulty getting up

7 not listening to others

E
1 stop laughing at his joke
2 Being a good daughter
3 bothering you this morning
4 spent, drawing the picture
5 My parents are busy decorating
6 My hobby is taking pictures of

Unit 18 p. 66

동명사와 to부정사

A	1 ordering	2 to turn off
	3 to tell, telling	4 to save
	5 asking	6 driving
	7 to give	

B	1 riding	2 to give
	3 seeing	4 failing
	5 to learn (learning)	6 walking
	7 to get	

C	1 ~할 것을	2 ~했던 것을
	3 ~했던 것을	4 ~할 것을
	5 열심히 노력	

D
1 finished writing a report
2 forgot to lock the gate
3 stopped to take a picture
4 how to avoid catching a cold
5 tried eating a frozen banana
6 was busy searching the Internet
7 finished shooting her new film

E
1 hoped to go back
2 mind changing
3 Avoid eating raw meat
4 tried hard to fix
5 forget watching the fireworks
6 keep bothering your puppy

Error Correction p. 68

1	Watching	주어, 동명사
2	singing	동명사
3	making	동명사
4	taking	보어, 동명사

5	is	단수
6	O / to dance	to부정사, 동명사
7	visiting	동명사
8	O	to부정사
9	meeting	동명사
10	O	to부정사
11	O	동명사
12	to solve	to부정사
13	drinking	동명사

1 066 Watching musicals is fun.

2 067 She enjoys singing loudly.

3 068 I am interested in making robots.

4 069 His hobby is taking pictures.

5 070 Using chopsticks is good for the brain.

6 071 Jane began dancing on the stage.

7 072 I remember visiting the museum before.

8 073 Remember to hand in your report tomorrow.

9 074 She forgot meeting you last year.

10 075 Don't forget to bring your lunch today.

11 076 We tried solving the puzzle for fun.

12 077 We tried to solve the puzzle to win a prize.

13 078 He stopped drinking water.

Chapter 07 | 분사

현재분사와 과거분사·분사의 형용사적 쓰임

A	**1** talking		**2** listening
	3 locked		**4** fried
	5 ringing		**6** parked
B	**1** cooked		**2** shaking
	3 getting		**4** filled
	5 amazing		**6** invited
C	**1** made of silk		**2** named Jack
	3 playing		**4** taken by my uncle

D **1** a message written by Adam
2 a fingerprint left on the window
3 wearing the blue sweater
4 geese flying in a V-formation
5 The flight attendant serving meals
6 adopted from the animal center
7 covered with chocolate

E **1** her smiling face
2 flying over there
3 baked potatoes
4 falling on the roof
5 touching his shoulder
6 made by the kids

감정을 나타내는 분사·현재분사와 동명사

A **1** amazing, amazed
2 satisfying, satisfied
3 disappointing, disappointed
4 interested, interesting
5 boring, bored

B	**1** 충격을 주는, ①		**2** 지루하게 하는, ①
	3 흥미를 느낀, ②		**4** 흥분을 느낀, ②
	5 놀람을 느낀, ②		
C	**1** singing room		**2** walking stick
	3 sleeping bag		**4** wrapping paper

D **1** 용도, 침낭
2 진행, 자고 있는 중인 아기

3	진행, 운전 중	
4	용도, 면허증	
5	용도, 대기실	
6	진행, 기다리는 중	

E
1 was pleased with
2 a raccoon washing
3 was disappointed
4 new washing machine
5 a frozen lake
6 interesting
7 swimming pool
8 Flying a kite
9 baby birds waiting for their mom

Unit 21 p. 77

분사구문

A
1 Chatting		**2** Being	
3 Although		**4** Visiting	

B
1 Getting married
2 Taking this bus
3 Waving goodbye
4 Living next door to Fred
5 Flying over the island

C
1 When he stayed in Korea
2 While I waited / was waiting for you
3 As she didn't have a seat
4 If you wear this coat
5 Although he looks tough

D
1 많이 먹지만, ④	**2** 지금 출발하면, ③
3 많이 읽어서, ①	**4** 방 청소를 할 때, ②

E
1 Walking under the same umbrella
2 Practicing hard
3 Saying sorry
4 Loving Chinese food

F
1 Saving the file
2 Being a vegetarian
3 Living alone in Spain
4 Waiting for the bus
5 Being satisfied with the food

Error Correction p. 79

1	moving	진행, 현재

2	used	수동, 과거
3	a robot moving underwater	뒤
4	O	유발하는, 느끼게 하다
5	boring	느끼게 하는, 현재
6	bored	느낀, 과거
7	O	잠자는 중, 현재분사
8	O	잠자는 용도, 동명사
9	삭제	주어, 함
10	Not	not, 앞
11	O	접속사
12	Reading	부사절, 동사원형 + -ing
13	Listening	부사절, 동사원형 + -ing

Sentence Writing p. 80

도전! 필수구문 156 p. 139

1 079	There is a moving robot.
2 080	I bought a used bike.
3 081	There is a robot moving underwater.
4 082	The book bores him.
5 083	The book is boring to him.
6 084	He is bored with the book.
7 085	Look at the sleeping lion.
8 086	I have a sleeping bag.
9 087	Reading a book, he puts on his glasses.
10 088	Not hearing the alarm, I kept sleeping.
11 089	Although having a driver's license, Emily never drives.
12 090	Reading this book, you will find the answer.
13 091	Listening to music, he searched the Internet.

Unit 22　　　p. 84
재귀대명사

A
1 you
2 ourselves
3 yourself
4 myself
5 herself
6 themselves

B
1 himself, 강조
2 yourself, 목적어
3 themselves, 강조
4 himself, 강조
5 yourself, 목적어

C
1 taught myself
2 Help yourself
3 enjoy ourselves
4 talking to myself

D
1 was disappointed with myself
2 He smiled at himself
3 doesn't feel any pain in itself
4 she often talks to herself
5 their projects for themselves
6 built its nest itself
　또는 itself built its nest

E
1 introduce myself
2 about himself
3 our airline tickets ourselves
4 cuts her own hair herself
　또는 herself cuts her own hair
5 the song itself
6 hung balloons around the house
　themselves 또는 themselves hung
　balloons around the house

Unit 23　　　p. 86
부정대명사 one, another, other(s)

A
1 one
2 it
3 Others
4 the others
5 the other
6 other

B
1 It
2 other
3 another
4 ones
5 others

C
1 others don't
2 the others weren't
3 the other was for her mom
4 another was a circle

D
1 the others are white
2 the other is a hamster
3 she wants to buy another
4 the others want chicken
5 others like instant food

E
1 another cup of coffee
2 want a smaller one
3 How about the white ones
4 my friends loved it
5 One lives, the other lives
6 Some animals live, others live

Unit 24　　　p. 88
부정대명사 all, both, each, every

A
1 Every
2 Each
3 All
4 can
5 Both
6 All

B
1 Each
2 every
3 all
4 both

C
1 looks
2 know
3 has
4 are
5 has

D
1 Both of us know
2 Both of my daughters are
3 Each of the three rooms has
4 All the windows were open
5 each student every morning
6 Every plant and animal needs

E
1 every Sunday
2 each of his books
3 all your problems
4 Each chapter has
5 Both glass and cans
6 every house has a colorful roof

Error Correction　　　p. 90

1 yourself　　　　같음, 재귀대명사

2	himself	himself
3	by themselves	by, themselves
4	for himself	for, himself
5	O	다른, one
6	another	같은, another
7	O	the other
8	others	others
9	need	복수
10	was	단수
11	O	복수
12	is	단수, 단수
13	student	단수, 단수

Sentence Writing p. 91

도전! 필수구문 156 p. 140

1 092	You must be proud of yourself.
2 093	Allen fixed the broken car himself.
3 094	Young children should not swim by themselves.
4 095	He always enjoys learning new things for himself.
5 096	This bag is too big. I need a smaller one.
6 097	I don't like this ring. Could you show me another?
7 098	I bought three pens. One is black, another is red, and the other is blue.
8 099	Some like going out, and others like staying at home.
9 100	All (of) the children need care and love.
10 101	All the advice was very helpful.
11 102	Both of them are high school students.
12 103	Each person is important for our team's victory.
13 104	Every student wants to get a good grade.

Chapter 09 | 비교표현

Unit 25 p. 94

원급, 비교급, 최상급

A	비교급	최상급
1	longer	longest
2	worse	worst
3	bigger	biggest
4	busier	busiest
5	less	least
6	more	most
7	better	best
8	closer	closest
9	more slowly	most slowly
10	more famous	most famous

B
1 hardest
2 not as
3 more often
4 long as
5 most
6 more delicious

C
1 big
2 smaller
3 oldest
4 hard
5 best
6 more expensive

D
1 can run faster than lions
2 not as cold as last week
3 the tallest in your family
4 as comfortable as the sofa
5 more pleasant than
6 the hottest month of the year

E
1 as often as you
2 the most helpful
3 as bad as mine
4 later than
5 the most difficult
6 more useful than

원급, 비교급, 최상급을 이용한 활용

A
1 as long as
2 higher
3 two times as fast
4 shorter
5 most popular
6 much
7 could
8 The bigger
9 tombs
10 the

B
1 much
2 The older
3 younger
4 two times more
5 most exciting
6 more and more crowded
7 well
8 heavier
9 the best, have ever taken
10 worse and worse

C
1 as young as possible
2 the most foolish mistake
3 a lot more than
4 The more, the healthier
5 four times as expensive as
6 one of the most diligent workers

D
1 as carefully as possible
2 the biggest fish, has ever caught
3 The less, the fewer
4 much (even, far, a lot, still) colder than
5 more and more difficult
6 the most popular tourist attractions

1	powerful	원급
2	not as	not as
3	lighter	비교급
4	more creative	more + 형용사
5	shortest	최상급

6	in	in
7	three times as	배수사 + as
8	O	원급
9	much	훨씬, much
10	smarter and smarter	비교급 + and + 비교급
11	the happier	the + 비교급
12	greatest	the + 최상급
13	have ever had	have ever p.p.

1
105 His speech is as powerful as his rival's.

2
106 Today is not as hot as yesterday.

3
107 Hot air is lighter than cold air.

4
108 Your idea is more creative than mine.

5
109 The thumb is the shortest of all five fingers.

6
110 Vatican City is the smallest nation in the world.

7
111 The KTX is three times as fast as the train.

8
112 Smile as often as possible.

9
113 I feel much healthier than before.

10
114 Cell phones are getting smarter and smarter.

11
115 The more we share, the happier we become.

12
116 The wheel is one of the greatest inventions in history.

13
117 This is the worst hairstyle that I have ever had.

시간 접속사·이유 접속사

A	**1** when	**2** until
	3 because	**4** while
	5 need	**6** since
	7 as	**8** Because
	9 After	
B	**1** since	**2** Because
	3 while	**4** before
	5 until	
C	**1** while	**2** After
	3 Because	
D	**1** arrive	**2** boils
	3 finishes	**4** come

E **1** while I cook lunch
2 since I visited Korea last
3 As the Earth rotates
4 until the sun came up
5 as it was too hot

F **1** as it was dark
2 before you swallow
3 While I was playing the violin
4 because (as, since) it is mysterious
5 After we made many mistakes

조건 접속사·양보 접속사·명령문 and / or

A	**1** unless	**2** If
	3 Although	**4** or
	5 Even though	**6** and
	7 finish	**8** or
B	**1** if	**2** unless
	3 Although	**4** and
C	**1** If	**2** unless
	3 and	**4** or
D	**1** set	**2** want
	3 returns	**4** ring

E **1** Unless a miracle happens
2 If you live alone
3 Even though the Gobi is a desert
4 or you will regret it
5 and you will strike high

F **1** (Al)though he is usually wrong
2 If you take this pill
3 and you will find
4 (Al)though it was freezing
5 Unless you use this game player

접속사 that·상관 접속사

A	**1** That	**2** likes
	3 but also	**4** and
	5 that	**6** either

B **1** It, that she went to Harvard University
2 It, that the little girl can sing so well
3 It, that he hasn't arrived yet
4 It, that Tom left his homework at home

C	**1** not only, but	**2** Neither, nor
	3 either, or	**4** both, and

D **1** 그녀가 운이 좋다는, ②
2 내가 늦은, ③
3 네가 이것을 좋아하는, ②

E **1** Not only he but also I
2 creative as well as interesting
3 that a gorilla escaped from the zoo
4 either by phone or by e-mail
5 that the police catch the criminal

F **1** neither liked nor disliked
2 Not only you but also Paula applied
3 that you did your best
4 that she found her missing dog
5 Their mom as well as the kids

1	When	갈 때, When
2	Until	할 때까지, Until
3	gets	시간, 미래, 현재

4	Because	자서, Because
5	take	조건, 미래, 현재
6	finish	If ~ not, 사용 불가
7	Though	했더라도, Though
8	and	and, 그러면
9	or	or, 그렇지 않으면
10	It	It
11	or	or, 둘 중 하나
12	nor	nor, 둘 모두 아닌
13	has	주어, B

1
118 When he goes fishing, I will join him.

2
119 Until she says, "Yes," her dog won't eat.

3
120 We will get home before it gets dark.

4
121 Because he didn't sleep enough, he had red eyes.

5
122 If you take a walk, you will feel better.

6
123 Unless we finish the meal, we will get hungry soon.

7
124 (Al)though I practiced a lot, I made a mistake.

8
125 Do your best, and you will succeed.

9
126 Water the plant, or it will die soon.

10
127 It is strange that it is snowing in May.

11
128 I will give this ticket to either Eric or Allen.

12
129 He was neither rude nor unkind.

13
130 Not only his brothers but also Tim has blond hair.

Chapter 11 | 관계사

관계대명사의 역할과 종류·주격과 목적격 관계대명사

A	**1** whom	**2** which
	3 which	**4** who

B
1 the money, which my uncle gave to me, 삼촌이 내게 준 (돈)
2 a reporter, who interviewed the president, 대통령을 인터뷰한 (기자)
3 the picture, which was in my room, 내 방에 있던 (사진)
4 The boy, who is playing the guitar, 기타를 치고 있는 (소년)
5 The rumor, that you heard, 네가 들었던 (소문)

C
1 This is the song which Becky made for me
2 The actor who (whom) you want to meet is not friendly
3 Ricky cooked spaghetti which smelled really good
4 I know a girl who can speak four languages
5 The Barbie doll which I bought yesterday is for you

D
1 who, he, 주격
2 whom, them, 목적격
3 which, it, 목적격

E
1 The flower which I want to buy
2 friends who will help you
3 The building which is standing on the hill
4 The writer whom I really like

F
1 which I want to watch
2 which the pianist played
3 who lived in Japan
4 whom he wanted to marry

소유격 관계대명사·관계대명사 that

A	**1** that	**2** whose
	3 that	**4** whose

5 that   **6** whose

B
1 whose dog saved his child
2 that (which) my mom bought
3 whose birthday is the same as mine
4 that I have
5 whose life was in danger

C
1 that is good for your health
2 whose car broke down
3 which (that) I am interested in
4 that you've ever seen

D
1 whose tail is very colorful
2 that you wrote to me
3 that you chose yesterday
4 whose hair is curly
5 that you learned today
6 whose writer won the prize

E
1 whose dog is missing
2 that my teacher has
3 whose father is a famous designer
4 whose hobby is bungee jumping
5 that I wanted
6 that you heard from her

관계대명사 생략·관계대명사 what

A
1 what   2 what
3 that   4 which
5 in which

B
1 which, ①   2 X
3 which was, ②   4 X
5 that, ①   6 who are, ②

C
1 what, 없음
2 What, 없음
3 that, 있음
4 that, 있음
5 what, 없음
6 that, 있음
7 what, 없음

D
1 I took on the wall
2 What King Sejong did
3 translated by my mom
4 I lived with last year

5 what you bought
6 which are made of glass

E
1 I bought last month
2 What I ate
3 given on this website
4 What I knew
5 I borrowed yesterday
6 what he wanted

관계부사 when, where, why, how

A
1 how   2 why
3 when   4 where

B
1 why she likes Max, for which
2 how people live, in which
3 when I first saw you, on which
4 where Mozart lived, in which

C
1 ⓓ   2 ⓐ   3 ⓑ   4 ⓒ

D
1 how he improved his grades
2 when we graduate from school
3 where my brother is working
4 why you punished your students
5 where his family stayed
6 how I can contact him

E
1 when we are the busiest
2 why the actor is popular
3 where we had lunch
4 how you can reduce stress
5 why he moved to Busan
6 when I made mistakes

1	which / that	사물, 주격
2	which / that	사물, 목적격
3	whose	소유격
4	that	that
5	O	that
6	that	that
7	O	가능

8	O	가능
9	what	없으므로, what
10	when	시간, when
11	where	장소, where
12	why	이유, why
13	삭제	방법, 없음

1
131 My teacher chose the book which (that) was written in English.

2
132 He posted a picture (which, that) he took yesterday on his blog.

3
133 He is from a country whose nature is very beautiful.

4
134 Look at the boy and the cat that are running.

5
135 I am the first girl that arrived here.

6
136 It is the very book that she wants.

7
137 We have to recycle the cans (which, that) we used.

8
138 The girl (who is) giving a speech is my sister.

9
139 Can you show me what is in your pocket?

10
140 9 o'clock is the time when our class starts.

11
141 This is the park where I usually exercise.

12
142 I don't know the reason why he was absent.

13
143 This is the way (how) he solved the puzzle.

Chapter 12 | 가정법

가정법 과거와 단순 조건문

A   **1** will   **2** wouldn't say
    3 played   **4** were
    5 will come

B   **1** knew   **2** will study
    3 would send   **4** takes
    5 had

C   **1** didn't eat, would have
    2 were not, could sleep
    3 lived, could visit
    4 were, would buy
    5 were, could learn
    6 would be, were

D   **1** ate, would be healthier
    2 is, will recommend it
    3 knew the truth, she would tell you
    4 doesn't look good, will give it
    5 listened to, would not fail
    6 spoke, would travel

E   **1** is fine, will go
    2 would, met
    3 had, would give you a ride
    4 were, would be late
    5 were good at, could see the movie
    6 paint, will look

I wish와 as if 가정법 과거

A   **1** had   **2** as if
    3 could   **4** were
    5 weren't   **6** were

B   **1** it didn't rain   **2** read
    3 didn't have to   **4** had
    5 were

C   **1** don't have   **2** isn't
    3 snows   **4** isn't surprised

D
1 I wish I knew
2 as if he were very thirsty
3 I wish my friend gave
4 as if he were not
5 as if the ground were shaking
6 I wish I were old enough

E
1 I had my own room
2 as if she knew
3 I wish my brother cleaned
4 as if today were the happiest day
5 I wish the people upstairs didn't walk
6 as if it were your last

Error Correction   p. 131

1	could	없는, could
2	were	없는, 과거
3	would	없는, would
4	O	없는, 과거
5	don't have	같음, 현재
6	get	있는, 현재
7	O	과거
8	were	과거
9	didn't make	과거
10	O	같음, 현재
11	knew	사실의 반대, 과거
12	were	사실의 반대, 과거
13	O	같음, 현재

Sentence Writing   p. 132

도전! 필수구문 156   p. 144

1
144 If my mom knew how to drive, she could pick me up.

2
145 If I were you, I would help the homeless.

3
146 If he got up early, he would not be late for class.

4
147 If I had enough time, I would visit you.

5
148 As I don't have enough time, I will not visit you.

6
149 If I get a bonus, I will treat you to dinner.

7
150 I wish I lived close to you.

8
151 I wish I were five years younger.

9
152 I wish you didn't make so much noise.

10
153 I am sorry you make so much noise.

11
154 He talks as if he knew the answer.

12
155 She treats me as if I were a baby.

13
156 In fact, I am not a baby.

Level 3

Grammar
ViSTA

Grammar ViSTA Series
STRUCTURE

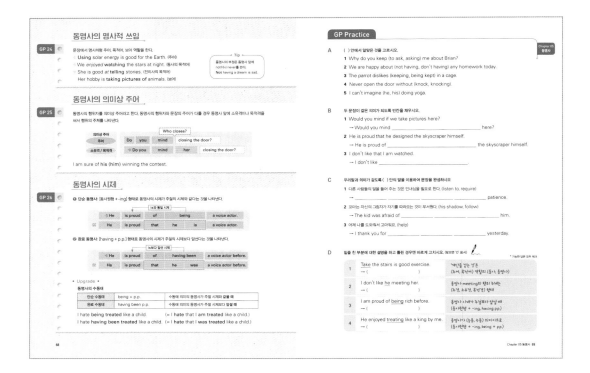

1 Grammar Point

● 문법패턴 도식화

총 177개의 핵심 문법을 도식화하여
시각적 학습 효과를 극대화시켰습니다.

● 대표 예문 선정

GP마다 대표 예문(☆)을 선정하여 문법 내용과
실전 예문을 동시에 학습할 수 있습니다.

● Tip과 Upgrade

주의해야 할 내용은 Tip으로,
심화 문법 내용은 Upgrade로 정리하였습니다.

2 GP Practice

● 선택형·단답형·서술형 문제

선택형, 단답형, 서술형 영작으로
단계적이고 반복적인 학습이 되도록 하였습니다.

● 오답 찾고 설명하기 문제

오답 찾기 방식으로 핵심 문법을 스스로 정리하고
자기 주도적 학습이 되도록 하였습니다.

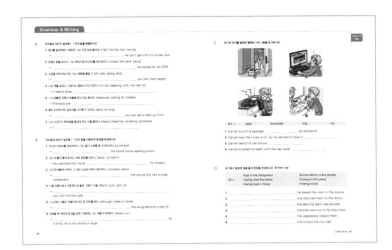

3 Grammar & Writing

• 단어 배열·문장 완성형 문제

학습한 문법 내용을 토대로 단어 배열 및
문장 완성을 통해 실질적인 쓰기 연습이
되도록 하였습니다.

• 구문 및 표현력 평가 문제

실생활을 소재로 한 대화나 삽화 문제를
구성함으로써 수행평가에 필요한 구문 작성 능력과
표현 능력을 키울 수 있도록 하였습니다.

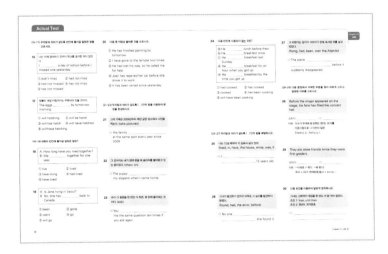

4 Actual Test

• 실전 문제

학습한 내용을 다양한 실전 문제를 통해서
다시 한 번 정리할 수 있도록 하였습니다.

• 내신 대비 서술형 문제

최신 내신 유형을 반영한 문제로 구성하여
서술형 내신을 완벽하게 대비할 수 있도록
하였습니다.

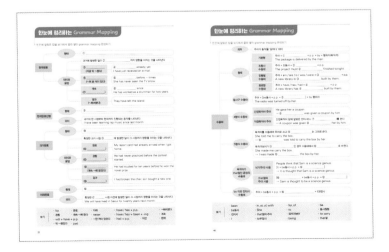

5 한눈에 정리하는 Grammar Mapping

• 문법 맵핑

학습한 문법 내용 전체를 한눈에 파악하고
핵심개념을 맵핑 이미지로 다시 한 번
정리할 수 있도록 하였습니다.

Workbook

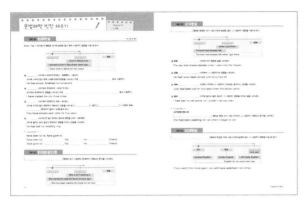

1 문법패턴 빈칸 채우기

- **노트 완성형 문제**

  노트 형태로 제시한 핵심 문법 사항의 빈칸을 채워 나가면서
  자기 주도적으로 학습할 수 있도록 하였습니다.

2 Workbook 연습문제

- **단계별 반복학습 문제**

  풍부하고 다양한 연습문제를 통해 문법과 쓰기 연습을
  극대화시켰습니다.

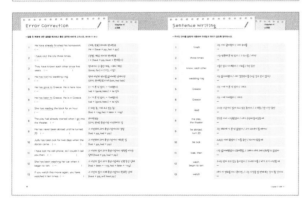

3 Error Correction & Sentence Writing

- **오답 찾고 설명하기 문제**

  학습한 문법 개념을 정확하게 이해하고 있는지
  시험해 볼 수 있는 자기 주도적 학습 방법입니다.

- **구문 영작 문제**

  학습한 문법 지식을 바탕으로 구문 단위로 영작을 능숙하게
  할 수 있는지 검증해 볼 수 있는 문제 유형입니다.

4 도전! 필수구문 156!

- **대표 예문 영작 문제**

  GP마다 선정한 대표 예문을 통문장으로 영작하고
  암기할 수 있도록 구성하였습니다.

* 본 교재는 대등한 쓰임의 단어들의 경우 ( )나 /로 구분 표기합니다.
(일반적 용도로도 사용)
  ex which (that): which 또는 that 사용 가능
  which / that: which 또는 that 사용 가능

* 본 교재는 문법 설명 파트에서 학습 요소의 강조를 위해 굵은 서체나
이탤릭체를 사용합니다. (일반적 용도로도 사용)

Grammar ViSTA Contents

Contents

Contents

시제

현재완료

GP 01

[have / has + 과거분사] 형태로 과거에 발생한 일이 현재 시점까지 영향을 미칠 때 쓴다.

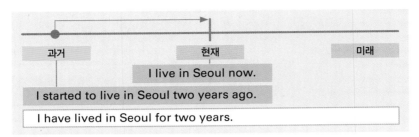

❶ 완료: (과거에 시작하여 현재는) ~완료했다, ~끝났다

과거에 시작한 일이 현재 시점에 완료되었음을 나타내고 주로 just, already, yet 등과 사용한다.

☆ He **has** *already* **finished** his homework.

❷ 경험: (과거부터 현재까지) ~해 본 적 있다

과거부터 현재까지의 경험을 나타내고 주로 ever, never, before, once, ~ times 등과 사용한다.

☆ I **have visited** the city *three times*.

❸ 계속: (과거부터 현재까지) 계속 ~해 왔다

과거에 시작한 일이 현재까지 계속되고 있음을 나타내고 [for + 기간] (~동안), [since + 과거 시점] (~이래로 계속),
how long(현재까지 얼마나 오래) 등과 쓴다.

☆ They **have known** each other *for* five years.

❹ 결과: (과거에 한 일이 현재의 결과에 영향을 미쳐) ~해버렸다

과거에 일어난 일의 결과가 현재까지 영향을 미치고 있음을 나타낸다.

☆ He **has lost** his wedding ring.

• **Upgrade** •

have been to vs. have gone to

[have been to]: '~에 갔다 왔다'라는 경험   ☆ He **has been to** Greece.

[have gone to]: '~에 가고 없다'라는 결과   ☆ He **has gone to** Greece.

현재완료진행

GP 02

[have / has + been + 현재분사] 형태로 과거 시점부터 현재까지 진행되는 동작을 나타낸다.

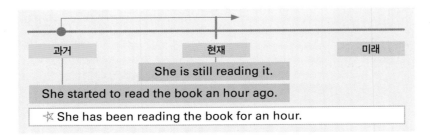

GP Practice

A ( ) 안에서 알맞은 것을 고르시오.

1 Where (were, have) you been today?

2 China (has invented, invented) paper money a long time ago.

3 Violent crime has decreased by 5% (for, since) 2017.

4 Miranda has (been, gone) to Hong Kong once.

5 The movie (is, has been) showing for three months.

B 다음 문장을 완료형 또는 완료진행형을 이용하여 바꿔 쓰시오.

1 It started to rain yesterday, and it is still raining.

→ It _____ since yesterday.

2 Brad went to a youth camp. He is at the camp now.

→ Brad _____ a youth camp.

3 I left my homework at home. I don't have it now.

→ I _____ my homework at home.

C 우리말과 의미가 같도록 ( ) 안의 말을 이용하여 문장을 완성하시오.

1 우리가 전에 만난 적 있나요? (ever, met)

→ _____ _____ _____ _____ before?

2 우리는 무엇을 살지 아직 결정하지 못했다. (not, decide)

→ We _____ _____ what to buy yet.

3 화산이 이틀째 폭발하고 있는 중이다. (erupt)

→ The volcano _____ _____ _____ _____ two days.

D 밑줄 친 부분에 대한 설명을 하고 틀린 경우엔 바르게 고치시오. (맞으면 'O' 표시)

* p.p.: 과거분사

1	The train <u>is running</u> since 10 a.m. → ( )	~이래로 (~하는 중, ~해 오고 있는 중) (is + -ing, has + been + -ing)
2	He has been in the army <u>for</u> last year. → ( )	(~동안 계속, ~부터 계속) 의미 (since, for) + (기간, 과거 시점)
3	We have <u>gone</u> to New York twice. → ( )	(~ 가 본 적 있다, ~ 가버렸다) have + (gone, been) + to + 장소
4	I <u>have never saw</u> a rainbow in my life. → ( )	(경험, 계속) 의미의 현재완료 주어 + (have + p.p., have + 과거동사)

과거완료

GP 03

[had + 과거분사] 형태로 특정한 과거 시점 이전에 발생한 일이 그 시점까지 영향을 미칠 때 쓴다.

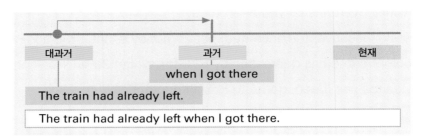

❶ **완료**: 특정 과거 시점 이전에 이미 완료된 일을 나타낸다.

※The play **had** already **started** *when I went into the theater.*

❷ **경험**: 특정 과거 시점 이전부터 그 시점까지의 경험을 나타낸다.

※He **had** never **been** abroad *until he turned 20.*

❸ **계속**: 특정 과거 시점 이전에 시작되어 그 시점까지 지속되는 동작이나 상태를 나타낸다.

※Judy **had been** sick for two days *when the doctor came.*

❹ **결과**: 특정 과거 시점 이전에 일어난 일의 결과가 그 시점까지 영향을 미치는 일을 나타낸다.

※I **had lost** my cell phone, *so I couldn't call you then.*

• Upgrade •

과거완료진행시제

[had + been + 현재분사] 형태로 특정 과거 시점 이전부터 그 시점까지 진행되는 동작을 나타낸다.

※She **had been washing** her car *when it began to rain.*

미래완료

GP 04

[will + have + 과거분사] 형태로 특정한 미래 시점 이전에 발생한 일이 그 시점까지 영향을 미칠 때 쓴다.

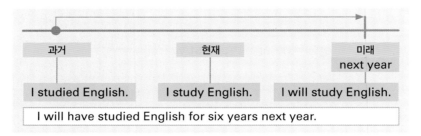

※*If you watch this movie again*, you **will have watched** it ten times.

GP Practice

A ( ) 안에서 알맞은 것을 고르시오.

1 He (has driven, had driven) the car for 20 years before it broke down.

2 The kid had been hiding for one hour before I (find, found) him.

3 The *Titanic* (has, had) been sailing to New York when it hit an iceberg.

4 By next year, I (will know, will have known) Kyle for 10 years.

5 The train (will have left, had left) by the time you arrive.

B 완료형 또는 완료진행형을 이용하여 문장을 완성하시오.

1 I _____ the book when I found a ten-dollar bill in it. (be reading)

2 He _____ raw fish before he turned 15. (not, eat)

3 We _____ there by tomorrow. (arrive)

4 He _____ in the sea when he saw a shark. (be swimming)

5 She _____ the test many times before she finally passed it. (fail)

C 우리말과 의미가 같도록 ( ) 안의 말을 이용하여 문장을 완성하시오.

1 우리가 도착했을 때 콘서트는 이미 시작되었다. (already, start)

→ The concert _____ _____ _____ when we arrived.

2 전화가 울릴 때 나는 공포영화를 2시간째 보는 중이었다. (watch)

→ I _____ _____ _____ a horror movie for two hours when the phone rang.

3 Jenny는 오늘밤이면 리포트를 다 끝냈을 것이다. (finish)

→ Jenny _____ _____ _____ her report by tonight.

D 밑줄 친 부분에 대한 설명을 하고 틀린 경우엔 바르게 고치시오. (맞으면 'O' 표시)

* p.p.: 과거분사

1	He <u>has just left</u> when I arrived home. → ( )	그 이전의 일이 과거 특정시점까지 영향을 미칠 때 (have + p.p., had + p.p.)
2	My brother had been the only son before I <u>am</u> born. → ( )	과거완료는 (과거, 현재) 특정시점 이전부터의 일
3	It <u>has been raining</u> for two days before it stopped. → ( )	그 이전의 일이 과거 특정시점에도 진행 중일 때 (had, has) + been + -ing
4	By next year, he <u>has become</u> a soldier. → ( )	미래 특정시점까지 완료된 일 (have + p.p., will have + p.p.)

A   우리말과 의미가 같도록 ( ) 안의 말을 배열하시오.

1 이 도시는 내가 떠난 이후로 많이 변해 왔다. (changed, has, since, a lot, I left)

→ The city _____.

2 너는 체중이 약간 늘었구나. 더욱 건강해 보인다. (gained, some weight, have)

→ You _____. You look healthier.

3 이것이 내가 지금껏 찾아오고 있던 것이다. (looking for, have, been)

→ That is what I _____.

4 네가 전화했을 때, 나는 네 생각을 해 오고 있는 중이었다. (thinking about, had, you, been)

→ I _____ when you called me.

5 그는 다음달이면 그 아프리카 소년을 5년째 후원하는 것이 된다. (sponsored, will, have, the African boy)

→ He _____ for five years next month.

6 나는 버스를 탔을 때, 버스를 잘못 탄 것을 알게 되었다. (had, I, gotten, found, I)

→ When I got on the bus, _____ on the wrong one.

B   우리말과 의미가 같도록 ( ) 안의 말을 이용하여 문장을 완성하시오.

1 내가 이 노래를 처음 들었을 때 이후로, 나는 이 노래를 좋아해 오고 있어. (love)

→ I _____ _____ _____ _____ since I heard it the first time.

2 비가 그쳤다. 우리는 우산이 이제 필요 없다. (stop, rain)

→ It _____ _____ _____. We don't need an umbrella now.

3 Jack은 선생님께서 그의 이름을 불렀을 때 수업 중에 자고 있는 중이었다. (sleep)

→ Jack _____ _____ _____ in class when his teacher called his name.

4 그가 깼을 때, 비행기는 중국 상공을 한 시간째 날고 있는 중이었다. (fly)

→ The plane _____ _____ _____ over China for an hour when he woke up.

5 나는 내 모든 양말을 세탁했기 때문에, 그때 신을 양말이 없었다. (wash, all)

→ I _____ _____ _____ _____ _____, so I had no socks to wear then.

6 네가 외출한 이후로 너의 강아지가 너를 기다리고 있는 중이다. (wait for)

→ Your dog _____ _____ _____ _____ _____ since you went out.

C 다음 표는 Ryan이 배우는 취미활동 종목과 기간이다. 보기에서 알맞은 말을 골라서 문장을 완성하시오.

배우는 종목	배우는 기간		
Swimming Lesson			
Drawing Lesson			
Yoga Lesson			
Piano Lesson			
	(April 1)	현재 (May 1)	(June 1)

보기	· has learned	· has been learning
	· will have learned	· had learned

1 Ryan _____ swimming until April 1.

2 Ryan _____ drawing since April 1.

3 Ryan _____ yoga since April 1.

4 Ryan _____ the piano for two months by June 1.

D 완료형 또는 완료진행형을 사용하여 두 문장을 한 문장으로 쓰시오.

1

Clara lost her ID card. She still doesn't have it.

→ Clara _____ her ID card.

2

Mr. Brown went to Canada. He is still there.

→ Mr. Brown _____ Canada.

3

I started to clean the house two hours ago. I am still cleaning.

→ I _____ the house for two hours.

4

He has met Kate three times.

→ If he meets Kate one more time, he _____ her four times.

(1–5) 빈칸에 들어갈 알맞은 말을 고르시오.

1 The singer _____ 100 concerts since 2002.

① holds   ② held

③ has held   ④ had held

⑤ will have held

2 He _____ as a reporter until he moved to Mexico.

① work   ② worked

③ has worked   ④ has been working

⑤ had worked

3 The fireworks _____ by the time you arrive.

① finish   ② finished

③ has finished ④ had finished

⑤ will have finished

4 She _____ a police officer last year.

① becomes   ② became

③ has become   ④ had become

⑤ will have become

5 Daniel _____ to India many times.

① was   ② been

③ has been   ④ gone

⑤ has gone

(6–7) 보기의 밑줄 친 부분과 같은 용법으로 쓰인 것은?

6 Scientists have searched for life in outer space for a long time.

① She has just eaten dinner.

② I haven't eaten anything since last night.

③ Have you ever tasted this fruit before?

④ He has just arrived at the station.

⑤ They have lost their house in the flood.

7 He has climbed the mountain two times.

① The airplane had just left when he arrived at the airport.

② I have never traveled alone so far.

③ She hasn't reserved a table yet.

④ Bob has gone to Dubai.

⑤ He has worked as a teacher for two years.

(8-9) 밑줄 친 부분이 어법상 **어색한** 것은?

8 ① Brian <u>hadn't visited</u> a foreign country until last year.

② I <u>haven't seen</u> her since yesterday.

③ He <u>will have recovered</u> from his illness by next month.

④ The lottery winner <u>has spent</u> all his money before two years passed.

⑤ He <u>has been hiding</u> the secret since he learned it.

9 ① He <u>has learned</u> yoga for three years.

② She <u>had read</u> the book twice before she returned it to me.

③ Mia <u>has won</u> three medals if she wins this time.

④ The dog <u>had been waiting for</u> its owner when I found it.

⑤ The hotdogs <u>had been sold out</u> when it was my turn to buy some.

10 빈칸에 들어갈 말이 **다른** 하나는?

① The party _____ been boring before Henry came.

② They _____ been married for five years when they had a baby.

③ I _____ lost my pen, so I need one.

④ He _____ not heard of me until then.

⑤ He _____ locked the door before he left home.

(11-12) 빈칸에 공통으로 들어갈 말로 알맞은 것은?

11 · Cindy _____ been to the island twice.

· He _____ been using the computer for three hours.

① have   ② has   ③ had

④ is   ⑤ will

12 · She has been interested in cars _____ she was a kid.

· I haven't eaten anything _____ lunch.

① since   ② for   ③ when

④ after   ⑤ before

(13-15) 주어진 문장과 같은 의미를 갖도록 빈칸을 채우시오.

13 He went to Paris for business. So he is not here.

⇨ He _____ Paris for business.

14 He started to run the restaurant two years ago. He is still running it.

⇨ He _____ the restaurant for two years.

15 Miranda forgot your name. She still doesn't remember it.

⇨ Miranda _____ your name.

(16–17) 우리말과 의미가 같도록 빈칸에 들어갈 알맞은 말을 고르시오.

16
> 나는 어제 결석하기 전까지 학교를 결석한 적이 없었다.
> I _____ a day of school before I missed one yesterday.

① didn't miss ② had not miss
③ had not missed ④ has not miss
⑤ has not missed

17
> 알들이 내일 아침까지는 부화되어 있을 것이다.
> The eggs _____ by tomorrow morning.

① will hatching ② will be hatch
③ will has hatch ④ will have hatched
⑤ will have hatching

(18–19) 대화의 빈칸에 들어갈 알맞은 말은?

18
> A: How long have you lived together?
> B: We _____ together for one year.

① live ② lived
③ have living ④ had lived
⑤ have lived

19
> A: Is Jane living in Seoul?
> B: No, she has _____ back to Canada.

① been ② gone
③ went ④ go
⑤ will go

20 다음 중 어법상 올바른 것을 고르시오.

① He has finished painting by tomorrow.
② I have gone to the temple two times.
③ He had lost his way, so he called me for help.
④ Joan has repaired her car before she drove it to work.
⑤ It has been rained since yesterday.

(21–23) 우리말과 의미가 같도록 ( ) 안의 말을 이용하여 문장을 완성하시오.

21
> 그의 가족은 2009년부터 매년 같은 장소에서 사진을 찍는다. (take pictures)

⇨ His family _____ at the same spot every year since 2009.

22
> 그 강아지는 내가 집에 왔을 때 슬리퍼를 물어뜯고 있는 중이었다. (chew on)

⇨ The puppy _____ my slippers when I came home.

23
> 네가 그 질문을 한 번만 더 하면, 열 번째 물어보는 것이다. (ask)

⇨ You _____ me the same question ten times if you ask again.

24 다음 빈칸에 사용되지 <u>않는</u> 것은?

> ⓐ He _____ lunch before then.
> ⓑ He _____ breakfast once.
> ⓒ He _____ breakfast last Sunday.
> ⓓ He _____ breakfast for an hour when you got up.
> ⓔ He _____ breakfast by the time you get up.

① had cooked   ② has cooked

③ cooked   ④ has been cooking

⑤ will have been cooking

(25-27) 우리말과 의미가 같도록 ( ) 안의 말을 배열하시오.

25 나는 12살 때부터 이 집에서 살고 있어.
(lived, in, have, this house, since, was, I)

⇨ I _____
_____ 12 years old.

26 그녀가 발견하기 전까지 아무도 그 실수를 발견하지 못했다.
(found, had, the error, before)

⇨ No one _____
_____ she found it.

27 그 비행기는 갑자기 사라지기 전에 대서양 위를 날고 있었다.
(flying, had, been, over the Atlantic)

⇨ The plane _____
_____ before it
suddenly disappeared.

(28-29) 다음 문장에서 어색한 부분을 찾아 바르게 고치고 알맞은 이유를 고르시오.

28 Before the singer appeared on the stage, his fans has filled the concert hall.

고치기: _____ ⇨ _____
이유: 가수가 무대에 등장했던 (현재, 과거)를
기준시점으로 그 이전의 일은
(have p.p., had p.p.)

29 They are close friends since they were first graders.

고치기: _____ ⇨ _____
이유: ~이래로 (~했다, ~해 왔다)
주어 + (과거, 현재완료)동사 + since ~

30 다음 조건을 이용하여 알맞게 영작하시오.

그녀는 그때까지 게임을 한 번도 져 본 적이 없었다.
조건 1: lose, until then
조건 2: 8단어, 과거완료

⇨ _____
_____ .

한눈에 정리하는 Grammar Mapping

빈칸에 알맞은 답을 보기에서 골라 넣어 grammar mapping 완성하기

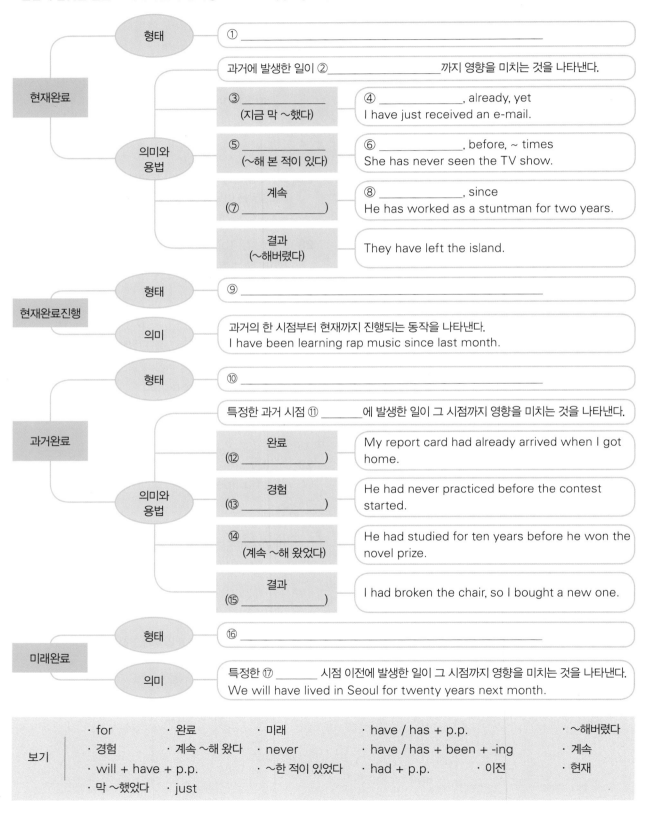

현재완료

형태 — ① _____

과거에 발생한 일이 ② _____까지 영향을 미치는 것을 나타낸다.

의미와 용법
- ③ _____ (지금 막 ~했다) — ④ _____, already, yet / I have just received an e-mail.
- ⑤ _____ (~해 본 적이 있다) — ⑥ _____, before, ~ times / She has never seen the TV show.
- 계속 (⑦ _____) — ⑧ _____, since / He has worked as a stuntman for two years.
- 결과 (~해버렸다) — They have left the island.

현재완료진행

형태 — ⑨ _____

의미 — 과거의 한 시점부터 현재까지 진행되는 동작을 나타낸다. / I have been learning rap music since last month.

과거완료

형태 — ⑩ _____

특정한 과거 시점 ⑪ _____에 발생한 일이 그 시점까지 영향을 미치는 것을 나타낸다.

의미와 용법
- 완료 (⑫ _____) — My report card had already arrived when I got home.
- 경험 (⑬ _____) — He had never practiced before the contest started.
- ⑭ _____ (계속 ~해 왔었다) — He had studied for ten years before he won the novel prize.
- 결과 (⑮ _____) — I had broken the chair, so I bought a new one.

미래완료

형태 — ⑯ _____

의미 — 특정한 ⑰ _____ 시점 이전에 발생한 일이 그 시점까지 영향을 미치는 것을 나타낸다. / We will have lived in Seoul for twenty years next month.

보기
- for
- 경험
- will + have + p.p.
- 막 ~했었다
- 완료
- 계속 ~해 왔다
- just
- 미래
- never
- ~한 적이 있었다
- have / has + p.p.
- have / has + been + -ing
- had + p.p.
- ~해버렸다
- 계속
- 현재
- 이전

22

Chapter

02

조동사

can, may

GP 05

❶ can + 동사원형

☆ He **can** (= **is able to**) speak five foreign languages. (능력: ～할 수 있다)

You **can** (= **may**) bring your own food. (허락: ～해도 된다)

That **can't** be Karl; he has gone to Spain. (부정적 추측: ～일 리가 없다)

cannot + have p.p. (현재를 기준으로 과거 사실에 대한 강한 의심: ～이었을(했을) 리가 없다)

The little girl **cannot have driven** the car.

My brother **can't have cleaned** his room. It is still messy.

❷ may + 동사원형

You **may** (= **can**) sit down or stand. (허락: ～해도 된다)

☆ He **may** like your idea. (약한 추측: ～일지도 모른다)

may + have p.p. (현재를 기준으로 과거 사실에 대한 약한 추측: ～이었을(했을)지도 모른다)

Olivia **may** (**might**) **have loved** me at that time.

You **may have heard** about 3D printers.

must, should

GP 06

❶ must + 동사원형

Drivers **must** (= **have to**) obey the traffic regulations. (의무: ～해야 한다)

☆ You **must not** take pictures in the museum. (～하면 안 된다)

☆ Children under seven **don't have to pay** an entrance fee. (～할 필요 없다)

Tony stayed up all night. He **must** be tired now. (강한 추측: ～임에 틀림없다)

must + have p.p. (현재를 기준으로 과거 사실에 대한 강한 추측: ～이었음(했음)이 틀림없다)

☆ You **must have practiced** very hard.

He didn't call me. He **must have forgotten** my phone number.

❷ should / ought to + 동사원형

☆ We **should** (= **ought to**) respect our parents. (도덕적 의무)

You **should not** (= **ought not to**) skip breakfast. (충고)

should + have p.p. (현재를 기준으로 과거 사실에 대한 후회나 유감: ～했어야 했는데 하지 못했다)

☆ I **should have done** my homework.

We **shouldn't have spent** all our money.

GP Practice

A ( ) 안에서 알맞은 것을 고르시오.

1 I have a problem. (Can, May) you help me?

2 He (can't, shouldn't) be Jane's brother. Jane is an only child.

3 She will (can, be able to) understand you when she grows up.

4 I can't find my key. I (should, may) have lost it.

5 He didn't eat anything today. He (must, have to) be hungry.

B 두 문장이 같은 의미가 되도록 빈칸을 채우시오.

1 I have an extra blanket. You can use it.

→ I have an extra blanket. You _____ use it.

2 Julie must practice her presentation on history.

→ Julie _____ practice her presentation on history.

3 Surprisingly, she could walk again.

→ Surprisingly, she _____ walk again.

C 우리말과 의미가 같도록 ( ) 안의 말을 이용하여 문장을 완성하시오.

1 우리는 모퉁이에서 좌회전을 했어야 했는데 못했다. (turn left)

→ We _____ _____ _____ _____ at the corner.

2 죄송합니다. 제가 전화를 잘못 건 것 같습니다. (dial)

→ Sorry. I _____ _____ _____ the wrong number.

3 그는 그 지루한 책을 읽었을 리가 없다. (can, read)

→ He _____ _____ _____ the boring book.

D 밑줄 친 부분에 대한 설명을 하고 틀린 경우엔 바르게 고치시오. (맞으면 'O' 표시)

* p.p.: 과거분사

1	He <u>must</u> be Chinese. He can't speak Chinese. → ( )	(~일 리가 없다, ~임에 틀림없다) (must not, cannot) + 동사원형
2	You will <u>can</u> use the service soon. → ( )	[조동사 + 조동사]는 (가능, 불가능) will + (can, be able to)
3	His room is clean. He must <u>clean</u> it. → ( )	(현재, 과거) 사실에 대한 강한 추측 must + (동사원형, have p.p.)
4	I am late. I should <u>come</u> earlier. → ( )	(현재, 과거) 사실에 대한 유감, 후회 should + (동사원형, have p.p.)

used to, would like to

GP 07

❶ **used to + 동사원형** (과거의 습관: ~하곤 했다 = would / 과거의 상태: ~이었다)

※ Mike **used to** collect foreign coins. (과거의 습관)

　= Mike **would** collect foreign coins.

※ He **used to** be my boyfriend, but he isn't now. (과거의 상태)

> ─○ Tip ○─
>
> ① [used to + 동사원형]: ~하곤 했다, ~이었다　　　Jack used to be very shy.
> ② [be used to + 동사원형]: ~하기 위해 사용되다　　It is used to cut metal.
> ③ [be used to + 동사원형ing]: ~하는 것에 익숙하다　He is used to living on the island.

❷ **would like to + 동사원형** (~하고 싶다)

We **would like to** invite you to our wedding.

I **would like to** leave a message for Mr. Ken.

had better, would rather, may as well

GP 08

❶ **had better + 동사원형** (~하는 것이 낫다)

※ You**'d better** take a window seat.

※ We **had better not** go out tonight because of the rain.

❷ **would rather + 동사원형** (차라리 ~하는 것이 낫다)

I **would rather** drink hot chocolate.

She**'d rather not** travel during the holidays.

• Upgrade •

would rather A than B: B하느니 차라리 A하겠다

※ I **would rather** play outside **than** watch TV at home.

❸ **may (might) as well + 동사원형** (차라리 ~하는 것이 낫다)

※ If there's nothing more to do, we **may as well** go home.

I **may as well not** speak to you if you don't listen.

GP Practice

A ( ) 안에서 알맞은 것을 고르시오.

1 You (had not better, had better not) go out after dark.

2 I (would, may) like to book a flight to San Francisco.

3 Paul is busy now. I (may as well, used to) visit him later.

4 I (would rather, may as well) walk than drive in heavy traffic.

5 There (would, used to) be a lot of mango trees in his yard.

B 보기에 주어진 말을 알맞게 고쳐 빈칸을 채우시오. (한 번씩만 사용)

| 보기 | had better | used to | would | would rather |

1 There _____ be more than 50 students in each class in the 1990s.

2 We _____ hide in the closet when we played hide-and-seek.

3 I _____ fail the test than cheat on it.

4 The food smells strange. You _____ not eat it.

C 우리말과 의미가 같도록 ( ) 안의 말을 이용하여 문장을 완성하시오.

1 나는 설거지를 하느니 차라리 요리를 하겠다. (cook)

→ I _____ _____ _____ than do the dishes.

2 너는 거짓말을 하지 않는 것이 낫겠다. (tell, better)

→ You _____ _____ _____ _____ a lie.

3 나의 늙은 개는 어렸을 때 매우 에너지가 넘쳤었다. (very energetic)

→ My old dog _____ _____ _____

_____ when it was young.

D 밑줄 친 부분에 대한 설명을 하고 틀린 경우엔 바르게 고치시오. (맞으면 'O' 표시)

1	He <u>would</u> be shy until he was ten. → ( )	과거의 (상태, 습관) 의미할 때는 (would, used to) + 동사원형
2	I <u>not had better</u> waste money. → ( )	had better의 부정형은 바로 (앞, 뒤)에 (don't, not)
3	You may as well <u>to go</u> to bed now. → ( )	(~하는 것이 낫다, ~하곤 했다) may as well + (동사원형, to부정사)
4	I would rather sleep <u>as</u> watch TV. → ( )	would rather A (as, than) B (A, B) 하느니 차라리 (A, B) 하겠다

A 우리말과 의미가 같도록 ( ) 안의 말을 배열하시오.

1 너는 너의 애완동물을 괴롭히면 안 된다. (bother, should, your, not, pet)

→ You _____.

2 주목해 주시겠습니까? (have, I, may, your, attention)

→ _____, please?

3 엄마는 나를 업어 주시곤 했었다. (carry, me, used to, on her back)

→ My mom _____.

4 Hillary는 어제 거기 있었을 리가 없다. 나와 함께 있었거든. (have, cannot, been, there)

→ Hillary _____ yesterday. She was with me then.

5 우리는 다른 사람 험담을 하지 않는 것이 좋겠다. (had better, speak ill of, not, others)

→ We _____.

6 너는 일정을 다시 확인했어야 했다. (should, checked, the schedule, have)

→ You _____ again.

B 우리말과 의미가 같도록 ( ) 안의 말을 이용하여 문장을 완성하시오.

1 Tiffany가 내 초콜릿을 먹은 것이 분명해. (must, eat)

→ Tiffany _____ _____ _____ _____ _____.

2 우리 반에 새 학생을 소개하겠습니다. (would, introduce)

→ I _____ _____ _____ _____ _____

_____ to our class.

3 나는 지하철을 타느니 차라리 걸어가겠다. (go on foot)

→ I _____ _____ _____ _____ _____ than take the

subway.

4 집에 분명히 누군가가 있어. 불이 켜져 있어. (must, someone)

→ There _____ _____ _____ _____ _____

_____. The light is on.

5 그는 친숙해 보여. 내가 그를 전에 봤을지도 몰라. (may, meet)

→ He looks familiar. _____ _____ _____ _____

_____.

6 너는 우산을 가져가는 것이 낫겠다. (had, take)

→ You _____ _____ _____ _____.

C 다음 주어진 말을 각 문장에 맞게 고쳐 빈칸을 채우시오.

1

| should / be | ⓐ The road is slippery. I _____ careful. |
| | ⓑ I fell down on the road. I _____ careful. |

2

cannot / be	ⓐ The dog _____ Jack's. It is barking at Jack.
	ⓑ She was sick yesterday.
	She _____ at the concert yesterday.

3

| must / be | ⓐ Brian is at home. He _____ bored. |
| | ⓑ Brian didn't call me. He _____ busy. |

4

| may / leave | ⓐ Mr. Smith is not here. You _____ a message for him. |
| | ⓑ I can't find my passport. I _____ it at home. |

D 다음 그림에서 두 가지의 상황을 비교합니다. 보기에서 알맞은 조동사를 골라 주어진 단어와 함께 문장을 완성하시오.

| before | now |
| have | buy, fix | put on |

| 보기 | would rather | had better | used to |

1 Matthew has stylish short hair. He _____ long hair.

2 I _____ a new chair than _____ the broken one.

3 This hat is too big for you. You _____ this cap.

(1–3) 빈칸에 들어갈 알맞은 말을 고르시오.

1 These glasses _____ be Cindy's. She doesn't wear glasses.

① may   ② could
③ cannot   ④ should
⑤ must

2 You will _____ get up at 6 a.m. starting tomorrow.

① had   ② should
③ must   ④ have to
⑤ will

3 He made the same mistake. He _____ have been more careful.

① would   ② can
③ must   ④ should
⑤ used to

(4–6) 빈칸에 들어갈 말로 알맞지 않은 것은?

4 He _____ help me with my homework last year.

① would   ② could
③ must   ④ used to
⑤ had to

5 Henry _____ have made this model airplane yesterday.

① cannot   ② must
③ will   ④ should not
⑤ may

6 The waves are high. We _____ stay away from the beach.

① ought to   ② had better
③ can   ④ must
⑤ should

(7–8) 다음 중 어법상 어색한 것을 고르시오.

7 ① I will be able to join you for the trip.
② I would rather to buy a used car.
③ You can use my computer for your homework.
④ The rumor may be true.
⑤ She might have missed the last bus.

8 ① He cannot have lied to me.
② Jake used to loving apple juice.
③ She must be a spy.
④ Nina should have handed in her report by last Friday.
⑤ You had better keep your promise.

(9–10) 빈칸에 공통으로 들어갈 말은?

9

> · You _____ not enter the staff-only room.
> · You _____ be Jake's twin brother.

① must   ② would

③ will   ④ used to

⑤ would rather

10

> · The boys _____ get together after school to play soccer.
> · I _____ like to order two sandwiches.

① could   ② must

③ should   ④ would

⑤ ought to

(11–13) 주어진 문장과 같은 의미를 갖도록 빈칸을 채우시오.

11 My dad used to drive his car to his office.

> ⇨ My dad _____ drive his car to his office.

12 I am sure that Tiffany knew the truth.

> ⇨ Tiffany _____ the truth.

13 We don't need to wash the dishes by hand.

> ⇨ We _____ wash the dishes by hand.

14 다음 중 어법상 올바른 것은?

① He can runs 100 meters in 11 seconds.

② You may as well as give up.

③ She was used to be very kind.

④ You ought to returning the book by then.

⑤ You had better go to bed now.

(15–16) 다음 우리말을 영어로 바르게 옮긴 것은?

15 분명히 그가 이 그림을 그렸을 거야.

① He had to draw this painting.

② He must draw this painting.

③ He might have drew this picture.

④ He must have drawn this picture.

⑤ He should have drawn this picture.

16 나는 음료수를 하나 더 마시지 않는 것이 낫겠다.

① I don't have to drink another soda.

② I had better not drink another soda.

③ I not need to drink another soda.

④ I must not drink another soda.

⑤ I had not better drink another soda.

17 다음 중 대화의 내용이 <u>어색한</u> 것은?

① A: Did Tom cheat on the test?
  B: No, he cannot have done that.

② A: My sister spilled water on my cell phone.
  B: You must have been upset.

③ A: Where is your wallet?
  B: I might have left it at the café.

④ A: His report is perfect.
  B: He should have worked hard.

⑤ A: Oh, dear. You broke your leg.
  B: I should have been careful.

(18–20) 우리말과 의미가 같도록 ( ) 안의 말을 배열하시오.

18 네가 그 문제에 책임을 질 필요는 없다.
(for, don't, responsible, to, have, be)

⇨ You _____

_____ that matter.

19 나는 예전에 복숭아에 알레르기가 있었다.
(be, to, allergic, used)

⇨ I _____

to peaches.

20 Andrew가 그런 어리석은 실수를 저질렀을 리가 없다.
(foolish, have, cannot, made, that, mistake)

⇨ Andrew _____

_____.

21 밑줄 친 부분의 의미로 <u>어색한</u> 것은?

① When you finish the work, you <u>may</u> go home. (허락)

② His decision <u>cannot</u> be wrong. (능력)

③ You <u>ought</u> to be there on time. (충고)

④ I <u>must</u> lower my voice here. (의무)

⑤ She <u>may</u> not like going to the zoo. (추측)

22 다음 두 문장의 의미가 서로 <u>다른</u> 것은?

① May I ask a favor of you?
  = Can I ask a favor of you?

② My answers cannot be wrong.
  = My answers must be correct.

③ He must send the e-mail right away.
  = He has to send the e-mail right away.

④ You should have helped your mom.
  = You must have helped your mom.

⑤ You should stay away from them!
  = You ought to stay away from them!

23 밑줄 친 부분의 쓰임이 나머지와 <u>다른</u> 것은?

① They <u>must</u> recycle the cans.

② He <u>must</u> be the eldest in his family.

③ We <u>must</u> wait for her answer.

④ She <u>must</u> make two copies of the papers.

⑤ I <u>must</u> look after my baby sister.

24 어법상 올바른 것으로만 짝지어진 것은?

ⓐ I had not better stay in the sun.
ⓑ It cannot be true at all.
ⓒ She must have studied abroad.
ⓓ I would rather sleep than watching that silly show.
ⓔ You should have go to the concert with us.

① ⓐ, ⓑ ② ⓐ, ⓒ
③ ⓑ, ⓒ ④ ⓑ, ⓓ
⑤ ⓓ, ⓔ

(25–27) 우리말과 의미가 같도록 ( ) 안의 말을 이용하여 문장을 완성하시오.

25 Beth는 그녀의 강아지들에게 먹이를 주어야 한다. (have, feed)

⇨ Beth _____ her puppies.

26 나는 하루 종일 방 안에만 있기보다는 산책을 하는 것이 낫겠다. (take a walk)

⇨ I _____ than stay in my room all day.

27 네가 그에게 사과를 했어야 했는데. (should, apologize)

⇨ You _____ to him.

(28–30) 다음 문장에서 어색한 부분을 찾아 바르게 고치고 알맞은 이유를 고르시오.

28 The lake would be quite clean. But it is not clean any more.

고치기: _____ ⇨ _____
이유: 현재와 다른 과거 (상태, 동작)이면 (would, used to) + 동사원형

29 You had not better take his advice.

고치기: _____ ⇨ _____
이유: had better의 부정형은 바로 (앞, 뒤)에 (don't, not)

30 They will must reserve the tickets in advance.

고치기: _____ ⇨ _____
이유: 조동사 뒤에는 (조동사, 동사원형) will + (must, have to)

31 다음 조건을 이용하여 알맞게 영작하시오.

나는 오늘 수영복을 가져왔어야 했는데 못 가져왔다.
조건 1: bring, swimsuit
조건 2: 7단어

⇨ _____

_____ .

한눈에 정리하는 Grammar Mapping

빈칸에 알맞은 답을 보기에서 골라 넣어 grammar mapping 완성하기

조동사

can
| 능력 | ~할 수 있다 (= be able to) |
| 허락 | ① _____ |

cannot
| 부정적 추측 | ② _____ (cannot + 동사원형)
~이었을 리가 없다 (③ _____) |

may
| 허락 | ~해도 된다 |
| 약한 추측 | ④ _____ (may + 동사원형)
~이었을지도 모른다 (⑤ _____) |

must
| 의무 | ~해야 한다 (= have to), must의 과거형 = had to |
| 강한 추측 | ⑥ _____ (must + 동사원형)
~이었음에 틀림없다 (⑦ _____) |

have to
| 의무 | ~해야 한다 (= must) |

Tips
| 금지 | ⑧ _____ (must not) |
| 불필요 | ⑨ _____ (don't have to) |

**should
ought to**
| 의무 / 충고 | (도덕적) ~해야 한다, ~하는 것이 좋다 (should + 동사원형.) |
| 유감 | ⑩ _____ (should + have + p.p.) |

used to
| 과거 습관 | ⑪ _____ (= would) |
| 과거 상태 | ⑫ _____ (≠ would) |

had better
| 강한 충고 | ⑬ _____ |
| 금지 충고 | ⑭ _____ ~하지 않는 것이 낫다 |

would rather
| 선택 | 차라리 ~하겠다
would rather A ⑮ _____ B: B하느니 차라리 A하겠다 |

may as well
| 선택 | 차라리 ~하는 것이 낫다 |

보기
- ~임에 틀림없다
- ~일지도 모른다
- ~하곤 했다
- ~할 필요가 없다
- had better not
- ~해도 된다
- must + have + p.p.
- ~하는 것이 낫다
- ~일 리가 없다
- ~이었다
- ~해서는 안 된다
- cannot + have + p.p.
- ~했어야 했는데 하지 못했다
- may + have + p.p.
- than

수동태

수동태의 의미와 기본 형태

GP 09

수동태는 [be동사 + 과거분사]의 형태로 주어가 동작의 영향을 받거나 당하는 대상이 될 때 쓴다.

능동태	주어 ❸	동사 ❷	목적어 ❶
수동태	목적어주어	be동사 과거분사	by 행위자

Columbus **discovered** America in 1492.
→ America **was discovered** in 1492 by Columbus.
This book **was not written** by George Orwell.

> **Tip**
> **[by + 행위자] 생략**
> ① 행위자가 일반인인 경우
>   The dollar is used in many countries.
> ② 행위자가 불분명하거나 중요하지 않은 경우
>   His bike was stolen.

수동태의 다양한 형태

GP 10

미래형 수동태	will (be going to) + be	과거분사
진행형 수동태	be동사 + being	과거분사
완료형 수동태	have (has / had) + been	과거분사
조동사 수동태	조동사 + be	과거분사

You **will be remembered** as a great leader. (미래형 수동태)
☆ Space elevators **are being built** by the company. (현재진행형 수동태)
☆ The road **has been closed** because of heavy snow. (현재완료형 수동태)
☆ These flowers **should be watered** every day. (조동사 수동태)

동사구 수동태

GP 11

두 개 이상의 단어로 이루어진 동사구는 하나의 단어 개념으로 생각하고 수동태로 바꾼다.

주어	동사	전치사	목적어	He looked after the puppy.
목적어주어	be동사 과거분사	전치사	by 행위자	☆ The puppy was looked after by him.

run over	~을 차로 치다	look after	~을 돌보다
turn on / off	~을 켜다 / 끄다	carry out	~을 실행하다
put off	~을 미루다	take care of	~을 돌보다
hand out	~을 나눠주다	make use of	~을 사용하다
laugh at	~을 비웃다	look up to	~을 존경하다

A ( ) 안에서 알맞은 것을 고르시오.

1 The street walls are (painting, being painted) by volunteers.

2 The dictionary app can (is, be) downloaded for free.

3 The math problem has not (was, been) solved yet.

4 These apples (are, were) picked yesterday.

5 Soda (is contained, contains) a lot of sugar.

B 다음 능동태 문장을 수동태로 바꿔 쓰시오.

1 The writer is writing the ending of the story.

→ The ending of the story _____ by the writer.

2 The tornado has damaged the whole town.

→ The whole town _____ by the tornado.

3 We should treat all people equally.

→ All people _____ equally.

C 우리말과 의미가 같도록 ( ) 안의 말을 이용하여 문장을 완성하시오.

1 얼음 한 덩어리가 그 아티스트에 의해서 조각되어지고 있는 중이다. (carve)

→ A block of ice _____ _____ _____ by the artist.

2 꿀은 기침에도 사용되어져 왔다. (use)

→ Honey _____ _____ _____ for coughs as well.

3 그의 새 앨범은 다음달에 출시될 것입니다. (release)

→ His new album _____ _____ _____ next month.

D 밑줄 친 부분에 대한 설명을 하고 틀린 경우엔 바르게 고치시오. (맞으면 'O' 표시)

* p.p.: 과거분사

1	The rules must is <u>obeyed</u>. → ( )	조동사 수동태는 must + (be + p.p., be동사 + p.p.)
2	Six gold medals <u>have are won</u> so far. → ( )	완료형 수동태는 have + (been + p.p., be동사 + p.p.)
3	The food is <u>being heating</u> again. → ( )	진행형 수동태는 be동사 + (being + -ing, being + p.p.)
4	The project <u>was carried</u> by her. → ( )	동사구 carry out(실행하다) 수동태는 be동사 + (carried, carried out)

4형식 문장의 수동태

GP 12

간접목적어와 직접목적어를 각각 주어로 하여 두 가지 형태의 수동태 문장으로 바꿀 수 있다.
직접목적어를 수동태의 주어로 만들면 간접목적어 앞에 전치사(to, for, of)를 쓴다.

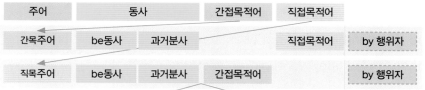

❶ 간접목적어와 직접목적어를 각각 주어로 쓰는 동사: give, offer, tell, teach...

She gave *him* two concert tickets.

→ *He* **was given** two concert tickets by her.

→ ☆ Two concert tickets **were given to** him by her.

❷ 직접목적어만을 주어로 쓰는 동사: make, buy, find, cook, write, pass...

My uncle bought me a nice backpack.

→ ☆ A nice backpack **was bought for** me by my uncle.

→ I **was bought** a nice backpack by my uncle. (×)

> ○ Tip ○
>
> 간접목적어 앞에 쓰는 전치사
> to: 대부분의 수여동사
> for: make, buy, find, cook...
> of: ask, inquire...

5형식 문장의 수동태

GP 13

능동태 문장의 목적어를 주어로 하고 목적격보어는 그대로 써서 수동태를 만든다.
단, 목적격보어가 동사원형이면 to부정사로 바꿔서 수동태를 만든다.

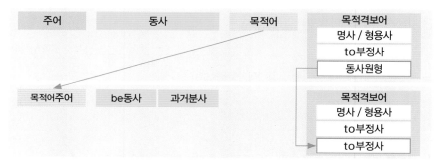

❶ 목적격보어가 명사 / 형용사 / to부정사인 경우: 그대로 쓴다.

They called her a walking dictionary.

→ ☆ She **was called** a walking dictionary.

He told us to sit down.

→ ☆ We **were told** to sit down by him.

> ○ Upgrade ○
>
> 지각동사의 목적격보어가 현재분사인 경
> 우 수동태에서 현재분사를 그대로 쓴다.
> I saw the dog swimmimg.
> The dog was seen swimmimg.

❷ 목적격보어가 동사원형인 경우: to부정사로 바뀐다.

(1) 사역동사: Jessica made me clean the room.

→ ☆ I **was made to clean** the room by Jessica.

(2) 지각동사: I saw the boy climb the tree.

→ ☆ The boy **was seen to climb (climbing)** the tree (by me).

GP Practice

A   ( ) 안에서 알맞은 것을 고르시오.

1 The secret message was sent (for, to) the wrong person.

2 I (taught, was taught) good habits by my parents.

3 The turtles were seen (lay, to lay) eggs on the beach.

4 We were made (standing, to stand) in line.

B   다음 능동태 문장을 수동태로 바꿔 쓰시오.

1 My mom made me take out the garbage.

→ I _____ the garbage by my mom.

2 They allowed us to enter the cave.

→ We _____ the cave.

3 They gave olive oil a lot of attention.

→ Olive oil _____ by them.

→ A lot of attention _____ by them.

C   우리말과 의미가 같도록 ( ) 안의 말을 이용하여 문장을 완성하시오.

1 지구는 움직이는 것이 느껴지지 않는다. (feel, move)

→ The Earth _____ _____ _____ _____ _____.

2 사람들은 이 과일을 '가난한 자의 음식'이라고 부른다. (call, poor man's food)

→ This fruit _____ _____ _____.

3 Jack의 엄마는 그를 위해 중고 바이올린을 사 주셨다. (buy)

→ A used violin _____ _____ _____ _____ by his mom.

D   밑줄 친 부분에 대한 설명을 하고 틀린 경우엔 바르게 고치시오. (맞으면 'O' 표시)

                                                * 간목: 간접목적어

1	He was seen <u>ride</u> a bike. → ( )	지각동사 see의 수동태는 be동사 + seen + (동사원형, to부정사)
2	He was made <u>stand up</u>. → ( )	사역동사 make의 수동태는 be동사 + made + (동사원형, to부정사)
3	Some yogurt was bought <u>of him</u>. → ( )	4형식 동사 buy의 수동태는 be동사 + bought + (for, of) + 간목
4	The ball was passed <u>for me</u> again. → ( )	4형식 동사 pass의 수동태는 be동사 + passed + (to, for) + 간목

목적어가 that절인 문장의 수동태

목적어가 that절인 문장은 두 가지 형태의 수동태를 만들 수 있다.

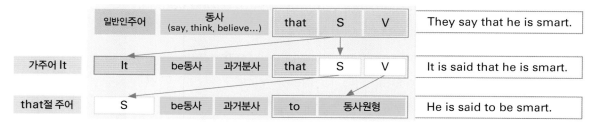

	일반인주어	동사 (say, think, believe...)	that	S	V	They say that he is smart.
가주어 It	It	be동사	과거분사	that	S	V	It is said that he is smart.
that절 주어	S	be동사	과거분사	to	동사원형	He is said to be smart.

People say that laughter brings good luck.
→ ☆ **It is said that** laughter brings good luck.
→ ☆ **Laughter is said to bring** good luck.

• Upgrade •

that절의 주어를 수동태의 주어로 할 때, 주절의 시제보다 that절의 시제가 앞서면 that절의 동사를 완료부정사(to have p.p.)로 바꾼다.
People **say** that she **is** an angel.　→ She is said **to be** an angel.
People **say** that she **was** an angel.　→ She is said **to have been** an angel.

by 이외의 전치사를 쓰는 수동태

주어	be동사	과거분사	by	The table is made by him.
			기타 전치사	The table is made of wood.

be interested in	~에 관심이 있다	be tired of	~에 싫증나다
be filled with	~로 가득 차 있다	be surprised at	~에 놀라다
be covered with	~로 덮여 있다	be known to	~에게 알려져 있다
be pleased with	~에 기뻐하다	be known as	~라고 알려지다
be satisfied with	~에 만족하다	be known for	~로 유명하다
be disappointed with	~에 실망하다	be made of / from	~로 만들어지다

The store **was filled with** toys for the Christmas sale.
☆ Korean popular music **is known as** K-pop.

GP Practice

A ( ) 안에서 알맞은 것을 고르시오.

1 This bakery is known (as, for) cheesecakes.

2 A monster is said (live, to live) in the lake called Loch Ness.

3 It (expects, is expected) that this summer will be very hot.

4 The poodle was covered (from, with) mud.

B 다음 능동태 문장을 수동태로 바꿔 쓰시오.

1 People believe that breaking a mirror brings bad luck.

→ It _____ breaking a mirror brings bad luck.

→ Breaking a mirror _____ bad luck.

2 They think that Mario is smart.

→ It _____ Mario is smart.

→ Mario _____ smart.

C 우리말과 의미가 같도록 ( ) 안의 말을 이용하여 문장을 완성하시오

1 목성은 60개 이상의 위성을 갖고 있다고 알려져 있다. (know, have)

→ Jupiter _____ _____ _____ _____ more than 60 moons.

2 초콜릿은 코코아콩으로 만들어진다. (make)

→ Chocolate _____ _____ _____ cocoa beans.

3 용의자는 키가 큰 남성이라고 보고되어졌다. (report, be)

→ The suspect _____ _____ _____ _____ a tall man.

D 밑줄 친 부분에 대한 설명을 하고 틀린 경우엔 바르게 고치시오. (맞으면 'O' 표시)

1	Lions are said <u>to sleep</u> about 20 hours. → ( )	'~한다고 이야기되어지다'는 be동사 + said + to (동사원형, have p.p.)
2	He is said <u>to be</u> an actor before. → ( )	'~이었다고 이야기되어지다'는 be동사 + said + to (동사원형, have p.p.)
3	It <u>believed</u> that the dog is 15 years old. → ( )	that절이 목적어인 문장의 수동태는 It + (believe, is believed) + that S + V
4	Her eyes are filled <u>in</u> hope. → ( )	'~로 가득 차다'는 be동사 + filled + (in, with)

A 우리말과 의미가 같도록 ( ) 안의 말을 배열하시오.

1 소포가 안전하게 배달이 되었다. (was, the package, delivered)

→ _____ safely.

2 그는 그 책을 다시 읽어 보라고 충고 받았다. (advised, was, he, to, read)

→ _____ the book again.

3 그녀는 우리를 실내에 머무르도록 했다. (were, we, to, stay, made, inside)

→ _____ by her.

4 새는 공룡에서 진화했다고 믿어진다. (to, are believed, have evolved)

→ Birds _____ from dinosaurs.

5 Sally가 피아노 치는 것이 들렸다. (was, heard, Sally, playing)

→ _____ the piano.

6 Sandra는 그녀의 새 자전거에 실망을 했다. (disappointed, was, with, new bike, her)

→ Sandra _____ .

B 우리말과 의미가 같도록 ( ) 안의 말을 이용하여 문장을 완성하시오.

1 그녀는 생각할 충분한 시간을 받았다. (give, enough)

→ She _____ _____ _____ _____ to think.

2 이 정보는 과학자들에 의해 비밀로 지켜졌다. (keep, secret)

→ The information _____ _____ _____ _____ the
scientists.

3 소금이 그녀에 의해 James에게 건네졌다. (salt, pass)

→ _____ _____ _____ _____ James by her.

4 내 컴퓨터는 아빠에 의해 수리되어지고 있는 중이다. (repair)

→ _____ _____ _____ _____ by my dad.

5 그의 작품은 박물관에 전시되어질 것이다. (display, artwork)

→ _____ _____ _____ _____ _____ at the
museum.

6 그의 초기 그림들은 사람들에게 비웃음을 당했다. (laugh at)

→ His early paintings _____ _____ _____ _____
_____ .

C 밑줄 친 부분을 주어로 시작하는 문장을 완성하시오.

1 They have canceled <u>the next flight from Busan</u>.

→ _____ by them.

2 I sent Joshua <u>a video file</u> by phone.

→ _____ by me by phone.

3 You must keep <u>your bed</u> clean and neat.

→ _____ clean and neat.

4 People have trained <u>dogs</u> in various ways.

→ _____ in various ways.

5 The teacher handed out <u>the tests</u> to the students.

→ _____ to the students by the teacher.

6 The boss made <u>him</u> attend the meeting every morning.

→ _____ every morning by the

boss.

D 그림에서 동그라미 표시된 사람이나 사물의 입장에서 문장을 완성하시오. (과거시제 사용)

name, Ace

give, a birthday gift

for, cook

1 The dog _____.

2 She _____ by him.

3 A birthday gift _____ her by him.

4 Some pancakes _____ Jane.

(1–4) 빈칸에 들어갈 알맞은 말을 고르시오.

1 All the windows must _____.

① close   ② closed

③ are closed   ④ be closing

⑤ be closed

2 The mystery has not _____ for centuries.

① be solved   ② been solve

③ been solved   ④ being solved

⑤ being solve

3 Students are made _____ school uniforms.

① wear   ② wears

③ worn   ④ to wear

⑤ wearing

4 The floor _____ by a robot cleaner.

① cleans   ② is cleaning

③ being cleaned ④ has being clean

⑤ is being cleaned

(5–6) 다음 중 어법상 어색한 것을 고르시오.

5 ① The money has been saved by her.

② The eggs are be boiled.

③ I am satisfied with your plan.

④ The fish will be fried for dinner.

⑤ The sun sets in the west.

6 ① Max is considered honest.

② A hat was seen fly in the air.

③ The headlights were turned off.

④ The mission was carried out by the team.

⑤ He was made to do the dishes.

(7–8) 빈칸에 공통으로 들어갈 말은?

7 · A puppy was heard _____ bark.

· He was asked _____ help Emma.

① to   ② of

③ for   ④ with

⑤ in

8 · We were tired _____ the long and boring speech.

· The bench is made _____ wood.

① to   ② of

③ for   ④ from

⑤ in

9 빈칸에 들어갈 말이 나머지와 <u>다른</u> 것은?

① The job was offered _____ Mr. Simpson.

② A glass of water was brought _____ me.

③ Her painting was sent _____ the art gallery.

④ A hair band was made _____ me by my aunt.

⑤ The baby pandas were shown _____ the public.

(10–12) ( ) 안의 말을 알맞은 형태로 고쳐 문장을 완성하시오.

10 Brian was made _____ the snow in front of his house. (sweep)

11 Leo is thought _____ a lot about Korea now. (know)

12 The desk was _____ papers. (cover)

13 다음 중 어법상 알맞은 것을 고르시오.

① He was not ran over by a car.

② Wine is made with grapes.

③ Brian was bought a bag by me.

④ I was told to finish my meal.

⑤ The fish tank put on the table.

(14–15) 두 문장의 의미가 같도록 빈칸에 들어갈 알맞은 말을 고르시오.

14
| It is known that coffee turns teeth yellow.
→ Coffee _____ teeth yellow. |

① known turn

② is known turn

③ is known turning

④ is known to turn

⑤ is known to turning

15
| They watched him hit a homerun.
→ He was watched _____ a homerun. |

① hit   ② to hit

③ be hitting   ④ be hit

⑤ is being hit

16 다음 우리말을 영어로 바르게 옮긴 것은?

> 그 종들은 2011년부터 수집되어져 왔다.

① The bells were collected since 2011.
② The bells have been collected since 2011.
③ The bells have collected since 2011.
④ The bells have are collected since 2011.
⑤ The bells are being collected since 2011.

(17–19) 주어진 문장과 같은 의미를 갖도록 빈칸을 채우시오.

17 People believed that the tree protected the town.

⇨ It _____
_____.

⇨ The tree _____
_____.

18 They gave the visitors a free lunch.

⇨ A free lunch _____
_____ by them.

19 Her test grades disappointed Clara.

⇨ Clara _____
_____.

20 밑줄 친 부분을 수동태의 주어로 쓸 수 없는 것은?

① He named his dog Snoopy.
② I watched her pack her bag.
③ She told them to drive slowly.
④ The news made her happy.
⑤ She taught me good manners.

(21–23) 우리말과 의미가 같도록 ( ) 안의 말을 배열하시오.

21 Tim이 주인공을 연기할 것으로 예상된다.
(expected, is, play, to, the main role, Tim)

⇨ _____
_____.

22 그의 휴대폰은 영화를 보는 동안 꺼졌다.
(turned, was, during, off, the movie)

⇨ His cell phone _____
_____.

23 그 조리법은 그 가문에서 전해 내려온 것이다.
(the recipe, been, has, passed down)

⇨ _____
_____ in the family.

24 어법상 올바른 것으로만 짝지어진 것은?

> ⓐ Many songs have been made by her.
> ⓑ It was said that Helen was a good driver.
> ⓒ The ring was bought of my mom.
> ⓓ He was elected class president.
> ⓔ You are allowed eat ice cream.

① ⓐ, ⓑ, ⓒ   ② ⓐ, ⓑ, ⓓ

③ ⓑ, ⓒ, ⓓ   ④ ⓑ, ⓓ, ⓔ

⑤ ⓒ, ⓓ, ⓔ

(25-27) 우리말과 의미가 같도록 ( ) 안의 말을 이용하여 문장을 완성하시오.

25 이 책은 많은 언어로 번역되어져 왔다.
(translate)

⇨ This book _____ _____ into many languages.

26 다람쥐가 나무를 오르는 것이 보였다.
(see, climb)

⇨ A squirrel _____ _____ the tree.

27 너의 등은 똑바르게 유지되어야 한다.
(must, keep)

⇨ Your back _____ straight.

28 다음 빈칸에 사용되지 않는 것은?

> ⓐ The city is known _____ clean air.
> ⓑ Some soup was cooked _____ him.
> ⓒ The basket is filled _____ apples.
> ⓓ The kitten is looked _____ by her.
> ⓔ She was watched _____ ride a bike.

① to   ② for

③ with   ④ after

⑤ of

(29-30) 다음 문장에서 어색한 부분을 찾아 바르게 고치고 알맞은 이유를 고르시오.

29 They were made wear life jackets on the ship.

고치기: _____ ⇨ _____

이유: 사역동사 make의 수동태는
be동사 + made + (동사원형, to부정사)

30 The party is be recorded by Jake now.

고치기: _____ ⇨ _____

이유: '~되어지는 중' 진행형 수동태는
be동사 + (be, being) + 과거분사

31 다음 조건을 이용하여 알맞게 영작하시오.

> 이 약은 아침식사 후에 복용되어져야 합니다.
> 조건 1: take, medicine
> 조건 2: 7단어, 조동사 수동태

⇨ _____

_____.

한눈에 정리하는 Grammar Mapping

빈칸에 알맞은 답을 보기에서 골라 넣어 grammar mapping 완성하기

수동태

의미 ── 주어가 동작을 '당하다' 의미

형태
- **기본형** : 주어 + ① _____ + p.p. + by + 행위자(목적격)
  The package is delivered by the man.
- **조동사 수동태** : 주어 + 조동사 + ② _____ + p.p.
  The project must ② _____ finished tonight.
- **진행형 수동태** : 주어 + am / are / is / was / were + ③ _____ + p.p.
  A new library is ③ _____ built by them.
- **완료형 수동태** : 주어 + have / has / had + ④ _____ + p.p.
  A new library has ④ _____ built by them.

동사구 수동태 : 주어 + [be동사 + p.p. + ⑤ _____] + by 행위자
The radio was turned off by her.

4형식 수동태
- **간접목적어 주어** : He gave her a coupon.
  → ⑥ _____ was given a coupon by him.
- **직접목적어 주어** : 간접목적어 앞에 알맞은 전치사(to, ⑦ _____)를 쓴다.
  → A coupon was given ⑧ _____ her by him.

5형식 수동태
- 목적어를 수동태의 주어로 쓰고 ⑨ _____ 는 그대로 쓴다.
  She told me to carry the box.
  → ⑩ _____ was told to carry the box by her.
- 목적격보어가 ⑪ _____ 인 경우 수동태에서 ⑫ _____ 로 바뀐다.
  She made me carry the box.
  → I was made ⑬ _____ the box by her.

목적어가 that절인 문장의 수동태
- **It(가주어) 사용** : People think that Sam is a science genius.
  [It + be동사 + p.p. + ⑭ _____]
  → It is thought that Sam is a science genius.
- **that절의 주어 사용** : [⑮ _____ + be동사 + p.p. + ⑫ _____]
  → Sam is thought to be a science genius.

by 이외 전치사 수동태 : 주어 + be동사 + p.p. + ⑯ _____ + (대)명사

보기
- been
- be동사
- 전치사
- I
- in, at, of, with
- She
- that절의 주어
- to부정사
- for, of
- to
- 목적격보어
- being
- be
- 동사원형
- to carry
- that절

48

부정사

to부정사의 명사적 쓰임

GP 16

❶ 명사적 쓰임

문장에서 명사처럼 주어, 목적어, 보어 역할을 한다.

(1) 주어 역할

　To have good habits is important.

(2) 목적어 역할

　I hope **to become** a robot scientist.

(3) 보어 역할

　Her job is **to create** game characters.

> **Tip**
>
> to부정사의 부정은 to부정사 앞에 not
> 이나 never를 쓴다.
> · I agreed to join the club.
> → I agreed not to join the club.

❷ 가주어와 가목적어 it

주어나 목적어로 쓰인 to부정사가 길어진 경우 보통 가주어, 가목적어 it을 쓰고 to부정사는 뒤로 보낸다.

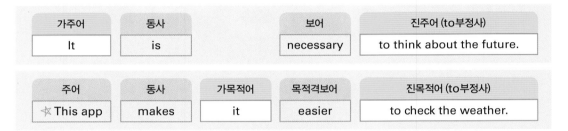

가주어	동사		보어	진주어 (to부정사)
It	is		necessary	to think about the future.

주어	동사	가목적어	목적격보어	진목적어 (to부정사)
☆ This app	makes	it	easier	to check the weather.

It is not easy **to make** new friends. (가주어 it)

He found **it** difficult **to say** no. (가목적어 it)

❸ 의문사 + to부정사

[의문사 + to부정사] 형태로 문장에서 명사처럼 쓰이며, [의문사 + 주어 + should + 동사원형]으로 바꿔 쓸 수 있다.

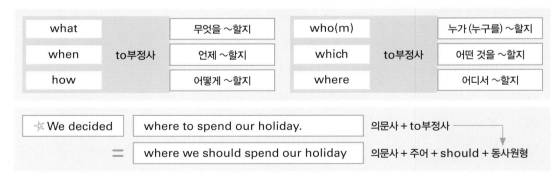

what		무엇을 ～할지	who(m)		누가 (누구를) ～할지
when	to부정사	언제 ～할지	which	to부정사	어떤 것을 ～할지
how		어떻게 ～할지	where		어디서 ～할지

☆ We decided	where to spend our holiday.	의문사 + to부정사
=	where we should spend our holiday	의문사 + 주어 + should + 동사원형

I don't know **when to start**.

　　　　 = when I should start

GP Practice

A ( ) 안에 알맞은 말을 고르시오.

1 The gentleman wanted (to leave, leave) a message.

2 Airplanes have made (it, this) easier to travel around the world.

3 I was nervous and forgot what (say, to say).

4 He found it fun (work, to work) with Elsa.

5 Can you teach me (how, why) to drive?

B 두 문장이 같은 의미가 되도록 빈칸을 채우시오.

1 To learn from mistakes is important.

→ _____ is important _____.

2 To develop good habits is not easy.

→ _____ is not easy _____.

3 We learned what we should do when an earthquake occurs.

→ We learned _____ when an earthquake occurs.

C 우리말과 의미가 같도록 ( ) 안의 말을 이용하여 문장을 완성하시오.

1 그들의 임무는 생존자들을 찾는 거였어. (mission, search for)

→ _____ _____ was _____ _____ _____ survivors.

2 그는 혼자 여행하는 것이 신나는 것임을 알게 되었다. (exciting, travel)

→ He found _____ _____ _____ _____ alone.

3 쥐들은 고양이 목에 어떻게 방울을 달 것인지를 논의했다. (how, hang)

→ The mice discussed _____ _____ _____ the bell around the cat's neck.

D 밑줄 친 부분에 대한 설명을 하고 틀린 경우엔 바르게 고치시오. (맞으면 'O' 표시)

1	<u>That</u> was fun to play tennis. → ( )	to부정사 주어가 길면 문장 앞에 (가주어, 진주어)인 (That, It) 사용
2	He agreed <u>don't</u> to buy a car. → ( )	to부정사의 부정은 (don't, not)을 to부정사 (앞, 뒤)에 사용
3	I thought <u>this</u> better to tell the truth. → ( )	주어 + 동사 + 가목적어 + 목적격보어 + 진목적어 (this, it) (to부정사, 동사원형)
4	I know how I <u>used</u> the machine. → ( )	'(무엇을, 어떻게) 할지'를 의미는 how + 주어 + (동사, should + 동사원형)

to부정사의 형용사적 쓰임

GP 17

❶ 명사 수식

문장에서 형용사처럼 명사를 수식한다. 이때 to부정사는 명사 뒤에서 명사를 수식한다.

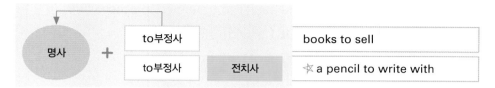

명사	+	to부정사		books to sell
		to부정사	전치사	☆ a pencil to write with

Give me *a chance* **to explain**.
Today, we have *something special* **to celebrate**.

❷ [be + to부정사] 용법

be동사 뒤에 to부정사를 사용하여 주어의 상태를 설명한다.

	주어	be동사 + to부정사			
예정	☆ We	are	to visit	Mexico next month.	～할 예정이다
가능	Nothing	was	to be seen	in the darkness.	～할 수 있다
의무	You	are	not to talk	during the test.	～해야 한다
운명	The spaceship	was	never to return	to the Earth.	～할 운명이다
의도	If you	are	to succeed,	do your best.	～하고자 하다

to부정사의 부사적 쓰임

GP 18

문장에서 부사처럼 동사, 형용사, 문장을 수식한다.

He works out hard **to burn** fat.　　　　　　　　(목적: ～하기 위해서)
　　　　　(= in order to, so as to)
We are happy **to hear** that.　　　　　　　　　　(감정의 원인: ～해서, ～하니)
☆ My password was easy **to remember**.　　　　　(형용사 수식: ～하기에)
She must be foolish **to trust** him.　　　　　　　(판단의 근거: ～하다니, ～으로 보아)
The boy grew up **to be** the president of the country.　(결과: ～해서, (결국) ～하다)
To turn left at the corner, you will find the bakery.　(조건: ～한다면)

GP Practice

A ( ) 안에서 알맞은 것을 고르시오.

1 I will show you a fun way (to learn, learn) English.

2 The dog must be angry (show, to show) its sharp teeth.

3 I found a nice hotel (to stay with, to stay at).

4 She would be surprised (hear, to hear) the results.

B 밑줄 친 [be + to부정사]의 알맞은 용법을 보기에서 골라 번호를 쓰시오. (한 번씩만 사용)

| 보기 | ① 가능 | ② 운명 | ③ 의무 | ④ 예정 | ⑤ 의도 | 용법 |

1 You <u>are to return</u> the book by tomorrow.　　　　　_____

2 No water <u>was to be found</u> on the planet.　　　　　_____

3 They <u>were never to meet</u> each other again.　　　　　_____

4 The bakery <u>is to open</u> next week.　　　　　_____

5 If you <u>are to meet</u> her, you should wait.　　　　　_____

C 우리말과 의미가 같도록 ( ) 안의 말을 이용하여 문장을 완성하시오.

1 내가 돌아올 때까지, 너희들은 여기에 있어야 해. (stay, be)

→ You _____ _____ _____ here until I come back.

2 그 기자는 무언가 쓸 것을 찾고 있어. (write about)

→ The reporter is looking for _____ _____ _____ _____.

3 연어는 알을 낳기 위해 그 강으로 돌아간다. (breed)

→ The salmon return to the river _____ _____.

4 나의 러시아 친구 이름은 철자를 쓰기가 어렵다. (difficult, spell)

→ My Russian friend's name is _____ _____ _____.

D 밑줄 친 부분에 대한 설명을 하고 틀린 경우엔 바르게 고치시오. (맞으면 'O' 표시)

1	There are chairs <u>to sit</u>. → (　　　　　　　　)	'(앉을, 위에 앉을) 의자'이므로 명사 + to부정사 + 전치사 (on, 없음)
2	You <u>are follow</u> the traffic rules. → (　　　　　　　　)	(가능, 의무)을·를 나타내며 be동사 + (동사, to부정사)
3	This robot is <u>conveniently</u> to use. → (　　　　　　　　)	(편리하게, 편리한) + 사용하기에 (부사, 형용사) + to부정사
4	The boy grew up <u>be</u> a comedian. → (　　　　　　　　)	(~하기 위해, 결국 ~하다) 의미는 grew up + (동사원형, to부정사)

목적격보어로 쓰이는 부정사

GP 19

동사의 종류에 따라 목적격보어로 to부정사나 원형부정사가 쓰인다.

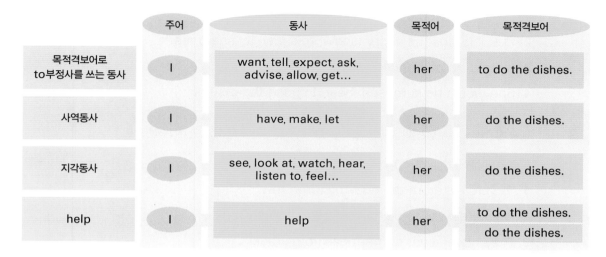

	주어	동사	목적어	목적격보어
목적격보어로 to부정사를 쓰는 동사	I	want, tell, expect, ask, advise, allow, get...	her	to do the dishes.
사역동사	I	have, make, let	her	do the dishes.
지각동사	I	see, look at, watch, hear, listen to, feel...	her	do the dishes.
help	I	help	her	to do the dishes. / do the dishes.

❶ 목적격보어로 to부정사를 쓰는 동사

☆ I *want* you **to listen to** me carefully.

My teacher *told* me **to hand in** the report online.

She *advised* me **not to use** my cell phone too much.

❷ 목적격보어로 원형부정사를 쓰는 동사

(1) 사역동사

☆ His funny joke *made* her **laugh**.

My mom *had* me **set** the table.

She *let* her kids **run** around the garden.

> **Tip**
> 사역동사의 의미
> ① let (허락): 원한다면 ~하게 하다
> ② have (명령, 권유): ~하게 하다
> ③ make (강제성): 강하게 ~하게 하다

(2) 지각동사

☆ She *watched* the kittens **play (playing)** with a ball.

We *heard* someone **ring (ringing)** the doorbell at midnight.

He *felt* a bug **crawl (crawling)** on his arm.

❸ 목적격보어로 to부정사와 원형부정사 둘 다 쓰는 동사: help

Smell *helps* us **taste (to taste)** food better.

• Upgrade •

get은 '~하게 하다'의 의미로 사역동사와 의미가 같지만 목적격보어로 to부정사를 쓴다.

She *got* me **to do** the dishes. = She *had* me **do** the dishes.

A ( ) 안에서 알맞은 것을 고르시오.

1 My mom told me (take, to take) out the garbage.

2 The makeup made her (look, to look) older.

3 He advised us (bring, to bring) a raincoat just in case.

4 I heard the birds (to sing, sing) early in the morning.

5 She got me (reserve, to reserve) a table at the restaurant.

B ( ) 안의 말을 알맞게 고쳐 빈칸을 채우시오.

1 I heard someone _____ at my door. (knock)

2 How did you make him _____ his mind? (change)

3 The driver asked his passengers _____ their seatbelts. (put on)

4 The picture helped him _____ the good old days. (remember)

C 우리말과 의미가 같도록 ( ) 안의 말을 이용하여 문장을 완성하시오.

1 판사는 그에게 벌금을 내도록 명령했다. (order, pay)

→ The judge _____ _____ _____ _____ a fine.

2 나는 모기가 내 팔을 무는 것을 느끼지 못했다. (feel, the mosquito, bite)

→ I didn't _____ _____ _____ _____ my arm.

3 그는 그의 고양이가 소파에서 자도록 내버려 뒀다. (let, sleep)

→ He _____ _____ _____ _____ on the sofa.

4 엄마는 내게 이면지를 재활용하도록 하셨다. (have, recycle)

→ My mom _____ _____ _____ the used paper.

D 밑줄 친 부분에 대한 설명을 하고 틀린 경우엔 바르게 고치시오. (맞으면 'O' 표시)

* 가능한 답은 모두 체크

1	We saw the seagulls <u>to follow</u> the boat. → ( )	주어 + see + 목적어 + 목적격보어 (원형부정사, to부정사)
2	She always makes me <u>to feel</u> special. → ( )	주어 + make + 목적어 + 목적격보어 (원형부정사, to부정사)
3	Joe helped me <u>fix</u> the door. → ( )	주어 + help + 목적어 + 목적격보어 (원형부정사, to부정사)
4	She asked Tom <u>marry</u> her. → ( )	주어 + ask + 목적어 + 목적격보어 (원형부정사, to부정사)

to부정사의 의미상 주어

GP 20

to부정사의 행위자를 to부정사의 의미상 주어라고 한다. to부정사의 행위자가 문장의 주어나 목적어와 다를 경우, to부정사 앞에 [for + 목적격] 또는 [of + 목적격] 형태로 행위 주체를 나타낸다.

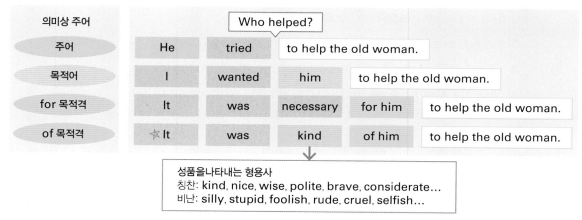

❶ for + 목적격: to부정사의 의미상의 주어는 대부분 [for + 목적격] 형태를 쓴다.

I held the door **for the next person** to come in.

❷ of + 목적격: 사람의 성품을 나타내는 형용사가 쓰이면 [of + 목적격] 형태를 쓴다.

It was *wise* **of her** to give you a second chance.

to부정사의 시제

GP 21

❶ 단순 부정사: [to + 동사원형] 형태로 to부정사의 시제가 주절의 시제와 같거나 미래를 나타낸다.

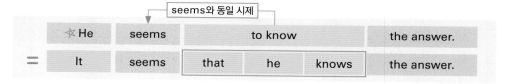

❷ 완료 부정사: [to + have p.p.] 형태로 to부정사의 시제가 주절의 시제보다 앞선다는 것을 나타낸다.

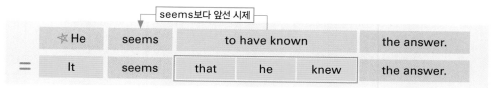

• Upgrade •

to부정사의 수동태

단순 수동태	to + be p.p.	수동태 의미의 to부정사가 주절 시제와 **같을 때**
완료 수동태	to + have been p.p.	수동태 의미의 to부정사가 주절 시제보다 **앞설 때**

I am happy **to be invited** by you. (= I am happy that I **am invited** by you.)

I am happy **to have been invited** by you. (= I am happy that I **was invited** by you.)

A ( ) 안에서 알맞은 것을 고르시오.

1 It was kind (of, for) you to bring me an extra blanket.

2 She seems (to have, to have had) a warm heart now.

3 This song is easy (of, for) you to sing.

4 I am sorry (to miss, to have missed) your call.

5 We don't want (to treat, to be treated) like children.

B 두 문장이 같은 의미가 되도록 빈칸을 채우시오.

1 It seems that my dog sometimes shares my feelings.

→ My dog sometimes seems _____ my feelings.

2 It seems that Mary left her passport at home.

→ Mary seems _____ her passport at home.

3 It seems that the artist is loved by Europeans.

→ The artist seems _____ by Europeans.

C 우리말과 의미가 같도록 ( ) 안의 말을 이용하여 문장을 완성하시오.

1 이 지도는 업그레이드 되어져야 한다. (upgrade)

→ This map needs _____ _____ _____.

2 이 가위는 왼손잡이 사람들이 쓰기에 편리해. (left-handed people, use)

→ These scissors are comfortable _____ _____ _____

_____ _____.

3 그 코끼리들은 쓰나미를 미리 감지했던 것 같아. (sense)

→ The elephants seemed to _____ _____ the tsunami in advance.

D 밑줄 친 부분에 대한 설명을 하고 틀린 경우엔 바르게 고치시오. (맞으면 'O' 표시)

1	It was wise <u>you</u> to make plans. → ( )	성품형용사가 (있으면, 없으면) 의미상 주어는 (of, for) + 목적격
2	He seems <u>to know</u> the answer now. → ( )	to부정사 시제가 주절과 같을 때 to + (동사원형, have p.p.)
3	I seem <u>to lose</u> my hand cream. → ( )	to부정사 시제가 주절보다 앞설 때 to + (동사원형, have p.p.)
4	The car needs <u>to wash</u>. → ( )	to부정사가 (능동, 수동) 의미이므로 to + (동사원형, be p.p.)

to부정사를 이용한 구문

GP 22

❶ 형용사 / 부사 + enough + to부정사

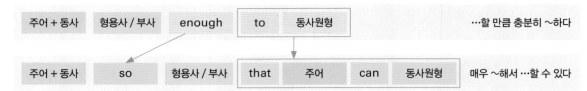

주어 + 동사	형용사 / 부사	enough	to	동사원형			…할 만큼 충분히 ~하다
주어 + 동사	so	형용사 / 부사	that	주어	can	동사원형	매우 ~해서 …할 수 있다

He was **lucky enough to marry** a woman like you.
→ He was **so lucky that he could marry** a woman like you.
The tornado is **powerful enough to destroy** houses.
→ The tornado is **so powerful that it can destroy** houses.

❷ too + 형용사 / 부사 + to부정사

주어 + 동사	too	형용사 / 부사	to	동사원형			…하기엔 너무 ~하다
주어 + 동사	so	형용사 / 부사	that	주어	can't	동사원형	매우 ~해서 …할 수 없다

The program was **too violent for him to watch**.
→ The program was **so violent that he couldn't watch** it.
She is **too young to go** to the movies alone.
→ She is **so young that she can't go** to the movies alone.

독립부정사

GP 23

to부정사의 표현이 숙어처럼 독립적 의미를 갖는 것이며, 문장 전체를 수식한다.

to begin with	우선, 먼저	to be frank with you	솔직히 말해서
to be sure	확실히	strange to say	이상한 이야기지만
so to speak	말하자면	not to mention	~은 말할 것도 없이
to tell the truth	사실대로 말하자면	to make matters worse	설상가상으로

To be sure, she is the smartest student in our school.
He is, **so to speak**, a musical genius.
To make matters worse, we felt tired and got lost in the woods.

GP Practice

A ( ) 안에서 알맞은 것을 고르시오.

1 Strange (saying, to say), I had the same dream twice last week.

2 The news was (so good, too good) to be true.

3 (To make, Making) matters worse, his cell phone died.

4 Her hair is long enough (that it reaches, to reach) the floor.

5 The rescue team arrived (enough fast, fast enough) to save the boy.

B 두 문장이 같은 의미가 되도록 빈칸을 채우시오.

1 The newborn puppy is so young that it can't open its eyes.

→ The newborn puppy is _____ its eyes.

2 My sister is so energetic that she can't stay still.

→ My sister is _____.

3 This bed is so large that it can hold three people.

→ This bed is _____ three people.

C 우리말과 의미가 같도록 ( ) 안의 말을 이용하여 문장을 완성하시오.

1 까마귀들은 도구를 사용할 만큼 영리하다. (smart, use)

→ Crows are _____ _____ _____ _____ tools.

2 안개가 너무 끼어서 그는 운전할 수 없었다. (foggy, drive)

→ It was _____ _____ for him _____ _____.

3 솔직히 말해서, 나는 우리 엄마의 음식을 좋아하지 않아. (frank with)

→ _____ _____ _____ _____ _____, I don't

like my mom's cooking.

D 밑줄 친 부분에 대한 설명을 하고 틀린 경우엔 바르게 고치시오. (맞으면 'O' 표시)

<small>* S: 주어, V: 동사</small>

1	The boy is <u>so</u> young to drive. → ( )	(~하기 충분한, 너무 ~해서) 의미일 때 (so, too) + 형용사 + to부정사
2	He worked <u>enough hard</u> to succeed. → ( )	(~하기 충분히, 너무 ~하게) 의미일 때 (enough + 부사, 부사 + enough) + to부정사
3	<u>To sure</u>, he is a great inventor. → ( )	(확실히, 확실하기 위해서) 의미일 때 to + (sure, be sure)
4	I am <u>too</u> busy that I can't meet you. → ( )	'매우 ~해서 ~할 수 없다' 의미일 때 S + V + (so, too) 형용사 that + S + can't + V

A 우리말과 의미가 같도록 ( ) 안의 말을 배열하시오.

1 야생동물의 사진을 찍는 것은 긴장감이 있었다. (thrilling, take pictures of, to)

→ It was _____ wild animals.

2 그는 나에게 그 공포영화를 안 보도록 충고했다. (to watch, advised, not, me)

→ He _____ the horror movie.

3 스테이크가 너무 익지 않아서 먹지를 못하겠다. (too, to, rare, eat, was)

→ The steak _____.

4 삭제되어야 할 파일을 선택하시오. (to, the file, be deleted)

→ Select _____.

5 네가 내 생일을 기억하다니 사려가 깊구나. (of, thoughtful, you, to, remember)

→ It was _____ my birthday.

6 Chris는 그의 바쁜 생활을 즐기는 것 같아 보인다. (to enjoy, his, seems, busy life)

→ Chris _____.

B 우리말과 의미가 같도록 ( ) 안의 말을 이용하여 문장을 완성하시오.

1 나는 네가 마음을 열어 주면 좋겠다. (want, open)

→ I _____ _____ _____ _____ your mind.

2 당신은 이 놀이공원에 방문한 100만 번째 손님입니다. (one millionth customer, visit)

→ You are the _____ _____ _____ _____ _____ this theme park.

3 너는 혼자서 여행하기에 너무 어리다. (young, travel)

→ You are _____ _____ _____ _____ alone.

4 그들은 비밀을 지키는 것이 어렵다는 것을 알게 되었다. (keep a secret)

→ They found it _____ _____ _____ _____ _____.

5 우리는 방콕에서 비행기를 갈아탈 예정입니다. (be, transfer)

→ We _____ _____ _____ in Bangkok.

6 그 작가는 많은 것들을 경험했던 것으로 보인다. (experience, things)

→ The writer seems _____ _____ _____ _____.

7 내 남동생은 절대로 내가 자신의 간식을 먹도록 하지 않는다. (let, eat, snacks)

→ My brother never _____ _____ _____ _____.

C 다음 문장을 to부정사를 이용하여 같은 의미를 갖는 문장으로 고치시오.

1 It seems that she enjoys her life.

→ She seems _____.

2 Ryan hasn't decided what he should wear to the party.

→ Ryan hasn't decided what _____.

3 Angela expects that her brother will become an actor.

→ Angela expects her brother _____.

4 The department store is going to hold a summer sale soon.

→ The department store is _____.

5 The box is so small that it can't hold the big teddy bear.

→ The box is too _____.

6 Her dog was so popular that it could appear in TV commercials.

→ Her dog was popular _____.

D 그림에 맞게 주어진 말을 이용하여 문장을 완성하시오. (과거시제 사용)

make /
set the table

tell /
wear sunscreen

advise /
wear green pants

help /
ride a bike

1 Peter's sister _____ in the morning.

2 Peter's sister _____.

3 Peter's sister _____.

4 Peter's sister _____.

(1-4) 빈칸에 들어갈 알맞은 말을 고르시오.

1
> I never let my cousin _____ my drone.

① touch   ② touches   ③ touched
④ to touch   ⑤ touching

2
> How kind _____ to bring me my lunch!

① she   ② her   ③ of her
④ for her   ⑤ of she

3
> They found a way _____ the virus.

① kill   ② killed   ③ to killed
④ to kill   ⑤ to have killed

4
> _____ the truth, I fell in love with Jane.

① Say   ② To say   ③ Tell
④ To tell   ⑤ To told

(5-6) 다음 빈칸에 들어갈 수 없는 것은?

5
> Mom _____ me stay inside the car.

① made   ② had   ③ saw
④ told   ⑤ let

6
> It was _____ for him to climb up the hill.

① easy   ② possible   ③ fun
④ foolish   ⑤ dangerous

7 빈칸에 들어갈 말이 바르게 짝지어진 것은?

> · To be _____, the singer has a great voice.
> · To make matters _____, it started raining.

① sure - bad   ② surely - bad
③ surely - badly   ④ surely - worse
⑤ sure - worse

(8-9) 다음 중 어법상 어색한 것을 고르시오.

8 ① She seems to have dyed her hair.
② Was it easy for you to lose weight?
③ He was careless enough to dive first.
④ I made it a rule to get up early.
⑤ He was enough shy to talk to her.

9 ① We got him see a doctor right away.
② He expects me to give him a bonus.
③ Did you make him read the book?
④ She helped me choose a bag.
⑤ We want you to be more careful.

10 어법상 올바른 것으로만 짝지어진 것은?

> ⓐ He seems to forget his promise yesterday.
> ⓑ This movie was boring of us to watch.
> ⓒ Let the boys play in the garden.
> ⓓ The elevator needs to be repaired.
> ⓔ He won't allow his son sleep late.

① ⓐ, ⓑ   ② ⓑ, ⓒ
③ ⓒ, ⓓ   ④ ⓒ, ⓔ
⑤ ⓓ, ⓔ

(11–13) ( ) 안의 말을 이용하여 문장을 완성하시오.

11 She expects you _____ on time. (arrive)

⇨ _____

12 It is important _____ the rules. (we, follow)

⇨ _____

13 He decided _____ a new car. (not, buy)

⇨ _____

(14–15) 밑줄 친 to부정사의 쓰임이 보기와 같은 것을 고르시오.

14
> I agreed <u>to babysit</u> my cousin.

① Joan has no reason <u>to say</u> no.
② I felt happy <u>to get</u> home safely.
③ Do you want <u>to order</u> now?
④ She lived <u>to be</u> 108 years old.
⑤ He wiped his glasses <u>to see</u> better.

15
> We <u>are to</u> thank our parents.

① The team <u>is to arrive</u> here by noon.
② No one <u>was to be seen</u> on the street.
③ Tom <u>is to visit</u> us next month.
④ You <u>are to save</u> energy.
⑤ They <u>were never to live</u> together.

(16–17) 빈칸에 공통으로 들어갈 말을 고르시오.

16
> · She helped me _____ my car.
> · I saw my cat _____ its face.

① wash   ② to wash   ③ washes
④ washed   ⑤ washing

17
> · I found it boring _____ a city tour.
> · It is better _____ the subway.

① take   ② to takes   ③ took
④ taking   ⑤ to take

(18-20) 우리말과 의미가 같도록 ( ) 안의 말을 이용하여 문장을 완성하시오.

18 Evan은 그녀가 Joan에게 속삭이는 것을 들었다. (hear, whisper)

⇨ Evan _____

_____ to Joan.

19 그 승무원은 우리에게 산소마스크 사용하는 방법을 보여 주었다. (how, use)

⇨The flight attendant showed us _____

_____ the oxygen mask.

20 그는 그의 모든 돈을 다 사용해버린 것 같다. (seem, spend)

⇨ He _____

all his money.

21 ( ) 안의 말이 밑줄 친 to부정사의 의미상 주어가 아닌 것은?

① (I) want to take a break.

② (She) was pleased to meet him.

③ It was careless (of you) to lose the bag.

④ (This book) is easy for me to read.

⑤ It is nice (of him) to help us.

(22-24) 우리말과 의미가 같도록 ( ) 안의 말을 배열하시오.

22 나는 마술을 배우는 것이 재미있다는 것을 알게 되었다. (to learn, fun, magic tricks)

⇨ I found it _____

_____.

23 커피는 내가 마시기에 너무 쓰다. (too, to, bitter, for, me, drink, is)

⇨ Coffee _____

_____.

24 그 탐정이 증거를 찾아냈던 것 같다. (to, the evidence, seems, have found)

⇨The detective _____

_____.

25 다음 우리말을 영어로 바르게 옮긴 것은?

그는 내게 팬케이크를 뒤집도록 시켰어.

① He made me to turn over the pancake.

② He had me turn over the pancake.

③ He told me turn over the pancake.

④ He got me turning over the pancake.

⑤ He let me to turn over the pancake.

26 짝지어진 두 문장의 의미가 서로 <u>다른</u> 것을 고르시오.

① It seems that she knows you.
　　→ She seems to have known you.

② He is going to hold a concert soon.
　　→ He is to hold a concert soon.

③ To display clothes is his job.
　　→ It is his job to display clothes.

④ The horse was so sick that it didn't eat.
　　→ The horse was too sick to eat.

⑤ He forgot what he should buy.
　　→ He forgot what to buy.

(27–28) 주어진 문장과 같은 의미를 갖도록 빈칸을 채우시오.

27 It seems that birds read the stars to find their way.

　⇨ Birds ＿＿＿＿＿＿＿＿＿＿＿＿＿＿
　　 the stars to find their way.

28 The umbrella was so small that it didn't cover his shoulders.

　⇨ The umbrella was ＿＿＿＿＿＿＿
　　 ＿＿＿＿＿＿＿＿＿＿ his shoulders.

(29–31) 다음 문장에서 어색한 부분을 찾아 바르게 고치고 알맞은 이유를 고르시오.

29 My sister made me to wash my running shoes.

고치기: ＿＿＿＿＿＿ ⇨ ＿＿＿＿＿＿
이유: make는 (목적어, 목적격보어)로
　　　(원형부정사, to부정사) 갖는 동사

30 The battery needs to changed.

고치기: ＿＿＿＿＿＿ ⇨ ＿＿＿＿＿＿
이유: 배터리가 (교체하다, 교체되다)이므로
　　　to부정사 (능동태, 수동태)

31 He seems to travel to many countries in his youth.

고치기: ＿＿＿＿＿＿ ⇨ ＿＿＿＿＿＿
이유: to부정사 시제가 주절의 시제와 / 시제보다
　　　(같을 때, 앞설 때) (to + 동사원형, to + have p.p.)

32 다음 조건을 이용하여 알맞게 영작하시오.

그 커튼은 햇빛을 가리기에 충분히 두꺼워.
조건 1: enough, thick, block
조건 2: 9단어

⇨ ＿＿＿＿＿＿＿＿＿＿＿＿＿＿＿＿
　 ＿＿＿＿＿＿＿＿＿＿＿＿＿＿＿ .

한눈에 정리하는 Grammar Mapping

빈칸에 알맞은 답을 보기에서 골라 넣어 grammar mapping 완성하기

형태와 역할 — to부정사는 [to + 동사원형] 형태로 문장에서 명사, 형용사, 부사로 쓰이며, 동사처럼 의미상 주어, 시제, 태를 갖는다. to부정사 구문을 이용하여 문장을 간단히 만들어 주며, 숙어처럼 사용되기도 한다.

쓰임

명사	① _____	She decided to help you.
	가주어 It, ② _____	I found it fun to read webtoons.
형용사	③ _____	The cat needs a box to play in.
	be동사 + to부정사	We are to follow the rules. (의무)
④ _____	목적, 감정의 원인, 형용사 수식, 결과, 판단의 근거, 조건	I am glad to hear the news. This machine is easy to use.
목적격보어	to부정사가 목적격보어	He asked me ⑤ _____ home.
	원형부정사가 목적격보어	She made us ⑥ _____ home.

cf. She helped me (to) carry the box.

동사적 성질

의미상 주어	⑦ _____ + 목적격	It is time for me to say goodbye.
	⑧ _____ + 목적격	It was foolish of you to trust him.
시제	단순형 (to + 동사원형)	He seems to be rich. = It seems that he is rich.
	완료형 (⑨ _____)	He seems to have been rich. = It seems that he was rich.
태	능동형 (to + 동사원형)	We are happy to invite you.
	수동형 (⑩ _____)	We are happy to be invited by you.

문장을 간단히

| to부정사 이용한 구문 | 형용사 / 부사 + ⑪ _____ + to부정사 | It is warm enough to eat outside. |
| | ⑫ _____ + 형용사 / 부사 + to부정사 | The soup is too spicy to eat. |

독립 부정사

| | not to mention to make matters worse | ⑬ _____ ⑭ _____ |

보기

- 설상가상으로
- too
- enough
- stay
- of
- ~은 말할 것도 없이
- to + have p.p.
- 부사
- to stay
- to + be p.p.
- 주어, 목적어, 보어
- 가목적어 it
- 명사 수식
- for

동명사

동명사의 명사적 쓰임

GP 24

문장에서 명사처럼 주어, 목적어, 보어 역할을 한다.

- ☆ **Using** solar energy is good for the Earth. (주어)
- ☆ We *enjoyed* **watching** the stars at night. (동사의 목적어)
- ☆ She is good *at* **telling** stories. (전치사의 목적어)
- Her hobby is **taking pictures of** animals. (보어)

> **Tip**
> 동명사의 부정은 동명사 앞에 not이나 never를 쓴다.
> **Not** having a dream is sad.

동명사의 의미상 주어

GP 25

동명사의 행위자를 의미상 주어라고 한다. 동명사의 행위자와 문장의 주어가 다를 경우 동명사 앞에 소유격이나 목적격을 써서 행위의 주체를 나타낸다.

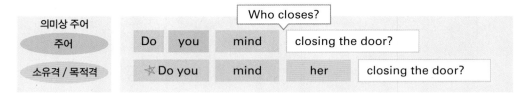

I am sure of **his (him)** winning the contest.

동명사의 시제

GP 26

❶ **단순 동명사**: [동사원형 + -ing] 형태로 동명사의 시제가 주절의 시제와 같다는 것을 나타낸다.

		is와 동일 시제			
☆ He	is proud	of	being		a voice actor.
= He	is proud	that	he	is	a voice actor.

❷ **완료 동명사**: [having + p.p.] 형태로 동명사의 시제가 주절의 시제보다 앞선다는 것을 나타낸다.

		is보다 앞선 시제			
☆ He	is proud	of	having been		a voice actor before.
= He	is proud	that	he	was	a voice actor before.

- Upgrade •

동명사의 수동태

단순 수동태	being + p.p.	수동태 의미의 동명사가 주절 시제와 **같을 때**
완료 수동태	having been p.p.	수동태 의미의 동명사가 주절 시제보다 **앞설 때**

I hate **being treated** like a child.   (= I **hate** that I **am treated** like a child.)
I hate **having been treated** like a child.   (= I **hate** that I **was treated** like a child.)

GP Practice

A   ( ) 안에서 알맞은 것을 고르시오.

1 Why do you keep (to ask, asking) me about Brian?

2 We are happy about (not having, don't having) any homework today.

3 The parrot dislikes (keeping, being kept) in a cage.

4 Never open the door without (knock, knocking).

5 I can't imagine (he, his) doing yoga.

B   두 문장이 같은 의미가 되도록 빈칸을 채우시오.

1 Would you mind if we take pictures here?

→ Would you mind _____ here?

2 He is proud that he designed the skyscraper himself.

→ He is proud of _____ the skyscraper himself.

3 I don't like that I am watched.

→ I don't like _____.

C   우리말과 의미가 같도록 ( ) 안의 말을 이용하여 문장을 완성하시오.

1 다른 사람들의 말을 들어 주는 것은 인내심을 필요로 한다. (listen to, require)

→ _____ _____ _____ _____ patience.

2 꼬마는 자신의 그림자가 자기를 따라오는 것이 무서웠다. (his shadow, follow)

→ The kid was afraid of _____ _____ _____ him.

3 어제 나를 도와줘서 고마워요. (help)

→ I thank you for _____ _____ _____ yesterday.

D   밑줄 친 부분에 대한 설명을 하고 틀린 경우엔 바르게 고치시오. (맞으면 'O' 표시)

* 가능한 답은 모두 체크

1	<u>Take</u> the stairs is good exercise. → ( )	'계단을 걷는 것'은 (주어, 목적어) 역할의 (동사, 동명사)
2	I don't like <u>he</u> meeting her. → ( )	동명사 meeting의 행위 주체는 (주격, 소유격, 목적격) 형태
3	I am proud of <u>being</u> rich before. → ( )	동명사 시제가 주절보다 앞설 때 (동사원형 + -ing, having p.p.)
4	He enjoyed <u>treating</u> like a king by me. → ( )	동명사가 (능동, 수동) 의미이므로 (동사원형 + -ing, being + p.p.)

동명사와 to부정사

GP 27

		주어	동사	목적어	
동명사만 목적어로 취하는 동사			enjoy, finish, mind, keep, give up, avoid, practice, quit, deny, admit, suggest...	동명사	
to부정사만 목적어로 취하는 동사			want, hope, agree, plan, expect, decide, learn, promise, refuse...	to부정사	
동명사와 to부정사를 모두 목적어로 취하는 동사	의미 차이 없는 경우	S	like, love, hate, begin, start, continue...	동명사 to부정사	
	의미 차이 있는 경우		remember / forget	동명사	~한 것을 기억하다 / 잊다
				to부정사	~할 것을 기억하다 / 잊다
			regret	동명사	~한 것을 후회하다
				to부정사	~하게 되어 유감이다
			try	동명사	시험 삼아 ~해 보다
				to부정사	~하려고 노력하다

❶ 동명사만 목적어로 취하는 동사

※ Did you *finish* **decorating** the Christmas tree?

I *suggested* **taking** a taxi as it was getting dark.

❷ to부정사만 목적어로 취하는 동사

※ Judy finally *agreed* **to accept** his offer.

She *refused* **to touch** my pet snake.

❸ 동명사와 부정사를 모두 목적어로 취하는 동사

(1) 의미 차이가 없는 동사

※ Evan *began* **playing (to play)** the guitar.

(2) 의미 차이가 있는 동사

※ He *forgot* **lending** me his umbrella. ((과거에) ~한 것을 잊다)

※ He *forgot* **to lend** me his umbrella. ((미래에) ~할 것을 잊다)

She *tried* **taking** pictures with her new phone. (시험 삼아 해 보다)

I *tried* **to solve** the math problem. (열심히 시도하다)

> **◦ Tip ◦**
> ① stop + to부정사: ~하기 위해 멈추다
> Tom stopped to talk to me.
> ② stop + 동명사: ~하는 것을 멈추다
> ※ Tom stopped talking to me.

동명사의 관용적 쓰임

GP 28

feel like -ing	~하고 싶다	spend 시간 / 돈 (in) -ing	~하는 데 ~을 소비하다
look forward to -ing	~을 고대하다	have difficulty (in) -ing	~하는 데 어려움이 있다
be worth -ing	~할 가치가 있다	be / get used to -ing	~하는 것에 익숙하다
It's no use -ing	~해도 소용없다	cannot help -ing	~하지 않을 수 없다

※ I *have difficulty* **making** decisions.

GP Practice

A ( ) 안에서 알맞은 것을 <u>모두</u> 고르시오.

1 The boxer wanted (to look, looking) strong and scary.

2 He gave up (to drink, drinking) coffee during weekdays.

3 Six months later, I began (to feel, feeling) homesick.

4 She spent her whole life (studying, to study) wild animals.

5 Olivia tried hard not (to eat, eating) at night.

B 보기의 말을 알맞게 고쳐 빈칸을 채우시오.

보기 ǀ	add	complain	get	use

1 Stop _____ about your food.

2 My parents finally agreed _____ a dog.

3 I am worried about your _____ the cell phone too often.

4 The chef forgot _____ salt to the soup and added more.

C 우리말과 의미가 같도록 ( ) 안의 말을 이용하여 문장을 완성하시오.

1 그녀는 나를 만났던 것을 기억하지 못했다. (remember, meet)

→ She didn't _____ _____ _____.

2 버스는 승객을 내려주기 위해 멈췄다. (stop, drop off)

→ The bus _____ _____ _____ _____ the passengers.

3 그는 TV 없이 사는 것이 익숙해졌다. (get used to, live)

→ He _____ _____ _____ _____ _____ a TV.

D 밑줄 친 부분에 대한 설명을 하고 틀린 경우엔 바르게 고치시오. (맞으면 'O' 표시)

* 가능한 답은 모두 체크

1	I know how to avoid <u>to catch</u> a cold. → ( )	주어 + avoid + 목적어 (to부정사, 동명사)
2	She promised <u>showing up</u> in time. → ( )	주어 + promise + 목적어 (to부정사, 동명사)
3	It started <u>rain</u> suddenly. → ( )	주어 + start + 목적어 (to부정사, 동명사)
4	Don't forget <u>calling</u> me later. → ( )	(~할 것을, ~했던 것을) 기억하다 forget + (to부정사, 동명사)

A   우리말과 의미가 같도록 ( ) 안의 말을 배열하시오.

1 파일을 다른 이름으로 저장해 보세요. (try, the file, name, a, different, saving, with)

→ _____.

2 닭구이가 맛있는 냄새가 났어. 그래서 먹지 않을 수 없었어. (couldn't, eating, help, I)

→ The grilled chicken smelled delicious. So _____ it.

3 그는 아이처럼 취급당하는 것을 싫어했다. (being, hated, treated, a child, like)

→ He _____.

4 그 여배우는 모피 코트를 입는 것을 거절했다. (a fur coat, refused, wear, to)

→ The actress _____.

5 너는 낯선 사람에게 말을 거는 것을 피해야 한다. (talking to, avoid, strangers)

→ You should _____.

6 이것의 임무는 화성에서 생명체를 탐사하는 것이다. (life, search for, to, on Mars, is)

→ Its mission _____.

B   우리말과 의미가 같도록 ( ) 안의 말을 이용하여 문장을 완성하시오.

1 이 영화는 두 번 볼 가치가 있다. (worth, watch)

→ The movie is _____ _____ _____ _____.

2 옆집 사람들은 밤늦게까지 계속 노래를 불렀어. (keep, until late)

→ The people next door _____ _____ _____ _____ at night.

3 그 영국의 두 가문은 30년 동안 지속적으로 싸웠다. (continue, fight)

→ The two English families _____ _____ _____ _____

_____ _____.

4 우리는 너를 곧 방문하기를 고대해. (forward, visit)

→ We _____ _____ _____ _____ _____ _____.

5 우리는 모든 티켓이 매진되었음을 알려드리게 되어 유감입니다. (regret, tell)

→ We _____ _____ _____ _____ that all the tickets are

sold out.

6 오른손으로 음식을 먹는 것은 인도에서는 무례하다고 생각되지 않아. (eat, with)

→ _____ _____ _____ _____ _____ _____ is

not considered rude in India.

C 다음 문장을 동명사를 이용하여 같은 의미를 갖는 문장으로 고치시오.

1 He is proud that he is the leader of his team.

→ He is proud of _____.

2 We are worried that she works too hard these days.

→ We are worried about _____.

3 I am sorry that I didn't invite you to the party.

→ I am sorry for _____.

4 She remembers that she visited the tower.

→ She remembers _____.

5 He regrets that he didn't keep his promise.

→ He regrets _____.

D Jake와 Cindy의 대화창의 일부이다. ( ) 안의 말을 이용하여 내용에 알맞은 문장을 완성하시오.

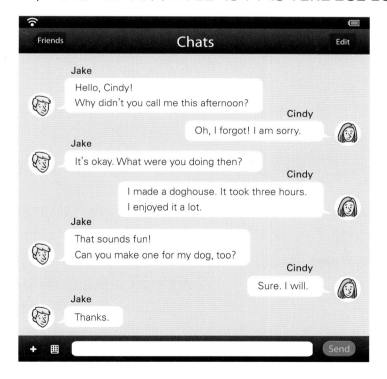

1 Cindy forgot _____ Jake this afternoon. (call)

2 Cindy was sorry for _____ Jake. (not, call)

3 Cindy spent three hours _____ a house for her puppy. (make)

4 Cindy enjoyed _____ the doghouse. (make)

5 Cindy promised _____ a house for Jake's dog. (make)

(1-5) 빈칸에 들어갈 알맞은 말을 고르시오.

1
Avoid _____ for three hours before you go to bed.

① eat ② ate
③ to eat ④ eating
⑤ having eaten

2
My mother was worried about _____ staying at home alone tonight.

① I ② my
③ mine ④ myself
⑤ for me

3
We agreed _____ the rules of the game.

① change ② changed
③ changing ④ to change
⑤ having changed

4
Don't forget _____ extra toppings on my pizza.

① put ② puts
③ to put ④ putting
⑤ having put

5
We couldn't help _____ the cute puppy.

① love ② loved
③ to love ④ loving
⑤ having loving

6 빈칸에 공통으로 들어갈 말을 고르시오.

· Jessy is looking forward to _____ you soon.
· He doesn't like _____ his talkative cousin.

① meet ② meets
③ met ④ to meet
⑤ meeting

(7-8) 다음 중 어법상 <u>어색한</u> 것을 고르시오.

7 ① I tried hard to avoid any mistakes.
② Are you good at playing the drum?
③ We started to pack our school bags.
④ I forgot paying the bill by tomorrow.
⑤ Her poem is worth reading.

8 ① She felt like traveling by train alone.
② I remember his taking us to a zoo.
③ Making movies is his job.
④ I hope to do some volunteer work.
⑤ He got used to sleep on the floor.

9 빈칸에 들어갈 말이 알맞게 짝지어진 것은?

> · She remembers _____ the temple last year.
> · Remember _____ your grandma tomorrow.

① visit - visit

② to visit - to visit

③ visiting - visiting

④ visiting - to visit

⑤ to visit - visiting

(10-11) 빈칸에 알맞지 <u>않은</u> 것을 고르시오.

10
> We _____ to visit the Great Pyramid the next year.

① planned   ② expected

③ wanted   ④ gave up

⑤ hated

11
> The queen _____ wearing casual clothes in public.

① enjoys   ② loves

③ keeps   ④ decides

⑤ avoids

(12-13) 우리말을 영어로 바르게 옮긴 것을 고르시오.

12
> Mike는 그녀가 정직한 것이 자랑스럽다.

① Mike is proud of be honest.

② Mike is proud of being honest.

③ Mike is proud of he being honest.

④ Mike is proud of she be honest.

⑤ Mike is proud of her being honest.

13
> 그는 내 기분을 상하게 하지 않으려 노력했다.

① He didn't try hurt my feelings.

② He didn't try to hurt my feelings.

③ He tried not hurt my feelings.

④ He tried not to hurt my feelings.

⑤ He tried not hurting my feelings.

14 밑줄 친 to의 쓰임이 나머지와 <u>다른</u> 것은?

① She left early <u>to</u> catch the bus.

② I am used <u>to</u> getting up early.

③ They forgot <u>to</u> feed the cat.

④ He refused <u>to</u> go out with us.

⑤ We decided not <u>to</u> eat junk food.

(15–16) 다음 중 어법상 올바른 것을 고르시오.

15 ① The fox had difficulty find food.
② We are proud of don't being lazy.
③ When did it stop to rain?
④ He is good at search the Internet.
⑤ He hopes to hear from you soon.

16 ① He hated do his homework.
② Let's keep to cheer for our team.
③ I am worried about be late.
④ We felt like going out for a walk.
⑤ He considered to quit his job.

(17–18) 우리말과 의미가 같도록 ( ) 안의 말을 이용하여 문장을 완성하시오.

17 새해를 맞이하기 위해 집 청소를 하는 것이 어때?
(clean)

⇨ How about _____ the house to welcome the new year?

18 그는 신발 끈을 묶기 위해 멈췄다.
(tie)

⇨ He stopped _____ his shoelaces.

(19–21) ( ) 안의 말을 이용하여 문장을 완성하시오.

19 Early people gathered food instead of _____ crops. (plant)

20 She practiced _____ for the speech contest. (speak)

21 He spent all his free time _____ fantasy novels. (read)

22 어법상 어색한 것으로만 짝지어진 것은?

ⓐ We enjoyed play on the beach.
ⓑ He regrets saying such a thing to you.
ⓒ She is busy cleaning her room.
ⓓ I suggested visiting the museum.
ⓔ Sending flowers to a sick person are not a good idea.

① ⓐ, ⓑ   ② ⓐ, ⓔ
③ ⓑ, ⓒ   ④ ⓑ, ⓓ
⑤ ⓓ, ⓔ

(23–25) 우리말과 의미가 같도록 ( ) 안의 말을 배열하시오.

23 그는 색종이로 배를 접어 보았다.
(he, tried, colored paper, folding, into a ship)

⇨ _____

_____ .

24 제가 당신의 옆자리에 앉아도 괜찮을까요?
(mind, do, you, sitting, my, next to, you)

⇨ _____

_____ ?

25 그는 그 잘못된 소문을 퍼트렸던 것을 부인한다.
(denies, he, the, rumor, false, spread, having)

⇨ _____

_____ .

(26–27) 주어진 두 문장을 한 문장으로 연결하시오.

26 · He was late for the meeting.
· He felt sorry about it.

⇨ He felt sorry about _____

_____ .

27 · He put the salad in the fridge.
· He forgot it.

⇨ He forgot _____ the
salad in the fridge.

(28–29) 다음 문장에서 어색한 부분을 찾아 바르게 고치고 알맞은 이유를 고르시오.

28 The machine suddenly stopped to work.

고치기: _____ ⇨ _____
이유: stop의 목적어는 (to부정사, 동명사)
(~하던 것을, ~하기 위해) 멈추다

29 He is proud of teaching the great scientist when he was young.

고치기: _____ ⇨ _____
이유: 동명사 시제가 주절 시제보다 앞서면
(단순 동명사, 완료 동명사)
(동사원형 + -ing, having p.p.)

30 다음 조건을 이용하여 알맞게 영작하시오.

우리는 그녀가 돌아와 주기를 고대해.
조건 1: look forward to
조건 2: 7단어, 동명사의 의미상 주어

⇨ _____

_____ .

한눈에 정리하는 Grammar Mapping

빈칸에 알맞은 답을 보기에서 골라 넣어 grammar mapping 완성하기

형태와 역할 — 동명사는 [동사원형 + -ing] 형태로 문장에서 명사처럼 주어, 목적어, 보어로 쓰인다. 이때 동명사와 to부정사는 특정 동사의 목적어로 쓰인다. 동사처럼 의미상 주어, 시제, 태를 가지며 숙어처럼 사용되기도 한다.

쓰임

명사
- 주어, 목적어, 보어 — I've finished cleaning my room.
- ① _____의 목적어 — She is fond of learning languages.

동사적 성질

의미상 주어
- ② _____ — Do you mind my (me) opening the box?

시제
- 단순형 (동사원형 + -ing) — He is proud of knowing the answer. = He is proud that he knows the answer.
- 완료형 (③ _____) — He is proud of having known the answer. = He is proud that he knew the answer.

태
- 능동형 (동사원형 + -ing) — I hate treating him like a baby.
- 수동형 (④ _____) — I hate being treated like a baby.

to부정사와 동명사

- ⑤ _____를 목적어로 갖는 동사 — We suggested taking a taxi. (⑥ _____, give up, ⑦ _____, suggest)
- ⑧ _____를 목적어로 갖는 동사 — We decided to take a taxi. (⑨ _____, plan, decide, ⑩ _____)

동명사, to부정사 모두 목적어로 갖는 동사
- 의미 차이가 ⑪ _____ 경우 — I love singing (to sing) on the stage. (love, hate, start, continue)
- 의미 차이가 ⑫ _____ 경우
  - She remembered meeting the man. (⑬ _____ 것을)
  - She remembered to meet the man. (⑭ _____ 것을)
  - He forgot visiting the website. (⑬ _____ 것을)
  - He forgot to visit the website. (⑭ _____ 것을)
  - I tried moving the table. (시험 삼아 ⑮ _____)
  - I tried to move the table. (⑯ _____)

관용적 쓰임

be used to -ing
cannot help -ing
- ⑰ _____
- ⑱ _____

* 중복 사용 가능

보기
- ~하는 데 익숙하다
- 동명사
- ~했던
- 있는
- ~해 보다
- 노력하다
- ~할
- having p.p.
- being p.p.
- 전치사
- ~하지 않을 수 없다
- 없는
- avoid
- agree
- refuse
- to부정사
- 소유격, 목적격
- keep

분사

현재분사와 과거분사

GP 29

분사는 [동사원형 + -ing] 형태의 현재분사와 [동사원형 + -ed] 형태의 과거분사가 있다. 현재분사는 능동, 진행의 의미를 갖고 과거분사는 수동, 완료의 의미를 갖는다.

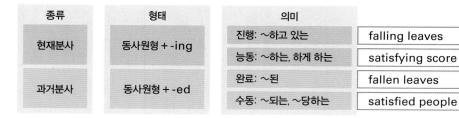

종류	형태	의미	
현재분사	동사원형 + -ing	진행: ~하고 있는	falling leaves
		능동: ~하는, 하게 하는	satisfying score
과거분사	동사원형 + -ed	완료: ~된	fallen leaves
		수동: ~되는, ~당하는	satisfied people

분사의 형용사적 쓰임

GP 30

❶ **명사 수식**: 명사 앞이나 뒤에서 명사를 수식한다. 보통 수식어와 함께 쓰이면 뒤에서 수식한다.

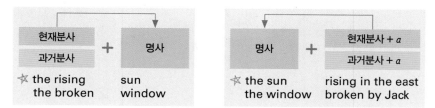

현재분사 / 과거분사	+	명사		명사	+	현재분사 + α / 과거분사 + α
☆ the rising / the broken		sun window		☆ the sun / the window		rising in the east / broken by Jack

The **growing** *desert* may cause more dust storms.
He gave me *a box* **filled** with candy.

❷ **보어 역할**: 주어나 목적어의 상태를 보충 설명한다.

주어	동사		주격보어	
He	sat		dozing.	현재분사
We	got		excited.	과거분사

주어	동사	목적어	목적격보어	
I	heard	a bird	singing.	현재분사
She	left	the door	locked.	과거분사

He got **injured** in the accident.
I found *the movie* **boring**.

◦ Tip ◦

감정을 나타내는 분사

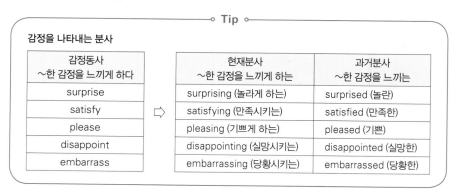

감정동사 ~한 감정을 느끼게 하다		현재분사 ~한 감정을 느끼게 하는	과거분사 ~한 감정을 느끼는
surprise		surprising (놀라게 하는)	surprised (놀란)
satisfy	⇨	satisfying (만족시키는)	satisfied (만족한)
please		pleasing (기쁘게 하는)	pleased (기쁜)
disappoint		disappointing (실망시키는)	disappointed (실망한)
embarrass		embarrassing (당황시키는)	embarrassed (당황한)

A ( ) 안에서 알맞은 것을 고르시오.

1 The island looks like a (sleeping, slept) lion.

2 My (recording, recorded) voice sounds strange to me.

3 She has a pet iguana (calling, called) Cutie.

4 She collects bells (making, made) in different countries.

5 His idea about the new product was (interesting, interested).

B 보기와 같이 두 문장을 같은 의미의 한 문장으로 고쳐 쓰시오.

> 보기 | I watched her hair. It was flying in the air.
> → I watched her hair flying in the air.

1 My dog found a wallet. It was buried in the snow.

→ My dog found a wallet _____ _____ _____ _____.

2 They rescued the family. They were caught in a storm.

→ They rescued the family _____ _____ _____ _____.

3 Who is the gentleman? He is wearing a red tie.

→ Who is the gentleman _____ _____ _____ _____?

C 우리말과 의미가 같도록 ( ) 안의 말을 이용하여 문장을 완성하시오.

1 그림 속에 숨겨진 다섯 마리의 동물을 찾아보세요. (animal, hide)

→ Find _____ _____ _____ _____ in the picture.

2 나는 해파리가 바다 위에 떠다니는 것을 보았다. (jellyfish, float)

→ I saw _____ _____ _____ in the sea.

3 치타는 130km/h의 놀라운 속도로 달릴 수 있다. (amaze, speed)

→ Cheetahs can run at an _____ _____ of 130km per hour.

D 밑줄 친 부분에 대한 설명을 하고 틀린 경우엔 바르게 고치시오. (맞으면 'O' 표시)

1	She is planning to buy a <u>using</u> car. → ( )	'중고의, 사용된' (진행, 수동) 의미 (현재분사, 과거분사)
2	Don't wake up the <u>sleeping</u> baby. → ( )	'감자고 있는' (진행, 수동) 의미 (현재분사, 과거분사)
3	His fashion style is never <u>bored</u>. → ( )	지루함을 (느끼게 하는, 느낀) 것이므로 (현재분사, 과거분사)
4	I have a <u>living in Brazil</u> friend. → ( )	[분사 + α]가 명사를 꾸밀 때 명사의 (앞, 뒤)에 위치

목적격보어로 쓰이는 분사

동사의 종류에 따라 목적격보어로 분사가 쓰이는데 목적어와 목적격보어의 관계가 능동이면 현재분사를, 수동이면 과거분사를 쓴다.

주어	동사	목적어	목적격보어	
	keep / find / leave	the girl	waiting.	능동관계
		his eyes	closed.	수동관계
S	see (지각동사)	the man	painting.	능동관계
		the house	painted.	수동관계
	have / get	his computer	fixed.	수동관계

❶ keep / find / leave + 목적어 + 현재분사: (목적어가 ~하는 것을) 계속하게 하다 / 발견하다 / 내버려 두다
　☆ He **kept** *the girl* **waiting**.
　They **found** *a six year-old boy* **living** in the mountains.
　He never **leaves** *his baby* **crying**.

❷ keep / find / leave + 목적어 + 과거분사: (목적어가 ~된 것을) 계속하게 하다 / 발견하다 / 내버려 두다
　☆ He **kept** *his eyes* **closed**.
　He **found** *the library* **closed**.
　He **left** *his food* **untouched**.

❸ 지각동사 + 목적어 + 현재분사: (목적어가 ~하는 것을) 보다 / 듣다 / 느끼다
　☆ He **saw** *the man* **painting** his house.
　She **heard** *the train* **coming** from a distance.

❹ 지각동사 + 목적어 + 과거분사: (목적어가 ~된 것을) 보다 / 듣다 / 느끼다
　☆ He **saw** *his house* **painted**.
　He **felt** his *shoulder* **touched** by someone.

❺ have / get + 목적어 + 과거분사: (목적어가 ~되도록) 하다
　He **had** *his computer* **fixed**.
　The girls **got** *their picture* **taken** together.

GP Practice

A ( ) 안에서 알맞은 것을 고르시오.

1 I heard people (praising, praised) you.

2 She had her hair (dyeing, dyed) brown again.

3 You can keep the food (freezing, frozen) up to two weeks.

4 He got the box (wrapping, wrapped) in colorful paper.

B 보기와 같이 목적어에 동그라미 하고, ( )에 주어진 목적격보어를 알맞은 형태로 바꾸시오.

> 보기 ┃   He saw his fans cheering for him. (cheer)

1 Max listened to her _____ in the snow. (walk)

2 Julia had her name _____ on all her books. (write)

3 He left the chair _____. (break)

4 I found my hamster _____ under the bed. (hide)

C 우리말과 의미가 같도록 ( ) 안의 말을 이용하여 문장을 완성하시오.

1 그 거짓말탐지기는 그녀가 거짓말을 하고 있는 것을 알아냈다. (find, tell)

→ The lie detector _____ _____ _____ a lie.

2 학생들은 그들의 키가 측정되도록 하였다. (their heights, measure)

→ The students had _____ _____ _____.

3 너는 외부에서 들려오는 소음을 들었니? (hear, come from)

→ Did you _____ _____ _____ _____ _____ outside?

4 그는 왼쪽 다리가 부러졌다. (have, break)

→ He _____ _____ _____ _____ _____.

D 밑줄 친 부분에 대한 설명을 하고 틀린 경우엔 바르게 고치시오. (맞으면 'O' 표시)

* p.p.: 과거분사

1	Mom kept me <u>stirring</u> the soup. → ( )	주어 + keep + 목적어 + (동사원형 + -ing, p.p.) 목적어가 (~하는 것을, ~된 것을) 계속 하게 하다
2	He heard him <u>played</u> the flute. → ( )	주어 + hear + 목적어 + (동사원형 + -ing, p.p.) 목적어가 (~하는 것을, ~된 것을) 듣다
3	She had her shoes <u>washing</u>. → ( )	주어 + have + 목적어 + (동사원형 + -ing, p.p.) 목적어가 (~하는 것을, ~되도록) 하다
4	I got my homework <u>doing</u>. → ( )	주어 + get + 목적어 + (동사원형 + -ing, p.p.) 목적어가 (~하는 것을, ~되도록) 하다

분사구문

분사구문은 [접속사 + 주어 + 동사]로 이루어진 부사절을 [동사원형 + -ing]의 부사구로 줄여 쓴 것을 말하고 문맥에 따라 시간, 이유, 양보, 조건 등의 의미를 가진다.

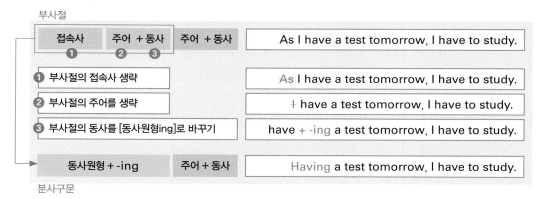

부사절

접속사 ❶	주어 + 동사 ❷ ❸	주어 + 동사	As I have a test tomorrow, I have to study.
❶ 부사절의 접속사 생략			~~As~~ I have a test tomorrow, I have to study.
❷ 부사절의 주어를 생략			~~I~~ have a test tomorrow, I have to study.
❸ 부사절의 동사를 [동사원형ing]로 바꾸기			have + -ing a test tomorrow, I have to study.
동사원형 + -ing	주어 + 동사		Having a test tomorrow, I have to study.

분사구문

❶ **시간: ~할 때, ~하는 동안, ~하기 전에**

When she saw me, she shouted with joy.

→ ☆ **Seeing** me, she shouted with joy.

> **Tip**
> 분사구문의 부정
> 분사구문 앞에 not이나 never를 쓴다.
> **Not having** time, he took a taxi.

❷ **이유: ~때문에**

As he didn't know how to say sorry, the boy just cried.

→ ☆ **Not knowing** how to say sorry, the boy just cried.

> **Tip**
> 의미를 명확하게 전달하기 위해 접속사를 생략하지 않을 수 있다.

❸ **양보: ~일지라도**

Although he lives near the school, he is always late for school.

→ **(Although) Living** near the school, he is always late for school.

❹ **조건: 만약 ~한다면**

If you take this bus, you will get to the airport.

→ **Taking** this bus, you will get to the airport.

❺ **동시동작: ~하면서**

As the singer waved to his fans, he disappeared from the stage.

→ **Waving** to his fans, the singer disappeared from the stage.

• Upgrade •

숙어처럼 쓰이는 분사구문

generally speaking	일반적으로 말해서	judging from	~로 판단하건대
frankly speaking	솔직히 말해서	considering (that)	~을 고려하면
strictly speaking	엄격히 말해서	compared with	~와 비교해 보면

Frankly speaking, I don't understand his explanation.

Judging from his looks, he must be in his twenties.

A ( ) 안에서 알맞은 것을 고르시오.

1 (To have, Having) a baby brother, Paula is good at babysitting.

2 (Walked, Walking) to school, he realized it was Sunday.

3 (Not being, Being not) hungry, I didn't eat lunch.

4 (To consider, Considering) the girl is only five, she is quite smart.

B 다음 밑줄 친 부분을 분사구문으로 고치시오.

1 <u>As he had poor eyesight</u>, he couldn't read the sign.

→ _____, he couldn't read the sign.

2 <u>If you take this bus</u>, you can go to the airport.

→ _____, you can go to the airport.

3 <u>Although he is not tall</u>, he is a great basketball player.

→ _____, he is a great basketball player.

C 보기에서 알맞은 접속사를 골라 밑줄 친 부분을 부사절로 고치시오.

보기	If	Because	While

1 <u>Cleaning my room</u>, I found some coins under the sofa.

→ _____, I found some coins under the sofa.

2 <u>Not feeling well</u>, he went to bed early.

→ _____, he went to bed early.

3 <u>Wearing these jeans</u>, you will look younger.

→ _____, you will look younger.

D 밑줄 친 부분에 대한 설명을 하고 틀린 경우엔 바르게 고치시오. (맞으면 'O' 표시)

1	<u>She watching</u> TV, she ate a snack. → ( )	주절과 같은 부사절의 (주어, 목적어)는 삭제 (함, 안 함)
2	<u>Turn</u> left, you can find the ATM. → ( )	부사절 시제가 주절 시제와 같을 때 부사절 동사를 (동사원형, 동사원형 + -ing)
3	<u>Being not</u> old enough, she can't drive. → ( )	분사의 부정은 (don't, not)을 분사 바로 (앞, 뒤)에 씀
4	<u>To judge from</u> his accent, he must be an Australian. → ( )	(~로 판단하기 위해, ~로 판단하건대) (To judge from, Judging from)

완료형 분사구문

GP 33

부사절의 시제가 주절의 시제보다 앞선 경우에 쓴다.

부사절		주절	
접속사	주어 + 동사	주어 + 동사	As I saw her before, I know her face.
	시제가 다를 경우		
Having + p.p.		주어 + 동사	☆ Having seen her before, I know her face.

수동 분사구문

GP 34

[being / having been + p.p.] 형태이며 being과 having been은 생략할 수 있다.

부사절	As	he	was	shocked	by the news,	he didn't say a word.
분사구문		☆ Being	shocked	by the news,		he didn't say a word.

부사절	As	it	was	written	in Latin,	the poem is hard to read.
분사구문		Having been	written	in Latin,		the poem is hard to read.

(Being) Kept in the aquarium, the dolphin gets stressed a lot.
(Having been) Built 30 years ago, the house is still in good condition.

주어가 있는 분사구문

GP 35

부사절의 주어와 주절의 주어가 다를 경우 부사절의 주어를 생략하지 않고 분사구문 앞에 쓴다.

		주어가 다를 경우			
부사절	As	it	rained	heavily yesterday,	the concert was canceled.
분사구문	☆	It	raining	heavily yesterday,	the concert was canceled.

School being over, they played baseball on the field.

with + 명사 + 분사

GP 36

[with + 명사 + 분사] 구문은 '~하면서, ~된 채로'의 의미로 동시동작을 나타낸다.

주어 + 동사 ~	with	명사	분사	
☆ He was sleeping	with	the alarm	ringing.	능동관계
☆ A pigeon flew to me	with	a message	tied to its leg.	수동관계

A ( ) 안에서 알맞은 것을 고르시오.

1 The birds flew south with winter (come, coming).

2 She went running with her dog (following, followed) her.

3 Frankly (speaking, spoken), I was not listening to you.

4 (Striking, Struck) by lightening, the tree fell down.

5 (Living, Having lived) alone before, he cooks very well.

B 분사구문을 이용하여 두 문장의 의미가 같도록 완성하시오.

1 As the bear slept through the winter, it is very hungry now.

→ _____, the bear is very hungry now.

2 When Medusa looked at him, he turned to stone.

→ _____, he turned to stone.

3 As the glasses were packed in a box, they were delivered safely.

→ _____, the glasses were delivered safely.

C 우리말과 의미가 같도록 ( ) 안의 말을 이용하여 문장을 완성하시오.

1 음식이 밀폐 용기 안에 보관되면 더욱 오래 지속될 수 있다. (keep, airtight container)

→ _____ _____ _____ _____ _____, food

can last longer.

2 나는 내 고양이가 키보드 위에 앉아 있는 상태에서 키보드를 사용하려 했다. (with, sit)

→ I tried to type on the keyboard _____ _____ _____

_____ on it.

3 짠 국을 먹었기 때문에 나는 지금 목이 마르다. (eat, salty soup)

→ _____ _____ _____ _____, I feel thirsty now.

D 밑줄 친 부분에 대한 설명을 하고 틀린 경우엔 바르게 고치시오. (맞으면 'O' 표시)

* p.p.: 과거분사

1	<u>Seeing</u> from space, the Earth looks blue. → (　　　　　　　)	'보여지면'은 (능동, 수동) 분사구문이며 (동사원형 + -ing, (Being) p.p.) 형태
2	<u>Working</u> hard, she finally succeeded. → (　　　　　　　)	부사절 시제가 주절보다 앞설 때 부사절 동사는 (동사원형 + -ing, having p.p.)
3	<u>Being</u> cloudy, I took an umbrella. → (　　　　　　　)	부사절 주어가 주절 주어와 다를 때 분사구문에서 주어 생략 (가능, 불가)
4	I slept with the light <u>turning</u> off. → (　　　　　　　)	with + 명사 + 분사 (동사원형 + -ing, p.p.) 해석은 명사가 (~하면서, ~된 채로)

A   우리말과 의미가 같도록 ( ) 안의 말을 배열하시오.

1 열쇠를 잃어버렸기 때문에, 그는 지금 집에 들어갈 수 없다. (his key, lost, having)

→ _____, he can't get into his house now.

2 은행이 문을 닫아서, 그는 현금지급기(ATM)를 찾아보았다. (closed, the bank, being)

→ _____, he looked for an ATM.

3 소금을 적게 먹는다면, 너는 체중을 줄일 수 있다. (salt, eating, less)

→ _____, you can lose weight.

4 나는 책을 읽었고, 고양이는 옆에서 자고 있었다. (my cat, sleeping, with, me, next to)

→ I read a book _____.

5 그 소년들은 감춰진 보물을 찾고 있는 중이다. (treasure, looking for, hidden)

→ The boys are _____.

6 빨리 도착하시면, 앞좌석을 차지할 수 있어요. (early, arriving)

→ _____, you can get a seat up front.

7 나는 누군가가 휘파람을 흥겹게 부는 것을 들었다. (heard, cheerfully, whistling, someone)

→ I _____.

B   우리말과 의미가 같도록 ( ) 안의 말을 이용하여 문장을 완성하시오.

1 자신의 리포트를 검토하면서, 그는 철자 오류를 몇 개 찾아냈다. (proofread)

→ _____ _____ _____, he found some spelling errors.

2 그는 눈물이 볼에 흐르는 채로 영화를 보았다. (tears, run down)

→ He watched the movie _____ _____ _____ his cheeks.

3 그의 또래들에 비하면, 그 어린 소년은 어휘가 풍부하다. (compare, peers)

→ _____ _____ _____ _____, the young boy has a large vocabulary.

4 다음 모퉁이에서 오른쪽으로 돌면, 카페가 있을 것입니다. (turn right, at)

→ _____ _____ _____ _____ _____ _____, you will find the cafe.

5 그 노래는 서둘러 만들어졌지만, 큰 히트를 했다. (although, make, in haste)

→ _____ _____ _____ _____, the song became a big hit.

6 어렸을 때 개에게 공격을 당했기 때문에, 그는 개를 두려워한다. (attack, by)

→ _____ _____ _____ _____ _____ as a child, he is still afraid of dogs.

C 보기의 단어를 알맞은 형태로 고쳐 그림을 묘사하시오.

보기 | open   download   ring   run

1 Daniel found his package _____ by someone.

2 Daniel liked the music a lot. So he wanted to have it _____.

3 Daniel heard his cell phone _____.

4 Daniel brushed his teeth with the tap water _____.

D 보기에서 알맞은 말을 골라 문장을 완성하시오. (한 번씩만 사용)

보기 |
· Kept in the refrigerator
· Having read the books
· Having lived in Tokyo
· Surrounded by many people
· Coming in first place
· It being windy

1 _____, he played the violin in the square.

2 _____, she returned them to the library.

3 _____, the dancing team was excited.

4 _____, the kids went out to fly their kites.

5 _____, the vegetables stayed fresh.

6 _____, she knows the city well.

(1–5) 빈칸에 들어갈 알맞은 말을 고르시오.

1
John heard his name _____ out in the crowd.

① call   ② calling
③ called   ④ to call
⑤ having called

2
The country is growing old at a _____ rate.

① surprise   ② to surprise
③ surprising   ④ surprised
⑤ being surprised

3
_____ near the school, Jack is always late for school.

① Lives   ② Live
③ To live   ④ Lived
⑤ Living

4
They all rushed out of the _____ house safely.

① burn   ② burning
③ burns   ④ burned
⑤ being burned

5
_____ her car, she reported it to the police.

① Lost   ② Losing
③ Having lost   ④ Being lost
⑤ Been lost

(6–7) 빈칸에 들어갈 말이 알맞게 짝지어진 것은?

6
· Spam mail is _____.
· She was _____ by the noise.

① annoy - annoy
② annoying - annoyed
③ annoying - annoying
④ annoyed - annoyed
⑤ annoyed - annoying

7
· _____ by his teacher, he studied even harder.
· _____ goodbye, he got on the train.

① Praise - Wave
② Praising - Waving
③ Praised - Waving
④ Praising - Waved
⑤ Praised - Waved

8 다음 중 어법상 옳은 문장은?

① Go to bed, she turned off the light.

② Being snowy, he wore a warm coat.

③ Generally spoken, instant food is not healthy.

④ Hurt by his joke, she didn't talk to him.

⑤ Felt nervous, he couldn't eat.

(9–10) 두 문장이 같은 의미를 갖도록 빈칸에 들어갈 말을 고르시오.

9

> If you have a bad memory, you had better write things down.
> → _____ a bad memory, you had better write things down.

① Have   ② To have

③ Had   ④ Having

⑤ Having had

10

> Being a doctor, she is not afraid of blood.
> → _____ she is a doctor, she is not afraid of blood.

① Because   ② Although

③ And   ④ But

⑤ Before

(11–13) ( ) 안의 단어를 알맞은 형태로 고쳐 빈칸을 완성하시오.

11 The watch _____ in Switzerland is very expensive. (make)

12 The panda _____ bamboo over there came from China. (eat)

13 He played the piano with his friends _____ him. (watch)

(14–15) 다음 중 어법상 어색한 문장은?

14 ① She had her skirts ironed.

② He got his homework done.

③ I heard Olivia playing the drums.

④ We felt the building shaking.

⑤ The kid had his face painting yellow.

15 ① Her singing voice is amazing.

② Did you buy the used computer?

③ He picked up the breaking glasses.

④ Stay away from the falling rocks.

⑤ He ordered some fried chicken.

16 밑줄 친 부분을 분사로 잘못 바꾼 것은?

① As the palace is covered with gold, it is shining in the sun.
→ Covered with gold,

② Because he was wearing earphones, he didn't hear the noise.
→ Wearing earphones,

③ As there was no hope, he was sad.
→ There being no hope,

④ When he drives his car, he never answers his phone.
→ Drives his car,

⑤ If you don't like the salad, you can pass it to me.
→ Not liking the salad,

(17–19) 우리말과 의미가 같도록 주어진 단어를 알맞게 바꾸시오.

17 긴 천으로 싸여 있었기 때문에, 그 미라는 무서워 보였어. (wrap)

⇨ _____ in a long cloth, the mummy looked scary.

18 거울을 들여다보면서, 그는 웃긴 표정을 지었다. (look)

⇨ _____ into the mirror, he made a funny face.

19 그의 발 크기로 판단해 보면, 그는 분명 키가 클 거야. (judge)

⇨ _____ from his foot size, he must be tall.

20 보기의 문장을 잘못 이해한 학생은?

보기 | Having learned sign language, he can communicate with the deaf.

① 율: 밑줄 친 분사구문은, 부사절 [접속사 + 주어 + 동사]로 고칠 수 있어.

② 아영: (As he learned)로 바꿀 수 있겠네.

③ 환: '수화를 배웠기 때문에'라고 해석하지.

④ 관우: 부사절과 주절의 시제가 다르니까 완료분사를 사용한 거지.

⑤ 승기: 맞아, 하지만 Having은 생략될 수 있어.

21 밑줄 친 부분을 [접속사 + 주어 + 동사]로 고칠 때, 접속사가 나머지와 다른 것은?

① Taking a shower, he sang a song.

② Calling my name, she smiled brightly.

③ Being rich, she doesn't waste money.

④ Opening the door, he let his dog in.

⑤ Entering the classroom, I turned off my cell phone.

22 다음 우리말을 영어로 옮길 때 빈칸에 알맞은 말은?

손으로 만져지면, 잎이 움츠러든다.
→ _____ by the hand, the leaves draw back.

① Touch
② Touching
③ Being touching
④ Touched
⑤ Having touched

23 어법상 올바른 것으로만 짝지어진 것은?

> ⓐ Don't feeling well, he stayed in bed.
> ⓑ Having spent all her money, she can't buy the book.
> ⓒ Frankly spoken, I love her idea.
> ⓓ Your plan sounds interesting.
> ⓔ I was sitting with my legs crossing.

① ⓐ, ⓑ   ② ⓑ, ⓒ
③ ⓑ, ⓓ   ④ ⓒ, ⓓ
⑤ ⓓ, ⓔ

(24-25) 밑줄 친 부사절을 분사구문으로 고치시오.

24 When bananas are left in the refrigerator, they turn brown.

⇨ _____ in the refrigerator, bananas turn brown.

25 As he lived in Italy, he has a good understanding of Italy.

⇨ _____ in Italy, he has a good understanding of Italy.

(26-27) 우리말과 의미가 같도록 ( ) 안의 말을 배열하시오.

26 나는 눈을 감았을 때 내 감각이 더 효과가 있다.
(my, closed, with, eyes)

⇨ My senses work better _____
_____.

27 날씨가 추워서, 우리는 실내에 머물렀다.
(being, it, cold)

⇨ _____,
we stayed inside.

(28-29) 다음 문장에서 어색한 부분을 찾아 바르게 고치고 알맞은 이유를 고르시오.

28 Having laid eggs, the seahorse got exhausting.

고치기: _____ ⇨ _____
이유: '매우 지쳤다'는 (수동, 능동) 상태이므로 exhaust의 (현재, 과거)분사

29 We saw a spider spins a web.

고치기: _____ ⇨ _____
이유: '거미가 거미줄을 짜고 있는'은 목적어의 (수동, 진행) 상태이므로 spin의 (현재, 과거)분사

30 다음 조건을 이용하여 알맞게 영작하시오.

> 피곤함을 느껴서, Max는 그의 방에서 쉬었다.
> 조건 1: tired, rest
> 조건 2: 7단어, 분사구문

⇨ _____
_____.

한눈에 정리하는 Grammar Mapping

빈칸에 알맞은 답을 보기에서 골라 넣어 grammar mapping 완성하기

형태와 역할	분사는 [① _____]의 현재분사와 [동사원형 + -ed]의 ② _____ 가 있고 현재분사는 ③ _____을, 과거분사는 ④ _____를 의미한다. 분사는 문장에서 형용사처럼 명사를 수식하거나 보어로 쓰이고 부사절을 간단히 표현할 때에도 쓰이는데 이런 분사를 분사구문이라고 한다.

현재분사	~하고 있는, ⑤ _____	boiling water, surprising story
과거분사	~하게 된, ⑥ _____	boiled water, surprised woman

쓰임	형용사	명사 수식	⑦ _____에서		the broken glass
			⑧ _____에서		the glass broken into pieces
		⑨ _____보어	현재분사	The service was satisfying.
			과거분사	The guest seemed satisfied.
		⑩ _____보어	현재분사	We found the service satisfying.
			과거분사	We found the guest satisfied.

분사구문	⑪ _____을 분사구문으로 만들기 부사절의 ⑫ _____ 생략 주절과 같은 ⑬ _____ 생략 동사원형 + -ing로 바꾸기	As he felt tired, he left the office early. ~~As~~ he felt tired, he left the office early. ~~he~~ felt tired, he left the office early. → Feeling tired, he left the office early.
	완료 분사구문	⑭ _____	Having failed again, he gave up. = As he had failed again, he gave up.
	수동 분사구문	(being) ⑮ _____	Being left alone, she locked the door.
		(having been) ⑮ _____	Having been born poor, he is rich now.
	주어 있는 분사구문	주어 + 분사구문	It being very foggy, I drove carefully.
	with + 명사 + ⑯ _____		With his eyes closed, he was lying still.

* 중복 사용 가능

보기	· 동사원형 + -ing	· 목적격	· 부사절	· 수동, 완료
	· p.p.	· ~하게 하는	· 주격	· 주어
	· 과거분사	· ~당하는	· 뒤	· 분사
	· 능동, 진행	· 앞	· having p.p.	· 접속사

비교표현

원급, 비교급, 최상급

GP 37

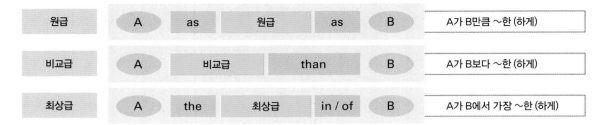

원급	A	as	원급	as	B	A가 B만큼 ~한 (하게)
비교급	A	비교급	than		B	A가 B보다 ~한 (하게)
최상급	A	the	최상급	in / of	B	A가 B에서 가장 ~한 (하게)

❶ 원급 비교

She is **as diligent as** my mom.

☆ My dog can run **as fast as** a cheetah.

☆ The rock band is **not as popular as** the girl group.

❷ 비교급 비교

☆ This cell phone is **cheaper than** that one.

The mobile game is **more exciting than** the arcade game.

❸ 최상급 비교

☆ The Sahara Desert is **the biggest** desert **in** the world.

Today is **the happiest** day **of** my life.

- Upgrade •

[A less + 원급 + than B]: A가 B보다 덜 ~한 (하게)

Joe is less tall than Andy.

= Joe is not as tall as Andy.

= Andy is taller than Joe.

> **Tip**
>
> 비교되는 대상은 문법적으로 동등한 것이어야 한다.
> · My little finger is shorter than her. (×)
> · My little finger is shorter than hers (her little finger). (O)

원급을 이용한 표현

GP 38

❶

| 배수사 | as | 원급 | as | | …보다 몇 배 ~한 (하게) |

This bridge is **two times as long as** that one.

(= This bridge is **two times longer than** that one.)

☆ This bike is **three times as light as** my old one.

❷

| as | 원급 | as | possible / 주어 can | 가능한 한 ~한 (하게) |

☆ Your point has to be **as specific as possible.** (= as specific as you can)

I needed the information **as soon as possible.** (= as soon as I could)

GP Practice

A   ( ) 안에서 알맞은 것을 고르시오.

1 Brian's room is as (clean, cleaner) as my room.

2 The horizon in Guam is (nicer, nicest) than that in Hawaii.

3 Johnny is the (more, most) creative student in the class.

4 She read (three time, three times) as many books as he.

B   두 문장이 같은 의미가 되도록 빈칸을 채우시오.

1 His salary is two times higher than mine.

→ His salary is two times _____ as mine.

2 Trekking is not as exciting as camping.

→ Camping is _____ than trekking.

3 They ran as fast as possible to catch the train.

→ They ran as fast as _____ to catch the train.

C   우리말과 의미가 같도록 ( ) 안의 말을 이용하여 문장을 완성하시오.

1 건강이 부유함보다 더 중요하다. (important)

→ Health is _____ _____ _____ wealth.

2 생쥐의 세포는 코끼리의 세포만큼 크다. (big)

→ A mouse's cells are _____ _____ _____ an elephant's.

3 나는 가능한 한 자주 운동하려고 노력한다. (often)

→ I try to exercise _____ _____ _____ _____

_____ .

4 1월은 한국에서 가장 추운 달이다. (cold)

→ January is _____ _____ _____ _____ Korea.

D   밑줄 친 부분에 대한 설명을 하고 틀린 경우엔 바르게 고치시오. (맞으면 'O' 표시)

1	The food is <u>good</u> than I expected. → ( )	(원급 + than, 비교급 + than)
2	The mall wasn't as <u>crowded</u> as usual. → ( )	(as + 원급 + as, as + 비교급 + as)
3	What is the <u>larger</u> country in the world? → ( )	the + (비교급, 최상급) + 명사 + in 장소명사
4	They should come as early as <u>can</u>. → ( )	as + 원급 + as + (can, possible)

비교급을 이용한 표현

GP 39

❶

| even, much, far, a lot, still | 비교급 | than | 훨씬 더 ~한 (하게) |

☆ Iron is **much heavier than** aluminum.

❷

| 비교급 | and | 비교급 | 점점 더 ~한 (하게) |

☆ Our world is becoming **smaller and smaller**.

❸

| the | 비교급 | (주어 + 동사) | , | the | 비교급 | (주어 + 동사) | ~할수록 더 ~하다 |

☆ **The darker** it grew, **the colder** it became.

• Upgrade •

'~보다'의 의미로 than 대신 to를 쓰는 형용사
· senior (junior) to: ~보다 연상인 (연하인)
· superior (inferior) to: ~보다 우월한 (열등한)

최상급을 이용한 표현

GP 40

❶

| one | of | the | 최상급 | 복수명사 | 가장 ~한 것들 중 하나 |

☆ Jennifer is **one of the most energetic girls** in her class.

❷

| the | 최상급 | 명사 | that | 주어 have ever p.p. | 지금껏 한 것 중 가장 ~한 |

☆ He is the bravest man **I have ever met**.

원급, 비교급을 이용한 최상급 의미

GP 41

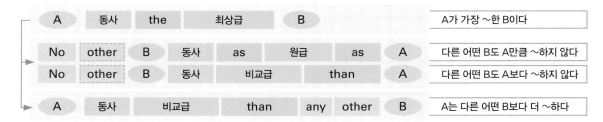

A	동사	the	최상급	B	A가 가장 ~한 B이다
No	other	B	동사	as	원급	as	A	다른 어떤 B도 A만큼 ~하지 않다
No	other	B	동사	비교급	than	A	다른 어떤 B도 A보다 ~하지 않다
A	동사	비교급	than	any	other	B	A는 다른 어떤 B보다 더 ~하다

The Nile is **the longest** river in the world.
= **No (other)** river in the world is **as long as** the Nile.
= ☆ **No (other)** river in the world is **longer than** the Nile.
= ☆ The Nile is **longer than any other** river in the world. (비교급 + than any other + 단수명사)

A ( ) 안에서 알맞은 것을 고르시오.

1 The (more, most) you practice, the better you will do.

2 This sofa is (much, very) more comfortable than the bed.

3 Soccer is one of the most popular (sport, sports) in Korea.

4 Winter is getting (cold and cold, colder and colder).

B 두 문장이 같은 의미가 되도록 빈칸을 채우시오.

1 Fresh water is the best drink.

→ _____ is as good as fresh water.

2 My brother is senior to me by three years.

→ My brother is _____ than me.

3 As you climb higher, you can see farther.

→ _____ you climb, _____ you can see.

C 우리말과 의미가 같도록 ( ) 안의 말을 이용하여 문장을 완성하시오.

1 그녀는 그녀의 언니보다 훨씬 사려 깊다. (much, thoughtful)

→ She is _____ _____ _____ than her sister.

2 적게 소비하면 할수록 더 많이 모을 수 있다. (much, little)

→ _____ we spend, _____ _____ _____ we can save.

3 체스는 전 세계에서 가장 인기 있는 보드게임 중에 하나이다. (popular)

→ Chess is _____ _____ _____ _____
board games in the world.

4 그것은 내가 지금까지 본 영화 중 가장 감동적이었다. (touching, watch)

→ That was _____ _____ _____ movie I've _____
_____ .

D 밑줄 친 부분에 대한 설명을 하고 틀린 경우엔 바르게 고치시오. (맞으면 'O' 표시)

1	Tests are getting <u>hard and hard</u>. → ( )	'점점 더 ~한' 의미는 (비교급 + and + 비교급, 원급 + and + 원급)
2	She looks <u>very</u> prettier without makeup. → ( )	'(매우, 훨씬)' 의미로 비교급을 강조할 때 (very, much) + 비교급
3	Paul is kinder than any other <u>boys</u> in the class. → ( )	'다른 어떤 …보다 더 ~한' 의미는 비교급 + than any other + (단수, 복수)명사
4	The more you practice, <u>the easy</u> it will become. → ( )	'~하면 ~할수록 더 ~하다' 의미는 the + 비교급, (비교급, the + 비교급)

A 우리말과 의미가 같도록 ( ) 안의 말을 배열하시오.

1 Jenny는 그의 오빠만큼 키가 크지 않다. (is, as, as, not, her, tall, brother)

→ Jenny _____ .

2 오늘은 내 생에 가장 행복한 날이다. (is, of, the, my, day, life, happiest)

→ Today _____ .

3 이것은 내가 읽은 것 중 최고의 만화이다. (I, the, ever, best, read, have, cartoon)

→ This is _____ .

4 여러분은 가능한 많은 에너지를 아껴 써야 합니다. (as, as, much, save, energy, possible)

→ You have to _____ .

5 중고차를 사는 것이 새 차를 사는 것보다 훨씬 덜 비싸다. (is, less, than, much, expensive)

→ Buying a used car _____ buying a new one.

6 바퀴벌레보다 세상에서 더 혐오스러운 곤충은 없다. (is, no, more, insect, than, disgusting)

→ _____ in the world _____ the cockroach.

B 우리말과 의미가 같도록 ( ) 안의 말을 이용하여 문장을 완성하시오.

1 농장을 방문하는 것이 책을 읽는 것보다 더 도움이 된다. (helpful)

→ Visiting a farm is _____ _____ _____ reading a book.

2 과학기술이 매년 점점 더 나아지고 있다. (get, good)

→ Technology is _____ _____ _____ _____ each year.

3 한글은 한국에서 가장 위대한 발명품 중 하나이다. (great, invention)

→ Hangeul is _____ _____ _____ _____ _____ in

Korea.

4 Dan은 나보다 두 배 더 빨리 수학 문제를 풀었다. (fast)

→ Dan solved the math questions _____ _____ _____

_____ I did.

5 그녀가 영어로 더 자주 말할수록, 더 많은 자신감을 얻을 거야. (often, confidence)

→ _____ _____ _____ she speaks English, _____

_____ _____ she gets.

6 엄마는 세상에서 다른 어떤 사람보다도 더 부지런하다. (any, diligent)

→ My mom is _____ _____ _____ _____ _____

person in the world.

C 다음 그림과 일치하도록 ( ) 안의 단어를 이용하여 문장을 완성하시오.

car			
Name	BMW	Ferrari	Bentley
Year	2017	2014	2014
Top Speed	260km/h	280km/h	290km/h
Price	$4,000	$6,000	$5,000
Popularity	★★★★	★★	★★★

1 The Ferrari is _____ the Bentley. (old)

2 The BMW is _____ car of the three. (popular)

3 The Bentley can run _____ than any _____. (fast)

4 The BMW is _____ than the Bentley. (expensive)

5 No _____ is _____ than the Ferrari. (expensive)

D 두 문장이 같은 의미가 되도록 빈칸을 채우시오.

1 The robot's arms are less efficient than I expected.

→ The robot's arms are not _____ _____ _____ I expected.

2 I think the whale is three times as big as the shark.

→ I think the whale is _____ _____ _____ _____ the shark.

3 They wrote their essays as clearly as possible.

→ They wrote their essays _____ _____ _____ _____.

4 As you read more books, you will gain more knowledge.

→ _____ _____ you read, _____ _____ _____ you will gain.

5 Venus is the brightest planet in the solar system.

→ _____ _____ planet in the solar system is _____ _____ Venus.

→ _____ _____ planet in the solar system is _____ _____ _____ Venus.

→ Venus is _____ _____ _____ _____ in the solar system.

(1–5) 빈칸에 들어갈 알맞은 말을 고르시오.

1 This backpack is as _____ as that one.

① light
② lighter
③ lightest
④ lightly
⑤ more light

2 The more you learn, _____ you become.

① wise
② wiser
③ wisest
④ the wiser
⑤ the wisest

3 This is _____ thing that I have ever done.

① great
② greater
③ greatest
④ the greatest
⑤ the greater

4 Using a smartphone is _____ than using a laptop.

① convenient
② as convenient
③ more convenient
④ convenienter
⑤ most convenient

5 No other teacher at my school is _____ as Ann.

① popular
② as popular
③ popularest
④ more popular
⑤ most popular

(6–7) 빈칸에 들어갈 말이 차례대로 짝지어진 것은?

6 · He is one of the _____ boys in his class.
· Call me as soon as you _____.

① tall - can
② tall - possible
③ taller - can
④ tallest - possible
⑤ tallest - can

7 · He is as _____ as you.
· *Ice Age* is the _____ movie I have ever watched.

① old - funnier
② old - funniest
③ older - funnier
④ older - funniest
⑤ oldest - funniest

8 빈칸에 들어갈 말로 알맞지 <u>않은</u> 것은?

Listening to music makes me _____ happier.

① much
② very
③ even
④ far
⑤ a lot

(9-10) 우리말을 영어로 바르게 옮긴 것을 고르시오.

9 헐크는 영화에서 가장 강한 영웅들 중 하나이다.

① The Hulk is one of the strongest heroes in the movies.
② The Hulk is one of the strongest hero in the movies.
③ The Hulk is one of the most strong heroes in the movies.
④ The Hulk is one of more stronger heroes in the movies.
⑤ The Hulk is one of the stronger hero in the movies.

10 더 많이 웃을수록 더 행복을 느낄 거야.

① You laugh more, you will feel happier.
② The more you laugh, you will feel happier.
③ The more you laugh, the happier you will feel.
④ You laugh more, the happier you will feel.
⑤ The more you laugh, the more happy you will feel.

11 밑줄 친 부분 중 어색한 것을 고르시오.

My mom loves me ① most ② than ③ anybody else ④ in the ⑤ world.

(12-14) 주어진 문장과 같은 의미가 되도록 빈칸을 채우시오.

12 No worker at the company is more intelligent than Jimmy.

⇨ Jimmy is _____ worker at the company.

13 The taxi fare is more expensive than the bus fare.

⇨ The bus fare is _____ as the taxi fare.

14 As you practice writing more, you will become better at it.

⇨ _____ you practice writing, _____ you will become at it.

15 다음 중 어법상 어색한 문장을 고르시오.

① This is more comfortable than that.
② Prices are getting cheaper and cheaper.
③ The trip was a lot more surprising than I had expected.
④ The deep she went into the ocean, the cold it became.
⑤ It was one of the most frightening dreams I have ever had.

(16–17) 우리말과 의미가 같도록 ( ) 안의 단어를 배열하시오.

16 이것은 내가 들었던 것 중 가장 재미없는 이야기이다.
(I, the, ever, heard, story, most, have, boring)

⇨ This is _____

_____ .

17 가격이 올라갈수록 우리는 더 적게 살 것이다.
(the, the, the, are, less, higher, prices)

⇨ _____

_____ we will buy.

(18–19) 주어진 문장과 같은 의미를 갖도록 빈칸을 채우시오.

18 Cheese pizza is less delicious than potato pizza.

⇨ Potato pizza is _____ delicious than cheese pizza.

19 You should gather as much information as you can.

⇨ You should gather as much information as _____ .

20 다음 중 어법상 옳은 것을 고르시오.

① Rice is the most common food of Asia.
② E-books are inferior than paper books.
③ Getting a job is very tougher than before.
④ The more she knows me, the much she loves me.
⑤ This car is three times more expensive than mine.

21 다음 중 나머지와 의미가 <u>다른</u> 문장을 고르시오.

① February is one of the shortest months of the year.
② February is shorter than any other month in the year.
③ February is the shortest month of the year.
④ No other month is as short as February.
⑤ No other month is shorter than February.

22 빈칸에 들어갈 말이 나머지와 <u>다른</u> 것은?

① The _____ he exercised, the stronger he became.
② This is _____ touching than any other book.
③ He reads a lot _____ than I do.
④ You can eat as _____ as you want.
⑤ We want to build a bridge which is even _____ fascinating.

23 다음 중 어법상 <u>어색한</u> 문장을 <u>모두</u> 고르시오.

① Matt is not as busy as Tim.

② This turtle is as twice old as Alex.

③ Actions speak much louder than words.

④ It is the worst hamburger that I have ever tried.

⑤ This has more functions than any other phones.

(24–26) 우리말과 의미가 같도록 ( ) 안의 말을 이용하여 문장을 완성하시오.

24 비타민 D가 감기약보다 훨씬 더 효과적이다.
(a lot, effective)

⇨ Vitamin D is _____
_____ cold medicine.

25 그녀는 역사상 가장 위대한 피겨 스케이터 중에 한 사람이다. (great, figure skater)

⇨ She is _____
_____ in history.

26 사람들이 우주에 점점 더 관심을 갖게 되었다.
(interested)

⇨ People got _____
_____ in space.

---

27 빈칸에 공통으로 들어갈 말을 쓰시오.

· The drama is getting _____ and _____ exciting.
· Do you agree that happiness is a lot _____ important than money?

⇨ _____

(28–29) 다음 문장에서 어색한 부분을 찾아 바르게 고치고 알맞은 이유를 고르시오.

28 No city in Australia is as more beautiful as Sydney.

고치기: _____ ⇨ _____
이유: as (비교급, 원급) as 사용

29 Greg is more talented than any other students in my class.

고치기: _____ ⇨ _____
이유: 비교급 + than + any other
+ (단수명사, 복수명사)

---

30 다음 조건을 이용하여 알맞게 영작하시오.

나는 가능한 한 조용히 집을 떠났다.
조건 1: leave, quietly, possible
조건 2: 7단어

⇨ _____
_____ .

한눈에 정리하는 Grammar Mapping

빈칸에 알맞은 답을 보기에서 골라 넣어 grammar mapping 완성하기

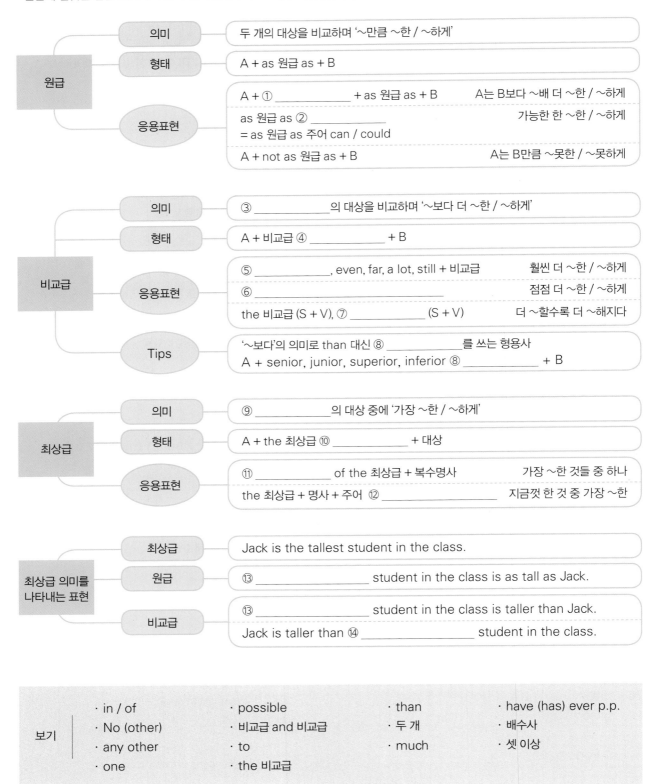

원급

| 의미 | 두 개의 대상을 비교하며 '~만큼 ~한 / ~하게' |

| 형태 | A + as 원급 as + B |

응용표현

A + ① _____ + as 원급 as + B	A는 B보다 ~배 더 ~한 / ~하게
as 원급 as ② _____ = as 원급 as 주어 can / could	가능한 한 ~한 / ~하게
A + not as 원급 as + B	A는 B만큼 ~못한 / ~못하게

비교급

| 의미 | ③ _____의 대상을 비교하며 '~보다 더 ~한 / ~하게' |

| 형태 | A + 비교급 ④ _____ + B |

응용표현

⑤ _____, even, far, a lot, still + 비교급	훨씬 더 ~한 / ~하게
⑥ _____	점점 더 ~한 / ~하게
the 비교급 (S + V), ⑦ _____ (S + V)	더 ~할수록 더 ~해지다

Tips

'~보다'의 의미로 than 대신 ⑧ _____를 쓰는 형용사
A + senior, junior, superior, inferior ⑧ _____ + B

최상급

| 의미 | ⑨ _____의 대상 중에 '가장 ~한 / ~하게' |

| 형태 | A + the 최상급 ⑩ _____ + 대상 |

응용표현

| ⑪ _____ of the 최상급 + 복수명사 | 가장 ~한 것들 중 하나 |
| the 최상급 + 명사 + 주어 ⑫ _____ | 지금껏 한 것 중 가장 ~한 |

최상급 의미를 나타내는 표현

| 최상급 | Jack is the tallest student in the class. |

| 원급 | ⑬ _____ student in the class is as tall as Jack. |

비교급

| ⑬ _____ student in the class is taller than Jack. |
| Jack is taller than ⑭ _____ student in the class. |

보기

- in / of
- No (other)
- any other
- one

- possible
- 비교급 and 비교급
- to
- the 비교급

- than
- 두 개
- much

- have (has) ever p.p.
- 배수사
- 셋 이상

접속사

부사절을 이끄는 접속사

GP 42

부사절은 [접속사 + 주어 + 동사] 형태로 부사처럼 다른 문장, 즉 주절을 수식한다.

부사절		주절
접속사	S + V ~	주어 + 동사 ~
☆ While	she was studying,	she listened to music.

❶ **시간 접속사**: when (~할 때), as (~함에 따라), while (~하는 동안), until (~할 때까지),
　　　　　　　since (~한 이래로 계속), as soon as (~하자마자), whenever (~할 때마다)...

☆ By law, you are a child **until** you are 18 years old.

☆ **When** he feels nervous, he bites his nails.

　While she blew out the candles, her hair caught on fire.

　She has changed a lot **since** I met her last year.

　As he grew up, he got more interested in history.

　As soon as it is ready, we will let you know.

　Whenever I try to use the Internet, the computer shuts down.

> **─ Tip ─**
> 접속사 while의 두 가지 의미
> ① ~하는 동안
> ② ~하는 반면에
> · While he is lazy, he is smart.

❷ **조건 접속사**: if, unless (= if not)...

　If I become a teacher, I will give my students little homework.

☆ **Unless** she leaves now, she will miss her flight.

　= **If** she does**n't** leave now, she will miss her flight.

❸ **이유 접속사**: because, as, since...

☆ He stopped watching the movie **because** it was too violent.

　As (Since) the pasta was too spicy, I couldn't finish it.

❹ **양보 접속사**: although, though, even though, even if...

☆ He didn't go to see the musical **although** he had a ticket.

　Even if you are poor, I will marry you.

• Upgrade •

시간 부사절과 조건 부사절의 시제

주절이 미래시제일 때에도 시간 부사절과 조건 부사절은 미래시제 대신 현재시제를 사용한다.

☆ I will speak to her **when** I meet (~~will meet~~) her the next time. (시간 부사절)

　If it rains (~~will rain~~) tomorrow, we will go to the movie. (조건 부사절)

GP Practice

A ( ) 안에서 알맞은 것을 고르시오.

1 Come and get your tea (if, while) it is still hot.

2 The dog waited (until, since) its owner said, "Eat!"

3 Let's end this meeting unless you (don't have, have) more questions.

4 The boat may turn over if you (lose, will lose) your balance.

5 (As soon as, Even if) I know the secret, I won't let her know it.

B 보기에서 알맞은 접속사를 골라 문장을 완성하시오.

보기	since	if	because	even though

1 I haven't eaten anything _____ I got up today.

2 _____ you don't leave now, you will be late for the movie.

3 _____ it has a bitter taste, it is good for colds.

4 _____ he told me a lie before, I don't trust him.

C 우리말과 의미가 같도록 ( ) 안의 말을 이용하여 문장을 완성하시오 .

1 내가 그 캔디 포장 껍질을 벗기자마자, 캔디를 땅에 떨어뜨렸어. (unwrap)

→ _____ _____ _____ _____ _____ the candy, I dropped it on the ground.

2 긴급한 일이 아니면, 내게 전화하지 말아 주세요. (it, an emergency)

→ Please don't call me _____ _____ _____ _____ _____ .

3 펭귄들은 날 수는 없지만, 헤엄을 매우 잘 치지. (penguins, fly)

→ _____ _____ _____ _____ , they are excellent swimmers.

4 그 서퍼는 커다란 파도가 올 때까지 기다리고 있는 중이다. (a huge wave)

→ The surfer is waiting _____ _____ _____ _____ _____ .

D 밑줄 친 부분에 대한 설명을 하고 틀린 경우엔 바르게 고치시오. (맞으면 'O' 표시)

1	<u>As</u> he looks scary, he is a nice man. → ( )	(~때문에, 비록 ~이지만) 의미의 (이유, 양보) 부사절 접속사
2	Whenever he <u>will see</u> me, he smiles. → ( )	'~할 때마다' 시간 (부사절, 주절)은 미래시제일 때 (현재, 미래)시제 사용
3	Unless he <u>is not</u> rude, I may like him. → ( )	unless는 (if, if ~ not) 의미로 not과 동시에 (사용, 사용 불가)

간접의문문

의문문이 다른 문장의 일부가 될 때 간접의문문이라고 하며, [주어 + 동사]의 어순을 갖는다.

❶ 의문사가 있는 경우: [의문사 + 주어 + 동사]

주어	동사	목적어	
		의문사	S + V ~
☆ I	don't know	where	he lives.

Where does he live?

Magicians never tell us **how they trick** people. (← How do they trick people?)

• Upgrade •

❶ 의문사가 주어인 경우 어순 변화가 없이 그대로 [의문사 + 동사]

I know. + **Who broke** this window?

→ ☆ I know **who broke** this window.

❷ 주절의 동사가 think, believe, guess, imagine 등인 경우, 의문사는 문장의 맨 앞에 위치한다.

Do you **think**? + What is his real job?

→ ☆ **What** do you think **his real job is**?

❷ 의문사가 없는 경우: [if / whether + 주어 + 동사]

주어	동사	목적어	
		if / whether	S + V ~
☆ I	don't know	if	she will win the contest.

Will she win the contest?

Tell me **if (whether) tomatoes are** vegetables. (← Are tomatoes vegetables?)

상관접속사

두 개 이상의 어구가 짝을 이루어 문법적으로 동일한 성질의 두 요소를 연결하는 접속사이다.

both	A	and	B	A와 B 둘 다
either	A	or	B	A와 B 둘 중 하나
neither	A	nor	B	A와 B 둘 다 아닌
not only	A	but (also)	B	A뿐만 아니라 B도
=	B	as well as	A	

☆ **Both** Jack **and** Jill are college students.

Either Daniel **or** you have to take care of the kitten.

☆ **Neither** the kids **nor** their mom likes meat.

Not only the body **but also** the mind needs exercise.

= The mind **as well as** the body needs exercise.

> ○ Tip ○
> 상관접속사의 수일치
> ① 복수 취급 both A and B
> ② B에 일치 either A or B
> neither A nor B
> not only A but also B
> = B as well as A

GP Practice

A ( ) 안에서 알맞은 것을 고르시오.

1 Cheerleaders can be (either, neither) girls or boys.

2 He asked her where (was she, she was) from.

3 We are not sure (if, what) the driverless car will be safe.

4 Chocolate is (both, not only) delicious but also good for your health.

5 (Do you think when, When do you think) he changed his mind?

B 두 문장을 '간접의문문'을 포함한 한 문장으로 고쳐 쓰시오.

1 Do you know? + Where is the Statue of Liberty?

→ Do you know _____ ?

2 She wonders. + Is he telling the truth?

→ She wonders_____ .

3 Do you think? + When will we have snow this year?

→ _____ do you think _____ ?

C 보기에서 알맞은 접속사를 골라 한 문장으로 고쳐 쓰시오.

| 보기 \| | neither ~ nor | both ~ and | either ~ or |

1 These sunglasses are for men. These are also for women.

→ These sunglasses are for _____ .

2 His idea is not creative. It is not interesting either.

→ His idea is _____ .

3 Usually, her phone is busy, or it is turned off.

→ Usually, her phone is _____ .

D 밑줄 친 부분에 대한 설명을 하고 틀린 경우엔 바르게 고치시오. (맞으면 'O' 표시)

* S: 주어, V: 동사

1	She asked me <u>what was my hobby</u>. → ( )	의문사 있는 간접의문문 어순 의문사 + (S + V, V + S)
2	I wonder <u>that he liked</u> the class. → ( )	의문사 없는 간접의문문 어순 (if / whether, that) + (S + V, V + S)
3	<u>Do you think why</u> she is angry? → ( )	주절에 think 있으면 간접의문문의 의문사는 문장 (앞, 중간)에 위치
4	Neither you nor I <u>are</u> wrong. → ( )	Neither A nor B가 주어일 때는 (A, B)에 동사의 단복수 일치

A 우리말과 의미가 같도록 ( ) 안의 말을 배열하시오.

1 알비노 쥐는 색소가 부족해서 하얀색 피부를 갖고 있다. (lacks, because, it)

→ An albino rat has white skin _____ pigment.

2 당신은 6개월을 등록하면 10% 할인을 받을 것입니다. (you, if, sign up, six months, for)

→ _____, you will get a 10% discount.

3 너는 이 나무를 누가 심었었는지 알고 있니? (do, planted, who, know, you)

→ _____ this tree?

4 우리 엄마뿐 아니라 아빠도 혈액형이 O형이셔. (as well as, my mom, my dad, has)

→ _____ blood type O.

5 그가 세차를 할 때마다 비가 온다. (every time, his car, washes, he)

→ _____, it rains.

6 당신이 회의에 참석할 수 있는지 아닌지를 알려 주시기 바랍니다. (attend, the meeting, you, can, if)

→ Please let us know _____.

B 우리말과 의미가 같도록 ( ) 안의 말을 이용하여 문장을 완성하시오.

1 배터리가 없었기 때문에 알람시계가 울리지 않았어. (battery, die)

→ The alarm clock didn't go off _____ _____ _____ _____.

2 Jessica와 나는 둘 다 곱슬머리이다. (both, curly hair)

→ _____ _____ _____ _____ _____ _____

_____.

3 그는 그의 꿈이 실현될지 안 될지 궁금해 한다. (come true)

→ He wonders _____ _____ _____ _____ _____

_____.

4 너는 내 주머니에 무엇이 있다고 생각하니? (guess, have)

→ _____ _____ _____ _____ _____

in my pocket?

5 나는 주로 디지털카메라를 사용하지만, 나는 필름카메라를 선호해. (use, usually)

→ _____ _____ _____ _____ a digital camera, I prefer a

film camera.

6 그는 그 컴퓨터가 세일할 때까지 기다릴 거야. (be, on sale)

→ He will wait _____ _____ _____ _____ _____ _____.

C　보기에서 알맞은 접속사를 골라 빈칸을 채우시오.

보기	· even though	· as	· both ~ and
	· neither ~ nor	· as well as	

1 Sandra is not at home now. Her sisters are not at home either.

→ _____ Sandra _____ her sisters are at home now.

2 This city is exciting. It is safe as well.

→ The city is safe _____ exciting.

3 The teacher was strict, but he loved his students a lot.

→ _____ the teacher was strict, he loved his students a lot.

4 Fruit has a lot of vitamin C. So it is good for you.

→ Fruit is good for you _____ it has a lot of vitamin C.

5 Leo enjoys water sports. His brother also enjoys water sports.

→ _____ Leo _____ his brother enjoy water sports.

D　Kate가 Drama club에 가입하기 위해 클럽 리더인 Steve에게 인터뷰를 받았다. Kate가 친구에게 인터뷰 내용을 전달하는 문장을 완성하시오.

1. Why do you want to join the club?
2. Are you good at dancing?
3. When did you decide to become an actress?
4. Who is your role model?
5. Can you act the part in the scenario?

1 Steve asked me _____ the club.

2 Steve wanted to know _____.

3 Steve asked _____ an actress.

4 Steve was curious about _____.

5 Steve asked me _____ in the scenario.

(1-5) 빈칸에 들어갈 알맞은 말을 고르시오.

1 I am not sure _____ the boy is Jason's younger brother.

① when   ② where

③ how   ④ unless

⑤ if

2 _____ it rains soon, the field will dry up.

① Unless   ② As

③ While   ④ As soon as

⑤ Since

3 _____ the singer earned a huge fortune, he is broke now.

① As   ② Whenever

③ Unless   ④ When

⑤ Even though

4 When do you _____ he will come?

① hear   ② think

③ want   ④ say

⑤ know

5 Neither blue _____ white is a warm color.

① and   ② or

③ nor   ④ not only

⑤ but

6 다음 중 어법상 옳은 것을 고르시오.

① She asked me that I liked her.

② Please tell me who is Mr. Kelly.

③ He knows what her favorite color is.

④ Do you think why you failed again?

⑤ Can you tell me where are canned foods?

(7-8) 밑줄 친 접속사 의미가 나머지와 다른 것은?

7 ① Lower the heat <u>when</u> the soup boils.

② He knows <u>when</u> the mart is closed.

③ Lizards lose their tails <u>when</u> they are threatened.

④ Let's start <u>when</u> you are ready.

⑤ <u>When</u> I was young, I was weak.

8 ① She asked me <u>if</u> I believed in love at first sight.

② You may look around <u>if</u> you want.

③ You can make it <u>if</u> you try your best.

④ What will happen <u>if</u> we break the rule?

⑤ <u>If</u> you miss this chance, you will regret it.

(9–10) 빈칸에 들어갈 말이 차례대로 짝지어진 것은?

9
· _____ California and Florida are famous for beautiful weather.
· _____ California but also Florida is famous for beautiful weather.

① Either - Both   ② Both - Both

③ Not only - Neither   ④ Both - Not

⑤ Both - Not only

10
· _____ the soup was cooking, the chef talked about the food.
· I want to know _____ he is our friend or enemy.

① Since - if   ② Even if - since

③ While - if   ④ While - as

⑤ When - until

(11–12) 주어진 문장과 같은 의미를 갖도록 빈칸을 채우시오.

11 If you are not careful, you will make the same mistake.

⇨ _____ you are careful, you will make the same mistake.

12 Jill is not only humorous but also generous.

⇨ Jill is generous _____ humorous.

13 다음 우리말을 영어로 바르게 옮긴 것을 고르시오.

너는 Emily가 왜 인기가 있다고 생각하니?

① Do you think why is Emily popular?

② Do you think why Emily is popular?

③ Why do you think is Emily popular?

④ Why do you think Emily is popular?

⑤ Why is Emily popular do you think?

(14–15) 밑줄 친 부분 중 어법상 어색한 것을 고르시오.

14 ① The dog barked loudly <u>until</u> someone came to save its owner.

② <u>As</u> he is an American, he likes kimchi.

③ <u>Even if</u> I am hungry, I won't eat fast food.

④ He spilled some tea <u>while</u> he was drinking it.

⑤ Catch me <u>if</u> you can.

15 ① Not Julie but her brothers <u>are</u> good at cooking.

② Both you and Jack <u>are</u> late for the movie.

③ I will wait here until she <u>will arrive</u>.

④ Jane as well as her friends <u>likes</u> the teacher.

⑤ If you <u>feed</u> your cat too much, it will get fat.

(16–17) 빈칸에 공통으로 들어갈 말을 쓰시오.
(대문자와 소문자 적용)

16
· _____ the watch is waterproof, I can wear it underwater.
· She has loved animals _____ she was a child.

⇨ _____ , _____

17
· Did you enjoy fishing _____ you were staying on the island?
· _____ Henry is shy, his brother is outgoing.

⇨ _____ , _____

(18–20) 두 문장을 한 문장으로 연결할 때 빈칸을 채우시오.

18
· Do you understand?
· What is he saying?

⇨ Do you understand _____ _____ ?

19
· Jerome doesn't look like his dad.
· His brother doesn't look like his dad either.

⇨ _____ _____ looks like their dad.

20
· I wonder.
· Is the trophy really made of gold?

⇨ I wonder _____ _____ gold.

21 밑줄 친 접속사와 바꿔 쓸 수 없는 것은?

① They call him a human bullet <u>as</u> he runs fast. (= since)
② It has been a year <u>since</u> we moved to this city. (= because)
③ <u>Whenever</u> he smiles, his dimples show. (= Every time)
④ I wonder <u>if</u> his long speech will ever end. (= whether)
⑤ <u>Although</u> I am young, I have a lot of gray hair. (= Though)

22 다음 중 올바른 것으로 짝지어진 것은?

ⓐ Even though he eats a lot, he is slim.
ⓑ I don't know why you are upset.
ⓒ He as well as I am your big fans.
ⓓ When do you know he will come?
ⓔ Unless you don't make a mistake, you will be the winner.

① ⓐ, ⓑ   ② ⓐ, ⓒ
③ ⓑ, ⓒ   ④ ⓑ, ⓓ
⑤ ⓓ, ⓔ

23 빈칸에 들어갈 말이 나머지와 다른 것을 고르시오.

① He didn't do his work _____ he had time.
② _____ he is a cook, he never cooks at home.
③ It started raining _____ it was sunny.
④ _____ the letters were too small, he couldn't read them.
⑤ _____ I ate a lot, I am still hungry.

(24–25) 우리말과 의미가 같도록 (   ) 안의 말을 배열하시오.

24 너는 저 소년이 누구라고 추측하니?
(do you guess, who, is, the boy)

⇨ _____

_____ ?

28 그 대통령은 백악관에 사는 동안 그의 음식 값을 지불했다. (the White House)

⇨ The president paid for his food _____

_____ .

(29–30) 다음 문장에서 어색한 부분을 찾아 바르게 고치고 알맞은 이유를 고르시오.

25 그 아이돌 그룹은 한국과 유럽 모두에서 인기가 있다.
(famous, in Korea, in Europe, both, and).

⇨ The idol group is _____

_____ .

29 Do you know how old is the castle?

고치기: _____ ⇨ _____
이유: 의문문이 문장의 일부가 되는
(직접, 간접)의문문 어순은
의문사 + (주어 + 동사, 동사 + 주어)

(26–28) 우리말과 의미가 같도록 (   ) 안의 말을 이용하여 문장을 완성하시오.

26 그녀는 성공한 작가이지만, 그녀는 겸손하다.
(successful writer)

⇨ _____

_____ , she is humble.

30 As soon as she will arrive, she will call you.

고치기: _____ ⇨ _____
이유: '~하자마자' 시간 부사절에서는
(현재, 미래)시제 대신 (현재, 미래)시제 사용

31 다음 조건을 이용하여 알맞게 영작하시오.

그 나노로봇은 더 작을 뿐만 아니라 더 영리하다.
조건 1: as well as, nano-robot
조건 2: 8단어

⇨ _____

_____ .

27 내가 그 빵집에 갈 때마다, 사람이 많았다.
(visit, the bakery)

⇨ _____

_____ , it was crowded.

한눈에 정리하는 Grammar Mapping

빈칸에 알맞은 답을 보기에서 골라 넣어 grammar mapping 완성하기

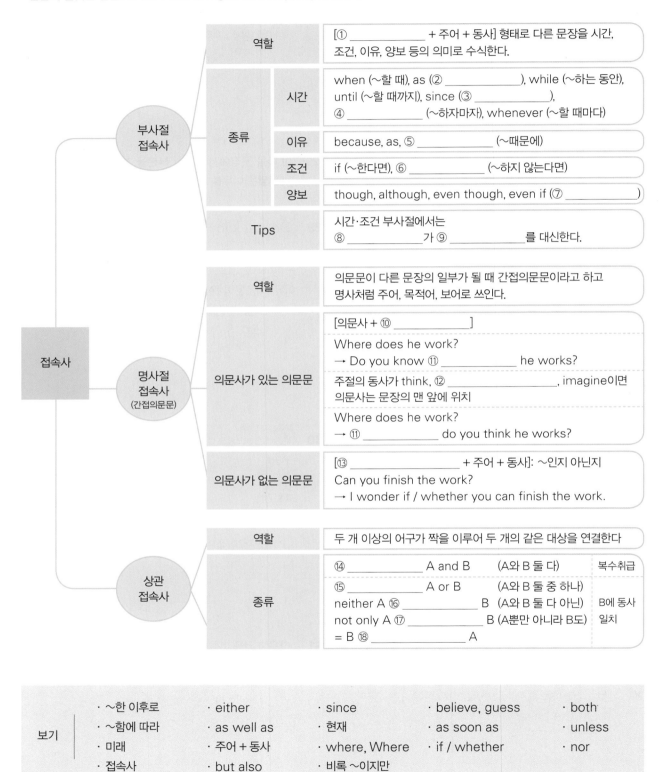

접속사

부사절 접속사

역할
[① _____ + 주어 + 동사] 형태로 다른 문장을 시간, 조건, 이유, 양보 등의 의미로 수식한다.

종류

시간
when (~할 때), as (② _____), while (~하는 동안), until (~할 때까지), since (③ _____),
④ _____ (~하자마자), whenever (~할 때마다)

이유
because, as, ⑤ _____ (~때문에)

조건
if (~한다면), ⑥ _____ (~하지 않는다면)

양보
though, although, even though, even if (⑦ _____)

Tips
시간·조건 부사절에서는
⑧ _____ 가 ⑨ _____ 를 대신한다.

명사절 접속사 (간접의문문)

역할
의문문이 다른 문장의 일부가 될 때 간접의문문이라고 하고 명사처럼 주어, 목적어, 보어로 쓰인다.

의문사가 있는 의문문
[의문사 + ⑩ _____]

Where does he work?
→ Do you know ⑪ _____ he works?

주절의 동사가 think, ⑫ _____, imagine이면 의문사는 문장의 맨 앞에 위치

Where does he work?
→ ⑪ _____ do you think he works?

의문사가 없는 의문문
[⑬ _____ + 주어 + 동사]: ~인지 아닌지
Can you finish the work?
→ I wonder if / whether you can finish the work.

상관 접속사

역할
두 개 이상의 어구가 짝을 이루어 두 개의 같은 대상을 연결한다

종류

⑭ _____ A and B (A와 B 둘 다) | 복수취급
⑮ _____ A or B (A와 B 둘 중 하나)
neither A ⑯ _____ B (A와 B 둘 다 아닌) | B에 동사
not only A ⑰ _____ B (A뿐만 아니라 B도) | 일치
= B ⑱ _____ A

보기
· ~한 이후로　· either　· since　· believe, guess　· both
· ~함에 따라　· as well as　· 현재　· as soon as　· unless
· 미래　· 주어 + 동사　· where, Where　· if / whether　· nor
· 접속사　· but also　· 비록 ~이지만

관계사

관계대명사 who, which, that

GP 45

접속사와 대명사 역할을 동시에 하고 관계대명사절은 형용사처럼 앞에 나오는 명사(선행사)를 수식한다.

선행사	주격 관계대명사	소유격 관계대명사	목적격 관계대명사
사람	who	whose	who(m)
동물, 사물	which	whose / of which	which
사람, 동물, 사물	that	-	that
선행사 없음	what	-	what

❶ 주격 관계대명사 who, which, that

접속사와 대명사	He is	a man.	+	He	is very polite to everyone.
관계대명사	He is	a man		who	is very polite to everyone.

☆ I bought a book **which (that)** is about space.

❷ 목적격 관계대명사 who(m), which, that

He is the man. + I respect him the most.

→ ☆ He is the man **who(m) (that)** I respect the most.

The cake **which (that)** she made for dessert was too sweet.

○─ Tip ─○

관계대명사 that을 주로 쓰는 경우
① 선행사가 [사람 + 사물], [사람 + 동물], -thing으로 끝나는 대명사인 경우
② 선행사가 최상급, 서수, the only, the very, the same, the last, all, every 등의 수식을 받는 경우

❸ 소유격 관계대명사 whose, of which

I know a man. + His daughter is a popular actress.

→ ☆ I know a man **whose** daughter is a popular actress.

We will invent a robot **whose** arms are very similar to a human's.

= We will invent a robot **of which** the arms are very similar to a human's.

❹ 관계대명사 what

관계대명사 what은 선행사를 포함하고 보통 '~하는 것'으로 해석한다. 관계대명사 what이 이끄는 절은 문장에서 주어, 목적어, 보어 역할을 한다.

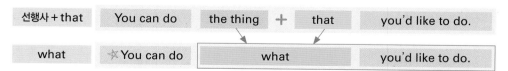

선행사 + that	You can do	the thing	+	that	you'd like to do.
what	☆You can do		what		you'd like to do.

I can't believe **what** you have just said. (what = the thing that)

GP Practice

A ( ) 안에서 알맞은 것을 고르시오.

1 He has a friend (who, whose) goal is to be a soccer player.

2 Is this the locker key (whom, which) you are looking for?

3 (That, What) he wants to know is how much his mom trusts him.

4 I saw a man and his dog (who, that) were running through the park.

B 두 문장을 관계대명사를 이용하여 한 문장으로 쓰시오.

1 Most of the people were very friendly. We met the people.

→ _____ .

2 The clothes cost more. They are made by famous designers.

→ _____ .

3 The person is called a zoologist. His job is studying animals.

→ _____ .

C 우리말과 의미가 같도록 ( ) 안의 말을 이용하여 문장을 완성하시오.

1 너는 내가 말하고 있는 것을 이해하니? (say)

→ Do you understand _____ _____ _____ _____ .

2 그녀가 파티에 초대했던 그 가수는 유명하지 않았다. (invite)

→ The singer _____ _____ _____ to the party was not famous.

3 나는 희귀한 물건을 수집하는 것이 취미인 한 소년을 안다. (hobby)

→ I know a boy _____ _____ _____ collecting rare items.

4 우리는 8시에 떠나는 기차를 탈 거야. (leave)

→ We are taking the train _____ _____ at 8 o'clock.

D 밑줄 친 부분에 대한 설명을 하고 틀린 경우엔 바르게 고치시오. (맞으면 'O' 불필요하면 '삭제' 표시)

1	He hired a woman <u>who</u> is very intelligent. → ( )	선행사가 (사람, 동물)일 때 (주격, 목적격) 관계대명사 + 동사
2	The girl whom I met <u>her</u> talked a lot. → ( )	(주격, 목적격) 관계대명사 뒤에 선행사를 가리키는 목적어를 (사용, 삭제)
3	<u>That</u> I want for lunch is a ham sandwich. → ( )	선행사가 없으므로 관계대명사 (What, That)
4	She is lying on the beach <u>which</u> sand is very soft. → ( )	선행사 + (주격, 소유격) 관계대명사 + 명사

관계부사 when, where, why, how

접속사와 부사 역할을 동시에 하고 관계부사절은 형용사처럼 앞에 나오는 명사(선행사)를 수식한다. 관계부사는 [전치사 + 관계대명사] 형태로 바꿀 수 있다.

	선행사	관계부사	전치사 + 관계대명사
시간	the time, the day…	when	at / in / on… which
장소	the place, the house…	where	at / in / on… which
이유	the reason	why	for which
방법	the way	how	in which

접속사와 부사(구)	I remember	the place.	+	I first met her	in	the place.

관계부사	I remember	the place	where	I first met her.
			in which	I first met her.

❶ **when**: 시간을 나타내는 the time, the day, the year 등이 선행사일 때

The day **when** (= on which) we can live on Mars will come.

Do you know the time **when** (= at which) his speech will end?

❷ **where**: 장소를 나타내는 the place, the house, the city 등이 선행사일 때

We visited a city **where** (= in which) the Olympic Games were held.

The restaurant **where** (= at which) we had dinner is closed on Sundays.

❸ **why**: 이유를 나타내는 the reason이 선행사일 때

The reason **why** (= for which) she likes me is mysterious.

Do you know the reason **why** (= for which) Rome collapsed?

❹ **how**: 방법을 나타내는 the way가 선행사일 때

The program shows **the way (= how)** people manage time wisely.

The program shows **the way in which** people manage time wisely.

The program shows the way how people manage time wisely. (X)

> **Tip**
> 선행사 the way와
> 관계부사 how는
> 같이 쓸 수 없다.

• Upgrade •

관계대명사 vs. 관계부사

관계대명사는 [접속사 + 대명사]의 역할을 하므로 관계대명사를 제외하면 주어, 목적어, 보어 중 하나가 빠져 있는 불완전한 문장을 이끈다. 관계부사는 [접속사 + 부사]의 역할을 하므로 관계부사를 제외하면 부사가 빠져 있는 완전한 문장을 이끈다.

This is the bridge **which** was built in the 19th century. (불완전한 문장)

This is the bridge **where** a car accident happened yesterday. (완전한 문장)

GP Practice

A ( ) 안에서 알맞은 것을 고르시오.

1 The resort (when, where) we stayed was very beautiful.

2 My students want to know (where, how) I entered university.

3 You should tell her the reason (why, how) you want to go there.

4 Do you remember the year (when, where) we graduated from elementary school?

B 두 문장을 관계부사를 이용하여 한 문장으로 쓰시오.

1 Australia is the country. My mom studied in the country.

→ _____ .

2 The reason is unknown. Dinosaurs disappeared for the reason.

→ _____ .

3 Tell us the way. You memorized English vocabulary so quickly in the way.

→ _____ .

C 우리말과 의미가 같도록 ( ) 안의 말을 이용하여 문장을 완성하시오.

1 나는 처음으로 만점을 받았던 그날을 잊을 수가 없다. (day)

→ I can't forget _____ _____ _____ I first got a perfect score.

2 그녀는 그 소방관이 많은 생명을 어떻게 구했는지 설명하고 있다. (save, firefighter)

→ She is explaining _____ _____ _____ _____ lots of lives.

3 나는 어제 그가 잠을 잘 수 없었던 이유를 알고 있다. (reason)

→ I know _____ _____ _____ he could not sleep last night.

4 이 공원은 그가 항상 주말을 보내는 곳이다. (place)

→ This park is _____ _____ _____ he always spends his weekends.

D 밑줄 친 부분에 대한 설명을 하고 틀린 경우엔 바르게 고치시오. (맞으면 'O' 불필요하면 '삭제' 표시)

1	I don't like the way <u>how</u> he treats me. → ( )	선행사 + 관계부사 (방법, 이유) (how, 없음)
2	One reason <u>why</u> I like this place is its clean air. → ( )	선행사 + 관계부사 (시간, 이유) (when, why)
3	Let me know the place <u>why</u> you learned to ski. → ( )	선행사 + 관계부사 (장소, 이유) (where, why)
4	Think about a time <u>how</u> you overcame some difficulties. → ( )	선행사 + 관계부사 (시간, 방법) (when, how)

관계대명사 생략

GP 47

❶ 목적격 관계대명사의 생략

The author (**whom**) I will visit is well known to everyone.

⚡The police found the bag (**that**) I had lost at the airport.

❷ [주격 관계대명사 + be동사]의 생략

I have a watch (**which was**) made in Switzerland fifty years ago.

The gentleman (**who is**) talking to my dad wears a suit all the time.

전치사 + 관계대명사

GP 48

관계대명사가 전치사의 목적어인 경우, 전치사는 관계대명사절 끝에 오거나 관계대명사 앞에 올 수 있다.

전치사가 관계대명사 앞에 오는 경우에는 관계대명사 that을 쓸 수 없다.

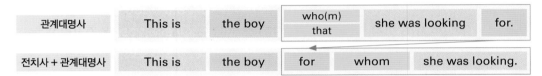

You are the person **who(m)** (**that**) I can rely **on**.

= ⚡You are the person **on whom** I can rely.

She displayed the trophies **which** (**that**) she feels very proud **of**.

= She displayed the trophies **of which** she feels very proud.

> **Tip**
>
> 전치사가 관계대명사 바로 앞에 올 경우에는 목적격 관계대명사를 생략할 수 없다.
> · She displayed the trophies of she feels very proud. (×)

관계사의 계속적 용법

GP 49

관계사의 계속적 용법은 [선행사 + comma(,) + 관계사절] 형태로 선행사에 대한 부가적인 설명을 한다.

❶ 관계대명사의 계속적 용법: who와 which만 가능하고 [접속사 (and, but, for) + 대명사]로 바꿔 쓸 수 있다.

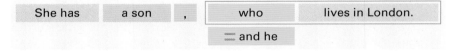

⚡We ordered some seafood dishes, **which** (= but they) tasted really awful.

＊ 계속적 용법의 which는 선행사로 단어뿐만 아니라 앞 문장 전체를 선행사로 취할 수 있다.

He plays loud music every night, **which** (= and it) makes sleeping difficult.

❷ 관계부사의 계속적 용법: when과 where만 가능하고 [접속사 (and, but) + 부사]로 바꿔 쓸 수 있다.

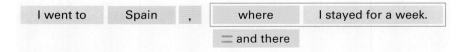

I will be free in the morning, **when** (= and then) you can come to see me.

A ( ) 안에서 알맞은 것을 고르시오.

1 I read the movie script (is written, written) by my aunt.

2 The teacher (whom, to whom) Bill is talking is from New Zealand.

3 She met a police officer, (who, which) gave her a ride to school.

4 We went to Yosemite Park, (where, when) we saw various cliffs and waterfalls.

B 두 문장의 의미가 같도록 관계사를 이용하여 빈칸을 채우시오.

1 This is Karl, and he is one of my closest friends.

→ This is Karl, _____.

2 We went to the toy fair on Monday, and then it was not crowded.

→ We went to the toy fair on Monday, _____.

3 I borrowed a bicycle, but my brother broke it the next day.

→ I borrowed a bicycle, _____.

C 우리말과 의미가 같도록 ( ) 안의 말을 이용하여 문장을 완성하시오.

1 네가 어제 보낸 그 이메일을 확인하지 못했다. (send)

→ I haven't checked _____ _____ _____ _____ me yesterday.

2 그는 유명한 배우인데, 아침마다 연습을 많이 한다. (practice)

→ He is a famous actor, _____ _____ a lot every morning.

3 폭풍에 의해 파괴되었던 그 집은 아직도 공사 중이다. (destroy, the storm)

→ The house _____ _____ _____ _____ is still being rebuilt.

4 오늘의 주제는 내가 관심 있는 인공지능에 관한 것이다. (be, interest)

→ Today's topic is about artificial intelligence, in _____ _____ _____ _____.

D 밑줄 친 부분에 대한 설명을 하고 틀린 경우엔 바르게 고치시오. (맞으면 'O' 표시)

* 관대: 관계대명사

1	This is the doll with <u>that</u> she wants to play. → ( )	전치사 + 관계대명사 (that, which)
2	<u>The boy playing</u> the piano is my brother. → ( )	선행사 + [주격 관대 + be동사] + -ing 생략 (가능, 불가능)
3	I said nothing, <u>that</u> made her angry. → ( )	comma(,) + 관계대명사 (that, which)
4	<u>The computer I bought</u> yesterday is not working. → ( )	선행사 + 목적격 관대 + 주어 + 동사 생략 (가능, 불가능)

복합관계대명사

GP 50

복합관계대명사는 관계대명사에 -ever를 붙인 형태로 명사절과 양보 부사절을 이끈다.

복합관계대명사	who(m)ever	whichever	whatever
선행사 + 관계대명사 (명사절)	~하는 누구든지	~하는 어느 것이든지	~하는 무엇이든지
	anyone who(m)	anything that	anything that
no matter + 관계대명사 (양보 부사절)	누가(누구를) ~하더라도	어느 것이(을) ~하더라도	무엇이(을) ~하더라도
	no matter who(m)	no matter which	no matter what

선행사 + 관계대명사	Anyone	who	wants to succeed	should be diligent.
복합관계대명사	☆ Whoever		wants to succeed	should be diligent.

❶ 명사절

I will give you **whichever** you choose. (← anything that)

My dad wants to buy my mom **whatever** she wants. (← anything that)

❷ 양보 부사절

Whomever you meet, be polite to them. (← No matter whom)

Whichever he may take, he will be satisfied. (← No matter which)

Whatever you do, don't do it halfway. (← No matter what)

복합관계부사

GP 51

복합관계부사는 관계부사에 -ever를 붙인 형태로 시간 / 장소 부사절이나 양보 부사절을 이끈다.

복합관계부사	whenever	wherever	however
선행사 + 관계부사 (시간 / 장소 부사절)	~하는 언제든지	~하는 어디든지	
	at any time when	at / in / to any place where	
no matter + 관계부사 (양보 부사절)	언제 ~하더라도	어디에서 ~하더라도	아무리 ~하더라도
	no matter when	no matter where	no matter how

❶ 시간 / 장소 부사절

I'll help you out **whenever** you are in trouble. (← at any time when)

☆The dog follows my dad **wherever** he goes. (← to any place where)

❷ 양보 부사절

Whenever she calls me, I always answer the phone. (← No matter when)

Wherever he may work, he'll get along with his co-workers. (← No matter where)

☆ **However smart** he is, he won't understand her tears. (← No matter how)

• Upgrade •

복합관계부사 however은 보통 [however + 형용사 / 부사 + 주어 + 동사] 형태로 쓴다.

GP Practice

A ( ) 안에서 알맞은 것을 고르시오.

1 (What, Whatever) the result is, I will accept it.

2 (Whoever, Whomever) breaks the rules will be punished.

3 (Whenever, However) hard it may be, don't give up.

4 (Wherever, However) he studies, he is always good at concentrating.

B 두 문장의 의미가 같도록 복합관계사를 이용하여 빈칸을 채우시오.

1 She smiles any time she sees me.

→ She smiles _____ she sees me.

2 I can give my old clothes to anyone who needs them.

→ I can give my old clothes to _____ needs them.

3 No matter what I decide to do, my family will support me.

→ _____ I decide to do, my family will support me.

C 우리말과 의미가 같도록 복합관계사를 이용하여 문장을 완성하시오.

1 그를 방문하는 누구든지 환영받을 것이다. (visit)

→ _____ _____ _____ will be welcomed.

2 우리가 만나면 언제든지, 우리는 한 시간 이상 이야기한다. (meet)

→ _____ _____ _____, we talk for over an hour.

3 시작이 있는 건 무엇이든 또한 끝이 있다. (have)

→ _____ _____ a beginning also has an end.

4 그 꽃들이 아무리 아름답다 하더라도, 오래가지 못할 것이다. (beautiful)

→ _____ _____ _____ _____ _____, they

will not last long.

D 밑줄 친 부분에 대한 설명을 하고 틀린 경우엔 바르게 고치시오. (맞으면 'O' 표시)

1	<u>Whenever</u> says that is a liar. → ( )	'~하는 건 누구든지' 의미는 (whenever, whoever)
2	Choose anything <u>whichever</u> you like. → ( )	선행사 + (관계대명사, 복합관계대명사)
3	<u>Whatever</u> you run away, he'll chase you. → ( )	'어디에 ~하더라도' 의미는 (Wherever, Whatever)
4	<u>Whenever</u> happens, I will be with you. → ( )	'~하는 무엇이든' 의미는 (Whenever, Whatever)

A 우리말과 의미가 같도록 ( ) 안의 말을 배열하시오.

1 내 옆에 앉았던 숙녀분이 지갑을 버스에 놓고 내렸다. (the, me, to, sat, who, next, lady)

→ _____ left her purse on the bus.

2 네가 해야 하는 것은 충분히 자는 거야. (to, do, you, have, what)

→ _____ is get enough sleep.

3 그는 그녀를 기다리지 않았던 이유를 설명하지 않았다. (he, the, why, wait, didn't, reason)

→ He didn't explain _____ for her.

4 어떤 방법을 선택하든, 좋은 면과 나쁜 면이 있다. (way, choose, you, whichever)

→ _____, there are a good side and a bad side.

5 지붕이 빨간색으로 칠해진 집은 멋있어 보였다. (was, the, red, roof, house, painted, whose)

→ _____ looked nice.

6 Mike는 학생들에게 구름이 형성되는 방법을 가르쳤다. (in, the, way, clouds, which, form)

→ Mike taught his students _____.

B 우리말과 의미가 같도록 ( ) 안의 말을 이용하여 문장을 완성하시오.

1 네가 전화했었던 저녁나절에 나는 집에 없었다. (call)

→ I wasn't at home in the evening _____ _____ _____.

2 너는 우리가 어제 샀던 빵을 먹었니? (buy)

→ Have you eaten the bread _____ _____ _____?

3 라면은 내가 요리할 수 있는 유일한 음식이다. (only)

→ Ramen is _____ _____ _____ _____ I can cook.

4 그는 가난한 사람들을 돕는데, 그것은 그를 행복하게 만든다. (make)

→ He helps the poor, _____ _____ _____ _____.

5 나의 부모님은 앞으로 내가 결혼하는 사람 누구라도 사랑하실 것이다. (marry)

→ My parents will love _____ _____ _____ in the future.

6 그녀는 시골에서 태어났고 거기서 그녀는 유년시절을 보냈다. (spend)

→ She was born in the country, _____ _____ _____ all of her childhood.

C 다음 그림과 일치하도록 주어진 말과 알맞은 관계사를 이용하여 문장을 완성하시오.

| 보기 | invented | screen was broken | lay eggs | wants to eat |

1 Pasta is ＿＿＿＿＿＿＿＿＿＿＿＿＿＿＿＿ right now.

2 He found a cell phone ＿＿＿＿＿＿＿＿＿＿＿＿＿＿ on the street.

3 The birds built a nest ＿＿＿＿＿＿＿＿＿＿＿＿＿＿.

4 Hangeul, ＿＿＿＿＿＿＿＿＿＿＿＿＿＿＿ in 1443, is a great writing
  system.

D 보기에서 알맞은 표현을 골라 문장을 완성하시오.

보기	· whatever is on this table	· what he told her
	· that came into his head	· wherever you go
	· in which the team could finally win the game	

1 Henry just said anything ＿＿＿＿＿＿＿＿＿＿＿＿＿＿＿.

2 You can take ＿＿＿＿＿＿＿＿＿＿＿＿＿＿.

3 She doesn't want to remember ＿＿＿＿＿＿＿＿＿＿＿＿＿.

4 This is the way ＿＿＿＿＿＿＿＿＿＿＿＿＿＿.

5 ＿＿＿＿＿＿＿＿＿＿＿＿＿, leave a note so that I know where you are.

(1–5) 빈칸에 들어갈 알맞은 말을 고르시오.

1
> The man _____ jacket is blue is my math teacher.

① who ② whom
③ whose ④ which
⑤ when

2
> Christina is my only friend _____ knows me well.

① which ② whose
③ whom ④ what
⑤ that

3
> Now is the time _____ you can change your mind.

① why ② how
③ what ④ where
⑤ when

4
> I will give this book to _____ needs it.

① whoever ② whichever
③ whatever ④ wherever
⑤ however

5
> I looked out of the window, _____ was facing the lake.

① who ② which
③ that ④ what
⑤ where

6 빈칸에 들어갈 말이 <u>다른</u> 것을 고르시오.

① We don't agree with _____ he suggested.
② Things are not always _____ they seem.
③ I thank her for _____ she has done to me.
④ The CEO will tell us _____ he spends his free time.
⑤ _____ I still don't understand is that he failed the exam.

(7–8) 밑줄 친 부분과 바꿔 쓸 수 있는 것을 고르시오.

7
> I sent her a letter, <u>which</u> didn't reach her.

① and it ② but it
③ for it ④ as it
⑤ because it

8
> I don't know the reason <u>why</u> people do fewer outdoor activities.

① at which ② in which
③ on which ④ for which
⑤ with which

(9-10) 다음 중 어법상 어색한 문장을 고르시오.

9 ① Take this ticket for which you paid.

② That's the reason why she got surprised.

③ I have a friend whose dream is to be a comedian.

④ Have you seen the woman who Sam is looking for?

⑤ Tell me the way how you answered the question.

10 ① Come to me whenever you feel like it.

② That is the village in which I was raised.

③ She can't forget the day which she first visited Greece.

④ Never put off till tomorrow what you can do today.

⑤ The actress looks beautiful in whatever she wears.

11 빈칸에 공통으로 들어갈 말을 고르시오.

· I really need a person _____ can help me with the project.
· Michelle wants to eat something _____ is not spicy.

① that
② who
③ whose
④ which
⑤ what

12 밑줄 친 부분을 생략할 수 없는 것을 고르시오.

① The boy who you met on the subway is my friend.

② I know the man who is standing near the bus stop.

③ She has a bag that was made in France.

④ The book which he lost yesterday is mine.

⑤ The house into which the thieves broke is owned by Mr. Cooper.

(13-15) 주어진 문장과 같은 의미를 갖도록 빈칸을 채우시오.

13 Charlie tells exactly the same story to anyone who listens.

⇨ Charlie tells exactly the same story to _____ listens.

14 The thing that is the most important in her life is her passion for art.

⇨ _____ is the most important in her life is her passion for art.

15 No matter how hard you run, you cannot catch me.

⇨ _____ hard you run, you cannot catch me.

(16–18) 두 문장을 한 문장으로 만들 때 빈칸에 알맞은 말을 쓰시오.

16
· I miss my old school days.
· I played basketball with my friends during my school days.

⇨ I miss my old school days _____ I played basketball with my friends.

17
· Did he change the subject?
· We should write a report about the subject.

⇨ Did he change the subject about _____ we should write a report.

18
· I respect Mother Theresa.
· She devoted her life to others.

⇨ I respect Mother Theresa, _____ devoted her life to others.

19 밑줄 친 부분 중 어법상 어색한 것을 고르시오.

① That's the doctor for whom Jack works.
② I visited the town in which my dad grew up.
③ Alex is the person with that I can share my happiness.
④ The picture at which she is looking is a fake.
⑤ The woman to whom my mom is talking is my teacher.

20 우리말을 영어로 바르게 옮긴 것을 모두 고르시오.

그는 시험을 잘 봤는데 그것은 아주 놀라운 일이었다.

① He did well on his exams, it was a big surprise.
② He did well on his exams, and it was a big surprise.
③ He did well on his exams, who was a big surprise.
④ He did well on his exams, that was a big surprise.
⑤ He did well on his exams, which was a big surprise.

(21–23) 우리말과 의미가 같도록 빈칸에 알맞은 말을 쓰시오.

21 나는 그 숙녀의 커피를 쏟아버려서 사과했다.

⇨ I apologized to the lady _____ coffee I spilled.

22 민지를 아는 누구라도 그녀를 좋아할 것이다.

⇨ _____ knows Minji will like her.

23 그 왕이 손대는 것은 무엇이라도 금으로 바뀌었다.

⇨ _____ the king touched turned into gold.

24 어법상 어색한 것으로 짝지어진 것은?

> ⓐ I know the reason why he was absent from class.
> ⓑ That is beautiful is not always good.
> ⓒ Tell me how you improved your English.
> ⓓ My cousin, whose age is 12, is a smart boy.
> ⓔ This is the store where my uncle built last year.

① ⓐ, ⓒ   ② ⓑ, ⓓ

③ ⓒ, ⓓ   ④ ⓑ, ⓔ

⑤ ⓐ, ⓔ

(25–27) 우리말과 의미가 같도록 ( ) 안의 말을 배열하시오.

25 그녀가 듣고 있는 음악은 록발라드이다.
(is, to, the, she, music, listening)

⇨ _____
_____ is a rock ballad.

26 그가 아무리 똑똑해도 최선을 다해야 한다.
(he, is, bright, however)

⇨ _____,
he should try his best.

27 네가 어디에 숨든지 간에, 난 너를 찾을 거야.
(no, you, where, hide, matter)

⇨ _____,
I'll find you.

28 빈칸에 공통으로 들어갈 말을 쓰시오.
(대문자와 소문자 적용)

> · _____ I need is a long vacation.
> · I think _____ Helen told me is a lie.

⇨ _____, _____

(29–30) 다음 문장에서 어색한 부분을 찾아 바르게 고치고 알맞은 이유를 고르시오.

29 The man who he lives upstairs is a college student.

고치기: _____ ⇨ _____

이유: (주격, 목적격) 관계대명사 뒤에는
선행사를 가리키는 주어 (사용, 삭제)

30 A pool where has no fence is a danger to children.

고치기: _____ ⇨ _____

이유: '울타리를 가지고 있지 않는' 의미이고
관계사절이 (완전, 불완전)하므로
(which, where)

31 다음 조건을 이용하여 알맞게 영작하시오.

> 인터넷은 사람들이 사는 방식을 바꿔왔다.
> 조건 1: change, the Internet
> 조건 2: 7단어, 완료시제와 관계부사

⇨ _____
_____.

한눈에 정리하는 Grammar Mapping

빈칸에 알맞은 답을 보기에서 골라 넣어 grammar mapping 완성하기

*S: 주어, V: 동사

관계사

① _____	관계대명사	S V
	관계부사	S V

관계대명사

역할
[접속사 + 대명사] 역할을 하면서 형용사처럼 명사를 수식

종류

선행사	[주격 + V]	[소유격 + 명사]	[목적격 + S + V]
사람	who	whose	who(m)
동물, 사물	which	whose / ② _____	which
사람, 동물, 사물	that	×	that
③ _____	what	×	what

that
선행사가 [④ _____], 서수, 최상급 등일 때 사용

what
선행사를 포함하고 ⑤ '_____'으로 해석

관계대명사 생략
⑥ _____ 관계대명사 생략
[주격 관계대명사 + ⑦ _____] 생략

전치사와 관계대명사
선행사 + [관계대명사 + 주어 + 동사 + ⑧ _____]
= 선행사 + [⑧ _____ + 관계대명사 + 주어 + 동사]
This is the novel which I talked about.
= This is the novel about which I talked.

계속적 용법
[⑨ _____ + who / which] → [접속사 + 대명사]
선행사를 ⑩ _____하고 앞에서부터 해석

관계부사

역할
[접속사 + 부사] 역할을 하면서 형용사처럼 명사를 수식

종류

when	the time (⑪ _____) + when 주어 + 동사
where	the place (⑫ _____) + where 주어 + 동사
why	the reason (⑬ _____) + why 주어 + 동사
how	the way (⑭ _____) + how 주어 + 동사 (the way, how 둘 중 하나는 반드시 ⑮ _____)

Tips
관계부사 = ⑧ _____ + 관계대명사
where = (in / on / at) + which

계속적 용법
[⑨ _____ + when / where] → [접속사 + then / there]
선행사를 ⑩ _____하고 앞에서부터 해석

복합관계사

역할
관계사에 -ever가 붙은 형태로 명사절과 부사절로 쓴다.

복합관계대명사
who(m)ever, ⑯ _____, whatever

복합관계부사
whenever, ⑰ _____, however

보기

· 이유	· 전치사	· 목적격	· 방법	· 선행사	· ~하는 것
· 장소	· 보충 설명	· 생략	· 시간	· 선행사 없음	· of which
· 사람 + 사물	· wherever	· be동사	· comma (,)	· whichever	

가정법

가정법 과거

GP 52

현재 사실과 반대되는 상황을 나타내거나 실현 불가능한 것을 가정할 때 쓴다.

☆ If he had a notebook,   he could lend it to me.

If she **were** tired, she **would** not **go** there with me.
→ As she isn't tired, she will go there with me.

> **Tip**
> 가정법 과거 문장에서 be동사는 인칭과 수에 관계없이 were를 쓴다.

• Upgrade •

단순 조건문은 [If + 주어 + 현재동사 ~, 주어 + will / can / may + 동사원형 ~] 형태로 실현 가능한 일을 가정할 때 쓴다.

☆ If you **miss** this chance, you **will regret** it.

가정법 과거완료

GP 53

과거 사실과 반대되는 상황을 나타내거나 실현 불가능한 것을 가정할 때 쓴다.

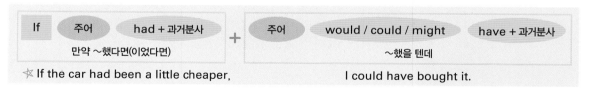

☆ If the car had been a little cheaper,   I could have bought it.

If you **had arrived** ten minutes earlier, you **could have gotten** a good seat.
→ As you didn't arrive ten minutes earlier, you could not get a good seat.

혼합가정법

GP 54

if절과 주절의 시제가 일치하는 않는 형태로 과거에 실현되지 못했던 일이 현재까지 영향을 미치는 것을 나타낼 때 쓴다.

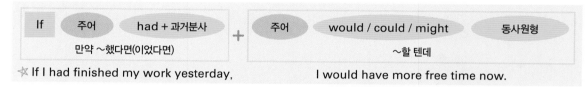

☆ If I had finished my work yesterday,   I would have more free time now.

If you **had taken** my advice, you **would be** in a better position now.
→ As you didn't take my advice, you are not in a better position now.

GP Practice

A ( ) 안에서 알맞은 것을 고르시오.

1 If she had a daughter, she (would, will) buy this dress for her.

2 If I meet Kate again, I (would, will) ask her to go to the movies.

3 If he had repaired his car, it would (have, have had) no problems now.

4 If I (didn't turn, hadn't turned) off my phone, I could have answered her call.

B 주어진 문장을 다음과 같이 바꿀 때 빈칸에 알맞은 말을 쓰시오.

1 He is sick now, so he can't enjoy the music festival.

→ If he _____ sick now, he _____ the music festival.

2 As the toy car was not cheap, I couldn't buy it.

→ If the toy car _____ cheap, I _____ it.

3 As he helped me, I am not in serious trouble these days.

→ If he _____ me, I _____ in serious trouble these days.

C 우리말과 의미가 같도록 ( ) 안의 말을 이용하여 문장을 완성하시오.

1 내일 날씨가 좋으면, 우리는 현장학습을 떠날 것이다. (be, go)

→ If the weather _____ nice tomorrow, we _____ _____ on a field trip.

2 그녀가 매일 산책을 했더라면, 더 건강했을 텐데. (take, be)

→ If she _____ _____ a walk every day, she _____ _____ _____ healthier.

3 Patrick이 충분한 경험을 가지고 있다면, 그들이 그를 고용할 텐데. (have, hire)

→ If Patrick _____ enough experience, they _____ _____ him.

4 내가 어제 더 열심히 연습을 했더라면 지금 긴장하지 않을 텐데. (practice, be)

→ If I _____ _____ harder yesterday, I _____ _____ _____ nervous now.

D 밑줄 친 부분에 대한 설명을 하고 틀린 경우엔 바르게 고치시오. (맞으면 'O' 표시)

* S: 주어, R: 동사원형, p.p.: 과거분사

1	If I <u>am</u> you, I would look for another job. → ( )	실현 가능성 (있는, 없는) 가정법 과거 If + S + (과거, 현재)동사, S + (will, would) + R
2	If you <u>leave</u> now, you will be home in one hour. → ( )	실현 가능성 (있는, 없는) 조건문 If + S + (과거, 현재)동사, S + (will, would) + R
3	If he had had a lawnmower, he could <u>cut</u> the grass. → ( )	실현 가능성 (있는, 없는) 가정법 과거완료 If + S + had p.p., S + could + (R, have p.p.)
4	If I had eaten lunch, I would not <u>have been</u> hungry now. → ( )	'만약 ~했다면, ~할 텐데'의 혼합가정법 If + S + had p.p., S + would + (R, have p.p.)

I wish + 가정법

현재에 이루기 힘든 것을 소망할 때나 과거에 이룰 수 없었던 것을 소망할 때 쓴다.

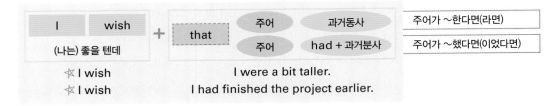

① I wish + 가정법 과거

I wish I **spoke** Chinese.

→ I am sorry (that) I don't speak Chinese.

② I wish + 가정법 과거완료

I wish she **had watched** the action movie with me.

→ I am sorry she didn't watch the action movie with me.

as if + 가정법

현재에 그렇지 않은 일을 그런 것처럼 가정할 때나 과거에 그렇지 않았던 일을 그랬던 것처럼 가정할 때 쓴다.

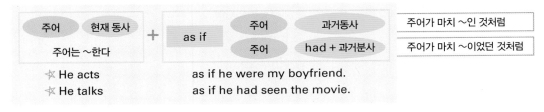

① as if + 가정법 과거

He looks **as if he were** surprised at the news.

→ In fact, he is not surprised at the news.

② as if + 가정법 과거완료

They talk **as if they had met** each other last month.

→ In fact, they didn't meet each other last month.

it's time + 가정법

이미 했어야 할 일을 하지 않은 것에 대한 유감을 나타낼 때 쓴다.

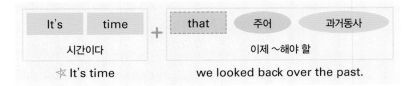

It's time we **had** dinner. It's almost seven.

A ( ) 안에서 알맞은 것을 고르시오.

1 I wish I (have, had) a younger sister now.

2 It's time she (took, takes) care of her little sister.

3 I wish he (has come, had come) to Jeju Island with me.

4 Paul treats me as if I (am, were) his private secretary.

B 주어진 문장을 다음과 같이 바꿀 때 빈칸에 알맞은 말을 쓰시오.

1 In fact, Jim doesn't like eating spaghetti.

→ It sounds as if Jim _____ eating spaghetti.

2 In fact, Jessica didn't go to Africa.

→ Jessica talks as if she _____ to Africa.

3 I'm sorry my brother plays loud music every night.

→ I wish _____ loud music every night.

4 I'm sorry that Kelly didn't show any interest in me.

→ I wish _____ a little interest in me.

C 우리말과 의미가 같도록 ( ) 안의 말을 이용하여 문장을 완성하시오.

1 이제 새 신발을 한 켤레 사야 할 때이다. (buy)

→ It _____ _____ I _____ a new pair of shoes.

2 당신이 마치 이 자리의 주인인 것처럼 말하는 군요. (be)

→ You talk _____ _____ you _____ the owner of this seat.

3 내가 엄마와의 대화 시간을 더 많이 가졌더라면 좋았을 텐데. (spend)

→ _____ _____ I _____ _____ more time talking
with my mom.

D 밑줄 친 부분에 대한 설명을 하고 틀린 경우엔 바르게 고치시오. (맞으면 'O' 표시)

* p.p.: 과거분사

1	I wish he <u>lent</u> some money to me yesterday. → ( )	과거에 이룰 수 없었던 것에 대한 소망은 I wish 주어 + (과거동사, had p.p.)
2	Rachel acts as if she <u>is</u> my sister. → ( )	현재 (사실, 사실의 반대) '처럼' 의미는 as if + 주어 + (과거동사, had p.p.)
3	My mom wishes she <u>had</u> a daughter. → ( )	현재에 이루기 힘든 것에 대한 소망은 I wish 주어 + (현재, 과거)동사
4	It's time that she <u>goes</u> to bed. → ( )	'이제 ~해야 할 시간이다' 의미는 It's time + (that) + 주어 + (현재, 과거)동사

if 생략 가정법

GP 58

if절 동사가 were나 had인 경우 if를 생략할 수 있고, 이때 주어와 동사가 도치된다.

If I were you   Were I you

* **Were I** you, I would accept the job offer.

  (← If I were you, ~)

* **Had she known** his phone number, she would have called him.

  (← If she had known his phone number, ~)

without, but for

GP 59

without / but for는 if절을 대신하는 표현으로 가정법 과거나 가정법 과거완료에 쓴다.

❶ 가정법 과거

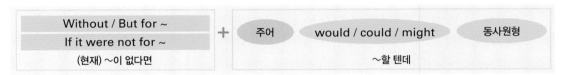

* **Without / But for** fire, we **couldn't live** normal lives.

= **If it were not for** fire, ~

= **Were it not for** fire, ~

❷ 가정법 과거완료

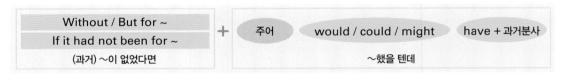

Without / But for your help, I **couldn't have made** my own blog.

= ☀ **If it had not been for** your help, ~

= **Had it not been for** your help, ~

• Upgrade •

if절이 없는 가정법 문장

주어, 부정사, 부사(구), 분사구문도 가정법의 if절을 대신할 수 있다.

An honest boy would admit his mistake immediately.

(← If he were an honest boy, he would admit his mistake immediately.)

It would be great **to have three days off each week**.

(← if we had three days off each week)

I used up my money; **otherwise**, I could have bought it for you.

(← if I had not used up my money)

A ( ) 안에서 알맞은 것을 고르시오.

1 (I were, Were I) your teacher, I would tell you to do better work.

2 (Without, With) a phone, I wouldn't know a single phone number.

3 (He had, Had he) told the truth, she would have forgiven him.

4 Were it not for a mirror, I couldn't (see, have seen) my own face.

B 주어진 문장을 다음과 같이 바꿀 때 빈칸에 알맞은 말을 쓰시오.

1 A true friend would understand my situation.

→ If _____, he would understand my situation.

2 Had they arrived on time, they would have seen the fireworks.

→ If _____ on time, they would have seen the fireworks.

3 Without his leadership, it would not have been successful.

→ If _____ his leadership, it would not have been successful.

C 우리말과 의미가 같도록 ( ) 안의 말을 배열하시오.

1 그녀가 내 여자친구라면, 그녀가 원하는 건 뭐든지 할 텐데. (my, she, were, girlfriend)

→ _____, I would do anything she wants.

2 너의 도움이 없었다면, 나는 면접에 떨어졌을 텐데. (for, but, help, your)

→ _____, I would have failed the interview.

3 그녀가 더 열심히 노력했다면, 더 좋은 성적을 거두었을 텐데. (she, tried, had, harder)

→ _____, she would have earned better grades.

4 돈이 없다면 가게에서 물건을 사기가 불가능할 텐데. (it, for, not were, money)

→ _____, it would be impossible to buy things at stores.

D 밑줄 친 부분에 대한 설명을 하고 틀린 경우엔 바르게 고치시오. (맞으면 'O' 표시)

* p.p.: 과거분사

1	<u>But</u> the song, she wouldn't have been famous. → ( )	'(~이 없었다면, ~이 없다면), ~했을 텐데' 의미는 (but, but for) + 명사
2	<u>I were</u> you, I would accept her invitation. → ( )	[If 주어 + were]에서 If를 생략하면 (주어 + were, Were + 주어) 어순
3	If it <u>had not been</u> for the fan, I couldn't sleep. → ( )	If it (were not, had not been) for + 명사, 주어 + could + 동사원형
4	<u>He had heard</u> the news, he would have been pleased. → ( )	[If 주어 + had p.p.]에서 If를 생략하면 (주어 + had p.p., Had + 주어 + p.p.) 어순

A   우리말과 의미가 같도록 ( ) 안의 말을 배열하시오.

1 나는 그가 좀 더 이성적이면 좋겠어. (I, he, be, more, wish, would, rational)

→ _____.

2 Chen은 오늘 직장에서 힘들었던 것처럼 보인다. (a, if, he, as, had, time, hard, had)

→ Chen looks _____ at work.

3 그들이 내말을 들었더라면 길을 잘못 들지 않았을 텐데. (to, me, had, they, listened)

→ _____, they wouldn't have gone the wrong way.

4 내가 하루 동안 대통령이 되면, 모든 것을 공짜로 만들 거야. (I, a, for, day, were, president)

→ _____, I would make everything free.

5 그녀가 한국어 말하는 걸 들으면, 너는 그녀를 외국인이라 생각지 못할 거야. (to, her, speak, hear, Korean)

→ _____, you wouldn't take her for a foreigner.

6 그의 충고가 없었다면, 나는 내 인생에서 아무것도 성취하지 못했을 텐데. (it, his, not, for, had, been, advice)

→ _____, I would have accomplished nothing in my life.

B   우리말과 의미가 같도록 ( ) 안의 말을 이용하여 문장을 완성하시오.

1 그녀의 의지가 없었더라면, 그녀는 금메달을 따지 못했을 텐데. (win)

→ _____ _____ her will, she _____ _____ _____
_____ the gold medal.

2 과거의 너 자신으로 돌아간다면 무엇을 할 것 같니? (go, do)

→ If you _____ back to yourself in the past, what _____ _____ _____?

3 이제 우리가 짐을 꾸리기 시작할 시간이야. 잠시 후에 떠나야 해. (time, start)

→ _____ _____ _____ _____ _____ packing. We have to
leave in a while.

4 만약 그가 내 생각에 동의했었다면, 그는 더 많은 돈을 기부했을 텐데. (agree, donate)

→ If he _____ _____ with my idea, he _____ _____ _____
more money.

5 전기가 없다면, 우리는 현대의 생활방식을 상상할 수 없을 거야. (imagine)

→ _____ _____ _____ _____ electricity, we _____
_____ _____ our modern lifestyles.

6 내가 지난주에 그 드레스를 샀다면, 오늘밤 그것을 입을 텐데. (buy, wear)

→ If I _____ _____ the dress last week, I _____ _____ it tonight.

C 주어진 말을 이용하여 그림의 인물이 말할 것 같은 문장을 완성하시오.

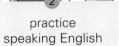

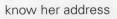

become
a fashion model

practice
speaking English

know her address

get a discount

1 Were I born again, I would _____.

2 I wish I _____ more before traveling.

3 If I _____, I would send her an invitation.

4 Had it not been for the coupon, I _____

at the store.

D 주어진 문장을 다음과 같이 바꿀 때 빈칸에 알맞은 말을 쓰시오.

1 In fact, she is not a close friend.

→ He talks about her _____ a close friend.

2 I am sorry I didn't read lots of books to pass the exam.

→ I _____ lots of books to pass the exam.

3 As the driver wasn't more careful, he couldn't avoid the car accident.

→ If the driver _____ more careful, he _____

the car accident.

4 Without my laptop, my team couldn't complete the assignment.

→ Were _____ my laptop, my team couldn't complete the

assignment.

5 As he didn't finish his chores, he can't go out and play with his friends today.

→ If he _____ his chores, he _____

and play with his friends today.

(1–6) 빈칸에 들어갈 알맞은 말을 고르시오.

1 If I _____ you, I wouldn't spend much time playing games.

① am   ② are
③ were   ④ had been
⑤ have been

2 If she had helped me, I _____ the project.

① finished   ② had finished
③ could finish   ④ can have finished
⑤ could have finished

3 If Paul had taken the medicine, he _____ better now.

① feel   ② felt
③ will feel   ④ would feel
⑤ would have felt

4 He talks as if he _____ raw fish when he was young.

① don't like   ② had liked
③ have liked   ④ will like
⑤ like

5 I _____ out the garbage if she washes the dishes.

① took   ② take
③ had taken   ④ will take
⑤ would take

6 You didn't tell them about it. I wish you _____ them about it.

① tell   ② told
③ will tell   ④ would told
⑤ had told

7 빈칸에 들어갈 말이 차례대로 짝지어진 것은?

· If it is sunny tomorrow, we _____ on a picnic.
· She isn't a doctor, but she talks as if she _____ a doctor.

① will go - is   ② would go - was
③ will go - were   ④ would go - is
⑤ would go - had been

8 빈칸에 들어갈 알맞은 말을 <u>모두</u> 고르시오.

_____ her support, I would not be able to complete my task.

① But   ② But for
③ Otherwise   ④ With
⑤ Without

(9-10) 우리말을 영어로 바르게 옮긴 것은?

9

> 지금 너를 만날 시간이 있으면 좋을 텐데.

① I wish I had time to meet you now.
② I wish I didn't have time to meet you now.
③ I wish I have time to meet you now.
④ I wish I don't have time to meet you now.
⑤ I wish I had had time to meet you now.

10

> 만약 내가 그 사실을 알았더라면 너에게 말해줬을 텐데.

① If I know the fact, I will tell it to you.
② If I knew the fact, I would tell it to you.
③ If I had known the fact, I would tell it to you.
④ If I knew the fact, I would have told it to you.
⑤ If I had known the fact, I would have told it to you.

11 다음 대화를 완성할 때 알맞은 것은?

> A: How was your trip to Mexico?
> B: It was great.
>   I wish you _____ with me.

① go   ② have gone
③ went   ④ had gone
⑤ would go

12 다음 중 의미가 나머지와 <u>다른</u> 것은?

① Without his decision, we wouldn't have taken those actions.
② But for his decision, we wouldn't have taken those actions.
③ If it had not been for his decision, we wouldn't have taken those actions.
④ If there were not his decision, we wouldn't have taken those actions.
⑤ Had it not been for his decision, we wouldn't have taken those actions.

13 주어진 말을 이용하여 빈칸에 알맞은 말을 쓰시오.

> If I had a car, I _____ him a ride. (give)

⇨ _____

(14-15) 주어진 문장과 같은 의미를 갖도록 빈칸을 채우시오.

14 If she had taken my advice, she wouldn't have made the mistake.

⇨ Had _____ my advice, she wouldn't have made the mistake.

15 Without any stress, our lives would be too boring.

⇨ If _____ any stress, our lives would be too boring.

(16-17) 다음 중 어법상 <u>어색한</u> 문장을 고르시오.

16 ① I wish she could speak English.

② He treats me as if I were a child.

③ Were I you, I would not do such a thing.

④ If I drank warm milk last night, I would have fallen asleep quickly.

⑤ But for the wakeup call, I would have been late for class.

17 ① It is time you had a haircut.

② I wish you can play the guitar.

③ He talks as if he had seen a UFO.

④ A gentleman would not use bad language.

⑤ Without water, all living things would die.

18 어법상 <u>어색한</u> 것으로 짝지어진 것은?

> ⓐ To be with you, I would be happy.
> ⓑ She is looking at me as if I am an alien.
> ⓒ If I spoke French well, I would go to live there.
> ⓓ I wish the weather would not be so freezing cold.
> ⓔ If he took the subway yesterday, he might have arrived on time.

① ⓐ, ⓒ   ② ⓑ, ⓓ

③ ⓒ, ⓓ   ④ ⓑ, ⓔ

⑤ ⓐ, ⓔ

(19-20) 다음 문장을 가정법 문장으로 바꿀 때 빈칸에 알맞은 말을 쓰시오.

19 As he injured his knee, he couldn't play in the soccer tournament.

⇨ If he _____,

he _____

in the soccer tournament.

20 I'm sorry you are feeling lonely today.

⇨ I wish you _____

lonely today.

(21-25) 우리말과 의미가 같도록 ( ) 안의 말을 배열하시오.

21 그가 우리의 반장으로 선출되었다면 좋을 텐데.
(I, he, had, wish, been, elected)

⇨ _____

as our class president.

22 잠시 쉴 시간이다.
(some, is, it, we, rest, time, got)

⇨ _____

for a while.

23 아빠가 성적표를 보았다면 실망했을 텐데.
(my, he, had, card, seen, report)

⇨ _____

_____, my dad would

have been disappointed.

24 아침을 거르지 않았더라면 지금 배고프지 않을 텐데.
(I, be, not, would, hungry)

⇨ If I had not skipped breakfast, _____

_____ now.

25 등대가 없다면 많은 배들이 바다에서 길을 잃을 거야.
(it, for, not, were, lighthouses)

⇨ _____,

many ships would get lost at sea.

(26–27) 우리말과 의미가 같도록 ( ) 안의 말을 이용하여 문
장을 완성하시오.

26 내가 아프지 않으면 대회에 참가할 수 있을 텐데.
(be, participate)

→ If I _____ _____ sick,

I _____ _____ in the

contest.

27 이제 네가 어떤 대학을 갈지 생각할 시간이다.
(think)

⇨ _____ _____ _____

_____ _____ about which

university to attend.

(28–29) 다음 문장에서 어색한 부분을 찾아 바르게 고치고
알맞은 이유를 고르시오.

28 Samuel isn't a policeman, but he acts
as if he is a policeman.

고치기: _____ ⇨ _____

이유: 현재 (사실, 사실의 반대) '처럼'일 때
as if + 주어 + (현재, 과거)동사

29 If you hadn't looked after the cat then,
it would have been dead by now.

고치기: _____ ⇨ _____

이유: '만약 ~했다면, ~할 텐데'의 혼합가정법
If + 주어 + (과거동사, had + 과거분사),
주어 + would + (동사원형, have + 과거분사)

30 다음 조건을 이용하여 알맞게 영작하시오.

우리가 한 달 동안 유럽 여행을 하면 좋을 텐데.
조건 1: wish, travel around Europe
조건 2: 9단어

⇨ _____

_____.

한눈에 정리하는 Grammar Mapping

빈칸에 알맞은 답을 보기에서 골라 넣어 grammar mapping 완성하기

가정법 과거	형태	[If + 주어 + 과거동사] + [주어 + ① _____ + 동사원형]
	의미	현재 사실의 반대: 만약 ~한다면, ~할 텐데 If you were diligent, you could get a job.
가정법 과거완료	형태	[If + 주어 + ② _____] + [주어 + 조동사 과거 + ③ _____]
	의미	과거 사실의 반대: 만약 ~했다면, ~했을 텐데 If he had read the book, he could have answered the question.
혼합 가정법	형태	[If + 주어 + ② _____] + [주어 + 조동사 과거 + ④ _____]
	의미	(과거에) 만약 ~했다면, (지금) ~할 텐데 If I had drunk more milk then, I would be taller now.
I wish 가정법 과거	형태	I wish + [주어 + 과거동사]
	의미	⑤ _____에 이루기 힘든 것을 소망: ⑥ _____ I wish I had no homework.
I wish 가정법 과거완료	형태	I wish + [주어 + had + p.p.]
	의미	⑦ _____에 이룰 수 없었던 것을 소망: ⑧ _____ I wish I had known how to get a ticket.
as if 가정법 과거	형태	주어 + 현재동사 + as if + [주어 + 과거동사]
	의미	현재에 그렇지 않은 일을 그런 것처럼: ⑨ _____ She acts as if she were a princess.
as if 가정법 과거완료	형태	주어 + 현재동사 + as if + [주어 + had + p.p.]
	의미	과거에 그렇지 않았던 일을 그랬던 것처럼: ⑩ _____ He talks as if he had gone abroad.
it's time 가정법	형태	It's time + [주어 + ⑪ _____]
	의미	했어야 할 일을 하지 않은 것에 대한 유감: ⑫ _____ It's time you studied harder.
if 생략 가정법	형태	[If + 주어 + 동사] → [⑬ _____] Were I in your position, I wouldn't do that.
without 가정법	형태	[without / but for + 명사구] + [주어 + 조동사 과거 + 동사원형] [주어 + 조동사 과거 + have + p.p.]
	의미	(현재에) ⑭ _____, ~할 텐데, (과거에) ⑮ _____, ~했을 텐데 Without / But for the sun, there could be no life. Without / But for your advice, I wouldn't have won the game.

보기	· 현재	· 과거	· 과거동사	· 동사원형	· 조동사 과거
	· had + p.p.	· have + p.p.	· 동사 + 주어	· ~이 없다면	· ~이 없었다면
	· ~라면 좋을 텐데	· ~했다면 좋을 텐데	· ~인 것처럼 …하다	· ~이었던 것처럼 …하다	· ~해야 할 시간이다

일치와 화법

수의 일치

❶ 단수 취급하는 경우

every / each + 단수명사	~one, ~thing, ~body	학문, 국가, 질병 등의 이름	**주어일 때**	단수동사
시간, 거리 등의 단위명사	구 (동명사, to부정사)	절 (that, whether, 의문사)	+	

☆ The Netherlands **is** famous for tulips and windmills.

Mathematics **is** a useful subject.

☆ Three dollars **is** enough to buy the milk.

Who made the underwater city **is** still a mystery.

❷ 복수 취급하는 경우

both A and B	the + 형용사 (~한 사람들)	a number of + 복수명사	**주어일 때**	복수동사
			+	

☆ The young **learn** things faster than the old.

☆ *A number of* people **are** resting on the beach. (많은: 복수 취급)

☆ *The number of* visitors to the blog **is** increasing. (~의 수: 단수 취급)

시제 일치와 예외

❶ 시제 일치

주절		종속절		
S	V (현재)	that	주어	동사 (모든 시제 가능)
S	V (과거)	that	주어	동사 (과거 / 과거완료)

☆ **I know** that my teacher **trusts / trusted / will trust / has trusted** me.

She **said** that her bird **laid / had laid** an egg.

❷ 시제 일치의 예외

종속절이 현재의 습관, 불변의 진리, 속담, 과학적 사실 등을 나타낼 때

주절		종속절		
S	V	that	주어	(항상) 현재시제 동사

종속절이 역사적 사실을 나타낼 때

주절		종속절		
S	V	that	주어	(항상) 과거시제 동사

☆ The book **said** that children **have** more bones than adults. (과학적 사실)

Jane **said** that she never **eats** instant food. (현재도 계속되는 습관)

☆ We **learned** that the Berlin Wall **fell** in 1989. (역사적 사실)

GP Practice

A ( ) 안에서 알맞은 것을 고르시오.

1 Every child (have, has) a natural talent.

2 Making promises (is, are) easier than keeping them.

3 Both Daisy and Julian (loves, love) Vietnamese food.

4 The rich (is, are) not always happy.

5 (Does, Do) anyone want any more cookies?

B ( ) 안의 말을 이용하여 빈칸을 채우시오.

1 Mike said that he _____ propose to Jessy the next day. (will)

2 She didn't know that light _____ faster than sound. (travel)

3 Do you know that the *Titanic* _____ in 1912? (sink)

4 We knew that it _____ going to rain that night. (be)

5 I heard that we _____ vitamin D through sunlight. (get)

C 우리말과 의미가 같도록 ( ) 안의 말을 이용하여 문장을 완성하시오.

1 그녀는 벽에도 귀가 있다고 말했다. (walls, have)

→ She said that the _____ _____ ears.

2 많은 사람들이 그 캠페인에 참여하고 있다. (number, be)

→ _____ _____ _____ _____ joining

the campaign.

3 이집트에서는, 죽은 자들은 약간의 빵과 함께 매장되었다. (dead, be buried)

→ In Egypt, _____ _____ _____ _____ with some bread.

D 밑줄 친 부분에 대한 설명을 하고 틀린 경우엔 바르게 고치시오. (맞으면 'O' 표시)

1	Economics <u>are</u> my favorite subject. → ( )	주어(학문명) + (단수, 복수)동사
2	A number of people <u>is</u> at the station. → ( )	a number of + 복수명사 + (단수, 복수)동사 (많은, ~의 수)
3	I <u>know</u> that he designed the statue. → ( )	주절 + 종속절 (현재, 과거)시제 [모든 시제 가능]
4	I learned that the Chinese <u>had invented</u> fireworks. → ( )	역사적 사실은 항상 (현재, 과거)시제

평서문의 간접화법 전환

GP 62

① 전달동사를 바꾼다. say (said), say to (said to) → tell (told)
② 콤마(,)와 인용부호(" ")를 없애고 접속사 that으로 연결한다.
③ 피전달문의 인칭, 시제, 부사 등을 전달자의 입장에 맞게 적절히 바꾼다.

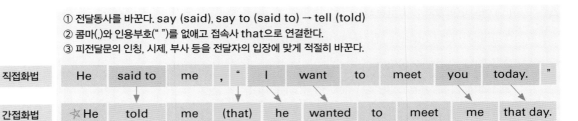

직접화법	He	said to	me	,	"	I	want	to	meet	you	today.	"
간접화법	☆ He	told	me		(that)	he	wanted	to	meet	me	that day.	

○ Tip ○

직접화법과 간접화법
직접화법은 인용 부호(" ")를 사용하여 다른 사람의 말을 그대로 전달하는 것이고, 간접화법은 다른 사람의 말을 전달자의 입장에 맞게 바꿔 전달하는 것이다.

She said to me, "I bought these earrings yesterday."
→ She **told** me **that she had bought those** earrings **the day before**.

○ Tip ○

간접화법으로 전환할 때 변하는 부사(구)
this (these) → that (those) / here → there / now → then / today → that day / ago → before
yesterday → the day before, the previous day / tomorrow → the next day, the following day

의문문의 간접화법 전환

GP 63

① 의문사가 있으면 ask + (목적어) + [의문사 + 주어 + 동사] 형태로 바꾼다.
② 의문사가 없으면 ask + (목적어) + [if (whether) + 주어 + 동사] 형태로 바꾼다.

직접화법	Jack	said to	me	,	"	Where	are	you	going	now	?	"
간접화법	☆ Jack	asked	me			where	I	was	going	then		.

Kate said to him, "Do you have any questions?"
→ ☆ Kate **asked** him **if (whether) he had** any questions.

명령문의 간접화법 전환

GP 64

① [tell, ask, advise, order + 목적어 + to부정사] 형태로 바꾼다.
② 부정명령문은 to부정사 앞에 not을 붙인다.

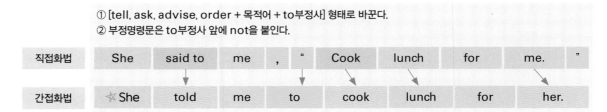

직접화법	She	said to	me	,	"	Cook	lunch	for	me.	"
간접화법	☆ She	told	me	to		cook	lunch	for	her.	

The teacher said to us, "Don't be late for school."
→ ☆ The teacher **ordered** us **not to be** late for school.

A ( ) 안에서 알맞은 것을 고르시오.

1 He asked me (where did I lived, where I lived).

2 She (said, told) us that she had watched the movie.

3 The waiter asked us (that, if) we were ready to order.

4 The police ordered the man (put up, to put up) his hands.

B 다음 문장을 간접화법 문장으로 바꿔 쓰시오.

1 Betty said to me, "I won't forget your help this time."

→ Betty _____ that time.

2 He said to her, "Why did you leave the party early?"

→ He _____ the party early.

3 The man said to me, "Do you remember me?"

→ The man _____ him.

4 She said to Paula, "Don't drive fast in a school zone."

→ She _____ in a school zone.

C 우리말과 의미가 같도록 ( ) 안의 말을 이용하여 문장을 완성하시오.

1 Mario는 우리를 그의 파티에 초대할 것이라고 우리에게 말했다. (tell, invite)

→ Mario _____ _____ _____ _____ _____

_____ to his party.

2 나는 그녀에게 무엇이 되고 싶은지를 물어봤다. (ask, want)

→ I _____ _____ _____ _____ _____ to be.

3 Rio는 내게 밝은색 셔츠를 입으라고 조언을 했다. (advise, wear)

→ Rio _____ _____ _____ _____ any brightly colored shirt.

D 밑줄 친 부분에 대한 설명을 하고 틀린 경우엔 바르게 고치시오. (맞으면 'O' 표시)

* S: 주어, V: 동사

1	She asked him <u>why was he</u> excited. → ( )	의문사 있는 의문문의 간접화법 ask him + 의문사 + (S + V, V + S)
2	Brad asked me <u>did I like</u> him. → ( )	의문사 없는 의문문의 간접화법 ask me + (if, that) + (S + V, V + S)
3	She told me <u>do</u> the laundry. → ( )	명령문의 간접화법 tell + 목적어 + (to부정사, 동사)
4	Mom told us <u>don't say</u> bad words. → ( )	부정명령문의 간접화법 tell + 목적어 + (not, don't) + to부정사

A   우리말과 의미가 같도록 (   ) 안의 말을 배열하시오.

1 하루에 사과 한 개씩 먹는 것은 의사를 멀리한다. (a, an, eating, keeps, apple, day)

→ _____ the doctor away.

2 Copernicus는 지구가 태양 주변을 돈다고 말했다. (the, that, said, moves, Earth)

→ Copernicus _____ around the sun.

3 실업자들의 수가 줄어들고 있다. (the, of, is, jobless, people, number)

→ _____ decreasing.

4 Ann은 내가 그때 매우 피곤해 보인다고 말했다. (looked, I, told, me, very, tired, that)

→ Anne _____ at that time.

5 그 요리사는 우리가 음식을 잘 먹었는지 물어보았다. (if, asked, us, we, had, enjoyed)

→ The chef _____ the food.

6 우리 선생님은 연습이 완벽함을 만든다고 말씀하셨다. (that, said, makes, practice, perfect)

→ My teacher _____ .

B   우리말과 의미가 같도록 (   ) 안의 말을 이용하여 문장을 완성하시오.

1 수영하는 방법을 아는 사람 있나요? (do, anyone)

→ _____ _____ _____ how to swim?

2 많은 학생들이 오늘 아침에 학교에 지각했다. (be late, number)

→ _____ _____ _____ _____ _____

for school this morning.

3 그녀는 내 장점들이 무엇이냐고 내게 물어보았다. (my strengths)

→ She _____ _____ _____ _____ _____ .

4 우리는 태양이 지구보다 약 109배 크다고 배웠다. (learn)

→ We _____ _____ _____ _____ about 109

times bigger than the Earth.

5 우리 엄마는 내게 오늘 따뜻한 코트를 입으라고 말씀하셨다. (tell, wear)

→ My mom _____ _____ _____ _____ a warm coat today.

6 Brian은 그가 내 사진을 찍어도 되는지를 내게 물어보았다. (take a picture, can)

→ Brian _____ _____ _____ _____ _____

_____ _____ _____ me.

C 다음 보기와 같이 직접화법을 전달자의 입장에 맞게 간접화법으로 바꿔 쓰시오.

> 보기 | He said to her, "Where do you work?"
> → He asked her <u>where she worked</u>.

1 The guide said to us, "Try the traditional food."

→ The guide advised us _____ .

2 She said to me, "Did you know the reason?"

→ She asked me _____ .

3 The policeman said to him, "Tell me the truth."

→ The policeman ordered him _____ .

4 The reporter said, "The first Olympic Games were held in 776 B.C."

→ The reporter said _____ .

5 My teacher said, "Athens is the capital of Greece."

→ My teacher said _____ .

D Miranda가 이모에게 요리를 배웠다. 그날의 일을 친구에게 전달하는 문장을 완성하시오.

1 My aunt asked me _____ .

2 My aunt asked me _____ .

3 My aunt said that _____ .

4 My aunt told me _____ .

5 My aunt ordered me _____ .

(1–4) 빈칸에 들어갈 알맞은 말을 고르시오.

1

> I learned that school uniforms
> _____ first invented in England.

① be   ② were

③ had been   ④ to be

⑤ have been

2

> Mike said that his school _____
> at nine. His school still starts at nine.

① start   ② starts

③ will start   ④ have started

⑤ has started

3

> She asked me _____ I wanted to
> join the soccer club.

① that   ② as

③ which   ④ if

⑤ unless

4

> My teacher told us _____ the
> whiteboard.

① look at   ② looked at

③ to look at   ④ to looked at

⑤ that I looked at

5 다음 빈칸에 공통으로 들어갈 말은?

> · They _____ me if I could speak
>   English.
> · A lady _____ me to hold the
>   elevator.

① advised   ② told

③ ordered   ④ asked

⑤ said

(6–7) 다음 중 어법상 어색한 문장을 고르시오.

6 ① I know that the drugstore is closed
     on Saturdays.

   ② She said that she breaks the printer
     by mistake.

   ③ My teacher told us to put away the
     book.

   ④ I think that he knew the secret.

   ⑤ Mr. Green said that laughter is the
     best medicine.

7 ① The color-blind are not able to see
     some colors.

   ② Both Jake and his sister are smart.

   ③ Seven kilograms were too heavy for
     me to lift.

   ④ To build houses is his job.

   ⑤ Each flower smells different.

(8–10) 빈칸에 들어갈 말로 알맞게 짝지어진 것은?

8
· Each piece of the cake _____ a different taste.
· Growing vegetables _____ not easy.

① have - be
② have - is
③ have - are
④ has - is
⑤ has - are

9
· There _____ a number of cars in the parking lot.
· The number of his pencils in the pencil case _____ 4.

① was - is
② were - are
③ was - are
④ was - be
⑤ were - is

10
· He said that he always _____ to school.
· We learned that the Sahara Desert _____ in Africa.

① walks - is
② walks - was
③ walks - will be
④ walked - was
⑤ walked - had been

11 빈칸에 들어갈 알맞은 말을 <u>모두</u> 고르시오.

Ray knew that she _____ dolls.

① collect
② collected
③ has collected
④ will collect
⑤ had collected

(12–14) 주어진 말을 이용하여 빈칸을 채우시오.

12 The Philippines _____ two official languages. (have)

13 We learned that the Great Wall of China _____ be seen from the moon. (can)

14 My dad said that he _____ come early that day. (will)

15 다음 중 간접화법으로 <u>잘못</u> 전환한 것은?

① She said, "I can help you."
   → She said that she could help me.
② I said to her, "What is your name?"
   → I asked her what my name was.
③ He said to me, "Are you okay?"
   → He asked me if I was okay.
④ The doctor said to me, "You should stay in bed today."
   → The doctor advised me to stay in bed that day.
⑤ Evan said to us, "Don't be shy."
   → Evan told us not to be shy.

16 다음 문장을 간접화법으로 바르게 전환한 것은?

> Tom said to me, "I passed the audition."

① Tom said that he passed the audition.

② Tom told me that he pass the audition.

③ Tom told to me that he had passed the audition.

④ Tom told me that he had passed the audition.

⑤ Tom told me to pass the audition.

17 다음 중 어법상 옳은 것을 고르시오.

① The United States have 50 states.

② Ten pounds of meat was cooked for the party.

③ I heard that you miss the train.

④ He asked me why was I busy.

⑤ Charlie told me turn on the light.

18 어법상 올바른 것으로만 짝지어진 것은?

> ⓐ What he said was interesting.
> ⓑ He asked me whether I was hungry.
> ⓒ I told my brother to cook pasta for me.
> ⓓ Two weeks are enough to read this book.
> ⓔ I knew that London was the capital of England.

① ⓐ, ⓑ, ⓒ   ② ⓐ, ⓑ, ⓓ

③ ⓑ, ⓒ, ⓓ   ④ ⓑ, ⓒ, ⓔ

⑤ ⓐ, ⓓ, ⓔ

(19–21) 우리말과 의미가 같도록 ( ) 안의 말을 배열하시오.

19 청각 장애우들은 의사소통을 위해 수화를 사용한다.
(use, deaf, sign language, the)

⇨ _____
for communication.

20 나는 그녀에게 제안이 있는지를 물어보았다.
(her, whether, I, asked, had, she)

⇨ _____
any suggestions.

21 엄마는 나에게 아침 식사를 건너뛰지 말라고 말씀하셨다.
(told, my mom, not, skip, to, me)

⇨ _____
breakfast.

(22–24) 우리말과 의미가 같도록 ( ) 안의 말을 이용하여 문장을 완성하시오.

22 나는 하마들이 그들의 땀을 썬스크린으로 사용한다는 것을 알게 되었다. (use, sweat)

⇨ I learned that hippos _____
_____ as sunscreen.

23 Daniel은 나에게 내가 그 그림을 직접 그렸었는지를 물어보았다. (ask, draw)

➡ Daniel _____

_____ the painting myself.

24 200달러가 자선단체에 기부되었다.
(be donated)

➡Two hundred dollars _____

to the charity.

(25–27) 다음 문장을 간접화법 문장으로 바꿔 쓰시오.

25 Julie said to him, "I like your present."

➡ Julie _____

_____.

26 The reporter said to her, "When is your next concert?"

➡The reporter _____

_____.

27 The doctor said to me, "Don't eat spicy food."

➡The doctor advised _____

_____.

(28–29) 다음 문장에서 어색한 부분을 찾아 바르게 고치고 알맞은 이유를 고르시오.

28 I didn't know that the South Pole was colder than the North Pole.

고치기: _____ ➡ _____
이유: 일반적, 과학적 사실은
항상 (현재, 과거)시제

29 A number of famous people is standing on the stage.

고치기: _____ ➡ _____
이유: a number of는
(많은, ~의 수)을·를 의미하며
주어로 쓰일 때 (단수, 복수) 취급

30 다음 조건을 이용하여 알맞게 영작하시오.

Mia는 한국전쟁이 1953년에 끝났다는 것을 배웠다.
조건 1: end, the Korean War
조건 2: 9단어

➡ _____

_____.

한눈에 정리하는 Grammar Mapping

빈칸에 알맞은 답을 보기에서 골라 넣어 grammar mapping 완성하기

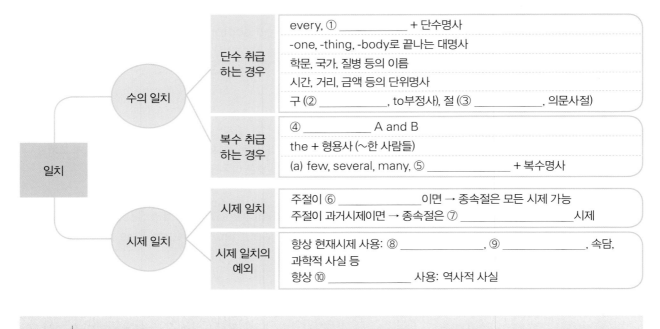

일치
- 수의 일치
  - 단수 취급 하는 경우
    - every, ① _____ + 단수명사
    - -one, -thing, -body로 끝나는 대명사
    - 학문, 국가, 질병 등의 이름
    - 시간, 거리, 금액 등의 단위명사
    - 구 (② _____, to부정사), 절 (③ _____, 의문사절)
  - 복수 취급 하는 경우
    - ④ _____ A and B
    - the + 형용사 (~한 사람들)
    - (a) few, several, many, ⑤ _____ + 복수명사
- 시제 일치
  - 시제 일치
    - 주절이 ⑥ _____이면 → 종속절은 모든 시제 가능
    - 주절이 과거시제이면 → 종속절은 ⑦ _____시제
  - 시제 일치의 예외
    - 항상 현재시제 사용: ⑧ _____, ⑨ _____, 속담, 과학적 사실 등
    - 항상 ⑩ _____ 사용: 역사적 사실

보기
- · 불변의 진리
- · a number of
- · 현재의 습관
- · 현재시제
- · both
- · 과거나 과거완료
- · that절
- · 동명사
- · 과거시제
- · each

화법 전환
- 평서문
  - 전달동사를 바꾼다. say → ① _____, say to → ② _____
  - 콤마(,)와 인용부호(" ")를 없애고 접속사 ③ _____으로 연결한다.
  - 피전달문의 인칭대명사와 시제를 전달자의 입장에 맞게 적절히 바꾼다.
  - 피전달문의 지시대명사와 부사를 전달자의 입장에 맞게 적절히 바꾼다.
- 의문문
  - 전달동사를 바꾼다. say, say to → ④ _____
  - 의문사가 없으면 [⑤ _____ + 주어 + 동사] 형태로 바꾼다.
  - 의문사가 있으면 [⑥ _____ + 주어 + 동사] 형태로 바꾼다.
  - 피전달문의 인칭, 시제, 부사 등을 전달자의 입장에 맞게 적절히 바꾼다.
- 명령문
  - 전달동사를 바꾼다. say to → tell / ask (부탁), ⑦ _____ (충고), order (명령)
  - 피전달문의 동사를 ⑧ _____로 바꾼다.
  - 부정명령문의 경우 don't를 ⑨ _____으로 바꿔 to부정사 앞에 놓는다.
  - 피전달문의 인칭, 부사 등을 전달자의 입장에 맞게 적절히 바꾼다.

보기
- · 의문사
- · that
- · not
- · ask
- · tell
- · say
- · if (whether)
- · advise
- · to부정사

특수구문

강조

❶ **동사 강조**: [do / does / did + 동사원형] 형태로 동사의 의미를 강조 한다.

주어	do / does / did	동사원형	
☆ Peter	does	like	the hip-hop group.

I **did** believe that she would fall in love with me.

❷ **[It is / was ~ that]에 의한 강조**: 강조 대상을 It is / was와 that 사이에 놓고 '~한 것은 바로 ~이다'로 해석한다.

주어	동사	목적어	장소 부사(구)	시간 부사(구)
Peter ❶	met	Alice ❷	in the park ❸	yesterday. ❹

	It	is (was)	강조 대상	that	나머지 문장
① 주어 강조	☆ It	was	Peter	that (who)	met Alice in the park yesterday.
② 목적어 강조	☆ It	was	Alice	that (whom)	Peter met in the park yesterday.
③ 장소 강조	☆ It	was	in the park	that (where)	Peter met Alice yesterday.
④ 시간 강조	It	was	yesterday	that (when)	Peter met Alice in the park.

Kelly will buy a new laptop tomorrow.

→ It is Kelly **that (who)** will buy a new laptop tomorrow.

→ It is a new laptop **that (which)** Kelly will buy tomorrow.

→ It is tomorrow **that (when)** Kelly will buy a new laptop.

> ○ **Tip** ○
> 강조 대상에 따라 that 대신 who(m), which, when, where 등의 관계대명사나 관계부사로 바꿔 쓸 수 있다.

부정표현

❶ **전체부정**: no, none, neither, nothing 등이 문장에 쓰여 '아무도(결코) ~않다'의 의미를 나타낸다.

☆ She had **nothing** to worry about.

(= She didn't have anything to worry about.)

None of my students likes English grammar.

(= All of my students don't like English grammar.)

> ○ **Tip** ○
> none: 셋 이상에 대한 부정어
> neither: 둘에 대한 부정어

❷ **부분부정**: 전체 중 일부만을 부정하는 것으로 '모두(항상) ~인 것은 아니다'의 의미를 나타낸다.

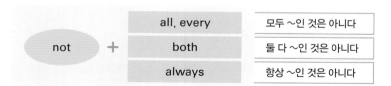

not +	all, every	모두 ~인 것은 아니다
	both	둘 다 ~인 것은 아니다
	always	항상 ~인 것은 아니다

Not all the students hate English grammar. (Not + all + 복수명사)

☆ **Not every** man enjoys talking about soccer. (Not + every + 단수명사)

☆ Rich people are **not always** happy.

A　( ) 안에서 알맞은 것을 고르시오.

1 He (do, does) like traveling by bike.

2 (It, This) was you that I saw at the mall last night.

3 (None, Neither) of those two stores closes on Sunday.

4 (No, Not) all the dancers in the ballroom are wearing high heels.

B　다음 밑줄 친 부분을 강조하여 다시 쓸 때 빈칸에 알맞은 말을 쓰시오.

1 Our school begins <u>at 9 o'clock</u>.

　→ It ＿＿＿＿＿＿＿＿＿＿＿＿＿＿＿＿＿＿＿＿＿ our school begins.

2 I <u>know</u> what happened to him.

　→ I ＿＿＿＿＿＿＿＿＿＿＿＿＿＿＿＿＿＿＿＿＿ what happened to him.

3 The idol group performed <u>a live concert</u>.

　→ It ＿＿＿＿＿＿＿＿＿＿＿＿＿＿＿＿＿＿＿＿＿ the idol group performed.

C　우리말과 의미가 같도록 ( ) 안의 말을 이용하여 문장을 완성하시오.

1 우리는 외계인이 존재한다고 정말로 믿고 있다. (believe)

　→ ＿＿＿＿＿＿＿ ＿＿＿＿＿＿＿ ＿＿＿＿＿＿ that aliens exist.

2 모든 학생이 장학금을 받을 수 있는 것은 아니다. (every)

　→ ＿＿＿＿＿＿＿ ＿＿＿＿＿＿＿ ＿＿＿＿＿＿ can get a scholarship.

3 그 선수들 중 누구도 앉아서 쉬고 있지 않다. (none)

　→ ＿＿＿＿＿＿ ＿＿＿＿＿＿ ＿＿＿＿＿ ＿＿＿＿＿ is sitting down and relaxing.

4 Tony가 현미경으로 본 것은 그의 머리카락이었다. (that)

　→ ＿＿＿＿＿ ＿＿＿＿＿ ＿＿＿＿＿ ＿＿＿＿＿ ＿＿＿＿＿ Tony looked at

　under the microscope.

D　밑줄 친 부분에 대한 설명을 하고 틀린 경우엔 바르게 고치시오. (맞으면 'O', 불필요하면 '삭제' 표시)

* S: 주어, V: 동사

1	I did <u>understood</u> what he said. → (　　　　　　　)	동사 강조는 do / does / did + (과거동사, 동사원형)
2	It was his mistake <u>what</u> Vicky laughed at.　→ (　　　　　　)	목적어를 강조할 때에는 It was + 목적어 + (that, what) + S + V
3	None of the girls <u>don't</u> likes me. → (　　　　　　)	부정어 none과 not을 함께 쓸 수 (있다, 없다)
4	<u>Not all</u> the candies taste good. → (　　　　　　)	부분부정 '모두 ~인 것은 아니다'는 (Not + all, All + not) + 복수명사

도치

GP 67

❶ **장소 / 방향 부사구 도치**: 장소나 운동의 방향을 나타내는 부사구가 강조되어 문장의 처음에 오면 [부사구 + 동사 + 주어]의 어순이 된다.

On the bed slept a cute baby.

From the ceiling hung an enormous spider.

• Upgrade •

주어가 대명사이면 도치가 이루어지지 않고 [주어 + 동사] 어순 그대로 쓴다.

The bus comes here. → Here comes the bus.

She comes here. → ☆ Here she comes.

❷ **부정어 도치**: not, never, little, seldom, hardly, only 등의 부정어가 강조되어 문장의 처음에 오면 [부정어 + 조동사 + 주어]나 [부정어 + be동사 + 주어]의 어순이 된다.

주어	부정어	동사		→	부정어	동사	주어	동사원형	
Bob	seldom	talks	to Janice.		☆ Seldom	does	Bob	talk	to Janice.

Little did I dream of meeting the movie star.

Not a single word could he say.

❸ **so [neither] + 동사 + 주어**: [so + 동사 + 주어]는 긍정문 뒤에, [neither + 동사 + 주어]는 부정문 뒤에 쓰이고 '역시 ~하다(하지 않다)'의 의미이다.

주어	일반동사 ~			do / does / did	주어	☆ I am sick of fast food, and so is my friend.
주어	be동사 ~	+	so	be동사	주어	I didn't hear your complaints, and neither did John.
주어	조동사 ~		neither	조동사	주어	☆ She won't go to the party, and neither will I.
주어	have p.p. ~			have	주어	A: Susan has been to America. B: So have I.

동격

GP 68

명사, 대명사의 의미를 보충하거나 바꿔 말하기 위해 한 번 더 설명해 주는 말을 그 (대)명사의 동격이라고 한다.

(대)명사	,	(대)명사	☆ Mr. Morgan, a doctor, advised me to eat more fruit.
the 명사 +	of	명사(구)	Spain considered the possibility of building a canal.
the 명사	that	주어 + 동사	I agreed with the idea that the rule should be changed.

GP Practice

A ( ) 안에서 알맞은 것을 고르시오.

1 On the bench (a gentleman sat, sat a gentleman).

2 His shirt is new, and so (his tie is, is his tie).

3 Never (has, does) she seen such a beautiful sky.

4 He gave up the idea (of, that) becoming a fashion model.

B 다음 문장을 바꿔 쓸 때 빈칸에 알맞은 말을 쓰시오.

1 The drone flew over my head.

→ Over my head _____.

2 He fell down on the ice.

→ Down on the ice _____.

3 Teenagers seldom write letters on paper.

→ Seldom _____.

C 우리말과 의미가 같도록 ( ) 안의 말을 이용하여 문장을 완성하시오.

1 불가사리는 바다 밑에서 산다. (a starfish)

→ Under the sea _____ _____ _____.

2 나는 그들이 헤어졌다는 소식을 들었다. (the news)

→ I heard _____ _____ _____ they had broken up.

3 그는 가족의 소중함을 거의 깨닫지 못했다. (little)

→ _____ _____ _____ realize the importance of his family.

4 나는 아침으로 빵과 우유를 먹는데 그녀도 또한 그렇다. (so)

→ I have bread and milk for breakfast, and _____ _____ _____.

D 밑줄 친 부분에 대한 설명을 하고 틀린 경우엔 바르게 고치시오. (맞으면 'O' 표시)

* S: 주어, V: 동사

1	In the attic <u>the kids hid</u>. → ( )	장소 부사구가 강조되어 문장의 처음에 오면 장소부사구 + (S + V, V + S)
2	Behind me <u>she stood</u>. → ( )	장소 부사구 도치에서 주어가 대명사이면 장소 부사구 + (S + V, V + S)
3	Nowhere <u>I could</u> find my USB. → ( )	부정어가 강조되어 문장의 처음에 오면 부정어구 + (S + 조동사, 조동사 + S)
4	He did well on the test, and <u>so I did</u>. → ( )	'역시 ~하다'의 의미는 긍정문 + (so, neither) + (S + V, V + S)

A 우리말과 의미가 같도록 ( ) 안의 말을 배열하시오.

1 그는 지루해 했었는데 나도 그랬었다. (so, and, I, did)

→ He felt bored, _____.

2 여기 그가 살았던 집이 있다. (is, he, the, lived, where, house)

→ Here _____.

3 모든 동물이 사나운 것은 아니다. (are, all, not, fierce, animals)

→ _____.

4 그 아이는 그의 신발 끈을 묶었다. (tie, his, did, the, child, shoelaces)

→ _____.

5 내가 너를 만나리라는 것은 꿈에도 생각하지 못했다. (I, of, did, you, dream, meeting)

→ Never _____ again.

6 우리가 어제 구경한 것은 바로 불꽃놀이었다. (it, we, was, that, watched, fireworks, yesterday)

→ _____.

B 우리말과 의미가 같도록 ( ) 안의 말을 이용하여 문장을 완성하시오.

1 그들 중 누구도 그 계획을 지지하지 않았다. (none, support)

→ _____ _____ _____ _____ the project.

2 Mike는 심각한 부상으로 정말 고통스러워했다. (suffer from)

→ Mike _____ _____ _____ severe injuries.

3 그녀는 가방 없이 집을 나간 적이 거의 없다. (leave home)

→ Rarely _____ _____ _____ _____ without her bag.

4 나에게 포기하지 말라고 충고한 분은 바로 나의 아빠였다. (it)

→ _____ _____ _____ _____ _____ advised me

not to give up.

5 그는 큰 실수를 했다는 사실을 부인했다. (fact, deny)

→ He _____ _____ _____ _____ he had made a big mistake.

6 나는 그것을 어떻게 하는지 설명할 수 없었고 나의 친구도 그랬다. (friend, neither)

→ I couldn't explain how to do it, and _____ _____ _____

_____.

C 다음은 그림을 묘사하는 문장이다. 주어진 말을 알맞게 배열하시오.

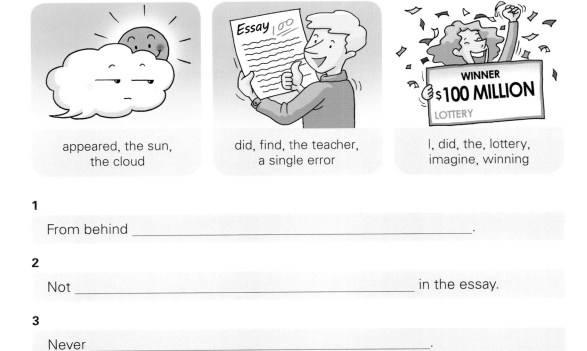

appeared, the sun,
the cloud

did, find, the teacher,
a single error

I, did, the, lottery,
imagine, winning

1

From behind _____ .

2

Not _____ in the essay.

3

Never _____ .

D 다음 Cindy의 일정표를 읽고, It ~ that 강조구문을 이용하여 물음에 답하시오.

Time	Things to do
8:00 a.m.	meet my friends at the school gate
1:00 p.m.	go to science class
5:00 p.m.	practice dancing for the school festival
7:00 p.m.	have dinner at a Mexican restaurant with my family

1 A: Will she meet her teachers at the school gate?

B: No, _____ .

2 A: Will she go to science class at 2 p.m.?

B: No, _____ .

3 A: Will she practice singing for the school festival?

B: No, _____ .

4 A: Will she have dinner at home with her family?

B: No, _____ .

(1–6) 빈칸에 들어갈 알맞은 말을 고르시오.

1 It was Mr. White _____ I wanted to see.

① which   ② what
③ when   ④ where
⑤ that

2 He _____ work out every day to improve his health.

① do   ② does
③ did   ④ will do
⑤ is

3 She loves sunbathing on the beach, and _____ .

① so do I   ② so am I
③ neither do I   ④ neither am I
⑤ nor do I

4 _____ country has a long history.

① Not all   ② All not
③ Not every   ④ Every not
⑤ No every

5 Never _____ to each other.

① they talked   ② talked they
③ they talk   ④ have they talked
⑤ they have talked

6 Seoul, _____ , is becoming a global city.

① the capital of Korea
② is the capital of Korea
③ the capital of Korea is
④ that the capital of Korea is
⑤ which the capital of Korea is

7 빈칸에 들어갈 알맞은 말을 <u>모두</u> 고르시오.

It was on Christmas _____ the first snow of the year fell.

① who   ② which
③ when   ④ where
⑤ that

(8–9) 다음 중 어법상 <u>어색한</u> 문장을 고르시오.

8 ① Here he comes.
② There goes my teacher.
③ Next to me sat a famous novelist.
④ Seldom knew I about the matter.
⑤ Not once did he try to do it.

9 ① She did promise that she would be here on time.

② It was Jack who joined a sports club.

③ It is my pen what I am looking for.

④ It was yesterday that the accident took place.

⑤ It is on the playground where the school festival will be held.

(10-11) 밑줄 친 부분의 쓰임이 나머지와 다른 것을 고르시오.

10 ① It was my glasses that he broke.

② It is chocolate that I want to eat.

③ It was Kelly that visited my house.

④ It was true that she blamed her friend.

⑤ It was yesterday that the printer was fixed.

11 ① Karl does want to have his own car.

② They did look tired after a long journey.

③ He usually does the cooking on the weekends.

④ She did calculate the distances precisely.

⑤ I do believe that he will understand me.

12 빈칸에 공통으로 들어갈 말을 쓰시오.

· It will improve your chances _____ succeeding the next time.
· This gave us the pleasure _____ eating a healthy diet.

⇨ _____

(13-15) 주어진 문장과 같은 의미를 갖도록 빈칸을 채우시오.

13 She doesn't do anything to prepare for the picnic.

⇨ She does _____ to prepare for the picnic.

14 I study with Andrew, but I sometimes study alone.

⇨ I _____ study with Andrew.

15 Some students consider English grammar difficult, but others don't.

⇨ _____ students consider English grammar difficult.

(16-17) 우리말을 영어로 바르게 옮긴 것을 고르시오.

16 부모님 두 분 다 내가 배우가 되기를 원하는 것은 아니다.

① All of my parents want me to be an actor.

② Both of my parents want me to be an actor.

③ Neither of my parents wants me to be an actor.

④ None of my parents wants me to be an actor.

⑤ Not both of my parents want me to be an actor.

17 Sally는 자원봉사를 할 계획인데 나도 그렇다.

① Sally is planning to do volunteer work, and so do I.

② Sally is planning to do volunteer work, and neither do I.

③ Sally is planning to do volunteer work, and so am I.

④ Sally is planning to do volunteer work, and neither am I.

⑤ Sally is planning to do volunteer work, and I am either.

(18-20) 우리말과 의미가 같도록 ( ) 안의 말을 배열하시오.

18 큰 초상화가 벽에 걸려 있었다.
(a, big, hung, portrait)

⇨ On the wall _____

_____ .

19 나는 그가 화났었다는 것을 거의 알아차리지 못했다.
(I, he, was, did, that, angry, notice)

⇨ Rarely _____

_____ .

20 나의 학생들 중 누구도 시험에서 부정행위를 하지 않았다.
(of, my, none, cheated, students)

⇨ _____

on the test.

21 다음 대화가 자연스럽지 <u>않은</u> 것을 고르시오.

① A: I enjoy Korean barbecue.
   B: So do I.

② A: I have never been abroad.
   B: Neither has my brother.

③ A: I couldn't download the file.
   B: Neither could I.

④ A: She has pimples on her face.
   B: So was her sister.

⑤ A: He didn't decide to stop smoking.
   B: Neither did my uncle.

(22-25) 밑줄 친 부분을 강조할 때 빈칸에 알맞은 말을 쓰시오.

22 I <u>little</u> dreamed that my friend would attend the program.

⇨ Little _____ that
my friend would attend the program.

23 His letter and present were <u>in the box</u>.

⇨ In the box _____

_____ .

24 He talked about <u>child safety</u> in the lecture.

⇨ It _____

he talked about in the lecture.

25 I <u>know</u> what we should do to protect the environment.

⇨ I _____ what we should

do to protect the environment.

26 어법상 올바른 문장의 개수를 고르시오.

ⓐ Scarcely he could recognize her.
ⓑ On the third floor is the laboratory.
ⓒ He does worry about his son's eating too much.
ⓓ Not only is he a math teacher, but he is also a popular writer.
ⓔ I was in biology class yesterday and so did my roommate.

① 1개   ② 2개

③ 3개   ④ 4개

⑤ 5개

(27–29) 다음 문장에서 어색한 부분을 찾아 바르게 고치고 알맞은 이유를 고르시오.

27 No every boy likes to play computer games.

고치기: _____ ⇨ _____

이유: 부분부정 '모두 ~인 것은 아니다'는 (no + every, not + every) + 단수명사

28 A: I have never told a lie to my parents.
B: So have I.

고치기: _____ ⇨ _____

이유: 부정문 + (so, neither) + 동사 + 주어

29 Never before the king has made such a thoughtful decision.

고치기: _____ ⇨ _____

이유: 부정어구 + (주어 + have + p.p., have + 주어 + p.p.)

30 다음 조건을 이용하여 알맞게 영작하시오.

내가 중국어를 배우기 시작한 것은 바로 지난 달이었다.
조건 1: start, learn Chinese
조건 2: 10단어, 강조 구문

⇨ _____

_____ .

한눈에 정리하는 Grammar Mapping

빈칸에 알맞은 답을 보기에서 골라 넣어 grammar mapping 완성하기

특수구문

강조

동사강조
[① ＿＿＿＿＿＿＿ + 동사원형] 형태로 '정말 ~하다'로 해석
Everyone does like him.

[It is ~ that] 강조
[It is / was + ② ＿＿＿＿＿ + that] 형태로 '~한 것은 바로 ~이다'로 해석
It was my dad that prepared breakfast for me.

부정표현

전체부정
no, none, neither, nothing 등이나 [not + ③ ＿＿＿＿＿＿＿]
의 형태로 '아무도(결코) ~않다'로 해석
I have nothing to give you.

부분부정
[not + ④ ＿＿＿＿＿＿＿＿＿＿] 형태로
'모두 (항상) ~인 것은 아니다'로 해석
Not all boys like playing outside.

도치

장소 부사구 도치
장소나 방향을 나타내는 부사구가 강조되어 문장의 처음에 오면 [부사구 + 동사 + 주어]의 어순이 된다. 단, 주어가 대명사이면 도치가 일어나지 않는다.
[⑤ ＿＿＿＿＿＿ + 장소 (방향) 부사구]
→ [장소 (방향) 부사구 + ⑥ ＿＿＿＿＿＿]
Down the corner stands city hall.

부정어 도치
부정어 (⑦ ＿＿＿＿＿＿＿＿＿＿＿＿＿)가 강조되어 문장의
처음에 오면 [부정어 + 동사 + 주어] 어순이 된다.
– be동사 있는 문장: [부정어 + ⑧ ＿＿＿＿＿＿]
– 조동사 있는 문장: [부정어 + ⑨ ＿＿＿＿＿＿ + 동사원형]
– 일반동사 있는 문장: [부정어 + do / does / did + 주어 + ⑩ ＿＿＿＿＿]
– 완료시제 있는 문장: [부정어 + ⑪ ＿＿＿＿＿＿ + 주어 + p.p.]
Little did I dream of getting a perfect score on the test.

so / neither 도치
앞 문장의 내용에 대해 ⑫ ＿＿＿＿＿를 나타내는 표현으로 [so / neither + 동사 + 주어] 형태이다. '역시 ~하다 / 하지 않다'로 해석
⑬ ＿＿＿＿＿ + [so + 동사 + 주어],
⑭ ＿＿＿＿＿ + [neither + 동사 + 주어]
I am the youngest son, and so is he.
Andrew hasn't watched the movie, and neither have I.

⑮ ＿＿＿＿＿
명사, 대명사의 의미를 보충하거나 바꿔 말하기 위해 한 번 더 설명해 주는 말
I can't believe the rumor ⑯ ＿＿＿＿＿ he will marry the actress.

보기
· 동격　　　· 동의　　　· 긍정문　　　· 부정문　　　· 동사원형
· 강조 대상　· 주어 + 동사　· 동사 + 주어　· 조동사 + 주어　· be동사 + 주어
· that　　　· have / has / had　· do / does / did　· all / every / both / always
· any / either / anything　· not, never, little, seldom, hardly

172

문장 형식을 결정짓는 동사들, 다 모여!

동사의 종류와 문장의 형식

자동사		타동사	
목적어가 필요 없는 동사		목적어가 필요한 동사	
is, rise, walk, jump, become, seem...		read, write, buy, give, show, find...	
run (달리다)	He **runs** very fast.	run (~를 운영하다)	He **ran** a *restaurant*.
grow (자라다)	My hair **grows** well.	grow (~를 재배하다)	My dad **grows** *rice*.

❶ 완전 자동사 (1형식 동사)

동사만으로 완전한 문장의 의미를 나타내므로 보어나 목적어가 필요 없고 다음과 같은 1형식 문장을 만든다. 이때 수식어는 문장의 형식에 영향을 미치지 않는다.

주어	완전 자동사	수식어
	go, come, run, live, fall, happen, arrive...	

The sun **rises** in the east.   They **lived** happily ever after.

❷ 불완전 자동사 (2형식 동사)

동사만으로는 문장의 의미가 완전하지 않아 주어를 보충 설명하는 보어를 필요로 하고 다음과 같은 2형식 문장을 만든다. 이때 주격보어는 명사와 형용사가 올 수 있다.

주어	불완전 자동사		주격보어
	상태동사	be동사, remain, stay, keep...	명사 / 형용사
	변화동사	become, get, turn, grow...	
	감각동사	look, feel, smell, sound...	형용사

He **was** *a famous singer*.   They **got** *surprised* by the noise.
You **look** *fashionable* in those pants.

❸ 완전 타동사 (3형식 동사)

동작의 대상이 되는 목적어가 있어야 문장의 의미가 완전해지는 동사이고 다음과 같은 3형식 문장을 만든다. 이때 목적어는 명사, 대명사, 동명사, to부정사, that절 등이 올 수 있다.

주어	완전 타동사	목적어
	enter, reach, discuss, resemble...	명사 / 대명사
	want, hope, expect, decide, plan...	to부정사
	enjoy, finish, mind, avoid...	동명사
	say, know, think, believe...	that절

I **discussed** *the problem* with David.   Pandas **like** *to eat* bamboo.
I **enjoyed** *traveling* by ship.   He **thinks** *that you are an angel*.

❹ 수여동사 (4형식 동사)

'~에게 …을 주다'의 의미로 두 개의 목적어를 필요로 하는 동사이고 다음과 같은 4형식 문장을 만든다. 이때 간접목적어는 '~에게'를 직접목적어는 '…을/를'을 의미한다.

주어	수여동사	간접목적어	직접목적어
	give, send, write, bring...	명사 / 대명사	명사
	make, buy, cook, find...		
	ask, inqure...		

Sally **gave** <u>me</u> <u>a big smile</u>. Can you **cook** <u>me</u> <u>some chicken soup</u>?

He **asked** <u>her</u> <u>the same question</u>.

* 4형식 문장의 3형식 문장으로의 전환

간접목적어와 직접목적어의 순서를 바꿀 수 있는데, 이때 간접목적어 앞에 전치사를 쓴다.

주어	수여동사	직접목적어	전치사	간접목적어
	give, send, write, bring...	명사 / 대명사	to	명사 / 대명사
	make, buy, cook, find...		for	
	ask, inqure...		of	

Sally **gave** a big smile *to me*. Can you **cook** some chicken soup *for me*?

He **asked** the same question *of her*.

❺ 불완전 타동사 (5형식 동사)

동작의 대상이 되는 목적어와 목적어를 보충 설명하는 목적격보어를 필요로 하는 동사로 다음과 같은 5형식 문장을 만든다. 이때 목적격보어는 동사의 종류에 따라 명사, 형용사, to부정사, 동사원형, 분사 등이 올 수 있다.

주어	불완전 타동사	목적어	목적격보어
	call, name, elect...	명사 / 대명사	명사
	make, keep, find...		형용사
	want, tell, ask, allow...		to부정사
	make, have, let...		동사원형
	see, watch, hear, feel...		동사원형 / 현재분사

People **call** Bangkok <u>the "City of Angels."</u>

Technology **has made** <u>the world</u> <u>smaller</u>.

Do you **want** <u>me</u> <u>to do</u> the dishes?

Evan never **lets** <u>his sister</u> <u>use</u> his computer.

Did you **see** <u>her</u> <u>dance / dancing</u> on the stage?

동사의 변신은 무죄!

① 동일한 동사이지만 의미에 따라 다른 형식의 문장을 만들 수 있다.

❶ make

	주어	동사	간접목적어	직접목적어	목적격보어	
3형식	He	made		a plan.		~를 만들다
4형식	Ken	made	me	a plane.		~에게 ~를 만들어주다
5형식	I	made		Tim	study.	~에게 ~하라고 시키다

❷ tell

	주어	동사	간접목적어	직접목적어	목적격보어	
3형식	He	told		a lie.		~를 말하다
4형식	He	told	us	the truth.		~에게 ~를 말해주다
5형식	He	told		us	to move.	~에게 ~하라고 말하다

❸ ask

	주어	동사	간접목적어	직접목적어	목적격보어	
3형식	Cindy	asked		a question.		~를 묻다
4형식	He	asked	me	a question.		~에게 ~를 묻다
5형식	She	asked		us	to go there.	~가 ~하라고 요청하다

❹ find

	주어	동사	간접목적어	직접목적어	목적격보어	
3형식	They	found		a diamond.		~를 찾다
4형식	She	found	me	my lost pen.		~에게 ~를 찾아주다
5형식	We	found		Jessy	honest.	~가 ~임을 알게 되다

② 감각동사 (2형식) VS. 지각동사 (5형식)

'보고', '듣고', '느끼는' 등의 감각과 관련된 동사는 문장의 형식에 따라 다양한 의미를 가진다.

❶ 감각동사

2형식	주어	감각동사	주격보어	
시각	You	look	tired.	~하게 보이다
청각	She	sounds	happy.	~하게 들리다
후각	It	smells	delicious.	~한 냄새가 나다
촉각	The air	felt	fresh.	~한 느낌이 들다

❷ 지각동사

5형식	주어	지각동사	목적어	목적격보어	
시각	I	saw	him	cook.	~가 ~하는 것을 보다
청각	She	heard	us	singing.	~가 ~하는 것을 듣다
후각	We	smelled	something	burning.	~가 ~하는 냄새를 맡다
촉각	He	felt	someone	pushing him.	~가 ~하는 것을 느끼다

A 3-level grammar embodiment project:
visualizing grammar and writing practice

Level 3

Grammar
ViSTA
workbook

DARAKWON

A 3-level grammar embodiment project:
visualizing grammar and writing practice

Level 3

Grammar
ViSTA
workbook

DARAKWON

목차

문법패턴 빈칸 채우기

GP 01 현재완료

*본 교재 GP 참조

[have / has + 과거분사] 형태로 과거에 발생한 일이 현재 시점까지 영향을 미칠 때 쓴다.

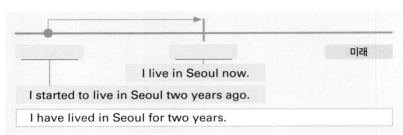

I live in Seoul now.

I started to live in Seoul two years ago.

I have lived in Seoul for two years.

미래

❶ _____ : (과거에 시작하여 현재는) ～완료했다, ～끝났다

과거에 시작한 일이 현재 시점에 완료되었음을 나타내고 주로 _____, _____, _____ 등과 사용한다.

He **has** *already* **finished** his homework.

❷ _____ : (과거부터 현재까지) ～해 본 적 있다

과거부터 현재까지의 경험을 나타내고 주로 _____, _____, _____, _____, _____ 등과 사용한다.

I **have visited** the city *three times*.

❸ _____ : (과거부터 현재까지) 계속 ～해 왔다

과거에 시작한 일이 현재까지 계속되고 있음을 나타내고 [_____] (～동안), [_____] (～이래로 계속), _____ (현재까지 얼마나 오래) 등과 쓴다.

They **have known** each other *for* five years.

❹ _____ : (과거에 한 일이 현재의 결과에 영향을 미쳐) ～해버렸다

과거에 일어난 일의 결과가 현재까지 영향을 미치고 있음을 나타낸다.

He **has lost** his wedding ring.

• Upgrade •

have been to vs. have gone to

[have been to]: '_____'라는 _____   He _____ Greece.

[have gone to]: '_____'라는 _____   He _____ Greece.

GP 02 현재완료진행

[_____] 형태로 과거 시점부터 현재까지 진행되는 동작을 나타낸다.

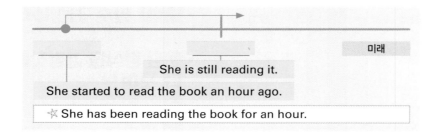

She is still reading it.

She started to read the book an hour ago.

☆ She has been reading the book for an hour.

미래

[_____] 형태로 특정한 과거 시점 이전에 발생한 일이 그 시점까지 영향을 미칠 때 쓴다.

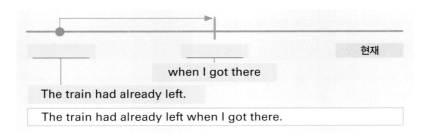

현재

when I got there

The train had already left.

The train had already left when I got there.

❶ 완료: _____ 이전에 이미 완료된 일을 나타낸다.

The play **had** already **started** *when I went into the theater*.

❷ 경험: _____ 이전부터 그 시점까지의 경험을 나타낸다.

He **had** never **been** abroad *until he turned 20*.

❸ 계속: _____ 이전에 시작되어 그 시점까지 지속되는 동작이나 상태를 나타낸다.

Judy **had been** sick for two days *when the doctor came*.

❹ 결과: _____ 이전에 일어난 일의 결과가 그 시점까지 영향을 미치는 일을 나타낸다.

I **had lost** my cell phone, *so I couldn't call you then*.

• Upgrade •

과거완료진행시제

[_____] 형태로 특정 과거 시점 이전부터 그 시점까지 진행되는 동작을 나타낸다.

She **had been washing** her car *when it began to rain*.

[_____] 형태로 특정한 미래 시점 이전에 발생한 일이 그 시점까지 영향을 미칠 때 쓴다.

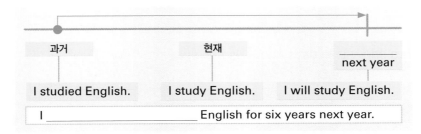

과거

현재

next year

I studied English.

I study English.

I will study English.

I _____ English for six years next year.

If you watch this movie again, you **will have watched** it ten times.

A ( ) 안에서 알맞은 것을 고르시오.

1 Your phone (is ringing, has been ringing) for ten minutes.

2 How (have, did) you been these days?

3 She (has checked not, hasn't checked) her mailbox since last month.

4 How long have you (working, been working) for the company?

5 There (was, has been) a lake in the town ten years ago.

6 Dylan (grew, has grown) taller. He looks different now.

7 He has been a police officer (since, for) seven years.

8 I have (been to, gone to) the theme park three times.

9 We (are waiting, have been waiting) for your call since this morning.

10 They have known each other (since, for) they were kids.

B 두 문장이 같은 의미를 갖도록 빈칸을 채우시오.

1 Joan was sick yesterday. She is still sick now.

→ Joan _____ yesterday.

2 I didn't eat anything last night. I still don't eat anything now.

→ I _____ since last night.

3 She started to eat dinner one hour ago. She is still eating now.

→ She _____ for one hour.

4 It started to snow two days ago. It is still snowing now.

→ It _____ for two days.

5 He started his diet last week. He is still on a diet now.

→ He _____ since last week.

6 Nancy bought a fancy backpack. She still has it now.

→ Nancy _____ a fancy backpack.

C 우리말과 의미가 같도록 ( ) 안의 말을 배열하시오.

1 그는 3년 동안 그의 집을 짓고 있다. (has, building, his house, been, for)

→ He _____ three years.

2 너는 얼마나 오랫동안 그 게임을 해 오고 있니? (have, how long, playing, you, been)

→ _____ the game?

3 그녀는 혼자서 여행을 해 본 적이 없다. (never, has, traveled)

→ She _____ alone.

4 마지막 손님이 아직 도착하지 않았다. (arrived, has, not, yet)

→ The last guest _____.

5 왜 바닷물이 짠지를 궁금해해 본 적 있나요? (have, ever, you, wondered)

→ _____ why sea water is salty?

6 우리 영어 선생님은 본국으로 가버리셨다. (has, to, gone, home country, his)

→ My English teacher _____.

D 우리말과 의미가 같도록 ( ) 안의 말을 이용하여 문장을 완성하시오.

1 나의 가족과 두 번 그 식당에 가 본 적 있다. (be)

→ I _____ _____ _____ _____ _____

with my family.

2 나의 이탈리아 친구는 김치를 이전에 먹어 본 적이 없었다. (try)

→ My Italian friend _____ _____ kimchi before.

3 그는 6시간 동안 계속 운전을 해 오는 중이어서, 지금 무척 피곤해 보인다. (drive)

→ He looks very tired now because he _____ _____ _____

_____ six hours.

4 그는 지난주 이후로 이 책을 계속 읽어 오고 있다. (read)

→ He _____ _____ _____ _____ _____ last week.

5 이런 종류의 버섯을 본 적이 있으세요? (ever, see)

→ _____ _____ _____ _____ this kind of mushroom?

6 그녀는 3년째 팀의 리더이다. (be, team's captain)

→ She _____ _____ _____ _____ _____ _____

three years.

A   ( ) 안에서 알맞은 것을 고르시오.

1 The sun (has, had) risen before I got up this morning.

2 After we had (missing, missed) the train, we had to wait for the next one.

3 By next year, I (will have, have) graduated from high school.

4 The couple had been (dating, dated) for one year before they got married.

5 The professor (has, had) started his lecture when I entered the classroom.

6 If you fail the driving test again, you (will have failed, have failed) three times.

7 I had not (knew, known) the reason before you told me.

8 He was late for work as his car (broke down, had broken down) on the way.

9 She had (worked, working) as a doctor before she became a singer.

10 I will have taught English for twelve years if I (taught, teach) one more year.

B   ( ) 안의 말을 완료형 시제로 고쳐 빈칸을 채우시오. (기준이 되는 특정시점: 이탤릭체)

1 I _____ a kebab *before I traveled to Turkey.* (not, eat)

2 He _____ the milk *before it went bad.* (drink)

3 We _____ the tower *by the end of this year.* (build)

4 The drugstore _____ *when I arrived.* (already, close)

5 *He knew the ending of the movie* because he _____ it.
(already, see)

6 It _____ for three months *before it finally rained that day.*
(not, rain)

7 The family _____ the bakery for 30 years *next week.* (run)

8 She _____ for this company for 20 years *before she quit.* (work)

9 The baby pandas _____ *by the time you visit them again.*
(grow up)

10 She _____ snow *until she moved to Korea.* (never, see)

C 우리말과 의미가 같도록 ( ) 안의 말을 배열하시오.

1 새끼 고양이는 엄마 고양이가 나타날 때까지 한동안 울고 있었다. (crying, had, been)

→ The kitten _____ for a while until its mom showed up.

2 나는 작년 이전에 부산에 갔다 온 적이 없었다. (had, been to, Busan, never)

→ I _____ before last year.

3 너는 여행에서 돌아올 때는 새로운 사람이 되어 있을 것이다. (have, a, will, become, new person)

→ You _____ by the time you come back from the trip.

4 우리는 다음달이면 10년째 함께 살고 있는 것이 될 것이다. (have been, will, living)

→ We _____ together for ten years by next month.

5 내가 이 박물관을 다시 방문하면, 열 번째 방문하는 것이 될 것이다. (visited, will, have, ten times, the museum)

→ I _____ when I visit it again.

6 그의 전화벨이 울렸을 때 그는 30분째 샤워를 하는 중이었다. (taking, had, a shower, been)

→ He _____ for 30 minutes when his phone rang.

D 우리말과 의미가 같도록 ( ) 안의 말을 이용하여 문장을 완성하시오.

1 네가 도착할 때 즈음, 나는 이곳을 떠나 있을 것이다. (leave)

→ By the time you arrive, I _____ _____ _____ here.

2 그 어린 형제들은 작년까지 침실을 같이 공유해 왔다. (share)

→ The young brothers _____ _____ a bedroom until last year.

3 이 돌고래는 인간에게 포획되기 전까지 바다에서 살아오고 있었다. (be living)

→ The dolphin _____ _____ _____ in the sea until it was captured by humans.

4 네가 깨어날 때면 이 기차는 포항에 도착했을 것이다. (arrive)

→ The train _____ _____ _____ in Pohang when you wake up.

5 이 배는 내일이면 열흘째 항해를 하고 있는 것이 될 것이다. (be sailing)

→ This ship _____ _____ _____ _____ for ten days tomorrow.

6 그녀는 차의 시동을 걸기 전에 안전벨트를 착용했다. (put on, seatbelt)

→ She _____ _____ _____ _____ _____ before she started her car.

■ 밑줄 친 부분에 대한 설명을 체크하고 틀린 경우엔 바르게 고치시오. (맞으면 'O' 표시)

1	He <u>have already finished</u> his homework. (→)	(계속, 완료) 의미의 현재완료 He + (have + p.p., has + p.p.)
2	I <u>have visit</u> the city three times. (→)	(경험, 계속) 의미의 현재완료 I + (have + p.p., have + 현재동사)
3	They have known each other <u>since</u> five years. (→)	현재까지 (~동안 계속, ~부터 계속) (since, for) + (기간, 시점)
4	He <u>has lost</u> his wedding ring. (→)	현재 여전히 반지를 잃어버린 상태이면 (과거, 현재완료)시제 (lost, has lost)
5	He <u>has gone</u> to Greece. He is here now. (→)	(~가 본 적 있다, ~가 가버렸다) has + (gone, been) + to 장소
6	He <u>has been</u> to Greece. He is in Greece. (→)	(~가 본 적 있다, ~가 가버렸다) has + (gone, been) + to 장소
7	She <u>has reading</u> the book for an hour. (→)	(~하는 중, ~해 오고 있는 중) (has + -ing, has + been + -ing)
8	The play had already started when I <u>go</u> into the theater. (→)	과거완료는 (과거, 현재) 특정시점 이전부터의 일
9	He <u>has never been</u> abroad until he turned 20. (→)	그 이전부터 과거 특정시점까지의 경험 (has + p.p., had + p.p.)
10	Judy <u>has been</u> sick for two days when the doctor came. (→)	그 이전부터 과거 특정시점까지 계속된 일 (has + p.p., had + p.p.)
11	I <u>have lost</u> my cell phone, so I couldn't call you then. (→)	그 이전의 일이 과거 특정시점까지 영향을 미치는 상태 (have + p.p., had + p.p.)
12	She <u>has been washing</u> her car when it began to rain. (→)	그 이전의 일이 과거 특정시점에도 진행 중인 상태 (had + been + -ing, has + been + -ing)
13	If you watch this movie again, you <u>have watched</u> it ten times. (→)	그 이전의 일이 미래 특정시점까지 완료된 상태 (have + p.p., will have p.p.)

Sentence writing

▪ 주어진 단어를 알맞게 이용하여 우리말과 의미가 같도록 영작하시오.

1	finish	그는 이미 끝마쳤다 / 그의 숙제를 →
2	three times	나는 방문해 본 적 있다 / 그 도시를 / 세 번 →
3	know, each other	그들은 알고 지내왔다 / 서로를 / 5년 동안 →
4	wedding ring	그는 잃어버렸다 / 그의 결혼반지를 (지금 갖고 있지 않다.) →
5	Greece	그는 ~에 가 본 적 있다 / 그리스 →
6	Greece	그는 ~에 가버렸다 / 그리스 →
7	read	그녀는 지금까지 읽어 오고 있는 중이다 / 그 책을 / 한 시간 동안 →
8	the play, the theater	연극은 이미 시작했었다 / 내가 극장에 들어갔을 때 →
9	be abroad, turn 20	그는 해외에 가 본 적 없었다 / 그가 20세가 될 때까지 →
10	be sick	Judy는 아파 왔었다 / 이틀 동안 / 의사가 왔을 때 →
11	lose, then	나는 잃어버렸었다 / 휴대폰을, / 그래서 네게 그때 전화할 수 없었다 →
12	wash, begin to rain	그녀는 닦아 오고 있는 중이었다 / 그녀의 차를 / 비가 오기 시작할 때 →
13	watch	네가 이 영화를 다시 본다면, / 너는 이것을 열 번째 보는 것이 될 것이다 →

GP 05 can, may

❶ can + 동사원형

He **can** (= _____) speak five foreign languages. (_____ : ~할 수 있다)

You **can** (= _____) bring your own food. (_____ : ~해도 된다)

That **can't** be Karl; he has gone to Spain. (_____ : ~일 리가 없다)

_____ (_____ 를 기준으로 _____ 에 대한 _____ : ~이었을(했을) 리가 없다)

The little girl **cannot have driven** the car.

My brother **can't have cleaned** his room. It is still messy.

❷ may + 동사원형

You **may** (= can) sit down or stand. (_____ : ~해도 된다)

He **may** like your idea. (_____ : ~일지도 모른다)

_____ (_____ 를 기준으로 _____ 에 대한 _____ : ~이었을(했을)지도 모른다)

Olivia **may (might) have loved** me at that time.

You **may have heard** about 3D printers.

GP 06 must, should

❶ must + 동사원형

Drivers **must** (= _____) obey the traffic regulations. (_____ : ~해야 한다)

You **must not** take pictures in the museum. (_____)

Children under seven **don't have to pay** an entrance fee. (_____)

Tony stayed up all night. He **must** be tired now. (_____ : ~임에 틀림없다)

_____ (_____ 를 기준으로 _____ 에 대한 _____ : ~이었음(했음)이 틀림없다)

You **must have practiced** very hard.

He didn't call me. He **must have forgotten** my phone number.

❷ should / ought to + 동사원형

We **should** (= _____) respect our parents. (도덕적 의무)

You **should not** (= _____) skip breakfast. (충고)

_____ (_____ 를 기준으로 _____ 에 대한 _____ 나 _____ : ~했어야 했는데 하지 못했다)

I **should have done** my homework.

We **shouldn't have spent** all our money.

❶ used to + 동사원형 (_____: ~하곤 했다 = _____ / _____: ~이었다)

Mike **used to** collect foreign coins. (과거의 습관)

= Mike **would** collect foreign coins.

He **used to** be my boyfriend, but he isn't now. (과거의 상태)

────────────○ Tip ○────────────
① [_____]: ~하곤 했다, ~이었다   Jack used to be very shy.
② [_____]: ~하기 위해 사용되다   It is used to cut metal.
③ [_____]: ~하는 것에 익숙하다   He is used to living on the island.

❷ _____ + 동사원형 (~하고 싶다)

We **would like to** invite you to our wedding.

I **would like to** leave a message for Mr. Ken.

❶ had better + 동사원형 (_____)

You**'d better** take a window seat.

We **had better not** go out tonight because of the rain.

❷ would rather + 동사원형 (_____)

I **would rather** drink hot chocolate.

She**'d rather not** travel during the holidays.

• Upgrade •

would rather A _____ B: _____ 하느니 차라리 _____ 하겠다

I **would rather** play outside **than** watch TV at home.

❸ may (might) as well + 동사원형 (_____)

If there's nothing more to do, we **may as well** go home.

I **may as well not** speak to you if you don't listen.

A 보기에서 알맞은 말을 골라 문장을 완성하시오. (한 번씩만 사용)

보기	be able to	should	must	can

1 They _____ be tired after a long walk.

2 You _____ have arrived earlier. The train has just left.

3 We will _____ swim well by the end of this swimming course.

4 The parking lot is empty. She _____ park there.

보기	had to	may	should	must

5 You _____ not touch the big dog without permission.

6 I was very full. So I _____ loosen my belt.

7 _____ I see your ticket, please?

8 The street is muddy. It _____ have rained a lot last night.

B 우리말과 의미가 같도록 밑줄 친 부분을 어법상 알맞게 고쳐 ( ) 안에 쓰시오.

1 우리는 달로 여행하는 것을 한동안은 기다려야 할 것이다.

→ We will <u>must</u> wait a long time before we can travel to the moon. (→   )

2 Ben은 그 수학문제를 풀 수 있었다.

→ Ben <u>be able to</u> solve the math problem. (→   )

3 그 소문은 사실일 리가 없다.

→ The rumor <u>must not</u> be true. (→   )

4 너는 돈을 지불할 필요가 없어, 내가 한턱낼게.

→ You <u>must not</u> pay the bill. I will treat you. (→   )

5 그 카페는 인기가 좋은 것이 분명해. 언제나 사람들로 붐벼.

→ The café <u>should</u> be popular. It is always crowded with people. (→   )

6 너는 그 연극을 봤어야 했어. 멋진 연극이었어.

→ You <u>must have seen</u> the play. It was awesome. (→   )

C 주어진 말을 알맞은 시제로 바꿔 문장을 완성하시오.

1 must / be   ⓐ He _____ busy now.

                               ⓑ He _____ busy yesterday.

2 should / call   ⓐ You _____ me tomorrow.

                               ⓑ You _____ me yesterday.

3 cannot / be   ⓐ He _____ at home now.

                               ⓑ He _____ at home one hour ago.

4 may / know   ⓐ Frank _____ the secret now.

                               ⓑ Frank _____ the secret already.

D 우리말과 의미가 같도록 ( ) 안의 말을 배열하시오.

1 나는 당신에게 충분히 감사할 수가 없군요. (cannot, I, thank you)

    → _____ enough.

2 책을 겉표지만 보고 판단하면 안 된다. (should, judge, a book, not, by its cover)

    → You _____.

3 그 영화는 대단한 것이 틀림없어, 별 5개를 받았어. (must, good, be, the movie)

    → _____. It was given a rating of five stars.

4 내가 문을 잠그지 않았을지도 몰라. (may, have, locked, not, the door)

    → I _____.

E 우리말과 의미가 같도록 ( ) 안의 말을 이용하여 문장을 완성하시오.

1 나는 이집트로 여행하기 위해 비자를 받을 필요가 없다. (have to, get, a visa)

    → I _____ _____ _____ _____ _____ _____ to travel to Egypt.

2 Lucy가 그런 것을 말했을 리가 없다. (can't, say, such a thing)

    → Lucy _____ _____ _____ _____ _____ _____.

3 여러분은 이번 여름 빅세일을 놓치면 안 됩니다. (must, miss)

    → You _____ _____ _____ _____ _____ _____ _____.

4 나의 앞니가 흔들린다. 나는 그 치아를 빼야 할 것이다. (will, pull)

    → My front tooth is loose. _____ _____ _____ _____ _____

        _____ _____.

A ( ) 안에서 알맞은 것을 고르시오.

1 You (would like to, had better) meet him in person.

2 This party is boring. We (used to, may as well) go home.

3 The actor (would, used to) be a troublemaker when he was young.

4 I (would like, would) to invite you to dinner on Saturday.

5 In the past, people (used to, had better) wish upon the full moon.

6 I would rather sleep (to, than) eat.

7 You (don't have better, had better not) blow your nose during meals.

B 보기에서 알맞은 말을 골라 문장을 완성하시오. (한 번씩만 쓰기)

보기 |	· would rather	· would like to	· had better not
	· may as well	· used to	

1 In the past, the air _____ be clean.

2 I _____ starve than steal.

3 Kate is a creative person. I _____ hear her opinion.

4 We _____ watch the movie. It is too violent.

5 If you don't understand the book, you _____ read another one.

C 우리말과 의미가 같도록 밑줄 친 부분을 어법상 알맞게 고쳐 쓰시오.

1 나는 클럽에 가입하고 싶습니다.

→ I <u>would rather</u> join the club.　　　　　　(→ 　　　　　　)

2 너는 다른 사람의 말을 끊지 않는 것이 좋겠다.

→ You <u>have better not</u> cut others off.　　　　(→ 　　　　　　)

3 예전에 이 산에는 호랑이가 많이 있었다.

→ There <u>would</u> be a lot of tigers in the mountains.　(→ 　　　　　　)

4 나는 다이어트를 하느니 차라리 운동을 하겠다.

→ I <u>would better</u> work out than go on a diet.　　(→ 　　　　　　)

5 너는 차라리 은행에 돈을 예금하는 것이 낫겠다.

→ You <u>may well</u> deposit the money in the bank.　(→ 　　　　　　)

D 우리말과 의미가 같도록 ( ) 안의 말을 배열하시오.

1 네가 계속 불평을 한다면, 너 혼자 하는 것이 낫겠다. (may as well, it, you, do, alone)

→ If you keep complaining, _____.

2 나는 기다리느니 그녀에게 전화하는 것이 낫겠다. (call, would rather, than, her)

→ I _____ wait.

3 너는 네 휴대폰을 먼저 충전하는 것이 낫겠다. (charge, had better, cell phone, your)

→ You _____.

4 사람들은 장거리 의사소통을 위해 봉화를 사용했었다. (signal fires, use, used to)

→ People _____ for long-distance communication.

5 우리 부모님은 학교에 점심을 가져가곤 하셨다. (would, their, bring, lunch, own)

→ My parents _____ to school.

6 침대에서 간식을 먹지 않는 것이 좋겠다. (had better, eat, snacks, not)

→ You _____ in bed.

E 우리말과 의미가 같도록 ( ) 안의 말을 이용하여 문장을 완성하시오.

1 우리는 이 식물들을 실외에 두지 않는 것이 낫겠다. (had, put)

→ We _____ _____ _____ _____ _____ _____ outside.

2 이 책 두 권을 대출하고 싶습니다. (would, check out)

→ I _____ _____ _____ _____ _____

_____ _____.

3 당신이 일을 즐기지 않는다면, 그만두는 것이 낫습니다. (may, quit)

→ If you don't enjoy your work, _____ _____ _____ _____.

4 저는 여러분들이 와 주신 것에 감사드리고 싶습니다. (thank, everyone)

→ I _____ _____ _____ _____ for coming.

5 그 기자는 십 년 동안 전업주부였다. (used, a housewife)

→ The reporter _____ _____ _____ _____ for ten years.

6 나는 그룹으로 일하느니 혼자 하는 것이 낫다. (work alone)

→ I _____ _____ _____ _____ than work in a group.

■ 밑줄 친 부분에 대한 설명을 체크하고 틀린 경우엔 바르게 고치시오. (맞으면 'O' 표시)

* 가능한 답은 모두 체크

1	He will can speak five foreign languages. (→)	[조동사 + 조동사]는 (가능, 불가능) will + (can, be able to)
2	He may likes your idea. (→)	(허락, 약한 추측)일 때 may + (동사, 동사원형)
3	You must not take pictures in the museum. (→)	조동사의 부정형은 조동사 (앞, 뒤)에 (not, don't)
4	Children under seven not have to pay an entrance fee. (→)	(~하면 안 된다, ~할 필요 없다) 의미일 때 (don't, not) + have to
5	Your speech was perfect. You must practice very hard. (→)	(현재, 과거) 사실에 대한 강한 추측일 때 must + (동사원형, have p.p.)
6	We ought respect our parents. (→)	(충고, 추측)일 때 ought + (동사원형, to + 동사원형)
7	I should do my homework yesterday. (→)	(현재, 과거) 사실에 대한 유감, 후회일 때 should + (동사원형, have p.p.)
8	Mike would collect foreign coins. (→)	과거의 (상태, 습관)일 때 (would, used to) + 동사원형
9	He would be my boyfriend, but he isn't now. (→)	과거의 (상태, 습관)일 때 (would, used to) + 동사원형
10	You have better take a window seat. (→)	(~하는 것이 낫다, ~해야만 한다) 의미일 때 (have, had) + better + 동사원형
11	We don't had better go out tonight because of the rain. (→)	had better의 부정형은 바로 (앞, 뒤)에 (don't, not) 사용
12	I would rather play outside as watch TV at home. (→)	would rather A (as, than) B (A, B) 하느니 차라리 (A, B) 하겠다
13	If there's nothing more to do, we may as well went home. (→)	(~하는 것이 낫다, ~하곤 했다) 의미일 때 may as well + (동사원형, 과거동사)

Sentence writing

▪ 주어진 단어를 알맞게 이용하여 우리말과 의미가 같도록 영작하시오.

1	speak, languages	그는 말할 수 있다 / 다섯 개의 외국어를 →
2	like	그는 좋아할지도 모른다 / 너의 아이디어를 →
3	take pictures	당신은 사진을 찍으면 안 됩니다 / 박물관에서 →
4	under seven, an entrance fee	7세 이하 아동은 / 지불할 필요가 없다 / 입장료를 →
5	practice	너는 분명히 연습했을 것이다 / 매우 열심히 →
6	respect	우리는 존경해야 한다 / 우리 부모님을 →
7	homework	나는 했어야만 했는데 (못해서 유감이다) / 내 숙제를 →
8	collect, foreign coins	Mike는 수집하곤 했었다 / 외국 동전을 →
9	boyfriend	그는 예전에 ~이었다 / 내 남자친구, / 하지만 그는 지금은 아니다 →
10	take a window seat	너는 ~갖는 것이 낫겠다 / 창가 자리를 →
11	because of the rain	우리는 나가지 않는 것이 좋겠다 / 오늘밤에 / 비 때문에 →
12	play outside, would rather, than	나는 차라리 나가서 놀겠다 / TV를 보는 것보다 / 집에서 →
13	there is nothing more, may	더 이상 할 것이 없다면, / 우리는 가는 것이 낫겠다 / 집에 →

문법패턴 빈칸 채우기

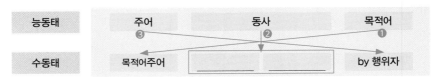

Chapter 03
수동태

GP 09 수동태의 의미와 기본 형태

수동태는 [_____]의 형태로 주어가 동작의 영향을 받거나 당하는 대상이 될 때 쓴다.

능동태	주어 ❸	동사 ❷	목적어 ❶
수동태	목적어→주어	_____ _____	by 행위자

Columbus **discovered** America in 1492.
→ America **was discovered** in 1492 by Columbus.
This book **was not written** by George Orwell.

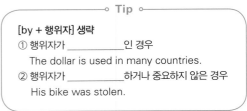

Tip
[by + 행위자] 생략
① 행위자가 _____인 경우
   The dollar is used in many countries.
② 행위자가 _____하거나 중요하지 않은 경우
   His bike was stolen.

GP 10 수동태의 다양한 형태

미래형 수동태	_____ (be going to) + _____	과거분사
진행형 수동태	_____ + _____	과거분사
완료형 수동태	_____ _____ + _____	과거분사
조동사 수동태	_____ + _____	과거분사

You **will be remembered** as a great leader. (_____ 수동태)
☆ Space elevators **are being built** by the company. (현재_____ 수동태)
☆ The road **has been closed** because of heavy snow. (현재_____ 수동태)
☆ These flowers **should be watered** every day. (_____ 수동태)

GP 11 동사구 수동태

두 개 이상의 단어로 이루어진 동사구는 하나의 단어 개념으로 생각하고 수동태로 바꾼다.

주어	동사 _____	목적어	He looked after the puppy.
목적어→주어	_____ _____ _____	by 행위자	☆ The puppy _____ him.

run over	_____	look after	_____
turn on / off	_____	carry out	_____
put off	_____		~을 돌보다
_____	~을 나눠주다	_____	~을 사용하다
_____	~을 비웃다	_____	~을 존경하다

GP 12 4형식 문장의 수동태

간접목적어와 직접목적어를 각각 주어로 하여 두 가지 형태의 수동태 문장으로 바꿀 수 있다.
_____를 수동태의 주어로 만들면 간접목적어 앞에 _____를 쓴다.

주어	동사	간접목적어	직접목적어
_____	be동사 과거분사	_____	by 행위자
_____	be동사 과거분사	_____	by 행위자

❶ 간접목적어와 직접목적어를 각각 주어로 쓰는 동사: give, offer, tell, teach...

She gave *him* two concert tickets.

→ *He* _____ two concert tickets by her.

→ Two concert tickets _____ him by her.

❷ _____만을 주어로 쓰는 동사: make, buy, find, cook, write, pass...

My uncle bought me a nice backpack.

→ A nice backpack _____ me by my uncle.

→ I **was bought** a nice backpack by my uncle. (×)

○─── Tip ───○
간접목적어 앞에 쓰는 전치사
_____ : 대부분의 수여동사
_____ : make, buy, find, cook...
_____ : ask, inquire...

GP 13 5형식 문장의 수동태

능동태 문장의 목적어를 주어로 하고 목적격보어는 그대로 써서 수동태를 만든다.
단, 목적격보어가 동사원형이면 _____로 바꿔서 수동태를 만든다.

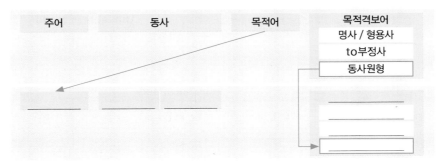

주어	동사	목적어	목적격보어
			명사 / 형용사
			to부정사
			동사원형
_____	_____	_____	_____
			_____

❶ 목적격보어가 명사 / 형용사 / to부정사인 경우: _____ 쓴다.

They called her a walking dictionary.

→ She **was called** a walking dictionary.

He told us to sit down.

→ We **were told** to sit down by him.

●─── Upgrade ───●
지각동사의 목적격보어가 현재분사인 경우 수동태
에서 현재분사를 _____ 쓴다.
I saw the dog swimmimg.
The dog was seen _____.

❷ 목적격보어가 _____인 경우: _____로 바뀐다.

(1) 사역동사: Jessica made me clean the room.

→ I **was made** _____ the room by Jessica.

(2) 지각동사: I saw the boy climb the tree.

→ The boy **was seen** _____ the tree (by me).

목적어가 that절인 문장은 두 가지 형태의 수동태를 만들 수 있다.

일반인주어	동사 (say, think, believe...)	that	S	V	They say that he is smart.
It	be동사	과거분사	___	___ ___	_____ he is smart.
S	be동사	과거분사	___	___	_____ smart.

People say that laughter brings good luck.

→ **It is said that** laughter brings good luck.

→ **Laughter** _____ good luck.

- Upgrade •

that절의 주어를 수동태의 주어로 할 때, 주절의 시제보다 that절의 시제가 앞서면 that절의 동사를 완료부정사(to have p.p.)로 바꾼다.

People **say** that she **is** an angel.　→ She is said _____ an angel.

People **say** that she **was** an angel.　→ She is said _____ an angel.

주어	be동사	과거분사	by	The table is made by him.
			_____	The table is made ____ wood.

be interested _____	~에 관심이 있다	be tired _____	~에 싫증나다
be filled _____	~로 가득 차 있다	be surprised _____	~에 놀라다
be covered _____	~로 덮여 있다	be known _____	~에게 알려져 있다
be pleased _____	~에 기뻐하다	be known _____	~라고 알려지다
be satisfied _____	~에 만족하다	be known _____	~로 유명하다
be disappointed _____	~에 실망하다	be made _____	~로 만들어지다

The store **was filled with** toys for the Christmas sale.

Korean popular music **is known** _____ K-pop.

A ( ) 안에서 알맞은 것을 고르시오.

1 We must not (forget, be forgotten) the war.

2 The light was (turn on, turned on) by Cindy.

3 The baby was (washing, being washed) by his mom.

4 The new product (was introduced, introduced) to the market.

5 This moment will (remember, be remembered) in my heart.

6 The park has (been, being) closed since May.

7 My house was (looked, looked after) by Nancy while I was on a trip.

B 주어진 문장을 수동태 문장으로 바꿔 쓰시오.

1 They discussed the issue at the meeting.

→ The issue _____.

2 Robots are making many of the products.

→ Many of the products _____.

3 People have spread the news by word of mouth.

→ The news _____.

4 The mother eagle took care of her eggs.

→ Her eggs _____.

5 We should save water.

→ Water _____.

6 Henry put off the meeting.

→ The meeting _____.

7 You must wash the sweaters by hand.

→ The sweaters _____.

8 She handed out sandwiches to homeless people.

→ Sandwiches _____.

C 다음 능동태 문장을 다양한 형태의 수동태로 바꿔 쓰시오.

능동태		Elena writes a report.
수동태	**1** 미래형	→ _____ Elena.
	2 (현재) 진행형	→ _____ Elena.
	3 (현재) 완료형	→ _____ Elena.
	4 조동사 수동태 (must)	→ _____ Elena.

D 우리말과 의미가 같도록 ( ) 안의 말을 배열하시오.

1 우리 형은 할아버지를 따라 이름 지어졌다. (was, my brother, named after)

→ _____ our grandfather.

2 키보드가 실수로 눌러지고 있는 중이다. (being, the keyboard, is, pressed)

→ _____ by mistake.

3 그의 글 스타일은 셰익스피어의 영향을 받아 왔다. (has, been, his writing style, influenced, by)

→ _____ Shakespeare.

4 그 이야기는 수년간 많은 아이들의 사랑을 받아 왔다. (loved, has been, the story, by)

→ _____ a lot of children for years.

5 그 도시에서 여론조사가 실시되었다. (carried out, the survey, was)

→ _____ in the city.

E 우리말과 의미가 같도록 ( ) 안의 말을 이용하여 문장을 완성하시오.

1 그의 가방은 어제 공원에서 발견되었다. (discover)

→ _____ _____ _____ _____ _____ _____ yesterday.

2 그 새로운 다리는 내년에 건설될 것이다. (the new bridge, build)

→ _____ _____ _____ _____ _____ next year.

3 당신의 햄버거는 2시까지 배달될 수 없습니다. (can, deliver)

→ _____ _____ _____ _____ by 2 p.m.

4 그는 과학자들에게 존경을 받는다. (look up to)

→ _____ _____ _____ _____ scientists.

5 쿠키가 오븐에서 구워지고 있는 중이다. (Cookies, bake)

→ _____ _____ _____ in the oven.

A 보기에서 알맞은 말을 골라 수동태 문장을 완성하시오. (중복 사용 가능)

보기 | to   for   of

1 The old pictures were shown _____ Tom.

2 A new toy was bought _____ my cat by me.

3 The same question was asked _____ all my classmates.

4 A job was offered _____ my sister.

B ( ) 안에서 알맞은 것을 고르시오.

1 Jane was allowed (use, to use) her computer.

2 The sink (keeps, is kept) dry at all times.

3 Tom was seen (to feed, feed) his dog by me.

4 We were made (picking up, to pick up) the trash on the street.

5 Charlie was asked (to change, change) seats with Jack.

6 A box of candies was sent (to, of) Kelly by Jason.

C 주어진 4형식 문장을 수동태 문장으로 바꿔 쓰시오.

1 I taught my dog some tricks.

→ My dog _____.

→ Some tricks _____.

2 He gave me a piece of advice.

→ I _____.

→ A piece of advice _____.

3 The deliveryman handed me a box of pizza.

→ _____ me by the deliveryman.

4 The interviewer asked him a difficult question.

→ _____ him by the interviewer.

5 They brought Dana a kid's meal.

→ _____ Dana.

D 주어진 5형식 문장을 수동태 문장으로 바꿔 쓰시오.

1 She made us read the book again.

→ We _____.

2 People called him a soccer genius.

→ He _____.

3 The police heard the boy shouting for help.

→ The boy _____.

4 The doctor advised him to rest for two weeks.

→ He _____.

E 우리말과 의미가 같도록 ( ) 안의 말을 배열하시오.

1 그 수제 가방은 벼룩시장에서 구입되었다. (bought, the handmade bag, was)

→ _____ at a flea market.

2 그들은 군대에서 복역하게 되었다. (were, they, to serve, made)

→ _____ in the military.

3 과거에 후추는 귀중한 것으로 여겨졌다. (was, valuable, considered, pepper)

→ _____ in the past.

4 그가 휘파람 부는 것이 들렸다. (was, he, heard, to, whistle)

→ _____.

F 우리말과 의미가 같도록 ( ) 안의 말을 이용하여 문장을 완성하시오.

1 Peter는 자신을 소개하도록 요청받았다. (ask, introduce)

→ Peter _____ _____ _____ _____ himself.

2 칠면조 요리가 손님들을 위해 요리되었다. (cook, the guests)

→ The turkey _____ _____ _____ _____ _____.

3 방콕은 종종 "천사들의 도시"라고 불려진다. (Bangkok, call)

→ _____ _____ _____ _____ the "City of Angels."

4 그 광고는 내가 그 제품에 대해 호기심을 갖도록 만들었다. (make, curious)

→ I _____ _____ _____ about the product by the ad.

A ( ) 안에서 알맞은 것을 고르시오.

1 Amanda (said, is said) to have leadership abilities.

2 We are interested (with, in) clean energy.

3 The hotel is known (to, for) its beautiful view.

4 The doctor is believed (to be, is) one of the best.

5 It (said, is said) that hair grows about one centimeter a month.

6 The bathtub was filled (with, of) hot water.

7 It is believed (to, that) cats are curious.

B 주어진 문장을 수동태 문장으로 바꿔 쓰시오.

1 They reported that the singer was missing.

→ It _____ .

→ The singer _____ .

2 People believe that elephants have good memories.

→ It _____ .

→ Elephants _____ .

3 They believed that the wizard had magical powers.

→ It _____ .

→ The wizard _____ .

4 They say that the city is safe and clean.

→ It _____ .

→ The city _____ .

5 People think that Paula has a sense of humor.

→ It _____ .

→ Paula _____ .

C 우리말과 의미가 같도록 ( ) 안의 말을 배열하시오.

1 까마귀들은 매우 영리하다고 알려져 있다. (known, are, to, very smart, be)

→ Crows _____.

2 인생은 경이로움으로 가득 차 있다. (filled, is, life, with)

→ _____ wonders.

3 스트레스가 모든 종류의 질병을 일으킨다고들 말한다. (said, that, is, it, causes, stress)

→ _____ all kinds of illnesses.

4 그 새 차는 휘발유를 덜 사용할 것으로 기대되어진다. (expected, is, to, use)

→ The new car _____ less gas.

5 산꼭대기는 눈으로 덮여 있다. (covered, is, with, the mountaintop)

→ _____ snow.

6 무슬림들은 하루에 다섯 번 기도하도록 요구되어진다. (required, are, pray, to)

→ Muslims _____ five times a day.

D 우리말과 의미가 같도록 ( ) 안의 말을 이용하여 문장을 완성하시오.

1 지구 온난화가 점점 나빠지고 있다고들 한다. (say, global warming)

→ It _____ _____ _____ _____ _____ is getting worse and worse.

2 이 3D 프린터는 유용하다고 알려져 있다. (know, useful)

→ The 3D printer _____ _____ _____ _____.

3 나는 너의 성공에 기분이 좋다. (please)

→ _____ _____ _____ _____ your success.

4 이 프로젝트는 성공할 것으로 예상되어진다. (expect, successful)

→ The project _____ _____ _____ _____.

5 그의 팬들은 그의 연기에 실망했다. (disappoint, fans)

→ _____ _____ _____ _____ _____ his acting.

6 그 왕관은 순금으로 만들어졌다. (make, pure gold)

→ The crown _____ _____ _____ _____.

Error Correction

■ 밑줄 친 부분에 대한 설명을 체크하고 틀린 경우엔 바르게 고치시오. (맞으면 'O' 표시)

* 가능한 답은 모두 체크
* to + V: to부정사, V + -ing: 현재분사

1	Space elevators <u>are being building</u> by the company. (→)	진행형 수동태는 be동사 + (being + -ing, being + p.p.)
2	The road <u>has closed</u> because of heavy snow. (→)	현재완료형 수동태는 has + (been + p.p., p.p.)
3	These flowers should <u>are watered</u> every day. (→)	조동사 수동태는 should + (be + p.p., be동사 + p.p.)
4	The puppy was <u>looked</u> by him. (→)	동사구 (look after(돌보다) 수동태는 be동사 + (looked, looked after)
5	Two concert tickets were given <u>of</u> him by her. (→)	4형식 동사 give의 수동태는 be동사 + given + (to, of) + 간접목적어
6	A nice backpack was bought <u>to</u> me by my uncle. (→)	4형식 동사 buy의 수동태는 be동사 + bought + (for, of) + 간접목적어
7	She was <u>call</u> a walking dictionary. (→)	5형식 동사 call의 수동태는 be동사 + (call, called) + 명사
8	We were told <u>sit</u> down by him. (→)	5형식 동사 tell의 수동태는 be동사 + told + (동사원형, to + V)
9	I was made <u>clean</u> a room by Jessica. (→)	사역동사 make의 수동태는 be동사 + made + (동사원형, to + V)
10	The boy was seen <u>climb</u> the tree. (→)	지각동사 see의 수동태는 be동사 + seen + (동사원형, to + V, V + -ing)
11	It <u>says</u> that laughter brings good luck. (→)	that절이 목적어인 문장의 수동태는 It + (says, is said) + that 주어 + 동사
12	Laughter is said <u>bring</u> good luck. (→)	that절이 목적어인 문장의 수동태는 that절의 주어 + is said + (동사원형, to + V)
13	Korean popular music is known <u>to</u> K-pop. (→)	(~라고 알려지다, ~에게 알려지다)이므로 be known + (for, as, to)

■ 주어진 단어를 알맞게 이용하여 우리말과 의미가 같도록 영작하시오.

1	space elevators, build	우주 엘리베이터가 / 건설되어지고 있는 중이다 / 그 회사에 의해 →
2	close, heavy snow	그 길은 / 폐쇄되어져 왔다 / 폭설 때문에 →
3	should, water	이 꽃들은 / 물을 줘야 한다 / 매일 →
4	look after	그 강아지는 / 보살펴졌다 / 그에 의해 →
5	concert tickets	두 장의 콘서트 티켓이 / 주어졌다 / 그에게 / 그녀에 의해 →
6	backpack	멋진 배낭이 / 구입되었다 / 나를 위해 / 나의 삼촌에 의해 →
7	a walking dictionary	그녀는 / 불려졌다 / 걸어 다니는 사전이라고 →
8	tell	우리는 / 지시되었다 / 앉으라고 / 그에 의해 →
9	make	나는 / 시켜졌다 / 방을 청소하라고 / Jessica에 의해 →
10	see, climb	그 소년은 / 보여졌다 / 나무를 오르고 있는 것이 →
11	It, laughter	~라고 이야기된다 / 웃음이 행운을 가져온다 →
12	laughter	웃음은 / ~한다고 이야기된다 / 행운을 가져온다고 →
13	popular music	한국의 대중음악은 / ~라고 알려져 있다 / K-pop →

문법패턴 빈칸 채우기

GP 16 to부정사의 명사적 쓰임

❶ 명사적 쓰임

문장에서 명사처럼 주어, 목적어, 보어 역할을 한다.

(1) _____ 역할

To have good habits is important.

(2) _____ 역할

I hope **to become** a robot scientist.

(3) _____ 역할

Her job is **to create** game characters.

> ○ **Tip** ○
>
> to부정사의 부정은 to부정사 _____에
> _____이나 _____를 쓴다.
> · I agreed to join the club.
> → I agreed not to join the club.

❷ 가주어와 가목적어 it

주어나 목적어로 쓰인 to부정사가 길어진 경우 보통 가주어, 가목적어 it을 쓰고 to부정사는 뒤로 보낸다.

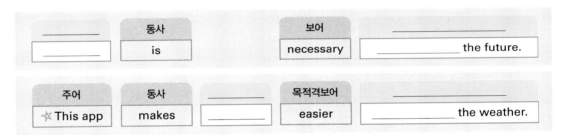

_____	동사		보어	_____
_____	is		necessary	_____ the future.

주어	동사	_____	목적격보어	_____
☆ This app	makes	_____	easier	_____ the weather.

It is not easy **to make** new friends. (가주어 it)

He found **it** difficult **to say** no. (가목적어 it)

❸ 의문사 + to부정사

[의문사 + to부정사] 형태로 문장에서 _____처럼 쓰이며, [의문사 + 주어 + should + 동사원형]으로 바꿔 쓸 수 있다.

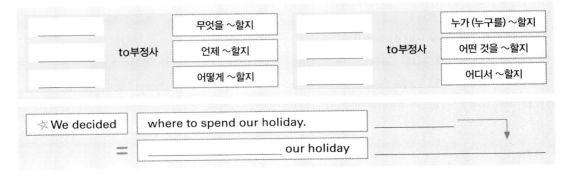

_____		무엇을 ~할지	_____		누가 (누구를) ~할지
_____	to부정사	언제 ~할지	_____	to부정사	어떤 것을 ~할지
_____		어떻게 ~할지			어디서 ~할지

☆ We decided	where to spend our holiday.	_____
=	_____ our holiday	

I don't know **when to start**.

= _____

❶ **명사 수식**

문장에서 형용사처럼 명사를 수식한다. 이때 to부정사는 명사 _____에서 명사를 수식한다.

		books to sell
	to부정사	☆ a pencil to write with

Give me *a chance* to explain.
Today, we have *something special* to celebrate.

❷ **[be + to부정사] 용법**

be동사 뒤에 to부정사를 사용하여 주어의 상태를 설명한다.

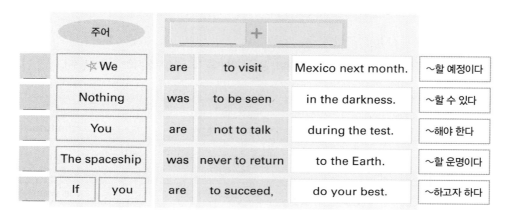

주어		_____ + _____		
☆ We	are	to visit	Mexico next month.	~할 예정이다
Nothing	was	to be seen	in the darkness.	~할 수 있다
You	are	not to talk	during the test.	~해야 한다
The spaceship	was	never to return	to the Earth.	~할 운명이다
If you	are	to succeed,	do your best.	~하고자 하다

문장에서 부사처럼 동사, 형용사, 문장을 수식한다.

He works out hard **to burn** fat.　　　　　　　　(_____ : ~하기 위해서)
　　　　　　　(= in order to, so as to)
We are happy **to hear** that.　　　　　　　　　(_____ : ~해서, ~하니)
My password was easy **to remember**.　　　　　(_____ : ~하기에)
She must be foolish **to trust** him.　　　　　　　(_____ : ~하다니, ~으로 보아)
The boy grew up **to be** the president of the country.　(_____ : ~해서, (결국) ~하다)
To turn left at the corner, you will find the bakery.　(조건: ~한다면)

동사의 종류에 따라 목적격보어로 to부정사나 원형부정사가 쓰인다.

	주어	동사	목적어	목적격보어
목적격보어로 _____를 쓰는 동사	I	____, ____, ____, ... advise, allow, get...	her	_____ the dishes.
_____동사	I	_____, _____, ____	her	_____ the dishes.
_____동사	I	____, _____, ____, ____, _____, ____...	her	_____ the dishes.
_____	I	help	her	_____ the dishes. _____ the dishes.

❶ 목적격보어로 _____를 쓰는 동사

I *want* you **to listen to** me carefully.

My teacher *told* me **to hand in** the report online.

She *advised* me **not to use** my cell phone too much.

❷ 목적격보어로 _____를 쓰는 동사

(1) _____동사

His funny joke *made* her **laugh**.

My mom *had* me **set** the table.

She *let* her kids **run** around the garden.

> ○ Tip ○
> **사역동사의 의미**
> ① let (허락): 원한다면 ~하게 하다
> ② have (명령, 권유): ~하게 하다
> ③ make (강제성): 강하게 ~하게 하다

(2) _____동사

She *watched* the kittens **play (playing)** with a ball.

We *heard* someone **ring (ringing)** the doorbell at midnight.

He *felt* a bug **crawl (crawling)** on his arm.

❸ 목적격보어로 _____와 _____ 둘 다 쓰는 동사: _____

Smell *helps* us **taste (to taste)** food better.

• Upgrade •

get은 '~하게 하다'의 의미로 사역동사와 의미가 같지만 목적격보어로 _____를 쓴다.

She *got* me _____ the dishes. = She *had* me **do** the dishes.

GP 20 to부정사의 의미상 주어

to부정사의 행위자를 _____라고 한다. to부정사의 행위자가 문장의 주어나 목적어와 다를 경우,
to부정사 앞에 [for + 목적격] 또는 [of + 목적격] 형태로 행위 주체를 나타낸다.

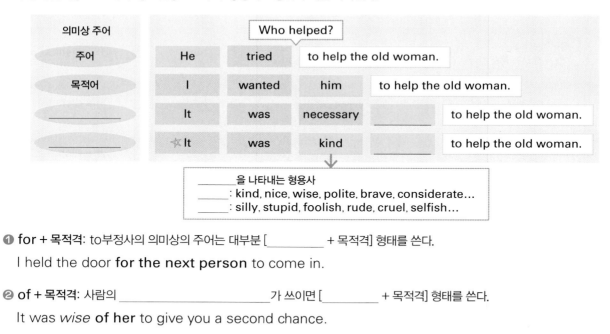

① for + 목적격: to부정사의 의미상의 주어는 대부분 [_____ + 목적격] 형태를 쓴다.

I held the door **for the next person** to come in.

② of + 목적격: 사람의 _____가 쓰이면 [_____ + 목적격] 형태를 쓴다.

It was *wise* **of her** to give you a second chance.

GP 21 to부정사의 시제

① 단순 부정사: [_____] 형태로 to부정사의 시제가 주절의 시제와 _____나 미래를 나타낸다.

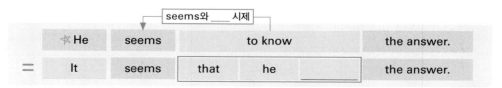

② 완료 부정사: [_____] 형태로 to부정사의 시제가 주절의 시제보다 _____는 것을 나타낸다.

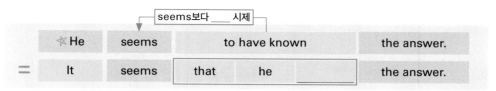

• Upgrade •

to부정사의 수동태

단순 수동태	to + _____	수동태 의미의 to부정사가 주절 시제와 **같을 때**
완료 수동태	to + _____	수동태 의미의 to부정사가 주절 시제보다 **앞설 때**

I am happy _____ by you.　　(= I **am** happy that I **am invited** by you.)

I am happy _____ by you.　　(= I **am** happy that I **was invited** by you.)

34

❶ 형용사 / 부사 + enough + to부정사

He was **lucky enough to marry** a woman like you.

→ He was _____ a woman like you.

The tornado is **powerful enough to destroy** houses.

→ The tornado is _____ houses.

❷ too + 형용사 / 부사 + to부정사

The program was **too violent for him to watch**.

→ The program was _____ it.

She is **too young to go** to the movies alone.

→ She is _____ to the movies alone.

to부정사의 표현이 숙어처럼 독립적 의미를 갖는 것이며, 문장 전체를 수식한다.

to begin with	_____	to be frank with you	_____
to be sure	_____	strange to say	_____
so to speak	_____	not to mention	_____
to tell the truth	사실대로 말하자면	to make matters worse	_____

To be sure, she is the smartest student in our school.

He is, **so to speak**, a musical genius.

To make matters worse, we felt tired and got lost in the woods.

A ( ) 안에서 알맞은 것을 고르시오.

1 My goal is (become, to become) the next Nobel Prize winner in my country.

2 He knew (what, how) to spell the word.

3 Can you tell me how (say, to say) thank you in German?

4 She wanted (to order, to orders) the soup of the day at the restaurant.

5 Science has made (it, this) possible for people to live longer.

6 (That, It) was not easy to remember all the rules.

7 (To prepare, Prepared) for the presentation was a lot of work.

8 He made it a rule (walked, to walk) his dog in the morning.

9 I didn't expect (to see, to saw) you here.

10 I'll tell you something. Will you promise (don't, not) to laugh?

B 두 문장이 같은 의미를 갖도록 to부정사를 이용하여 문장을 완성하시오.

(1–3) 가주어 It ~ 진주어 to부정사

1 To download the app takes only 10 seconds.

→ _____ the app.

2 To deliver pizza by drone is a great idea.

→ _____ by drone.

3 To swim across the stream is dangerous.

→ _____ the stream.

(4–6) 의문사 + to부정사

4 He sometimes doesn't know when he should stop talking.

→ He sometimes doesn't know _____.

5 I don't know whom I should ask.

→ I don't know _____.

6 Please tell me when I should turn off the oven.

→ Please tell me _____ the oven.

C   ( ) 안의 말을 [의문사 + to부정사]로 바꿔 문장을 완성하시오.

1 그 아기는 걷는 방법을 배우기 시작했어. (walk)

→ The baby began to learn _____ _____ _____ .

2 다음엔 어디로 가야 하는지를 말해 주시겠어요? (go)

→ Can you tell me _____ _____ _____ next?

3 그 요리사는 손님들을 위해 무엇을 요리할지에 대해 생각하고 있다. (cook)

→ The chef is thinking about _____ _____ _____ for the guests.

4 너는 내일 첫 기차를 타기 위해 언제 일어나야 할지를 알고 있니? (get up)

→ Do you know _____ _____ _____ _____ to catch the first train

tomorrow?

D   우리말과 의미가 같도록 ( ) 안의 말을 배열하시오.

1 그의 첫 번째 파트타임 일은 펭귄에게 먹이를 주는 일이었어. (feed, to, penguins, was)

→ Her first part-time job _____ .

2 나는 어떻게 수화를 하는지를 배울 예정이다. (sign language, to use, how)

→ I am going to learn _____ .

3 때로는 아니라고 말할 필요가 있었다. (necessary, is, it, say no, to)

→ Sometimes _____ .

4 그는 아기를 깨우지 않기 위해 조용히 걸었다. (wake up, to, not, the baby)

→ He walked quietly _____ .

E   우리말과 의미가 같도록 ( ) 안의 말을 이용하여 문장을 완성하시오.

1 그 영화는 한국 역사를 이해하는 것을 쉽게 만들었다. (easy, understand)

→ The movie made it _____ _____ _____ _____ _____ .

2 가을에 낙엽 위를 걷는 것은 즐겁다. (walk, fallen leaves)

→ It is pleasant _____ _____ _____ _____ _____ in autumn.

3 그 프로젝트는 바다 아래로 터널을 건설하는 것이다. (the project, build)

→ _____ _____ _____ _____ _____ a tunnel under the sea.

4 우리는 캠핑카를 빌리는 것을 계획하고 있다. (plan, rent)

→ We are _____ _____ _____ a camping car.

A 문장의 밑줄 친 부분의 해석을 ( ) 안에 쓰시오.

1 He was the first person <u>to arrive</u>. (→   )

2 Brad is a great <u>roommate to live with</u>. (→   )

3 We are <u>glad to hear</u> that. (→   )

4 They were <u>excited to find</u> the fossils of mammoths. (→   )

5 You <u>are to leave</u> now. (→   )

6 There is no easy <u>way to succeed</u>. (→   )

7 This robot cleaner is <u>easy to use</u>. (→   )

B 두 문장을 to부정사를 이용하여 같은 의미를 갖는 한 문장으로 쓰시오.

1 I saw you again. I was happy.

→ I was happy _____.

2 You trust Paula. So you cannot be wise.

→ You cannot be wise _____.

3 The boy grew up. He became the president of the country.

→ The boy grew up _____.

4 She carries a membership card. She wants to get a discount.

→ She carries a membership card _____.

C [be동사 + to부정사]를 이용하여 두 문장이 같은 의미를 갖도록 빈칸을 채우시오.

1 You must wear a helmet when you ride a mountain bike.

→ _____ when you ride a mountain bike.

2 The volcano is going to erupt any minute.

→ _____ any minute.

3 No water can be found on the planet.

→ _____ on the planet.

4 If you intend to meet her, you need to wait here.

→ If _____ her, you need to wait here.

D 우리말과 의미가 같도록 ( ) 안의 말을 배열하시오.

1 그는 프리랜서 일을 하기 위해 그의 정규직 직업을 포기했어. (freelance work, do, to)

　→ He gave up his regular job ＿＿＿＿＿＿＿＿＿＿＿＿＿＿＿＿＿＿＿＿.

2 꽃은 곤충을 유인하기 위해 달콤한 향이 난다. (attract, in order to, insects)

　→ The flower smells sweet ＿＿＿＿＿＿＿＿＿＿＿＿＿＿＿＿＿＿＿＿.

3 사막에서 아무것도 들려질 수가 없었어. (be, to, heard, was)

　→ Nothing ＿＿＿＿＿＿＿＿＿＿＿＿＿＿＿＿＿＿＿ in the desert.

4 그 텐트는 들어가서 자기에 매우 안락해. (sleep in, very cozy, to)

　→ The tent is ＿＿＿＿＿＿＿＿＿＿＿＿＿＿＿＿＿.

5 그 소년은 놀이터에서 같이 놀 친구들을 만났어. (many friends, play with, to)

　→ The boy met ＿＿＿＿＿＿＿＿＿＿＿＿＿＿＿＿ on the playground.

6 여러분들은 인터뷰에서 개인적인 질문을 하시면 안 됩니다. (are, to ask, not, personal, questions)

　→ You ＿＿＿＿＿＿＿＿＿＿＿＿＿＿＿＿＿＿ at the interview.

E 우리말과 의미가 같도록 ( ) 안의 말을 이용하여 문장을 완성하시오.

1 지금이 알프스를 방문하기에 최적의 시간이다. (the best time, visit)

　→ Now is ＿＿＿＿ ＿＿＿＿ ＿＿＿＿ ＿＿＿＿ ＿＿＿＿ the Alps.

2 따뜻하고 건강한 상태로 있기 위해 그 곰은 먹이를 많이 먹었다. (a lot of, stay)

　→ The bear ate ＿＿＿＿ ＿＿＿＿ ＿＿＿＿ ＿＿＿＿ ＿＿＿＿

　＿＿＿＿ warm and healthy.

3 그의 목소리는 흉내내기가 매우 쉽다. (easy, imitate)

　→ His voice ＿＿＿＿ ＿＿＿＿ ＿＿＿＿ ＿＿＿＿ ＿＿＿＿.

4 나는 그 진실을 알고 있는 유일한 사람이지. (the only person, the truth)

　→ I am ＿＿＿＿ ＿＿＿＿ ＿＿＿＿ ＿＿＿＿ ＿＿＿＿ ＿＿＿＿

　＿＿＿＿.

5 상담원과 통화를 하시려면 0번을 누르세요. (be, talk with)

　→ If you ＿＿＿＿ ＿＿＿＿ ＿＿＿＿ ＿＿＿＿ our counselor, please press 0.

6 그 학교는 매년 소방 훈련을 실시할 예정이야. (be, hold, a fire drill)

　→ The school ＿＿＿＿ ＿＿＿＿ ＿＿＿＿ ＿＿＿＿ ＿＿＿＿

　every year.

A ( ) 안에서 알맞은 것을 고르시오.

1 I want you not (to make, made) the same mistake.

2 She advised me (accepting, to accept) his apology.

3 He never lets his children (to eat, eat) any instant food.

4 The tall basketball player made others (to look, look) small.

5 His neighbors asked him (babysitting, to babysit) their baby for an hour.

6 Did you hear your dog (to sing, sing)?

7 I had him (taking, take) a cooking class.

B ( ) 안의 말을 알맞게 고쳐 빈칸을 채우시오.

1 He felt the ground _____ as the train passed by. (shake)

2 I didn't expect him _____ his homework. (complete)

3 I will let you know _____ the bus. (where, get off)

4 The teacher ordered us _____ to each other. (not, talk)

5 The professor advised him _____ out of college. (not, drop)

6 He was shocked to watch the accident _____. (happen)

7 She got her sister _____ home early. (come)

C 보기에서 알맞은 말을 골라 알맞은 형태로 고쳐 문장을 완성하시오.

보기	brush	do	keep	paint

1 Brian helped me _____ the house.

2 The dentist advised me _____ my teeth carefully.

3 We expect you _____ it a secret.

4 Mom made me _____ the dishes.

보기	drive	stop	listen to	wash

5 She never lets me _____ her car.

6 I saw him _____ his sneakers.

7 The general ordered his soldiers _____ firing.

8 My uncle advised me _____ others first.

D 우리말과 의미가 같도록 ( ) 안의 말을 배열하시오.

1 어떤 아이들에게도 부모 중에서 고르라고 요청하면 안 된다. (any child, ask, to, choose)

→ Don't _____ between parents.

2 나는 내 여동생이 잠꼬대 하는 것을 들었다. (heard, talking, my sister)

→ I _____ in her sleep.

3 그는 Betty에게 그녀의 결정에 대해 다시 생각하도록 시켰다. (had, think again, Betty)

→ He _____ about her decision.

4 그는 우리에게 약속을 깨지 말라고 말했다. (told, not, us, to, our promise, break)

→ He _____.

5 너는 내가 사실을 말하기를 원하니? (want, the truth, me, to tell)

→ Do you _____?

6 잠자는 개가 누워 있도록 내버려 둬. (the sleeping dog, let, lie)

→ _____.

E 우리말과 의미가 같도록 ( ) 안의 말을 이용하여 문장을 완성하시오.

1 많은 사람들이 소방관이 불을 끄는 것을 도왔다. (help, put out)

→ Many people _____ _____ _____ _____ _____ the fire.

2 Mike는 땀이 그의 등에 흐르는 것을 느꼈다. (sweat, felt, run)

→ Mike _____ _____ _____ down his back.

3 우리는 누군가가 해변을 따라 걷고 있는 것을 보았다. (see, walk along)

→ We _____ _____ _____ _____ the beach.

4 선생님은 우리에게 자신을 따라서 말하도록 시키셨다. (make, repeat after)

→ The teacher _____ _____ _____ _____ him.

5 그녀는 그에게 뒷좌석에 앉으라고 말했다. (tell, get in)

→ She _____ _____ _____ _____ _____ the backseat.

6 은행은 사람들에게 돈을 빌리도록 권장한다. (encourage, borrow)

→ Banks _____ _____ _____ _____ _____.

7 엄마는 내가 아침식사를 거르는 것을 허락하지 않으셔. (allow, skip)

→ My mom doesn't _____ _____ _____ _____.

A ( ) 안에서 알맞은 것을 고르시오.

1 How kind (of, for) you to listen to my problem.

2 There is no chance (for she, for her) to forgive him.

3 She didn't want (to be disturbed, to disturb) by anyone.

4 Your dog seems (likes, to like) the cat.

5 It is not possible (of him, for him) to cancel his trip.

6 It is dangerous (for you, of you) to touch any wild plants.

7 Clara seems (to have visited, to visit) the city before.

8 Do you like (to call, to be called) by your nickname?

B 밑줄 친 부분 중 어법상 틀린 것은 바르게 고쳐 쓰시오. (맞으면 'O' 표시)

1 It was not easy of the reporter to interview shy people.   (→   )

2 It was brave of her to take the risk.   (→   )

3 Wasn't it difficult you to learn Chinese?   (→   )

4 The bed was too hard for he to sleep on.   (→   )

5 He designed a bridge to be build next year.   (→   )

6 The brothers were lucky to find the treasure last year.   (→   )

C 두 문장이 같은 의미를 갖도록 빈칸을 채우시오.

1 It seems that my brother likes Linda.

→ My brother _____ Linda.

2 It seems that my teacher enjoys teaching.

→ My teacher _____ teaching.

3 It seems that Tom is very good at numbers.

→ Tom _____ numbers.

4 It seems that I heard about the scientist.

→ I _____.

5 It seems that he was a baseball player in his youth.

→ He _____ in his youth.

D 우리말과 의미가 같도록 ( ) 안의 말을 배열하시오.

1 내가 문을 열어 둔 것은 부주의했었어. (careless, to leave, me, of)

→ It was _____ the door open.

2 이 박스는 포장이 되어져야 한다. (be, needs, wrapped, to)

→ This box _____.

3 그는 그의 직업을 즐기는 것처럼 보여. (enjoy, to, seems, his job)

→ He _____.

4 그가 잠비아의 두 소년을 후원하는 것은 관대한 것이었다. (of, generous, to, him, sponsor)

→ It was _____ two children from Zambia.

5 너는 그 상을 두 번 받은 유일한 선수다. (the prize, to have won, player, the only)

→ You are _____ twice.

6 그 구멍은 운석에 의해 만들어진 것으로 보인다. (seems, created, to have been)

→ This hole _____ by a meteor.

E 우리말과 의미가 같도록 ( ) 안의 말을 이용하여 문장을 완성하시오.

1 그가 내 수프를 데워 준 것은 사려 깊었어. (thoughtful, warm up)

→ It was _____ _____ _____ _____ _____ _____ my soup.

2 내가 동시에 두 가지 일을 하는 것은 어려웠어. (hard, do, two things)

→ It was _____ _____ _____ _____ _____ _____

_____ at the same time.

3 그는 할 일이 너무 많은 것으로 보여. (seem, have)

→ He _____ _____ _____ too much work to do.

4 너의 자전거를 고장 냈던 것 미안해. (sorry, break)

→ I am _____ _____ _____ _____ your bike.

5 그 여배우는 데뷔 이래로 많이 변해 온 것 같아. (seem, change)

→ The actress _____ _____ _____ _____ a lot since her debut.

6 내가 노력해도 소용이 없었다. (useless, try)

→ It was _____ _____ _____ _____ _____.

7 그는 Jessica에게 초대를 받게 되어서 흥분했어. (thrilled, invite)

→ He was _____ _____ _____ _____ by Jessica.

A ( ) 안에서 알맞은 것을 고르시오.

1 (Begin, To begin) with, I would like to thank you for coming.

2 (To be sure, To sure), his idea will change the way we live.

3 She was (enough kind, kind enough) to give me a ride to school.

4 The truck was too big (parked, to park) in the garage.

5 It is never (late too, too late) to learn.

6 This game is (so, too) exciting that I can't stop playing it.

7 So (speak, to speak), the dog was part of his childhood.

8 (To tell, To be) the truth, I like Miranda.

B 두 문장이 같은 의미를 갖도록 빈칸을 채우시오.

1 It was so foggy that he couldn't drive this morning.

→ It was _____ _____ _____ _____ _____ _____ this morning.

2 The book was so popular that it became a bestseller.

→ The book was _____ _____ _____ _____ _____ _____.

3 The dog was so fat that it couldn't pass through the hole.

→ The dog was _____ _____ _____ _____ _____
_____ _____.

4 The city is so small that it can be toured in three hours.

→ The city is _____ _____ _____ _____ _____
_____ _____.

5 This cake is so beautiful that I can't eat it.

→ This cake is _____ _____ _____ _____ _____ _____.

6 This dress is so old fashioned that I can't wear it.

→ This dress is _____ _____ _____ for me _____ _____.

7 She was so smart that she could solve the quiz.

→ She was _____ _____ _____ _____ _____ _____.

C ( ) 안의 말과 [too ~ to] 또는 [enough to] 구문을 이용하여 문장을 완성하시오.

1 그 강아지는 내 손안에 알맞을 만큼 충분히 작았다. (small, fit)

→ The puppy was _____ _____ _____ _____ in my hand.

2 용의자는 알리바이를 갖고 있을 만큼 영리했다. (smart, have an alibi)

→ The suspect was _____ _____ _____ _____ _____ _____.

3 신발이 그가 착용하기에는 너무 작았다. (small, wear)

→ The shoes were _____ _____ _____ _____ _____.

4 어젯밤에 너의 코골이가 너무 시끄러워서 나를 깨울 정도였다. (loud, wake me up)

→ Your snoring was _____ _____ _____ _____ _____

_____ last night.

5 이 피자는 너무 커서 내가 혼자 다 먹을 수 없다. (big, for me, finish)

→ This pizza is _____ _____ _____ _____ _____ _____ by myself.

6 이 차는 여섯 명이 타기에는 너무 좁다. (small, ride in)

→ The car is _____ _____ _____ _____ _____ _____ _____.

D 우리말과 의미가 같도록 ( ) 안의 말을 배열하시오.

1 이상한 이야기이지만, 그 웃긴 노래가 큰 히트가 되었다. (to say, strange, became, the funny song)

→ _____, _____ a big hit.

2 바다가 매우 짜서 내가 물 위에 뜨게 한다. (enough, salty, to float, for me)

→ The sea is _____ on the water.

3 솔직히, 그는 내 타입이 아니야. (to be, he, is, frank with, you, not)

→ _____, _____ my type.

4 내 여동생은 영리하고, 귀여운 것은 말할 것도 없지. (to mention, not, cute, she, is)

→ My sister is smart. _____, _____.

5 포도가 수확되기에 충분히 익었다. (enough, ripe, to, be picked)

→ The grapes are _____.

6 설상가상으로, 비가 내리기 시작했다. (matters, to, make, worse, began, it)

→ _____, _____ to rain.

7 그 광고는 너무 단순해서 사람들 시선을 끌지 못했다. (simple, catch, too, to, the eyes)

→ The advertisement was _____ of people.

Error Correction

■ 밑줄 친 부분에 대한 설명을 체크하고 틀린 경우엔 바르게 고치시오. (맞으면 'O' 표시)

1	This app makes <u>this</u> easier to check the weather. (→)	주어 + 동사 + 가목적어 + 목적격보어 + 진목적어 (this, it) (to부정사, 동사)
2	We decided where <u>spend</u> our holiday. (→)	(어디서, 어떻게) ~할지를 where + (동사, to부정사)
3	I need a pencil <u>to write</u>. (→)	(쓸, 가지고 쓸) 연필이므로 명사 + to부정사 + 전치사 (없음, with)
4	We are <u>visit</u> Mexico next month. (→)	(예정, 운명)일 때 be동사 + (동사, to부정사)
5	My password was <u>easily</u> to remember. (→)	기억하기에 (쉽게, 쉬운) 의미이며 (부사, 형용사) + to부정사 어순
6	I want you <u>listen</u> to me carefully. (→)	주어 + want + 목적어 + 목적격보어 (원형부정사, to부정사)
7	His funny joke made her <u>to laugh</u>. (→)	주어 + 사역동사(make) + 목적어 + 목적격보어 (원형부정사, to부정사)
8	She watched the kittens <u>to play</u> with a ball. (→)	주어 + 지각동사(watch) + 목적어 + 목적격보어 (원형부정사, to부정사)
9	It was kind <u>of him</u> to help the old woman. (→)	성품형용사가 (있으면, 없으면) 의미상 주어는 (of, for) + 목적격
10	He seems <u>to knew</u> the answer now. (→)	to부정사 시제가 주절과 같을 때 to + (동사원형, have p.p.)
11	He seems <u>have known</u> the answer before. (→)	to부정사 시제가 주절보다 앞설 때 to + (동사원형, have p.p.)
12	He was <u>enough lucky</u> to marry a woman like you. (→)	(~하기 충분한, 너무 ~한) 의미일 때 (enough + 형용사, 형용사 + enough) + to부정사
13	The program was <u>violent too</u> for him to watch. (→)	(~하기 충분한, 너무 ~해서) 의미일 때 (too + 형용사, 형용사 + too) + to부정사

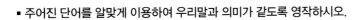
■ 주어진 단어를 알맞게 이용하여 우리말과 의미가 같도록 영작하시오.

1	app, it, check	이 앱은 / 만든다 / 이것을 / 더 쉬운 상태로 / 날씨를 확인하는 것을 →
2	spend one's holiday	우리는 결정했다 / 어디에서 보낼지를 / 우리의 휴가를 →
3	write	나는 필요하다 / 연필을 / 가지고 쓸 →
4	Mexico	우리는 / 방문할 예정이다 / 멕시코를 / 다음달에 →
5	password, remember	내 비밀번호는 / 쉬웠다 / 기억하기에 →
6	listen to, carefully	나는 / 원한다 / 네가 / 내 말을 듣기를 / 주의깊게 →
7	joke, laugh	그의 재미있는 농담은 / 만들었다 / 그녀가 / 웃도록 →
8	watch, the kittens	그녀는 / 보았다 / 새끼 고양이들이 / 노는 것을 / 공을 가지고 →
9	it, the old woman	친절했다 / 그가 도왔던 것은 / 할머니를 →
10	seems to	그는 / 알고 있는 것처럼 보인다 / 답을 →
11	seems to	그는 / 알고 있었던 것처럼 보인다 / 답을 →
12	marry a woman	그는 / 충분히 운이 좋았다 / ~와 결혼할 만큼 / 당신 같은 여성 →
13	violent	그 프로그램은 / 너무 폭력적이었다 / 그가 시청하기에 →

문법패턴 빈칸 채우기

GP 24 동명사의 명사적 쓰임

문장에서 명사처럼 주어, 목적어, 보어 역할을 한다.

　Using solar energy is good for the Earth. (＿＿＿＿＿＿)

　We *enjoyed* **watching** the stars at night. (동사의 ＿＿＿＿＿)

　She is good *at* **telling** stories. (전치사의 ＿＿＿＿＿)

　Her hobby is **taking pictures of** animals. (＿＿＿＿＿)

> ∘ Tip ∘
> 동명사의 부정은 동명사 ＿＿＿에 ＿＿＿＿이나 ＿＿＿＿를 쓴다.
> **Not** having a dream is sad.

GP 25 동명사의 의미상 주어

동명사의 행위자를 ＿＿＿＿＿＿라고 한다. 동명사의 행위자와 문장의 주어가 다를 경우 동명사 앞에 ＿＿＿＿＿＿이나 ＿＿＿＿＿을 써서 행위의 주체를 나타낸다.

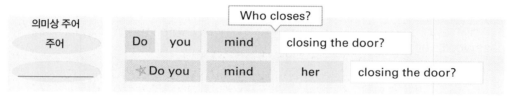

I am sure of **his (him)** winning the contest.

GP 26 동명사의 시제

❶ 단순 동명사: [＿＿＿＿＿＿＿＿] 형태로 동명사의 시제가 주절의 시제와 ＿＿＿＿＿는 것을 나타낸다.

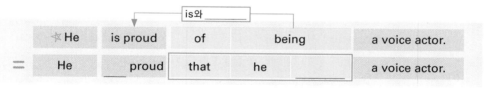

❷ 완료 동명사: [＿＿＿＿＿＿＿＿] 형태로 동명사의 시제가 주절의 시제보다 ＿＿＿＿＿는 것을 나타낸다.

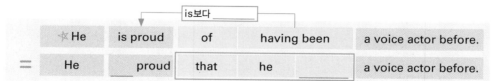

● Upgrade ●

동명사의 수동태

단순 수동태		수동태 의미의 동명사가 주절 시제와 ＿＿＿＿ 때
완료 수동태		수동태 의미의 동명사가 주절 시제보다 ＿＿＿ 때

I hate ＿＿＿＿＿＿＿＿ like a child.　(＝ I **hate** that I **am treated** like a child.)

I hate ＿＿＿＿＿＿＿＿ like a child.　(＝ I **hate** that I **was treated** like a child.)

주어	동사	목적어
_____만 _____로 취하는 동사	_____, _____, _____, _____, quit, deny, admit, suggest...	_____
_____만 _____로 취하는 동사	_____, _____, _____, _____, promise, refuse...	_____
	의미 차이 ___ 경우	S	_____, love, _____, _____, start, _____...	동명사 / to부정사
_____와 _____를 ___ 목적어로 취하는 동사			_____ / _____	동명사 _____ / to부정사 _____
	의미 차이 ___ 경우		_____	동명사 _____후회하다 / to부정사 _____유감이다
			_____	동명사 _____ / to부정사 _____

❶ 동명사만 목적어로 취하는 동사

Did you *finish* **decorating** the Christmas tree?

I *suggested* **taking** a taxi as it was getting dark.

❷ to부정사만 목적어로 취하는 동사

Judy finally *agreed* **to accept** his offer.

She *refused* **to touch** my pet snake.

❸ 동명사와 부정사를 모두 목적어로 취하는 동사

(1) 의미 차이가 없는 동사

Evan *began* **playing (to play)** the guitar.

(2) 의미 차이가 있는 동사

He *forgot* **lending** me his umbrella. ((_____) ~한 것을 잊다)

He *forgot* **to lend** me his umbrella. ((_____) ~할 것을 잊다)

She *tried* **taking** pictures with her new phone. (시험 삼아 해 보다)

I *tried* **to solve** the math problem. (열심히 시도하다)

○ Tip ○

① stop + to부정사: _____ 멈추다

Tom stopped to talk to me.

② stop + 동명사: _____ 멈추다

Tom stopped talking to me.

feel like -ing	_____	spend 시간 / 돈 (in) -ing	_____
look forward to -ing	_____	have difficulty (in) -ing	_____
be worth -ing	_____	be / get used to -ing	_____
It's no use -ing	_____	cannot help -ing	_____

I *have difficulty* **making** decisions.

A ( ) 안에서 알맞은 것을 고르시오.

1 (Studying, Study) the stars is one of my favorite hobbies.

2 He punished (her, she) for having told a lie.

3 Do you mind my (take, taking) a bite of your instant noodles?

4 She is proud of (is, being) the mother of five children.

5 My brother wore my sneakers without (asking, to ask) me.

6 Forgive me for (not remembering, don't remembering) your name.

7 Don't be ashamed of (having been, being) poor before.

8 You can enjoy (picking, being picked) strawberries at my farm.

B 두 문장이 같은 의미를 갖도록 빈칸을 채우시오.

1 Do you mind if you take a picture of me?

→ Do you mind _____ of me?

2 Do you mind if I take a picture of you?

→ Do you mind _____ of you?

3 He was proud that he became the school president.

→ He was proud of _____.

4 He was proud that she became the school president.

→ He was proud of _____.

5 She feels sorry that she is late for the meeting.

→ She feels sorry for _____.

6 She feels sorry that she was late for the meeting.

→ She feels sorry for _____.

7 He denies that he is interested in Emily.

→ He denies _____ Emily.

8 He denies that he was interested in Emily.

→ He denies _____ Emily.

C ( ) 안의 말을 알맞게 고쳐 빈칸을 채우시오.

1 The fish was not afraid of _____ by people. (touch)

2 I insist on _____ being innocent. (he)

3 We are sure of _____ the election next time. (win)

4 He suggested her _____ the leader of our club. (become)

5 I am sorry for _____ having hurt your feeling. (she)

D 우리말과 의미가 같도록 ( ) 안의 말을 배열하시오.

1 그에게는 돈을 버는 것이 돈을 지키는 것보다 쉽다. (money, making, easier, is)

→ For him, _____ than keeping it.

2 그 유명인은 잊혀지는 것이 두려웠다. (being, was afraid of, by people, forgotten)

→ The celebrity _____.

3 우리는 날아다니는 차를 타는 것을 상상할 수 있다. (a flying car, riding, imagine, in)

→ We can _____.

4 그는 내게 거짓말을 했던 것을 사과했다. (lied, apologized for, having)

→ He _____ to me.

5 아이들은 누군가가 그들에게 어떤 것도 가르치지 않아도 배울 수 있다. (anyone, teaching, them)

→ Children can learn without _____ anything.

E 우리말과 의미가 같도록 ( ) 안의 말을 이용하여 문장을 완성하시오.

1 그 운전사는 빨간불에 멈추지 않았던 것을 인정했다. (not, stop)

→ The driver admitted _____ _____ _____ at the red light.

2 집에 머무는 대신에 캠핑 가자. (instead of, stay)

→ Let's go camping _____ _____ _____ _____.

3 당신은 요리하는 것과 먹는 것 중에 무엇을 잘하십니까? (or)

→ Are you better at _____ _____ _____?

4 일찍 일어나는 것의 장점이 무엇인가요? (the advantage of, get up)

→ What is _____ _____ _____ _____ _____?

5 불을 줄이고 이것을 5분 동안 계속 휘저으세요. (keep, stir)

→ Lower the heat and _____ _____ _____ _____

_____.

A ( ) 안에서 알맞은 것을 고르시오.

1 The ancient Romans loved (to eat, eating) peacocks.

2 The two countries agreed to stop (to fight, fighting).

3 How about (be, being) honest with me?

4 She tried really hard (helping, to help) you out this time.

5 Don't forget (to bring, bringing) your student ID card the next time.

6 The boy had trouble (to open, opening) the bottle.

7 The model practiced (to pose, posing) in front of a mirror.

8 Do you remember (riding, to ride) the pony when you were young?

9 The club members agreed (holding, to hold) a meeting.

10 He couldn't help (crying, to cry) at the sad thought.

B ( ) 안의 말을 알맞게 고쳐 빈칸을 채우시오.

1 I am planning _____ my fashion style. (change)

2 He tried _____ nicknames for his classmates for fun. (make)

3 He didn't feel like _____ at that moment. (talk)

4 Why do you hate _____ online? (shop)

5 He couldn't help _____ of her. (think)

6 She is getting used to _____ glasses. (wear)

7 We didn't expect _____ this time. (win)

8 Don't forget _____ hello to your mom for me. (say)

9 Please stop _____ me the same questions. (ask)

10 The dog keeps _____ its tail when it is happy. (wag)

C 두 문장이 같은 의미를 갖도록 빈칸을 채우시오.

1 She remembers that she should turn off the printer.

→ She _____ the printer.

2 Do you remember that you told me the secret?

→ Do you _____ ?

3 Don't forget that you should return the book to me.

→ Don't _____ to me.

4 I regret that I ate a heavy dinner tonight.

→ I _____ tonight.

D 우리말과 의미가 같도록 ( ) 안의 말을 배열하시오.

1 잠이 안 올 때는 양을 세 보는 것이 어때? (try, sheep, counting, why don't you)

→ _____ when you can't fall asleep?

2 엄마는 동물보호소에서 개를 입양하는 것을 제안하셨다. (adopting, a, suggested, dog)

→ My mom _____ from the animal shelter.

3 그는 피자를 주문한 것을 잊어버리고 저녁 외식을 나갔다. (forgot, pizza, ordering)

→ He _____ and went out for dinner.

4 나는 지금 그 문제를 논의하고 싶은 기분이 아니다. (feel like, the issue, discussing)

→ I don't _____ now.

E 우리말과 의미가 같도록 ( ) 안의 말을 이용하여 문장을 완성하시오.

1 그 운전사는 타이어를 체크하기 위해서 멈춰 섰다. (stop, check)

→ The driver _____ _____ _____ _____ _____ .

2 그 영화는 다시 볼 가치가 있다. (be worth, watch)

→ The movie _____ _____ _____ _____ .

3 그는 그때 그 귀여운 인형을 구입하지 않았던 것을 후회한다. (regret, buy)

→ He _____ _____ _____ _____ _____ then.

4 우리 할머니는 사람들의 말을 잘 못 들으신다. (difficulty, hear)

→ My grandma _____ _____ _____ people.

■ 밑줄 친 부분에 대한 설명을 체크하고 틀린 경우엔 바르게 고치시오. (맞으면 'O' 표시)

* 가능한 답은 모두 체크

1	<u>Use</u> solar energy is good for the Earth. (→)	주어 + 동사 + 주격보어 (동사, 동명사)
2	We enjoyed <u>to watch</u> the stars at night. (→)	주어 + enjoy + 목적어 (to부정사, 동명사)
3	She is good at <u>tell</u> stories. (→)	주어 + 동사 + 전치사 + 목적어 (to부정사, 동명사)
4	Do you mind <u>she</u> closing the door? (→)	동명사 closing의 행위 주체는 (주격, 소유격, 목적격) 형태
5	He is proud of <u>be</u> a voice actor now. (→)	동명사 시제가 주절과 같을 때 (동사원형 + -ing, having p.p.)
6	He is proud of <u>be</u> a voice actor before. (→)	동명사 시제가 주절보다 앞설 때 (동사원형 + -ing, having p.p.)
7	Did you finish <u>to decorate</u> the Christmas tree? (→)	주어 + finish + 목적어 (to부정사, 동명사)
8	Judy finally agreed <u>accepting</u> his offer. (→)	주어 + agree + 목적어 (to부정사, 동명사)
9	Evan began <u>play</u> the guitar. (→)	주어 + begin + 목적어 (to부정사, 동명사)
10	He forgot <u>lending</u> me his umbrella. (→)	'~했던 것을 잊다' 의미일 때 forget + (to부정사, 동명사)
11	He forgot <u>lend</u> me his umbrella. (→)	'~할 것을 잊다' 의미일 때 forget + (to부정사, 동명사)
12	Tom stopped <u>talking</u> to me. (→)	'~하던 것을 멈추다' 의미일 때 stop + (to부정사, 동명사)
13	I have difficulty <u>to make</u> decisions. (→)	'~하는 데 어려움이 있다' 의미일 때 have difficulty + (to부정사, 동명사)

Sentence writing

▪ 주어진 단어를 알맞게 이용하여 우리말과 의미가 같도록 영작하시오.

1	use solar energy	태양열을 이용하는 것은 / 지구에 좋다 →
2	watch the stars	우리는 즐겼다 / 별을 보는 것을 / 밤에 →
3	be good at, tell stories	그녀는 잘한다 / 이야기하는 것을 →
4	mind, close	당신은 꺼려하시나요 / 그녀가 닫는 것을 / 문을? →
5	proud, a voice actor	그는 자랑스러워 한다 / ~인 것을 / 성우 →
6	proud, a voice actor	그는 자랑스러워 한다 / ~이었던 것을 / 성우 →
7	finish, decorate	너는 끝냈니 / 장식하는 것을 / 크리스마스트리를? →
8	accept one's offer	Judy는 / 마침내 동의했다 / 받아들이는 것을 / 그의 제안을 →
9	begin	Evan은 / 시작했다 / 연주하는 것을 / 기타를 →
10	lend me	그는 잊었다 / 빌려주었던 것을 / 내게 / 그의 우산을 →
11	lend me	그는 잊었다 / 빌려줄 것을 / 내게 / 그의 우산을 →
12	talk to	Tom은 멈췄다 / 말하던 것을 / 내게 →
13	difficulty, make decisions	나는 ~하는 데 어려움이 있다 / 결정하는 것을 →

문법패턴 빈칸 채우기

GP 29 현재분사와 과거분사

분사는 [동사원형 + -ing] 형태의 현재분사와 [동사원형 + -ed] 형태의 과거분사가 있다. 현재분사는 _____, _____의 의미를 갖고 과거분사는 _____, _____의 의미를 갖는다.

종류	형태	의미	
현재분사	_____	_____ : ~하고 있는	falling leaves
		_____ : ~하는, 하게 하는	satisfying score
과거분사	_____	_____ : ~된	fallen leaves
		_____ : ~되는, ~당하는	satisfied people

GP 30 분사의 형용사적 쓰임

❶ _____ : 명사 앞이나 뒤에서 명사를 수식한다. 보통 _____와 함께 쓰이면 _____에서 수식한다.

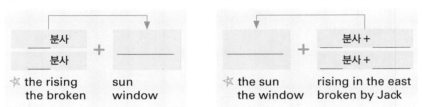

⭐ the rising   sun   ⭐ the sun   rising in the east
the broken   window   the window   broken by Jack

The **growing** desert may cause more dust storms.
He gave me a box **filled** with candy.

❷ _____ : 주어나 목적어의 상태를 보충 설명한다.

_____	동사		_____	
He	sat		dozing.	
We	got		excited.	

주어	동사	_____	_____	
I	heard	a bird	singing.	
She	left	the door	locked.	

He got **injured** in the accident.
I found the movie **boring**.

─○ Tip ○─

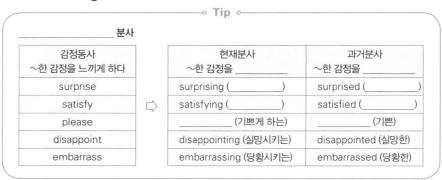

_____ 분사		
감정동사 ~한 감정을 느끼게 하다	현재분사 ~한 감정을 _____	과거분사 ~한 감정을 _____
surprise	surprising (_____)	surprised (_____)
satisfy	satisfying (_____)	satisfied (_____)
please	_____ (기쁘게 하는)	_____ (기쁜)
disappoint	disappointing (실망시키는)	disappointed (실망한)
embarrass	embarrassing (당황시키는)	embarrassed (당황한)

동사의 종류에 따라 목적격보어로 분사가 쓰이는데 목적어와 목적격보어의 관계가 능동이면 _____를, 수동이면 _____를 쓴다.

주어	동사	목적어	목적격보어	
	keep / find / leave	the girl	waiting.	_____ 관계
		his eyes	closed.	_____ 관계
S	see (지각동사)	the man	painting.	_____ 관계
		the house	painted.	_____ 관계
	have / get	his computer	fixed.	_____ 관계

❶ keep / find / leave + _____ + _____ (_____) 계속하게 하다 / 발견하다 / 내버려 두다

　He *kept the girl* waiting.
　They *found a six year-old boy* living in the mountains.
　He never *leaves his baby* crying.

❷ keep / find / leave + _____ + _____ (_____) 계속하게 하다 / 발견하다 / 내버려 두다

　He *kept his eyes* closed.
　He *found the library* closed.
　He *left his food* untouched.

❸ 지각동사 + _____ + _____ : (_____) 보다 / 듣다 / 느끼다

　He *saw the man* painting his house.
　She *heard the train* coming from a distance.

❹ 지각동사 + _____ + _____ : (_____) 보다 / 듣다 / 느끼다

　He *saw his house* painted.
　He *felt* his *shoulder* touched by someone.

❺ have / get + _____ + _____ : (_____) 하다

　He *had his computer* fixed.
　The girls *got their picture* taken together.

분사구문은 [접속사 + 주어 + 동사]로 이루어진 부사절을 [동사원형 + -ing]의 부사구로 줄여 쓴 것을 말하고 문맥에 따라 시간, 이유, 양보, 조건 등의 의미를 가진다.

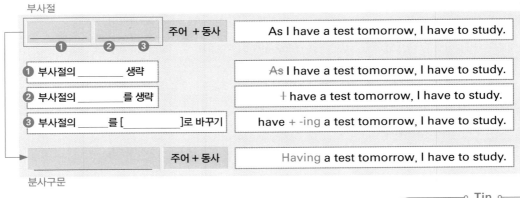

① 시간: ~할 때, ~하는 동안, ~하기 전에

_____ me, she shouted with joy.

→ _____ me, she shouted with joy.

② 이유: ~때문에

_____ how to say sorry, the boy just cried.

→ _____ how to say sorry, the boy just cried.

③ 양보: ~일지라도

_____ near the school, he is always late for school.

→ (_____) _____ near the school, he is always late for school.

④ 조건: 만약 ~한다면

_____ this bus, you will get to the airport.

→ _____ this bus, you will get to the airport.

⑤ 동시동작: ~하면서

_____ to his fans, he disappeared from the stage.

→ _____ to his fans, the singer disappeared from the stage.

> **○ Tip ○**
> 분사구문의 부정
> 분사구문 _____에 _____이나
> _____를 쓴다.
> **Not having** time, he took a taxi.

> **○ Tip ○**
> 의미를 명확하게 전달하기 위해 접속사를 생략하지 않을 수 있다.

• **Upgrade** •

숙어처럼 쓰이는 분사구문

generally speaking		judging from	
frankly speaking		considering (that)	
strictly speaking	엄격히 말해서	compared with	~와 비교해 보면

Frankly speaking, I don't understand his explanation.

Judging from his looks, he must be in his twenties.

GP 33 완료형 분사구문

부사절의 시제가 주절의 시제보다 _____ 경우에 쓴다.

부사절		주절	
접속사	주어 + ◯	주어 + ◯	As I saw her before, I know her face.

시제가 ____ 경우

| | 주어 + 동사 | ☆ Having seen her before, I know her face. |

GP 34 수동 분사구문

[_____ + _____] 형태이며 being과 having been은 생략할 수 있다.

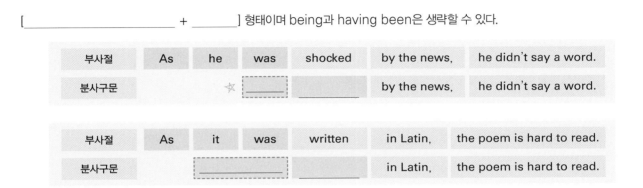

부사절	As	he	was	shocked	by the news,	he didn't say a word.
분사구문	☆	_____	_____		by the news,	he didn't say a word.

부사절	As	it	was	written	in Latin,	the poem is hard to read.
분사구문	_____				in Latin,	the poem is hard to read.

(Being) Kept in the aquarium, the dolphin gets stressed a lot.
(Having been) Built 30 years ago, the house is still in good condition.

GP 35 주어가 있는 분사구문

부사절의 주어와 주절의 주어가 다를 경우 부사절의 주어를 생략하지 않고 분사구문 앞에 쓴다.

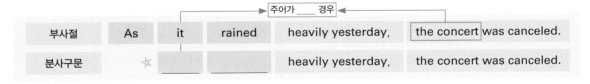

주어가 ____ 경우

부사절	As	it	rained	heavily yesterday,	the concert was canceled.
분사구문	☆	_____	_____	heavily yesterday,	the concert was canceled.

School being over, they played baseball on the field.

GP 36 with + 명사 + 분사

[with + 명사 + 분사] 구문은 '_____'의 의미로 동시동작을 나타낸다.

주어 + 동사 ~	with	_____	_____	
☆ He was sleeping	_____	the alarm	ringing.	관계
☆ A pigeon flew to me	_____	a message	tied to its leg.	관계

A ( ) 안에서 알맞은 것을 고르시오.

1 The chef sprinkled some (slicing, sliced) onions on the pizza.

2 Look at the (talking, talked) bird in the cage.

3 Ice and snow are just (freezing, frozen) water.

4 We couldn't open the (locking, locked) door.

5 Did you hear anyone (knocking, knocked) on the door last night?

6 You have an (amazing, amazed) talent at painting.

7 Don't sit on the (breaking, broken) chair.

B 주어진 말을 어법상 알맞게 고쳐 문장을 완성하시오.

감정 유발 동사	⇨	감정을 나타내는 분사

1 disappoint   The test results are _____ to Tom.

Tom is _____ with the test results.

2 surprise   My success was _____ to my friends.

My friends were _____ at my success.

3 amaze   The sci-fi movie was _____.

We were _____ by the sci-fi movie.

4 frighten   The earthquake is a _____ disaster.

We were _____ by the earthquake.

5 interest   The new game is _____ to him.

He is _____ in the new game.

C ( ) 안의 말을 알맞게 고쳐 빈칸을 채우시오.

1 He is planning to buy a _____ computer. (use)

2 There was no trash _____ behind on the street. (leave)

3 Who is the girl _____ for you? (wait)

4 My dad cooked _____ rice for dinner. (fry)

5 The newly _____ couple love each other. (marry)

6 We watched the parade cars _____. (pass by)

7 They ran away from the _____ hurricane. (oncome)

D 주어진 두 문장을 현재분사나 과거분사를 이용하여 한 문장으로 쓰시오.

1 Olivia has an uncle. He is living in Canada.

→ Olivia has an uncle _____.

2 He ran after the balloon. It was flying up into the sky.

→ The boy ran after the balloon _____.

3 The girl is my niece. She is riding a scooter.

→ The girl _____ is my niece.

4 The sweater is very warm. It was knitted by my mom.

→ The sweater _____ is very warm.

E 우리말과 의미가 같도록 ( ) 안의 말을 배열하시오.

1 나는 깃털로 채워진 베개를 사지 않을 거야. (filled with, the pillows, feathers)

→ I won't buy _____.

2 그 연설자는 무대 위에서 당황해 했다. (felt, the speaker, embarrassed)

→ _____ on the stage.

3 Sanders 씨, 당신에게 남겨진 두 개의 메시지가 있습니다. (left, two messages, you, for)

→ Mr. Sanders, we have _____.

4 다른 새의 둥지에 알을 낳고 있는 저 새는 뻐꾸기이다. (its eggs, laying, the other bird's, in, nest)

→ The bird _____ is the cuckoo.

F 우리말과 의미가 같도록 ( ) 안의 말을 이용하여 문장을 완성하시오.

1 그는 덫에 걸린 사슴을 구해 주었다. (catch, in, a trap)

→ He saved the deer _____ _____ _____ _____.

2 에스키모들은 그들의 음식을 얼렸다. (get, freeze)

→ The Eskimos _____ _____ _____.

3 나는 천둥소리에 깜짝 놀랐다. (surprise, at, sound)

→ I was _____ _____ _____ _____ of the thunder.

4 벽에 걸린 저 그림을 봐. (hang, on, the wall)

→ Look at the picture _____ _____ _____ _____.

Unit 16 목적격보어로 쓰이는 분사

A 다음 문장에서 목적보어의 쓰임을 체크하시오.

	주어 + 동사	목적어	목적격보어	목적어와 목적격보어 관계
1	I will never keep	you	waiting again.	(~하고 있는, ~된)
2	The boy watched	the plane	taking off.	(~하고 있는, ~된)
3	You will see	the roses	blooming soon.	(~하고 있는, ~된)
4	Look at	the butterfly	flying.	(~하고 있는, ~된)
5	I saw	Jessica	fixing her car.	(~하고 있는, ~된)
6	We left	the box	unopened.	(~하고 있는, ~된)
7	Emily had	her hair	cut.	(~하고 있는, ~된)
8	He found	his shoes	stolen.	(~하고 있는, ~된)
9	We got	the room	cleaned.	(~하고 있는, ~된)
10	The news made	me	excited.	(~하고 있는, ~된)

B 우리말과 의미가 같도록 ( ) 안의 단어를 이용하여 문장을 완성하시오.

1 과학자들은 빙하가 빠르게 녹고 있는 것을 알게 되었다. (melt)

→ The scientists found the iceberg _____ fast.

2 그는 파마가 다른 스타일로 되어지도록 했다. (do)

→ He had a perm _____ in a different style.

3 그녀는 흰머리를 뽑았다. (pull out)

→ She had her gray hair _____.

4 너는 너의 눈이 검사되도록 해야 한다. (check)

→ You should have your eyes _____.

5 그녀는 누군가 창문을 노크하고 있는 것을 들었다. (knock)

→ She heard someone _____ on the window.

6 그는 양파수프가 타고 있는 냄새를 맡았다. (burn)

→ He smelled the onion soup _____.

7 Jake는 과학 수업이 흥미롭다는 것을 알게 되었다. (interest)

→ Jake found the science class _____.

C ( ) 안의 말을 알맞게 고쳐 빈칸을 채우시오.

1 The sport star had his picture _____ with his fans. (take)

2 The audience found his concert _____. (bore)

3 I want to have milk _____ again. (deliver)

4 Keep the water _____ and put in some pasta. (boil)

5 She heard her brother _____ the guitar. (play)

D 우리말과 의미가 같도록 ( ) 안의 말을 배열하시오.

1 내가 그를 보았을 때, 나는 내 심장이 빨리 뛰는 것을 느꼈다. (beating, my heart)

→ When I saw him, I felt _____ rapidly.

2 그 락가수는 그의 귀에 피어싱을 했다. (got, pierced, his ears)

→ The rock singer _____.

3 그 신사는 그의 신발이 닦여지도록 하였다. (polished, his shoes)

→ The gentleman got _____.

4 그녀는 그녀의 아이들이 숨바꼭질 하는 것을 보았다. (playing, her kids)

→ She watched _____ hide-and-seek.

5 그 작가는 그녀의 소설이 영화로 만들어지도록 하였다. (her, made, novel)

→ The writer had _____ into a movie.

E 우리말과 의미가 같도록 ( ) 안의 말을 이용하여 문장을 완성하시오.

1 너희는 조별 과제 다 했니? (do, your group project)

→ Did you get _____ _____ _____ _____?

2 그녀는 밤에 문이 잠겨지도록 했다. (lock, the door)

→ She had _____ _____ _____ at night.

3 그 영화음악은 그 영화를 신나게 만들었다. (excite, the movie)

→ The film music made _____ _____ _____.

4 우리는 Jason이 홈런을 치는 것을 보았다. (hit, Jason)

→ We watched _____ _____ a homerun.

5 그는 그의 개가 오리들을 쫓아 뛰는 것을 보았다. (run after, his dog)

→ He watched _____ _____ _____ _____ the ducks.

A 문장의 밑줄 친 부분을 분사구문으로 바꿔 쓰시오.

1 <u>As she felt cold</u>, she turned on the heater.

→ _____, she turned on the heater.

2 <u>When you make a decision</u>, you should think it over.

→ _____, you should think it over.

3 <u>While using my phone</u>, I dropped it by mistake.

→ _____, I dropped it by mistake.

4 <u>Because he didn't know English</u>, he couldn't read the warning.

→ _____, he couldn't read the warning.

5 <u>If you take notes</u>, you will understand the lesson better.

→ _____, you will understand the lesson better.

6 <u>Although he is almost 80 years old</u>, he still enjoys outdoor activities.

→ _____, he still enjoys outdoor activities.

B 밑줄 친 부분을 [접속사 + 주어 + 동사] 형태의 부사절로 바꿔 쓰시오. (접속사 한 번만 사용)

| 보기 | Although | Because | When |

1 <u>Loving animals</u>, Jennifer has five dogs.

→ _____, she has five dogs.

2 <u>Being a used TV</u>, it works very well.

→ _____, it works very well.

3 <u>Crossing the street</u>, the kids raised their right arms.

→ _____, they raised their right arms.

| 보기 | While | If | Because |

4 <u>Taking this shortcut</u>, you can arrive there faster.

→ _____, you can arrive there faster.

5 <u>Feeling hungry</u>, he ordered a second sandwich.

→ _____, he ordered a second sandwich.

6 <u>Eating lunch</u>, the campers thought about their dinner plans.

→ _____, they thought about their dinner plans.

C 우리말과 의미가 같도록 ( ) 안의 말을 배열하시오.

1 너는 충분한 과일을 먹기 때문에, 비타민을 복용할 필요 없다. (enough, eating, fruit)

→ _____, you don't have to take vitamins.

2 조심성이 없어서 그는 또 접시를 깼다. (being, careful, not)

→ _____, he broke a dish again.

3 태양이 구름 뒤에서 나오면서 밝게 빛났다. (from behind, coming out, the cloud)

→ _____, the sun shone brightly

4 관중들은 박수를 치고 환호하면서 일어났다. (and, clapping, cheering)

→ The audience stood up, _____.

5 "네"라고 말하면서, 그녀는 손가락으로 오케이 사인을 만들었다. (saying, "Yes")

→ _____ she made the okay sign with her fingers.

6 버스에 탄 후에 그는 빈 좌석을 발견했다. (the bus, getting, on)

→ _____, he found an empty seat.

D 우리말과 의미가 같도록 ( ) 안의 말을 이용하여 문장을 완성하시오.

1 상자를 연 후에, 그는 오래된 일기장을 발견했다. (open)

→ _____ _____ _____, he found an old diary.

2 그는 게으르기 때문에 일을 절대 완성하지 않는다. (be, lazy)

→ _____ _____, he never completes things.

3 새들은 가벼운 뼈를 갖고 있기 때문에 날 수가 있다. (have, bones)

→ _____ _____ _____, birds can fly.

4 집에 들어가자마자, Chris는 자신의 방으로 뛰어들어갔다. (enter)

→ _____ _____ _____, Chris rushed into his room.

5 창피함을 느껴서, 그의 얼굴은 빨갛게 변했다. (feel, embarrassed)

→ _____ _____, his face turned red.

6 실수를 하기를 원치 않아서, 그는 일정표를 다시 확인했다. (not, want, make mistakes)

→ _____ _____ _____ _____ _____, he checked the

schedule again.

A   ( ) 안에서 알맞은 것을 고르시오.

1 (Save, Saved) by the lifeguard, she was taken to the hospital.

2 (Gaining, Having gained) too much weight, I have to buy new clothes.

3 He was sitting on the chair with his arms (folding, folded).

4 (Decorate, Decorated) with flowers, the hall was very beautiful.

5 Strictly (spoken, speaking), his novel is not creative.

6 Generally (speaking, speak) Japanese food is beautiful.

7 (Asking, Asked) about the secret, he replied right away.

8 The weather (is, being) cold, the boys kept playing soccer.

B   문장의 밑줄 친 부사절을 분사구문으로 바꿔 쓰시오.

1 Although it was daytime, the street was empty.

→ _____ _____ _____, the street was empty.

2 Because he watched the movie, he knows the ending.

→ _____ _____ _____ _____, he knows the ending.

3 When the button was touched, the robot began to move.

→ _____ _____ _____ _____, the robot began to move.

4 Because I reserved a seat, I don't have to wait in line.

→ _____ _____ _____ _____, I don't have to wait in line.

5 Even though I slept enough, I am still sleepy.

→ _____ _____ _____, I am still sleepy.

6 Because the dog is loved by its owner, it always looks happy.

→ _____ _____ _____ _____, the dog always looks happy.

7 As his report was written in a hurry, it had many spelling errors.

→ _____ _____ _____ _____, his report had many spelling errors.

C 우리말과 의미가 같도록 [with + 명사 + 분사] 형태로 문장을 완성하시오.

1 새 한 마리가 다리 하나를 다친 채로 교실로 날아들었다. (its leg, hurt)

→ A bird flew into my classroom _____ _____ _____ _____.

2 그들은 해가 질 때 집으로 향했다. (the sun, set)

→ They started for home _____ _____ _____ _____.

3 그 소년은 눈을 감고 소원을 빌었다. (his eyes, close)

→ The boy made a wish _____ _____ _____ _____.

4 그 축구 선수는 관중들이 환호하는 상황에서 골을 넣었다. (spectators, cheer)

→ The soccer player scored a goal _____ _____ _____.

D 우리말과 의미가 같도록 ( ) 안의 말을 배열하시오.

1 나는 충분히 잤지만 여전히 졸리다. (slept, enough, having)

→ _____, I am still sleepy.

2 훈련을 받아 왔기 때문에, 우리는 그 기술에 매우 능숙해졌어. (been, trained, having)

→ _____, we became very skillful.

3 중국에서 교육을 받았기 때문에, 그녀는 중국 문화를 잘 알아. (having, educated, been)

→ _____ in China, she knows Chinese culture well.

4 긴 근무시간을 고려하면, 그의 수입은 적다. (his, considering, working hours, long)

→ _____, his income is small.

E 우리말과 의미가 같도록 ( ) 안의 말을 이용하여 문장을 완성하시오.

1 예전에 벌에 쏘였기 때문에, 나는 조심스럽다. (be, sting)

→ _____ _____ _____ by a bee before, I am cautious.

2 그녀의 기억을 잃어버렸기 때문에, 그녀는 과거를 기억 못한다. (lost, memory)

→ _____ _____ _____ _____, she doesn't remember her past.

3 일기예보를 확인하지 않았었기 때문에, 나는 우산이 없다. (not, check)

→ _____ _____ _____ the weather report, I don't have an umbrella.

4 내 고양이와 비교하면, 너의 개는 매우 살갑다. (compare to)

→ _____ _____ _____ _____, your dog is very friendly.

■ 밑줄 친 부분에 대한 설명을 체크하고 틀린 경우엔 바르게 고치시오. (맞으면 'O' 표시)

* V + -ing: 현재분사, p.p.:과거분사

1	Look at the <u>rise</u> sun. (→)	'떠오르고 있는'은 (진행, 수동) 의미이므로 (현재분사, 과거분사) 사용
2	Look at <u>the rising in the east sun.</u> (→)	[분사 + α]가 명사를 꾸밀 때 명사의 (앞, 뒤)에 위치
3	He kept the girl <u>waited.</u> (→)	S + keep + 목적어 + (V + -ing, p.p.) 목적어가 (~하는 것을, ~된 것을) 계속하게 하다
4	He kept his eyes <u>closing.</u> (→)	S + keep + 목적어 + (V + -ing, p.p.) 목적어가 (~하는 것을, ~된 것을) 계속하게 하다
5	He saw the man <u>painted</u> his house. (→)	S + see + 목적어 + (V + -ing, p.p.) 목적어가 (~하는 것을, ~된 것을) 보다
6	He saw his house <u>painted.</u> (→)	S + see + 목적어 + (V + -ing, p.p.) 목적어가 (~하는 것을, ~된 것을) 보다
7	<u>See</u> me, she shouted with joy. (→)	부사절 시제가 주절 시제와 같을 때 부사절 동사를 (동사원형, V + -ing)으로 바꿈
8	<u>Don't knowing</u> how to say sorry, the boy just cried. (→)	분사의 부정은 (don't, not)을·를 분사 바로 (앞, 뒤)에 사용
9	<u>Seeing</u> her before, I know her face. (→)	부사절 시제가 주절보다 앞설 때 부사절 동사를 (V + -ing, Having p.p.)로 바꿈
10	<u>Shocking</u> by the news, he didn't say a word. (→)	'충격을 받아서'는 (능동, 수동) 분사구문이므로 (V + -ing, (Being) p.p.) 형태
11	<u>Raining</u> heavily yesterday, the concert was canceled. (→)	부사절 주어가 주절 주어와 다를 때 부사절의 주어 생략 (가능, 불가)
12	He was sleeping with the alarm <u>rung.</u> (→)	with + 명사 + 분사 (V + -ing, p.p.) 명사가 (~하면서, ~된 채로) 의미
13	A pigeon flew to me with a message <u>tied</u> to its leg. (→)	with + 명사 + 분사 (V + -ing, p.p.) 명사가 (~하면서, ~된 채로) 의미

■ 주어진 단어를 알맞게 이용하여 우리말과 의미가 같도록 영작하시오.

1	look at, rise	~를 보아라 / 떠오르는 / 태양 →
2	rise, in the east	~를 보아라 / 저 태양 / 동쪽에서 떠오르는 →
3	keep, wait	그는 계속하게 했다 / 소녀가 기다리는 것을 →
4	keep, close	그는 계속 유지했다 / 그의 눈이 감긴 채로 →
5	see, paint	그는 보았다 / 그 남자가 페인트칠을 하는 것을 / 그의 집을 →
6	see, paint	그는 보았다 / 그의 집이 페인트칠 된 것을 →
7	see, with joy	나를 보자마자, / 그녀는 기뻐서 소리질렀다 →
8	how to say sorry	몰랐기 때문에 / 어떻게 미안하다고 할지를, / 소년은 그냥 울었다 →
9	before, know	그녀를 이전에 보았었기 때문에, / 나는 그녀의 얼굴을 안다 →
10	shock, by	그 소식에 충격을 받아서, / 그는 한마디도 하지 않았다 →
11	it, heavily, be canceled	어제 비가 심하게 내려서, / 그 콘서트가 취소되었다 →
12	the alarm, ring	그는 잠을 자고 있었다 / 알람이 울리면서 →
13	pigeon, a message, tie	비둘기 한 마리가 내게 날아왔다 / 메시지가 묶여진 채로 / 다리에 →

GP 37 원급, 비교급, 최상급

원급	A			B	A가 B만큼 ~한 (하게)
비교급	A			B	A가 B보다 ~한 (하게)
최상급	A			B	A가 B에서 가장 ~한 (하게)

❶ 원급 비교

She is **as diligent as** my mom.

My dog can run **as fast as** a cheetah.

The rock band is **not as popular as** the girl group.

❷ 비교급 비교

This cell phone is **cheaper than** that one.

The mobile game is **more exciting than** the arcade game.

❸ 최상급 비교

The Sahara Desert is **the biggest** desert **in** the world.

Today is **the happiest** day **of** my life.

> ○ **Tip** ○
> 비교되는 대상은 문법적으로 동등한 것이어야 한다.
> · My little finger is shorter than her. (×)
> · My little finger is shorter than hers (her little finger). (O)

• Upgrade •

[A less + 원급 + than B]: A가 B보다 덜 ~한 (하게)

Joe is less tall than Andy.

= Joe is not as tall as Andy.

= Andy is taller than Joe.

GP 38 원급을 이용한 표현

❶

This bridge is **two times as long as** that one.

(= This bridge is **two times longer than** that one.)

This bike is **three times as light as** my old one.

❷

as	원급	as		

Your point has to be **as specific as possible**. (= as specific as _____)

I needed the information **as soon as possible**. (= as soon as _____)

GP 39 비교급을 이용한 표현

❶
| ____ , ____ , ____ , ____ , | ____ | than | 훨씬 더 ～한 (하게) |

* Iron is **much heavier than** aluminum.

❷
| 비교급 | and | 비교급 | 점점 더 ～한 (하게) |

* Our world is becoming **smaller and smaller**.

❸
| ____ | (주어 + 동사) , | ____ | (주어 + 동사) | ～할수록 더 ～하다 |

* **The darker** it grew, **the colder** it became.

• Upgrade •

'～보다'의 의미로 than 대신 to를 쓰는 형용사
· senior (junior) to: ～보다 연상인 (연하인)
· superior (inferior) to: ～보다 우월한 (열등한)

GP 40 최상급을 이용한 표현

❶
| one | of | the | 최상급 | ____ | ____ |

* Jennifer is **one of the most energetic girls** in her class.

❷
| the | 최상급 | 명사 | ____ | ____ | ____ |

* He is the bravest man **I have ever met**.

GP 41 원급, 비교급을 이용한 최상급 의미

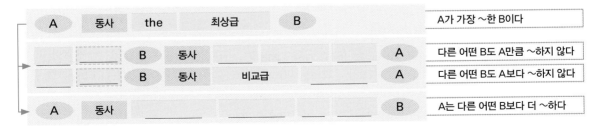

A	동사	the	최상급	B	A가 가장 ～한 B이다
____	____	B	동사	____ ____	A	다른 어떤 B도 A만큼 ～하지 않다
____	____	B	동사	비교급	A	다른 어떤 B도 A보다 ～하지 않다
A	동사	____	____	B	A는 다른 어떤 B보다 더 ～하다

The Nile is **the longest** river in the world.
= **No (other)** river in the world is **as long as** the Nile.
= **No (other)** river in the world is **longer than** the Nile.
= The Nile is **longer than any other** river in the world. (비교급 + than any other + _____)

A   ( ) 안에서 알맞은 것을 고르시오.

1 The firefighter is as (brave, braver) as a soldier.

2 This backpack is (heavier, heaviest) than the other one.

3 This problem is less (hard, harder) than that one.

4 Charlie is the funniest boy (in, of) the class.

5 You must be (not as rich as, as not rich as) Mansour.

6 This new album is more popular (as, than) the old one.

7 Let me know the results as soon as (possible, you possible).

8 The dictionary is (two thicker than, twice as thick as) my textbook.

B   ( ) 안의 말을 알맞게 고쳐 빈칸을 채우시오.

1 What is the _____ way to succeed? (good)

2 I spent as _____ money as you did. (little)

3 The air in Beijing is _____ than that in Auckland. (dirty)

4 Seoul is _____ city in Korea. (crowded)

5 My method is _____ than hers. (practical)

6 She is _____ member in the group. (thin)

7 Weekends tend to be not so _____ as weekdays. (busy)

8 The thumb is _____ of all the five fingers. (short)

C   두 문장의 의미가 같도록 빈칸을 채우시오.

1 He went into his room as quietly as possible.

→ He went into his room _____ he could.

2 The little wolf doesn't look as fierce as I expected.

→ The little wolf looks _____ than I expected.

3 Chris drank three times as much coffee as I did.

→ Chris drank three times _____ than I did.

D 우리말과 같은 뜻이 되도록 ( ) 안의 말을 배열하시오.

1 가능한 한 빨리 연락하겠습니다. (as, as, soon, possible)

→ I will contact you _____.

2 신용카드는 현금보다 더 편리하다. (more, cash, than, convenient)

→ Credit cards are _____.

3 우리 마을은 시골만큼 조용하지는 않다. (as, as, the, not, quiet, country)

→ Our town is _____.

4 나는 그보다 두 배 더 많은 돈을 가지고 있었다. (as, as, he, did, much, twice, money)

→ I had _____.

5 서울의 겨울은 제주도의 겨울보다 덜 따뜻하다. (of, than, that, warm, less, Jeju Island)

→ The winter in Seoul is _____.

6 그는 내 친구 중에서 가장 모험심이 강한 사람이다. (the, all, of, most, person, adventurous, my friends)

→ He is _____.

E 우리말과 같은 뜻이 되도록 ( ) 안의 말을 이용하여 문장을 완성하시오.

1 나는 내 사무실에서 가장 바쁜 사람이다. (busy, person)

→ I am _____ _____ _____ _____ my office.

2 가능한 한 자주 웃으려고 해라. (often)

→ Try to smile _____ _____ _____ _____ _____.

3 Jason은 Amy보다 두 배 많은 티셔츠를 가지고 있다. (T-shirts)

→ Jason has _____ _____ _____ _____ as Amy.

4 쓰레기를 줄이는 것이 그 어떤 것보다 더 중요하다. (important)

→ Reducing trash is _____ _____ _____ anything else.

5 이것이 검색 엔진 중에서 가장 편리하다. (convenient)

→ This is _____ _____ _____ _____ all the search engines.

6 그것의 평균 수명은 사람의 수명보다 세 배 더 길다. (long)

→ Its average lifespan is _____ _____ _____ _____

that of humans.

A ( ) 안에서 알맞은 것을 고르시오.

1 I've been feeling (very, much) better than yesterday.

2 The rarer the diamond is, the (more, much) valuable it is.

3 Computers are getting (small and small, smaller and smaller).

4 They are the (stranger, strangest) couple I have ever met.

5 Although he is five years junior (to, than) me, I admire him.

6 The (fast, faster) you drive, the more gas your car uses.

7 Usain Bolt is faster than any other (runner, runners) in the world.

8 A tornado is one of the most threatening natural (disaster, disasters).

B ( ) 안의 말을 알맞게 고쳐 빈칸을 채우시오.

1 The more he exercises, _____ he becomes. (strong)

2 Alison is getting _____ as she grows up. (tall)

3 He's _____ person I've ever talked with. (humorous)

4 Clayton Kershaw is one of _____ in the Major Leagues. (good, pitcher)

5 Drowsy driving is _____ than drunk driving. (even, dangerous)

C 두 문장이 같은 의미를 갖도록 빈칸을 채우시오. (4번은 같은 의미의 세 문장을 쓸 것)

1 My mom is two years senior to my dad.

→ My mom is two years _____ my dad.

2 As you exercise more, you become healthier.

→ _____ you exercise, _____ you become.

3 I have never studied a more difficult subject than this.

→ This is the most difficult subject that _____.

4 Ann is the most curious girl at my school.

→ No (other) girl at my school is _____ Ann.

→ No (other) girl at my school is _____ Ann.

→ Ann is _____ than _____ at my school.

D 우리말과 의미가 같도록 ( ) 안의 말을 배열하시오.

1 눈송이는 얼음보다 훨씬 더 빨리 녹는다. (ice, than, more, much, quickly)

→ Snowflakes melts _____.

2 그녀는 내가 아는 가장 현명한 사람 중 한 명이다. (of, one, the, people, wisest)

→ She is _____ I've ever known.

3 빈펄 리조트는 다른 어떤 리조트보다도 좋은 서비스를 제공한다. (any, than, better, other, service, resort)

→ The Vin Pearl Resort provides _____.

4 그것은 내가 먹어 본 것 중에서 가장 맛있는 음식이다. (the, I, ever, most, have, food, eaten, delicious)

→ It is _____.

5 Ms. Jackson 선생님이 우리 학교에서 가장 다정하시다. (is, no, as, as, other, friendly, teacher, at, my school)

→ _____ Ms. Jackson.

6 더 많은 책을 읽을수록, 너는 더 많은 아이디어를 얻을 것이다. (the, will, you, get, ideas, more)

→ The more books you read, _____.

E 우리말과 의미가 같도록 ( ) 안의 말을 이용하여 문장을 완성하시오.

1 그의 목소리가 점점 더 커지고 있다. (loud)

→ His voice is getting _____ _____ _____.

2 나의 의견이 너의 것보다 훨씬 더 논리적이다. (logical, far)

→ My opinion is _____ _____ _____ than yours.

3 이것은 내가 지금껏 본 것 중에서 가장 웃긴 연극이다. (watch, ever)

→ This is the funniest play _____ _____ _____ _____.

4 여름이 가까워질수록, 낮 시간이 더 길어진다. (close, long)

→ _____ _____ summer gets, _____ _____ the
daytime grows.

5 목성은 태양계에서 가장 큰 행성이다. (big)

→ Jupiter is _____ _____ _____ _____ planet in the
solar system.

6 그는 세계에서 가장 인기 있는 과학자들 중 한 명이다. (famous, scientist)

→ He is _____ _____ _____ _____
_____ in the world.

■ 밑줄 친 부분에 대한 설명을 체크하고 틀린 경우엔 바르게 고치시오. (맞으면 'O' 표시)

1	My dog can run as <u>faster</u> as a cheetah. (→)	(as + 원급 + as, as + 비교급 + as)
2	The rock band is <u>not as</u> popular as the girl group. (→)	(as not, not as) + 원급 + as
3	This cell phone is <u>cheap</u> than that one. (→)	(원급 + than, 비교급 + than)
4	The Sahara Desert is the <u>bigger</u> desert in the world. (→)	the + (비교급, 최상급) + 명사 + in 장소명사
5	This bike is <u>as three times</u> light as my old one. (→)	'~보다 몇 배 ~한' (as + 배수사, 배수사 + as) + 원급 + as
6	Your point has to be as specific as <u>can</u>. (→)	'가능한 ~한 (하게)' as + 원급 + as + (can, possible)
7	Iron is <u>very</u> heavier than aluminum. (→)	비교급 강조는 (매우, 훨씬) (very, much) + 비교급
8	Our world is becoming <u>small and small</u>. (→)	'점점 더 ~한' (비교급 + and + 비교급, 원급 + and + 원급)
9	The darker it grew, <u>colder</u> it became. (→)	'~하면 ~할수록 더 ~하다' the + 비교급, (비교급, the + 비교급)
10	Jennifer is one of the most energetic <u>girls</u> in her class. (→)	'가장 ~한 것들 중 하나' one of the 최상급 + (단수명사, 복수명사)
11	He is the bravest man I <u>met</u>. (→)	'~한 것 중 가장 ~한' the + 최상급 + 명사 + 주어 + (과거, have ever p.p.)
12	<u>Any</u> other river in the world is longer than the Nile. (→)	'다른 어떤 …보다 더 ~한' (No, Any) other + 단수명사 + 동사 + 비교급 than
13	The Nile is longer than any other <u>rivers</u> in the world. (→)	'다른 어떤 …보다 더 ~한' 비교급 + than any other + (단수명사, 복수명사)

Sentence writing

• 주어진 단어를 알맞게 이용하여 우리말과 의미가 같도록 영작하시오.

1	run, fast, a cheetah	나의 개는 / 빠르게 달릴 수 있다 / 치타만큼 →
2	the rock band, popular, the girl group	록 밴드는 / 유명하지 않다 / 걸 그룹만큼 →
3	cell phone, cheap	이 폰이 / 더 싸다 / 저 폰(것)보다 →
4	the Sahara Desert, big, desert	사하라 사막은 / 가장 큰 사막이다 / 세계에서 →
5	three times, light, as	이 자전거는 / 세 배 더 가볍다 / 나의 오래된 자전거보다 →
6	point, has to, specific	너의 요점은 / 구체적이어야 한다 / 가능한 한 →
7	iron, heavy, aluminum	철은 / 훨씬 더 무겁다 / 알루미늄보다 →
8	become, small	우리의 세상은 / 점점 더 작아지고 있다 →
9	it, grow, become	날이 어두워질수록, / 더 추워졌다 →
10	energetic, class	Jennifer는 / 한 명이다 / 가장 활동적인 소녀들 중 / 그녀의 반에서 →
11	brave, ever, meet	그는 / 가장 용감한 남자이다 / 지금껏 내가 만난 →
12	the Nile, long, no	세계에서 다른 어떤 강도 / 더 길지 않다 / 나일 강(the Nile)보다 →
13	the Nile, long, any	나일 강은 / 더 길다 / 세계에서 다른 어떤 강보다 →

GP 42 부사절을 이끄는 접속사

부사절은 [접속사 + 주어 + 동사] 형태로 _____처럼 다른 문장, 즉 주절을 _____한다.

접속사	_____	+	주절 주어 + 동사 ~
☆ While	she was studying,		she listened to music.

❶ 시간 접속사: when (~할 때), as (~함에 따라), while (_____), until (_____),
since (_____), as soon as (_____), whenever (_____)...

By law, you are a child **until** you are 18 years old.

When he feels nervous, he bites his nails.

While she blew out the candles, her hair caught on fire.

She has changed a lot **since** I met her last year.

As he grew up, he got more interested in history.

As soon as it is ready, we will let you know.

Whenever I try to use the Internet, the computer shuts down.

> **Tip**
> 접속사 while의 두 가지 의미
> ① ~하는 동안
> ② ~하는 반면에
> · While he is lazy, he is smart.

❷ 조건 접속사: if, unless (= _____)...

If I become a teacher, I will give my students little homework.

Unless she leaves now, she will miss her flight.

= **If** she does**n't** leave now, she will miss her flight.

❸ 이유 접속사: because, as, _____...

He stopped watching the movie **because** it was too violent.

As (Since) the pasta was too spicy, I couldn't finish it.

❹ 양보 접속사: _____, _____, _____, even if...

He didn't go to see the musical **although** he had a ticket.

Even if you are poor, I will marry you.

• Upgrade •

시간 부사절과 조건 부사절의 시제

주절이 미래시제일 때에도 _____ 부사절과 _____ 부사절은 _____ 대신 _____를 사용한다.

I will speak to her **when** I meet (~~will meet~~) her the next time. (_____)

If it rains (~~will rain~~) tomorrow, we will go to the movie. (_____)

GP 43 간접의문문

의문문이 다른 문장의 일부가 될 때 _____이라고 하며, [_____]의 어순을 갖는다.

❶ _____가 있는 경우: [_____]

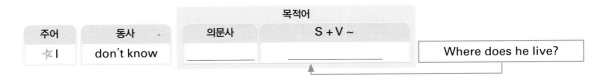

주어	동사	목적어	
		의문사	S + V ~
☆ I	don't know	_____	_____

Where does he live?

Magicians never tell us **how they trick** people. (← How do they trick people?)

• Upgrade •

❶ 의문사가 주어인 경우 어순 변화가 없이 그대로 [의문사 + 동사]

I know. + **Who broke** this window?

→ ☆ I know **who broke** this window.

❷ 주절의 동사가 _____, _____, _____, _____ 등인 경우, 의문사는 문장의 _____에 위치한다.

Do you **think**? + What is his real job?

→ **What** do you think **his real job is?**

❷ _____가 없는 경우: [_____ + 주어 + 동사]

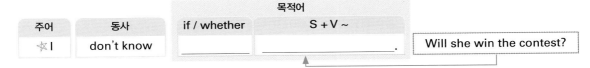

주어	동사	목적어	
		if / whether	S + V ~
☆ I	don't know	_____	_____ .

Will she win the contest?

Tell me **if (whether) tomatoes are** vegetables. (← Are tomatoes vegetables?)

GP 44 상관접속사

두 개 이상의 어구가 짝을 이루어 문법적으로 동일한 성질의 두 요소를 연결하는 접속사이다.

_____	A	_____	B	A와 B 둘 다
_____	A	_____	B	A와 B 둘 중 하나
_____	A	_____	B	A와 B 둘 다 아닌
_____	A	_____	B	A뿐만 아니라 B도
=	B	_____	A	

☆ **Both** Jack **and** Jill are college students.
Either Daniel **or** you have to take care of the kitten.
☆ **Neither** the kids **nor** their mom likes meat.
Not only the body **but also** the mind needs exercise.
= The mind **as well as** the body needs exercise.

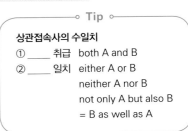

── ○ Tip ○ ──
상관접속사의 수일치
① _____ 취급   both A and B
② _____ 일치   either A or B
　　　　　　 neither A nor B
　　　　　　 not only A but also B
　　　　　　 = B as well as A

A   ( ) 안에서 알맞은 말을 고르시오.

1   I caught a cold (as soon as, if) my holiday started.

2   Could you take care of my baby (although, while) I cook?

3   (Since, Although) he was a student, he got a student discount.

4   When I (will meet, meet) my nephew, I will give him a big hug.

5   It will be great if she (goes, will go) with us.

6   I haven't met Paul (when, since) he moved to another city.

7   Joan spoke to him (if, even though) she didn't know him.

B   보기에서 알맞은 접속사를 골라 문장을 완성하시오. (한 번씩만 사용)

보기	while	even though	until	if

1   _____ you go, I will go, too.

2   He wore sunscreen _____ it was cloudy.

3   Please watch my luggage _____ I come back.

4   _____ there is life, there is hope.

보기	since	as soon as	although	because

5   _____ I opened the book, I fell asleep.

6   She has collected teddy bears _____ she was ten years old.

7   _____ I don't know his face, I remember his voice.

8   Some animals are in danger _____ people hunt them for money.

보기	if	unless	when	until

9   Flip the pancake _____ the bottom starts to turn golden brown.

10   _____ you sunbathe too long, you'll get burned.

11   He waited _____ his name was finally called.

12   _____ the actress wears makeup, people don't recognize her.

C 우리말과 의미가 같도록 ( ) 안의 말을 배열하시오.

1 네가 하이킹을 간다면, 향수를 뿌리지 않는 것이 좋을 거야. (go for, if, you, a hike)

→ _____, you had better not wear any perfume.

2 Patrick은 우산을 가져갈 때마다 잃어버린다. (an umbrella, takes, every, time, Patrick)

→ _____, he loses it.

3 네가 열기를 참을 수 없다면, 주방을 떠나라. (cannot, the heat, stand, if, you)

→ _____, get out of the kitchen.

4 나의 여름방학이 시작된 이래로 시간이 빠르게 지나갔다. (my, since, started, summer vacation)

→ Time has flown _____.

5 그녀가 나를 볼 때, 그녀의 눈은 반짝인다. (she, when, me, looks at)

→ _____, her eyes twinkle.

6 그 새 과자는 출시되자마자 모두 팔렸다, (was, released, as, as, it, soon)

→ The new snack sold out _____.

D 우리말과 의미가 같도록 ( ) 안의 말을 이용하여 문장을 완성하시오.

1 그 아이스크림은 딱딱해서, 나는 이것을 나이프로 먹었다. (the ice cream)

→ _____ _____ _____ _____ _____, I ate it with a knife.

2 네가 괴물 복장을 벗지 않으면 아이들이 울 것이다. (take off, the monster costume)

→ _____ _____ _____ _____ _____ _____ _____,

the kids will start crying.

3 그가 공부하려고 노력하는 동안에 그를 방해하지 마. (try to)

→ Don't bother him _____ _____ _____ _____ _____.

4 버스에서 내리실 때 발을 조심하세요. (get off)

→ Watch your step _____ _____ _____ _____ _____.

5 내가 중학교를 졸업한 지 일 년째다. (graduate from)

→ It has been a year _____ _____ _____ _____ _____.

6 이 다이아몬드는 가짜임에도 불구하고 진짜처럼 보인다. (the diamond, fake)

→ _____ _____ _____ _____ _____, it looks like a real one.

7 그는 민트 잎이 어두운색으로 변할 때까지 튀겼다. (they, turn dark)

→ He fried the mint leaves _____ _____ _____ _____.

A ( ) 안에서 알맞은 것을 고르시오.

1 Can you tell on the map (where are we, where we are) now?

2 Both Tom and Jack (was, were) absent from school yesterday.

3 Neither you nor he (seem, seems) to know the answer.

4 How old do you guess (is the actor, the actor is)?

5 I wonder (that, if) he agrees with us.

6 Do you know (how tall the Eiffel Tower is, how the Eiffel Tower is tall)?

7 When do you (think, know) she will arrive?

B 주어진 두 문장을 간접의문문을 포함한 한 문장으로 쓰시오.

1 Do you know? + How big is the moon?

→ Do you know _____?

2 Do you think? + How big is the moon?

→ _____?

3 I am not sure. + Does she like my suggestion?

→ I am not sure _____.

4 I wonder. + Are you coming to the party?

→ I wonder _____.

5 I want to know. + What does my cat want to say?

→ I want to know _____.

6 Do you believe? + What caused the ice age?

→ _____ the ice age?

7 Can you tell me? + Who cooked the delicious pasta?

→ Can you tell me _____?

8 Dad, do you remember? + When did Mom propose to you?

→ Dad, do you remember _____?

C 주어진 두 문장을 상관접속사를 포함한 한 문장으로 쓰시오.

1 Britain has public schools. Britain has private schools, too. (both ~ and)

→ Britain has _____.

2 Max is ready for the exam. I am ready for the exam, too. (not only ~ but also)

→ _____ for the exam.

3 His illness is not getting better. It is not getting worse either. (neither ~ nor)

→ His illness is getting _____.

4 You can cook. Or you can do the dishes after the meal. (either ~ or)

→ You can _____ after the meal.

D 우리말과 의미가 같도록 ( ) 안의 말을 배열하시오.

1 나는 이 상징이 무엇을 의미하는지를 배웠다. (learned, what, I, the symbol, meant)

→ _____.

2 우리 삼촌은 흡연도 안 하고 음주도 안 하셔. (neither, my uncle, drinks, smokes, nor)

→ _____.

3 우리는 부모님을 사랑할 뿐 아니라 존경해. (love, respect, not only, but also, we)

→ _____ our parents.

4 누가 진실을 이야기하고 있다고 믿니? (is telling the truth, do you believe, who)

→ _____ ?

E 우리말과 의미가 같도록 ( ) 안의 말을 이용하여 문장을 완성하시오.

1 나는 너 또는 내가 승자가 될 거라고 추측해. (be, the winner)

→ I guess _____ _____ _____ _____ _____

_____ _____ .

2 나는 Emily뿐만 아니라 너도 파티에 초대하고 싶어. (invite, as)

→ I want to _____ _____ _____ _____ _____ _____ to the party.

3 너는 누가 저 유리집을 설계했는지 알고 있니? (design, the glass house)

→ Do you know _____ _____ _____ _____ _____ ?

4 나는 그가 그의 약속을 지킬지 의문이 든다. (keep)

→ I doubt _____ _____ _____ _____ _____ .

Error Correction ✏

▪ 밑줄 친 부분에 대한 설명을 체크하고 틀린 경우엔 바르게 고치시오. (맞으면 'O' 표시)

1	While she was studying, she listened to music. (→)	(~하는 동안, ~하는 반면) 의미의 (시간, 양보) 부사절 접속사
2	By law, you are a child <u>until</u> you are 18 years old. (→)	(~할 때까지, ~하는 동안) 의미의 시간 부사절 접속사 (until, while)
3	<u>Although</u> he feels nervous, he bites his nails. (→)	(~할 때, 비록 ~이지만) 의미의 (시간, 양보) 부사절 접속사
4	Unless she <u>doesn't leave</u> now, she will miss her flight. (→)	unless는 (if, if ~ not)의 의미로 not과 동시 (사용, 사용 불가)
5	He stopped watching the movie <u>even if</u> it was too violent. (→)	(~때문에, 비록 ~이지만) 의미의 (이유, 양보) 부사절 접속사
6	He didn't go to see the musical <u>because</u> he had a ticket. (→)	(~때문에, 비록 ~이지만) 의미의 (이유, 양보) 부사절 접속사
7	I will speak to her when I <u>will meet</u> her the next time. (→)	'~할 때' 의미의 시간 (부사절, 주절)은 미래시제 대신 (현재, 미래)시제
8	I don't know where <u>does he live</u>. (→)	의문사 있는 간접의문문 어순 의문사 + (주어 + 동사, 동사 + 주어)
9	I know <u>who broke</u> this window. (→)	주어 역할의 의문사가 있는 간접의문문 의문사 + (주어 + 동사, 동사)
10	<u>Do you think what</u> his real job is? (→)	주절에 think가 있으면 간접의문문의 의문사는 문장 (앞, 중간)에 위치
11	I don't know <u>that</u> she will win the contest. (→)	의문사가 없는 간접의문문 (if, whether, that) + 주어 + 동사
12	Both Jack and Jill <u>is</u> college students. (→)	Both A and B가 주어일 때 항상 (단수, 복수) 취급
13	Neither the kids nor their mom <u>like</u> meat. (→)	Neither A nor B가 주어일 때 (A, B)에 동사의 단복수 일치

■ 주어진 단어를 알맞게 이용하여 우리말과 의미가 같도록 영작하시오.

1	listen to	그녀가 공부하고 있는 동안, / 그녀는 음악을 들었다 →
2	by law	법에 따르면, / 너는 아동이다 / 네가 18세가 될 때까지 →
3	nervous, bite	그가 초조함을 느낄 때, / 그는 손톱을 물어뜯는다 →
4	unless, her flight	그녀가 지금 떠나지 않으면, / 그녀는 비행기를 놓칠 것이다 →
5	stop watching, violent	그는 영화를 보는 것을 멈췄다 / 이것이 너무 폭력적이어서 →
6	go to see the musical	그는 뮤지컬을 보러 가지 않았다 / 그가 티켓을 갖고 있었음에도 →
7	speak to	나는 그녀에게 말을 걸 것이다 / 내가 그녀를 다음번에 만나면 →
8	where	나는 모른다 / 그가 어디에 사는지를 →
9	who	나는 안다 / 누가 창문을 깼었는지를 →
10	real job	너는 무엇이라고 생각하니 / 그의 진짜 직업이? →
11	win the contest	나는 모르겠다 / 그녀가 콘테스트에서 이길지 아닐지를 →
12	college students	Jack과 Jill 모두 / 대학교 학생들이다 →
13	kids, neither	그 아이들과 그들의 엄마 모두 ~하지 않는다 / 좋아한다 / 고기를 →

GP 45 관계대명사 who, which, that, what

_____와 _____ 역할을 동시에 하고 관계대명사절은 형용사처럼 앞에 나오는 _____를 _____한다.

선행사	주격 관계대명사	소유격 관계대명사	목적격 관계대명사
사람	_____	_____	_____
동물, 사물	_____	/ of which	_____
사람, 동물, 사물	_____	-	_____
선행사 없음	_____	-	_____

❶ _____ 관계대명사 who, which, that

접속사와 대명사	He is	a man.	+	_____	is very polite to everyone.
관계대명사	He is	a man		_____	is very polite to everyone.

※ I bought a book **which (that)** is about space.

❷ _____ 관계대명사 who(m), which, that

He is the man. + I respect him the most.

→ ※ He is the man **who(m) (that)** I respect the most.

The cake **which (that)** she made for dessert was too sweet.

◦ Tip ◦

관계대명사 that을 주로 쓰는 경우
① 선행사가 [사람 + _____], [사람 + _____], _____으로 끝나는 대명사인 경우
② 선행사가 _____, _____, _____, the very, the same, the last, all, every 등의 수식을 받는 경우

❸ 소유격 관계대명사 whose, of which

I know a man. + His daughter is a popular actress.

→ ※ I know a man **whose** daughter is a popular actress.

We will invent a robot **whose** arms are very similar to a human's.

= We will invent a robot **of which** the arms are very similar to a human's.

❹ 관계대명사 what

관계대명사 what은 _____를 포함하고 보통 '_____'으로 해석한다. 관계대명사 what이 이끄는 절은 문장에서 _____, _____, _____ 역할을 한다.

선행사 + that	You can do	_____	+	_____	you'd like to do.
what	☆ You can do	_____			you'd like to do.

I can't believe **what** you have just said. (what = the thing that)

GP 46 관계부사 when, where, why, how

접속사와 부사 역할을 동시에 하고 관계부사절은 형용사처럼 앞에 나오는 _____를 _____한다.
관계부사는 [_____] 형태로 바꿀 수 있다.

선행사		관계부사	전치사 + 관계대명사
시간	the time, the day…	_____	_____ … which
장소	the place, the house…	_____	_____ … which
이유	the reason	_____	_____ which
방법	the way	_____	_____ which

접속사와 부사(구)	I remember	the place.	I first met her	_____ _____
관계부사	I remember	the place	_____	I first met her.
			_____ _____	I first met her.

❶ **when:** _____을 나타내는 the time, the day, the year 등이 선행사일 때

The day **when** (= on which) we can live on Mars will come.

Do you know the time **when** (= at which) his speech will end?

❷ **where:** _____를 나타내는 the place, the house, the city 등이 선행사일 때

We visited a city **where** (= in which) the Olympic Games were held.

The restaurant **where** (= at which) we had dinner is closed on Sundays.

❸ **why:** _____를 나타내는 the reason이 선행사일 때

The reason **why** (= for which) she likes me is mysterious.

Do you know the reason **why** (= for which) Rome collapsed?

❹ **how:** _____을 나타내는 the way가 선행사일 때

The program shows **the way (= how)** people manage time wisely.

The program shows **the way in which** people manage time wisely.

The program shows the way how people manage time wisely. (X)

> **Tip**
> 선행사 _____와
> 관계부사 _____는
> 같이 쓸 수 _____.

• Upgrade •

관계대명사 vs. 관계부사

관계대명사는 [접속사 + 대명사]의 역할을 하므로 관계대명사를 제외하면 주어, 목적어, 보어 중 하나가 빠져 있는 _____을 이끈다. 관계부사는 [접속사 + 부사]의 역할을 하므로 관계부사를 제외하면 부사가 빠져 있는 _____을 이끈다.

This is the bridge **which** was built in the 19th century. (불완전한 문장)

This is the bridge **where** a car accident happened yesterday. (완전한 문장)

❶ _____의 생략

The author (**whom**) I will visit is well known to everyone.

The police found the bag (**that**) I had lost at the airport.

❷ [_____ + _____]의 생략

I have a watch (**which was**) made in Switzerland fifty years ago.

The gentleman (**who is**) talking to my dad wears a suit all the time.

GP 48 전치사 + 관계대명사

관계대명사가 전치사의 목적어인 경우, 전치사는 관계대명사절 끝에 오거나 관계대명사 앞에 올 수 있다. 전치사가 관계대명사 앞에 오는 경우에는 관계대명사 that을 쓸 수 _____.

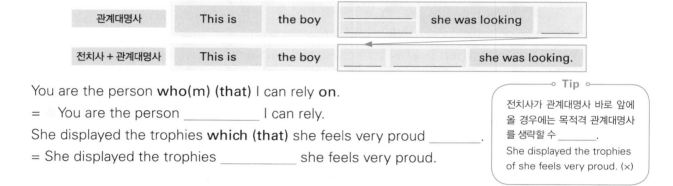

| 관계대명사 | This is | the boy | _____ | she was looking | _____ |
| 전치사 + 관계대명사 | This is | the boy | _____ | she was looking. | |

You are the person **who(m)** (**that**) I can rely **on**.

= You are the person _____ I can rely.

She displayed the trophies **which** (**that**) she feels very proud _____.

= She displayed the trophies _____ she feels very proud.

> ─○ Tip ○─
> 전치사가 관계대명사 바로 앞에 올 경우에는 목적격 관계대명사를 생략할 수 _____.
> She displayed the trophies of she feels very proud. (×)

GP 49 관계사의 계속적 용법

관계사의 계속적 용법은 [선행사 + _____ + _____] 형태로 선행사에 대한 부가적인 설명을 한다.

❶ **관계대명사의 계속적 용법**: who와 which만 가능하고 [_____ (and, but, for) + _____]로 바꿔 쓸 수 있다.

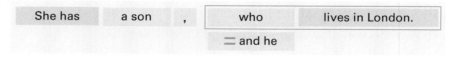

| She has | a son | , | who | lives in London. |
| | | | ≡ and he | |

We ordered some seafood dishes, **which** (= but they) tasted really awful.

＊ 계속적 용법의 which는 선행사로 단어뿐만 아니라 앞 문장 전체를 선행사로 취할 수 있다.

He plays loud music every night, **which** (= and it) makes sleeping difficult.

❷ **관계부사의 계속적 용법**: when과 where만 가능하고 [접속사 (and, but) + 부사]로 바꿔 쓸 수 있다.

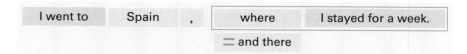

| I went to | Spain | , | where | I stayed for a week. |
| | | | ≡ and there | |

I will be free in the morning, **when** (= and then) you can come to see me.

GP 50 복합관계대명사

복합관계대명사는 _____에 _____를 붙인 형태로 _____과 _____을 이끈다.

복합관계대명사	who(m)ever	whichever	whatever
선행사 + 관계대명사 (명사절)	~하는 누구든지	~하는 어느 것이든지	~하는 무엇이든지
	anyone who(m)	anything that	anything that
no matter + 관계대명사 (양보 부사절)	누가(누구를) ~하더라도	어느 것이(을) ~하더라도	무엇이(을) ~하더라도
	no matter who(m)	no matter which	no matter what

선행사 + 관계대명사	Anyone who	wants to succeed	should be diligent.
복합관계대명사	☆ _____	wants to succeed	should be diligent.

❶ 명사절

I will give you **whichever** you choose. (← anything that)
My dad wants to buy my mom **whatever** she wants. (← anything that)

❷ 양보 부사절

Whomever you meet, be polite to them. (← No matter _____)
Whichever he may take, he will be satisfied. (← No matter _____)
Whatever you do, don't do it halfway. (← No matter _____)

GP 51 복합관계부사

복합관계부사는_____에 _____를 붙인 형태로 시간 / 장소 부사절이나 양보 부사절을 이끈다.

복합관계부사	whenever	wherever	however
선행사 + 관계부사 (시간 / 장소 부사절)	~하는 언제든지	~하는 어디든지	
	at any time when	at / in / to any place where	
no matter + 관계부사 (양보 부사절)	언제 ~하더라도	어디에서 ~하더라도	아무리 ~하더라도
	no matter when	no matter where	no matter how

❶ 시간 / 장소 부사절

I'll help you out **whenever** you are in trouble. (← at any time when)
The dog follows my dad **wherever** he goes. (← to any place where)

❷ 양보 부사절

Whenever she calls me, I always answer the phone. (← No matter when)
Wherever he may work, he'll get along with his co-workers. (← No matter where)
However smart he is, he won't understand her tears. (← No matter how)

• Upgrade •

복합관계부사 however은 보통 [however + 형용사 / 부사 + 주어 + 동사] 형태로 쓴다.

A ( ) 안에서 알맞은 것을 고르시오.

1 That is the very question (that, whom) I want to ask him.

2 I interviewed a writer (whom, whose) book became a bestseller.

3 The safari tour (which, who) my mom recommended was amazing.

4 Cindy is a great person (who, which) donates lots of money to a charity.

5 Did you understand (that, what) she wanted to point out in her presentation?

B 보기에서 알맞은 말을 골라 문장을 완성하시오.

보기	· whose design is unique	· what I expected
	· who stole my cell phone	· that live next door

1 The service was different from _____.

2 My sister likes the cat and its owner _____.

3 The assignment is to find the building _____.

4 The police caught the man _____.

C 두 문장을 관계대명사를 이용하여 한 문장으로 만드시오. (that은 써야 할 경우에만 사용)

1 The woman is my mother. She is singing on the stage.

→ _____.

2 I lost the sneakers. I bought them at a flea market.

→ _____.

3 There are many people. Their opinions are different from yours.

→ _____.

4 The data might be inaccurate. You gathered them on the Internet.

→ _____.

5 The team is looking for the pilot and the plane. They crashed into the sea.

→ _____.

D 선행사 여부를 표시하고, 빈칸에 관계대명사 what 또는 that을 써서 문장을 완성하시오.

1 All _____ you have to do is take some vitamin C.   선행사 (있음, 없음)

2 _____ is important now is hard work and patience.   선행사 (있음, 없음)

3 We visited the tower _____ is open 24 hours a day.   선행사 (있음, 없음)

4 I can understand _____ Andy is trying to say.   선행사 (있음, 없음)

5 She wants to get a job _____ can inspire people.   선행사 (있음, 없음)

6 _____ surprises me is that she likes lizards.   선행사 (있음, 없음)

E 우리말과 의미가 같도록 ( ) 안의 말을 배열하시오.

1 효과가 좋은 약이 있나요? (any, well, works, which, medicine)

→ Do you have _____?

2 우리가 안다는 것은 우리가 행동하는 것과 다르다. (we, we, do, know, what, what)

→ _____ is different from _____.

3 그들은 청소하도록 프로그램 되어 있는 로봇을 발명했다. (a, is, that, robot, programmed)

→ They invented _____ to clean up.

4 나는 내가 필기 노트를 빌린 반 친구에게 감사했다. (I, the, notes, whose, borrowed, classmate)

→ I thanked _____.

F 우리말과 의미가 같도록 ( ) 안의 말을 이용하여 문장을 완성하시오.

1 나는 더 많은 메모리 용량이 있는 노트북이 필요하다. (have, memory)

→ I need a laptop _____ _____ _____ _____.

2 당신이 가장 필요로 하는 것은 유머감각이다. (most, need)

→ _____ _____ _____ is a sense of humor.

3 Peter는 내가 비밀에 대해 말할 수 있는 유일한 친구이다. (tell)

→ Peter is the only friend _____ _____ _____ _____

about my secret.

4 이것은 가격이 합리적인 훌륭한 여행 상품이다. (price, reasonable)

→ It is a great travel package _____ _____ _____.

A 보기에서 알맞은 말을 골라 문장을 완성하시오.

보기	when	where	why	how

1 Africa is a place _____ a lot of animals live in the wild.

2 Tell me _____ the child was rescued from the burning house.

3 Do you know the reason _____ the old couple looks that happy.

4 There was a time _____ the field used to be underwater.

B [관계부사]와 [전치사 + 관계대명사]를 이용하여 두 문장을 한 문장으로 만드시오.

1 I can't forget the day. + She left me alone on the day.

→ I can't forget the day _____. (관계부사)

→ I can't forget the day _____. (전치사 + 관계대명사)

2 Where is the hotel? + Your family stayed at the hotel.

→ Where is the hotel _____? (관계부사)

→ Where is the hotel _____? (전치사 + 관계대명사)

3 I know the reason. + He became popular for the reason.

→ I know the reason _____. (관계부사)

→ I know the reason _____. (전치사 + 관계대명사)

4 We'll study the way. + People reduce stress in the way.

→ We'll study _____. (관계부사)

→ We'll study _____. (전치사 + 관계대명사)

C ( ) 안에서 알맞은 것을 고르고, 밑줄 친 부분이 완전한 문장인지 불완전한 문장인지 체크하시오.

1 Sunday is the only day (that, when) <u>he can get enough rest</u>. (완전, 불완전)

2 He runs a shopping mall (which, where) <u>sells fashionable clothes</u>. (완전, 불완전)

3 Show me (which, how) <u>you put out the fire with an extinguisher</u>. (완전, 불완전)

4 I remember the days (which, when) <u>we spent together</u>. (완전, 불완전)

D   우리말과 의미가 같도록 ( ) 안의 말을 배열하시오.

1 Juliet은 사람들에게 어떻게 보이는지 신경쓰지 않는다. (to, she, how, people, looks)

→ Juliet doesn't care _____ .

2 봄은 우리가 새로운 시작을 하는 때이다. (a, we, new, when, make, start, the time)

→ Spring is _____ .

3 그가 그녀와 헤어진 이유는 아무도 모른다. (he, her, with, why, broke up, the reason)

→ No one knows _____ .

4 내가 주로 공부하는 도서관은 월요일에 문을 닫는다. (I, study, where, usually, the library)

→ _____ is closed on Monday.

5 놀부는 그의 동생을 대했던 방식에 대해 후회했다. (he, his, had, brother, treated, the way)

→ Nolbu regretted _____ .

6 그녀가 보석을 보관하는 상자는 서랍에 있다. (she, her, keeps, where, jewelry, the box)

→ _____ is in the drawer.

E   우리말과 의미가 같도록 ( ) 안의 말을 이용하여 문장을 완성하시오.

1 그가 너에게 전화했던 이유는 미안하다고 말하기 위해서였어. (call)

→ The reason _____ _____ _____ _____ was to say sorry.

2 4월 1일은 사람들이 서로를 속이는 날이야. (play tricks)

→ April 1 is a day _____ _____ _____ on one another.

3 연어는 그들이 태어났던 장소로 돌아간다. (be born)

→ Salmon return to the places _____ _____ _____ .

4 그녀는 사람들에게 그녀가 어떻게 지진에서 생존했는지 말했다. (survive)

→ She told people _____ _____ _____ the earthquake.

5 여기는 여동생과 내가 자랐던 집이다. (grow up)

→ This is the house _____ _____ _____ in with my sister.

6 우리와 함께 가는 것을 거절했던 이유를 말해 주겠니? (refuse, go)

→ Could you tell me the reason _____ _____ _____

_____ with us?

A ( ) 안에서 알맞은 것을 고르시오.

1 There are few friends on (who, whom) he can depend.

2 Bill sent her flowers, (who, which) touched her heart.

3 The hotel (at that, at which) I stayed last night was terrible.

4 The picture (was painted, painted) by Julia is hanging on the wall.

5 The music (which, to which) we listened yesterday was really impressive.

6 I'm proud of my uncle, (who, that) won a gold medal at the Olympic Games.

B 생략할 수 있는 부분에 밑줄을 긋고 그 이유를 보기에서 고르시오. (생략이 없으면 'X' 표시)

보기 │ ① 목적격 관계대명사	② 주격 관계대명사 + be동사	이유
1 Dogs can smell things that people can't.		_____
2 This is the road which leads to city hall.		_____
3 The kid who are playing here are very noisy.		_____
4 The man who I wanted to see was not in the office.		_____
5 Science is the subject in which I'm interested.		_____

C 두 문장이 같은 의미를 갖도록 관계사를 이용하여 빈칸을 채우시오.

1 My mom gave away my books. They were only two years old.

　→ My mom gave away my books, _____.

2 We arrived there on Christmas Eve. It was very cold at that time.

　→ We arrived there on Christmas Eve, _____.

3 They climbed Mt. Halla. Doing so made them very tired.

　→ They climbed Mt. Halla, _____.

4 I went to a small restaurant. I ran into my childhood friend there.

　→ I went to a small restaurant, _____.

5 I read a story about Helen Keller. She overcame her physical difficulties.

　→ I read a story about Helen Keller, _____.

D 우리말과 의미가 같도록 ( ) 안의 말을 배열하시오.

1 지금 사진을 찍고 있는 그 남자는 나의 삼촌이다. (a, the, man, photo, taking)

→ _____ now is my uncle.

2 내가 어젯밤에 잤던 새 침대는 매우 편안했다. (I, in, the, bed, slept, new)

→ _____ last night was very comfortable.

3 그가 앉아 있는 의자는 나무로 만들어졌다. (is, he, on, the, chair, which)

→ _____ sitting is made of wood.

4 나의 형은 2015년에 유학을 갔었는데 그때 16살이었다. (he, old, was, years, when, sixteen)

→ My brother went abroad to study in 2015 _____.

5 그녀는 그 남자에게 물었으나 그는 그녀에게 정답을 말해 주지 않았다. (her, the, not, tell, did, who, answer)

→ She asked the man, _____.

6 나는 성격이 급한데 그런 점이 종종 날 어려움에 빠뜨린다. (me, into, often, which, gets, trouble)

→ I have a bad temper, _____.

E 우리말과 의미가 같도록 ( ) 안의 말을 이용하여 문장을 완성하시오. (생략 가능한 관계사는 생략)

1 Andy는 가난했지만 자기 생활에 만족했다. (poor)

→ Andy, _____ _____ _____, was satisfied with his life.

2 레게머리(Dreadlocks) 그가 관심을 갖고 있는 스타일이다. (be)

→ Dreadlocks are the style _____ _____ _____ _____

interested.

3 내가 원했던 그 선수의 운동복은 다 팔렸었다. (want)

→ The player's jersey _____ _____ was sold out.

4 나는 자주 인스턴트 음식을 먹는데 그것은 건강에 나쁜 영향을 미친다. (have)

→ I often eat junk food, _____ _____ a bad effect on health.

5 우리는 당신이 함께 일할 수 있는 숙련된 몇몇 작가들이 있어. (work)

→ We have a few experienced writers _____ _____ _____

_____ with.

6 그녀는 영국으로 갔는데 거기서 스무 살까지 살았다. (live)

→ She moved to England, _____ _____ _____ until the age of 20.

A 보기에서 알맞은 말을 골라 문장을 완성하시오.

보기	whatever	whoever	whenever	however

1 _____ busy you are, you have to attend the meeting.

2 _____ comes first will get a discount coupon.

3 _____ I may say, my parents won't believe me.

4 _____ my dad comes home, he brings something to eat.

보기	whichever	whomever	wherever	however

5 We can eat _____ food we love.

6 _____ you look, there is beauty.

7 _____ he likes to play with, I don't mind.

8 _____ she judges me, I want to tell her how I feel about her.

B 두 문장이 같은 의미를 갖도록 빈칸에 알맞은 복합관계사를 쓰시오.

1 Anything that you like is fine with me.

→ _____ you like is fine with me.

2 No matter which train you take, you will be late.

→ _____ train you take, you will be late.

3 He makes new friends no matter where he goes.

→ He makes new friends _____ he goes.

4 No matter when you are in trouble, you can ask for my help.

→ _____ you are in trouble, you can ask for my help.

5 I feel sorry for anyone whom I might have hurt unintentionally.

→ I feel sorry for _____ I might have hurt unintentionally.

6 No matter how brilliant the scientist is, he won't be able to solve the mystery.

→ _____ brilliant the scientist is, he won't be able to solve the mystery.

C 우리말과 의미가 같도록 ( ) 안의 말을 배열하시오.

1 무슨 일이 일어나더라도 마음을 바꾸지 않을 것이다. (no, may, what, happen, matter)

→ I won't change my mind _____.

2 오늘밤 어느 팀이 이기든 결승전에 갈 것이다. (wins, team, tonight, whichever)

→ _____ will go to the final.

3 그 차가 아무리 비싸더라도 아빠는 그것을 살 것이다. (is, the, car, expensive, however)

→ _____, my dad will buy it.

4 그 문제에 대한 해결책을 찾는 누구든지 보상받을 것이다. (a, to, the, finds, problem, whoever, solution)

→ _____ will be rewarded.

5 네가 다른 사람을 위해 한 것은 무엇이든 너에게 되돌아올 것이다. (do, you, for, others, whatever)

→ _____ will come back to you.

6 여유 시간이 있을 때마다 Maggie는 헬스클럽에 간다. (has, she, free, some, time, whenever)

→ Maggie goes to the gym _____.

D 우리말과 의미가 같도록 복합관계사와 ( ) 안의 말을 이용하여 문장을 완성하시오.

1 그녀가 필요한 건 어느 것이든 그녀에게 줄 것이다. (need)

→ I will give her _____ _____ _____.

2 갈증이 날 때마다 음료수 말고 물을 마셔라. (feel thirsty)

→ Drink water, not soda, _____ _____ _____ _____.

3 그 자리에 그가 추천하는 누구라도 고용할 것이다. (recommend)

→ I will hire _____ _____ _____ for the position.

4 그가 아무리 부자라도, 행복을 살 수는 없다. (rich)

→ _____ _____ _____ _____, he cannot buy happiness.

5 네가 요리하는 건 무엇이든지 정성을 다해라. (cook)

→ Put your heart into _____ _____ _____.

6 당신이 어디에 있든지, 당신은 혼자가 아니라는 것을 명심해라. (be)

→ _____ _____ _____, keep in mind that you are not alone.

■ 밑줄 친 부분에 대한 설명을 체크하고 틀린 경우엔 바르게 고치시오. (맞으면 'O' 표시)

1	I bought a book <u>who</u> is about space. (→)	선행사 (사물, 동물) 관계대명사 (주격, 목적격) + 동사
2	He is the man whom I respect <u>him</u> the most. (→)	(주격, 목적격) 관계대명사 뒤 선행사를 가리키는 목적어 (사용, 삭제)
3	I know a man <u>who</u> daughter is a popular actress. (→)	선행사 + (주격, 소유격) 관계대명사 + 명사 + 동사
4	You can do <u>that</u> you'd like to do. (→)	선행사가 없으므로 관계대명사 (what, that)
5	The day <u>where</u> we can live on Mars will come. (→)	선행사 + 관계부사 (시간, 장소) (when, where)
6	Do you know the reason <u>at</u> which Rome collapsed? (→)	선행사 + 전치사 + which (시간, 이유) (at, for)
7	The program shows a way <u>how</u> people manage time wisely. (→)	선행사 + 관계부사 (방법, 이유) (how, 없음)
8	The police found <u>the bag I had lost</u> at the airport. (→)	선행사 + 목적격 관계대명사 + 주어 + 동사 생략 (가능, 불가능)
9	You are the person on <u>that</u> I can rely. (→)	전치사 + 관계대명사 (that, who, whom)
10	We ordered some seafood dishes, <u>that</u> tasted really awful. (→)	comma(,) + 관계대명사 (that, which)
11	<u>Who</u> wants to succeed should be diligent. (→)	'~하는 누구든지'의 복합관계대명사는 (Who, Whoever)
12	The dog follows my dad <u>whatever</u> he goes. (→)	'어디에 ~하더라도'의 복합관계부사는 (wherever, whatever)
13	<u>Whenever</u> smart he is, he won't understand her tears. (→)	'아무리 ~하더라도'의 복합관계부사는 (Whenever, However)

Sentence writing

■ 주어진 단어를 알맞게 이용하여 우리말과 의미가 같도록 영작하시오.

1	buy, space	나는 샀다 / 책을 / 우주에 관한 →
2	respect, the most	그는 남자다 / 내가 가장 존경하는 →
3	popular, actress	나는 안다 / 남자를 / 그의 딸이 유명한 여배우인 →
4	would like to, do	너는 할 수 있다 / 네가 하고 싶은 것을 →
5	on Mars, come	그날이 / 우리가 화성에 살 수 있는 / 올 것이다 →
6	Rome, collapse	너는 아니 / 이유를 / 로마가 멸망했던? →
7	show, a way, manage	그 프로그램은 보여 준다 / 방식을 / 사람들이 시간을 현명하게 관리하는 →
8	find, lose	경찰은 찾았다 / 가방을 / 공항에서 내가 잃어버렸던 →
9	the person, rely, on	너는 사람이다 / 내가 의지할 수 있는 →
10	seafood dishes, taste, awful	우리는 주문했다 / 해산물 요리를, / 그런데 그것은 정말로 맛이 없었다 →
11	want, succeed, diligent	성공하기를 원하는 누구든지 / 부지런해야 한다 →
12	follow, go	그 개는 아빠를 따라간다 / 그가 가는 데는 어디든지 →
13	smart, tears	그가 아무리 똑똑하더라도, / 그는 이해하지 못할 것이다 / 그녀의 눈물을 →

GP 52 가정법 과거

_____과 반대되는 상황을 나타내거나 실현 불가능한 것을 가정할 때 쓴다.

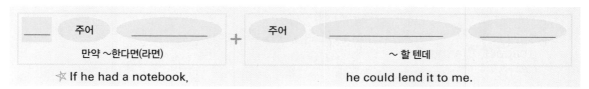

_____	주어	_____	+	주어	_____	_____
만약 ~한다면(라면)					~ 할 텐데	

☆ If he had a notebook,　　　　　he could lend it to me.

If she **were** tired, she **would** not **go** there with me.
→ As she isn't tired, she will go there with me.

> **Tip**
> 가정법 과거 문장에서 be동사는 인칭과 수에 관계없이 _____를 쓴다.

• Upgrade •

단순 조건문은 [If + 주어 + 현재동사 ~, 주어 + will / can / may + 동사원형 ~] 형태로 실현 가능한 일을 가정할 때 쓴다.
If you **miss** this chance, you **will regret** it.

GP 53 가정법 과거완료

_____과 반대되는 상황을 나타내거나 실현 불가능한 것을 가정할 때 쓴다.

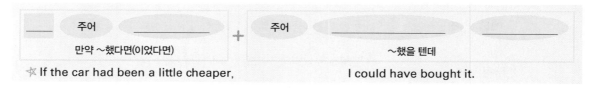

_____	주어	_____	+	주어	_____	_____
만약 ~했다면(이었다면)					~했을 텐데	

☆ If the car had been a little cheaper,　　　　　I could have bought it.

If you **had arrived** ten minutes earlier, you **could have gotten** a good seat.
→ As you didn't arrive ten minutes earlier, you could not get a good seat.

GP 54 혼합가정법

if절과 주절의 시제가 일치하는 않는 형태로 _____에 실현되지 못했던 일이 현재까지 영향을 미치는 것을 나타낼 때 쓴다.

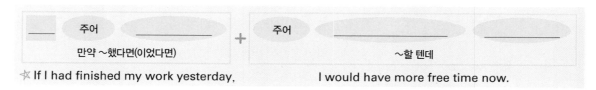

_____	주어	_____	+	주어	_____	_____
만약 ~했다면(이었다면)					~할 텐데	

☆ If I had finished my work yesterday,　　　　　I would have more free time now.

If you **had taken** my advice, you **would be** in a better position now.
→ As you didn't take my advice, you are not in a better position now.

GP 55 I wish + 가정법

현재에 이루기 힘든 것을 소망할 때나 과거에 이룰 수 없었던 것을 소망할 때 쓴다.

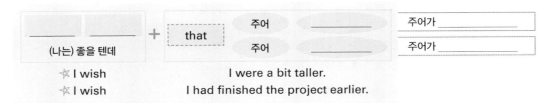

① I wish + _____

I wish I spoke Chinese.

→ I am sorry (that) I don't speak Chinese.

② I wish + _____

I wish she had watched the action movie with me.

→ I am sorry she didn't watch the action movie with me.

GP 56 as if + 가정법

현재에 그렇지 않은 일을 그런 것처럼 가정할 때나 과거에 그렇지 않았던 일을 그랬던 것처럼 가정할 때 쓴다.

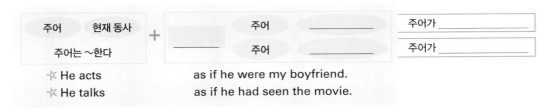

① as if + 가정법 과거

He looks **as if he were** surprised at the news.

→ In fact, he is not surprised at the news.

② as if + 가정법 과거완료

They talk **as if they had met** each other last month.

→ In fact, they didn't meet each other last month.

GP 57 it's time + 가정법

_____을 하지 않은 것에 대한 유감을 나타낼 때 쓴다.

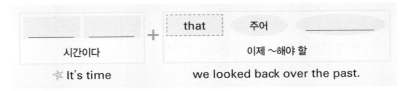

It's time we had dinner. It's almost seven.

GP 58 if 생략 가정법

if절 동사가 were나 had인 경우 if를 생략할 수 있고, 이때 _____와 _____가 _____된다.

Were I you, I would accept the job offer.
(← If I were you, ~)
Had she known his phone number, she would have called him.
(← If she had known his phone number, ~)

GP 59 without, but for

without / but for는 if절을 대신하는 표현으로 가정법 과거나 가정법 과거완료에 쓴다.

❶ 가정법 과거

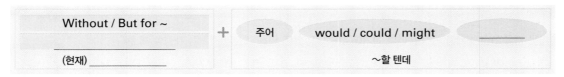

Without / But for fire, we couldn't live normal lives.
= If it were not for fire, ~
= Were it not for fire, ~

❷ 가정법 과거완료

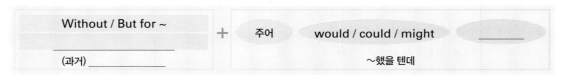

Without / But for your help, I couldn't have made my own blog.
=   If it had not been for your help, ~
= Had it not been for your help, ~

• Upgrade •

if절이 없는 가정법 문장
주어, 부정사, 부사(구), 분사구문도 가정법의 if절을 대신할 수 있다.
An honest boy would admit his mistake immediately.
(← If he were an honest boy, he would admit his mistake immediately.)
It would be great **to have three days off each week**.
(← if we had three days off each week)
I used up my money; **otherwise**, I could have bought it for you.
(← if I had not used up my money)

A ( ) 안에서 알맞은 것을 고르시오.

1 If I (were, am) a child, I would play outside all day.

2 We (had, will have) to take a taxi if we finish work late at night.

3 If she had married me, she would (lead, have led) a happier life.

4 Tell me what you would do if you (were, had been) me in that situation.

5 If Harry (missed, had missed) the chance, he would wait one more year.

6 If he had taken his coach's advice, he might (be, have been) a winner today.

B ( ) 안의 말을 알맞게 고쳐 빈칸을 채우시오.

1 If I had stayed up all night, I _____ very tired now. (be)

2 If he _____ enough friends, he would not feel lonely. (have)

3 If they were not busy today, they _____ the school union. (visit)

4 If she had known a lot about the computer, she _____ it herself. (fix)

5 If you _____ yourself, I will take you to the amusement park. (behave)

6 I could have enjoyed my school life if I _____ the college I wanted. (enter)

C 두 문장이 같은 의미를 갖도록 빈칸을 채우시오.

1 As he isn't honest, he cheats others.

  → If he _____ honest, he would not _____ others.

2 As it rained yesterday, we couldn't go on a picnic.

  → If it _____ yesterday, we _____ on a picnic.

3 As they don't live close to each other, they can't meet often.

  → If they _____ close to each other, they _____ often.

4 As we didn't catch the last bus, we walked home.

  → If we _____ the last bus, we _____ home.

5 As we didn't make a reservation, we have to wait for a table.

  → If we _____ a reservation, we _____ to wait for

  a table.

D 우리말과 의미가 같도록 ( ) 안의 말을 배열하시오.

1 그가 너무 수줍어하지 않는다면 훌륭한 배우가 될 텐데. (he, he if, be, not, were, would)

→ _____ so shy, _____ a great actor.

2 그녀가 여동생이 있다면, 그녀와 인형놀이를 할 텐데. (if, she, she, dolls, had, play, could)

→ _____ a younger sister, _____ with her.

3 그 소문에 대해 내가 너에게 얘기하면 너는 놀랄 텐데. (I, if, you, you, be, told, would)

→ _____ surprised _____ about the rumor.

4 내가 그의 청혼을 수락했더라면, 지금 내가 그의 부인일 텐데. (I, I, if, be, had, would, accepted)

→ _____ his proposal, _____ his wife now.

5 그가 열심히 일하지 않았더라면 승진하지 못했을 텐데. (if, he, he, not, not have, had, gotten, could, worked)

→ _____ hard, _____ a promotion.

6 그녀가 내 말을 들었더라면, 그녀는 그런 실수는 안 했을 텐데. (if, she, she, not, had, have, made, listened, would)

→ _____ to me, _____ such a mistake.

E 우리말과 의미가 같도록 ( ) 안의 말을 이용하여 문장을 완성하시오.

1 내가 부자라면 해변에 있는 집을 살 텐데. (be, buy)

→ If I _____ wealthy, I _____ _____ a beach house.

2 그들이 다음주에 돌아온다면 우리는 환영파티를 열 것이다. (come, hold)

→ If they _____ back next week, we _____ _____ a welcome party.

3 그가 그녀를 무시하지 않는다면, 그녀는 화내지 않을 텐데. (ignore, get)

→ If he _____ _____ her, she _____ _____ _____ angry at him.

4 눈이 많이 왔었다면, Jessy는 큰 눈사람을 만들 수 있었을 텐데. (snow, make)

→ If it _____ _____ heavily, Jessy _____ _____ _____ a big snowman.

5 그가 더 일찍 진료를 받았었다면, 그의 건강은 지금 더 나빠지지 않았을 텐데. (see, be)

→ If he _____ _____ a doctor earlier, his health _____ _____

_____ _____ now.

6 Jordan이 열쇠를 잃어버리지 않았다면, 나는 사물함을 열 수 있었을 텐데. (lose, open)

→ If Jordan _____ _____ _____ the key, I _____ _____

_____ my locker.

A ( ) 안에 알맞은 것을 고르시오.

1 I wish I (don't, didn't) wear glasses now.

2 It's time you (left, will leave) for the airport.

3 I wish I (took, had taken) the online class for free yesterday.

4 He treats me as if I (am, were) a maid even though I am his sister.

5 It is about time we (said, will say) goodbye to this year.

6 Kelly is a new classmate, but she talks as if she (saw, had seen) me before.

B ( ) 안의 말을 알맞게 고쳐 빈칸을 채우시오.

1 I wish you _____ more generous to your brother now. (be)

2 I couldn't contact you. I wish I _____ your cell phone number. (lose, not)

3 It's almost ten o'clock. It's time you _____ the math test. (finish)

4 I needed more sleep. I wish he _____ playing the guitar at night. (stop)

5 She is not pretty, but she acts as if she _____ a princess. (be)

6 The result was not announced, but he talked as if he _____ it. (know)

C 주어진 문장을 가정법 문장으로 바꿀 때 빈칸에 알맞은 말을 쓰시오.

1 I'm sorry she didn't go shopping with us.

→ _____ shopping with us.

2 In fact, my foreign friends don't like spicy food.

→ My foreign friends are talking to her as if _____.

3 It's time for you to tell me why you fought with your sister.

→ It's time _____ why you fought with your sister.

4 I'm sorry he doesn't pay attention to people around him.

→ _____ to people around him.

5 In fact, my mother found out about my poor grades.

→ My mother acts as if _____.

D 우리말과 의미가 같도록 ( ) 안의 말을 배열하시오.

1 나는 하늘을 날고 있는 기분이 들어. (I, sky, as, the, in, were, if, flying)

→ I feel _____.

2 이제 나의 진로를 결정할 시기이다. (I, my, it's time, decided, career path)

→ _____.

3 그녀는 그녀의 집에 수영장이 있기를 바란다. (a, her, wishes, pool, she, house, had, swimming)

→ _____.

4 그는 백만장자였던 것처럼 이야기한다. (he, as, been, if, had, a, millionaire)

→ He talks _____.

5 내가 그때 그에게 아무 말도 하지 않았더라면 좋았을 텐데. (I, I, said, him, wish, to, had, nothing)

→ _____ then.

6 나는 네가 모든 결정을 스스로 내릴 수 있기를 바란다. (I, you, all, make, wish, could, the decisions)

→ _____ on your own.

E 우리말과 의미가 같도록 ( ) 안의 말을 이용하여 문장을 완성하시오.

1 Billy는 마치 가수인 것처럼 노래한다. (be)

→ Billy sings _____ _____ _____ _____ _____.

2 Olivia가 나의 새 영어 선생님이시라면 좋겠다. (be)

→ I wish _____ _____ _____ _____ _____ _____.

3 쓰레기를 줄이는 더 좋은 방법을 우리가 찾아야 할 때이다. (find)

→ _____ _____ _____ _____ _____ a better way to reduce waste.

4 내가 어렸을 때 춤추는 것을 배웠더라면 좋았을 텐데. (learn)

→ _____ _____ _____ _____ _____ to dance when I was young.

5 더 많은 사람들이 대중교통을 이용하면 좋을 텐데. (use)

→ _____ _____ _____ _____ _____ public transportation.

6 아빠는 화가 나지 않았던 것처럼 웃고 계신다. (get)

→ My dad is smiling _____ _____ _____ _____ _____ _____ upset.

A ( ) 안에 알맞은 것을 고르시오.

1 (I were, Were I) you, I would work out every day.

2 (With, Without) the tip, he couldn't pass the job interview.

3 It would be fantastic (win, to win) first place in the contest.

4 (With, Without) this ticket, you could have entered the rap concert.

5 (If were, Were) it not for a car, it would take much longer to travel.

6 (Have, Had) he been more careful, the accident wouldn't have happened.

B 주어진 문장을 if로 시작하는 가정법 문장으로 고쳐 쓰시오.

1 Without his message, I might have been waiting for him.

→ _____ for his message, I might have been waiting for him.

2 To taste her food, you would think that she is a chef.

→ _____ her food, you would think that she is a chef.

3 But for life jackets, nobody could swim in the sea.

→ _____ life jackets, nobody could swim in the sea.

4 Had it not rained yesterday, I would have held the party in my garden.

→ _____ yesterday, I would have held the party in my garden.

C 주어진 문장을 if를 생략한 가정법 문장으로 고쳐 쓰시오.

1 If I were president, I would ban all tests.

→ _____, I would ban all tests.

2 If he had gotten up earlier, he could have seen the beautiful sunrise.

→ _____ earlier, he could have seen the beautiful sunrise.

3 If it were not for the app, we couldn't find the route easily.

→ _____ the app, we couldn't find the route easily.

4 If it had not been for the traffic jam, he wouldn't have been late for the seminar.

→ _____ the traffic jam, he wouldn't have been late for the

seminar.

D 우리말과 의미가 같도록 ( ) 안의 말을 배열하시오.

1 내가 네 입장이라면 그런 바보 같은 짓은 하지 않을 텐데. (your, I, were, in, shoes)

→ _____, I wouldn't do such a silly thing.

2 핸드폰이 없다면 나는 전화번호를 하나도 모를 거야. (would, my, I, phone, without, cell)

→ _____, _____ not know a single phone number.

3 KTX가 없다면 매주 만나기는 어려웠을 거야. (for, it, KTX, were, not, the)

→ _____, it would be difficult to meet every weekend.

4 어제 폭풍우가 내렸었다면 그 비행은 취소되었을 텐데. (stormed, had, yesterday, it)

→ _____, the flight would have been canceled.

5 인터넷이 없다면, 우리는 책 읽는데 더 많은 시간을 보낼 텐데. (we, the, but, Internet, for, would)

→ _____, _____ spend more time reading books.

6 그 감독이 없었다면 이 영화는 만들어지지 않았을 텐데. (had, the, been, director, for, it, not)

→ _____, this movie could have never been made.

E 우리말과 의미가 같도록 ( ) 안의 말을 이용하여 문장을 완성하시오.

1 한국인이라면 젓가락을 사용할 텐데. (use)

→ A Korean _____ _____ chopsticks.

2 네가 투명인간이라면 무엇을 할 것 같니? (do)

→ _____ _____ an invisible man, what _____ you _____?

3 법이 없다면 세상은 매우 혼란스러울 거야. (laws, be)

→ _____ _____, the world _____ _____ very chaotic.

4 내가 너라면 나는 중간고사 대비 일정을 짤 텐데. (plan)

→ _____ _____ _____, I _____ _____ a schedule for the
midterm exam.

5 그가 더 많은 야채를 먹었더라면 감기에 쉽게 걸리지 않았을 텐데. (eat, get)

→ _____ _____ _____ more vegetables, he _____ _____
_____ _____ a cold.

6 방범 카메라가 없었다면, 그들은 그 절도범을 잡지 못했을 텐데. (catch)

→ _____ _____ _____ _____ for security cameras, they
_____ _____ _____ _____ the burglar.

Error Correction

■ 밑줄 친 부분에 대한 설명을 체크하고 틀린 경우엔 바르게 고치시오. (맞으면 'O' 표시)

* S: 주어, R: 동사원형, p.p.: 과거분사

1	If he <u>has</u> a notebook, he could lend it to me. (→)	실현 가능성 (있는, 없는) 가정법 과거 If + S + (과거, 현재)동사, S + (can, could) + R
2	If you <u>miss</u> this chance, you will regret it. (→)	실현 가능성 (있는, 없는) 조건문 If + S + (과거, 현재)동사, S + (will, would) + R
3	If the car had been a little cheaper, I could <u>bought</u> it. (→)	실현 가능성 (있는, 없는) 가정법 과거완료 If + S + had p.p., S + could + (R, have p.p.)
4	If I had finished my work yesterday, I would <u>have had</u> more free time now. (→)	'만약 ~했다면, ~할 텐데'의 혼합 가정법 If + S + had p.p., S + would + (R, have p.p.)
5	I wish I <u>were</u> a bit taller. (→)	현재에 이루기 힘든 것에 대한 소망은 I wish + S + (현재, 과거)동사
6	I wish I <u>finished</u> the project earlier. (→)	과거에 이룰 수 없었던 것에 대한 소망은 I wish + S + (과거동사, had p.p.)
7	He acts as if he <u>is</u> my boyfriend. (→)	현재 (사실, 사실의 반대) '~처럼' as if + S + (과거동사, had p.p.)
8	He talks as if he <u>saw</u> the movie. = In fact, he didn't see the movie. (→)	과거 (사실, 사실의 반대) '~처럼' as if + S + (과거동사, had p.p.)
9	It's time we <u>look</u> back over the past. (→)	'이제 ~해야 할 시간이다' It's time + (that) + S + (현재, 과거)동사
10	<u>I were</u> you, I would accept the job offer. (→)	[If 주어 + 과거동사]에서 If 생략하면 (주어 + 동사, 동사 + 주어) 어순
11	<u>She had</u> known his phone number, she would have called him. (→)	[If 주어 + had p.p.]에서 If 생략하면 (주어 + had p.p., Had + 주어 + p.p.) 어순
12	<u>But</u> fire, we couldn't live normal lives. (→)	'(~이 없었다면, ~이 없다면), ~할 텐데' (But, But for) + 명사
13	If it <u>were not</u> for your help, I couldn't have made my own blog. (→)	If it (were not, had not been) for + 명사, 주어 + could + have p.p.

Sentence writing

▪ 주어진 단어를 알맞게 이용하여 우리말과 의미가 같도록 영작하시오.

1	a notebook, lend, to	만약 그가 공책이 있다면, / 그는 나에게 빌려줄 텐데 →
2	miss, this chance, regret	네가 이 기회를 놓친다면, / 너는 후회할 거다 →
3	a little, cheaper, buy	이 차가 조금 더 쌌더라면, / 나는 그것을 구입했을 텐데 →
4	finish, work, free time	만약 내가 끝냈더라면 / 나의 일을 / 어제, / 나는 가질 텐데 / 더 많은 자유 시간을 / 지금 →
5	a bit, taller	나는 좋을 텐데 / 내가 좀 더 크다면 →
6	finish, the project, earlier	나는 좋을 텐데 / 내가 이 프로젝트를 더 일찍 끝냈었다면 →
7	act, boyfriend	그는 행동한다 / 마치 나의 남자친구인 것처럼 →
8	talk, see, the movie	그는 말한다 / 마치 그 영화를 봤던 것처럼 →
9	time, look back over	이제 시간이다 / 과거를 돌아봐야 할 →
10	be, accept, the job offer	내가 너라면, / 나는 받아들일 텐데 / 일자리 제안을 →
11	his phone number, call	그녀가 알았더라면 / 그의 전화번호를, / 그녀는 그에게 전화했을 텐데 →
12	but, fire normal lives	불이 없으면, / 우리는 살 수 없을 텐데 / 정상적인 삶을 →
13	if, it, help, own, blog	만약 없었더라면 / 너의 도움이, / 나는 만들 수 없었을 텐데 / 나만의 블로그를 →

문법패턴 빈칸 채우기

GP 60 수의 일치

❶ 단수 취급하는 경우

_____ + 단수명사	~one, ~thing, ~body	____, ____, 등의 이름	+	_____ 동사
시간, 거리 등의 _____	(동명사, to부정사)	(that, whether, 의문사)		

☆ The Netherlands **is** famous for tulips and windmills.
   Mathematics **is** a useful subject.
☆ Three dollars **is** enough to buy the milk.
   Who made the underwater city **is** still a mystery.

❷ 복수 취급하는 경우

both A and B	the + 형용사 (~한 사람들)	a number of + 복수명사	+	_____ 동사

☆ The young **learn** things faster than the old.
☆ *A number of* people **are** resting on the beach. (_____: _____ 취급)
☆ *The number of* visitors to the blog **is** increasing. (_____: _____ 취급)

GP 61 시제 일치와 예외

❶ 시제 일치

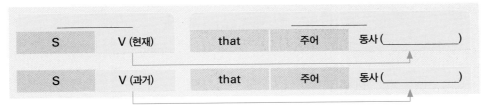

S	V (현재)	that	주어	동사(_____)
S	V (과거)	that	주어	동사(_____)

☆ **I know** that my teacher **trusts / trusted / will trust / has trusted** me.
☆ She **said** that her bird **laid / had laid** an egg.

❷ 시제 일치의 예외

종속절이 _____, _____, _____, _____ 등을 나타낼 때

		종속절		
S	V	that	주어	(항상) _____ 시제 동사

종속절이 역사적 사실을 나타낼 때

S	V	that	주어	(항상) _____ 시제 동사

☆ The book **said** that children **have** more bones than adults. (과학적 사실)
☆ Jane **said** that she never **eats** instant food. (현재도 계속되는 습관)
☆ We **learned** that the Berlin Wall **fell** in 1989. (역사적 사실)

GP 62 평서문의 간접화법 전환

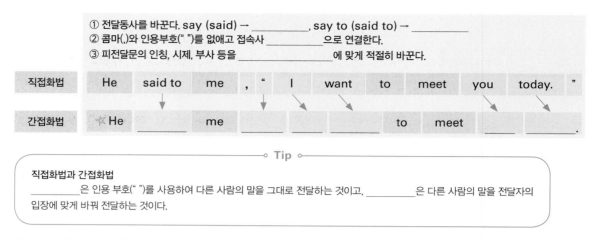

① 전달동사를 바꾼다. say (said) → _____ , say to (said to) → _____
② 콤마(,)와 인용부호(" ")를 없애고 접속사 _____ 으로 연결한다.
③ 피전달문의 인칭, 시제, 부사 등을 _____에 맞게 적절히 바꾼다.

| 직접화법 | He | said to | me | , | " | I | want | to | meet | you | today. | " |

| 간접화법 | ☆ He | | me | | | | | | to | meet | | |

— Tip —

직접화법과 간접화법
_____은 인용 부호(" ")를 사용하여 다른 사람의 말을 그대로 전달하는 것이고, _____은 다른 사람의 말을 전달자의 입장에 맞게 바꿔 전달하는 것이다.

She said to me, "I bought these earrings yesterday."
→ She **told** me **that she had bought those** earrings **the day before**.

— Tip —

간접화법으로 전환할 때 변하는 부사(구)
this (these) → _____ / here → _____ / now → _____ / today → _____ / ago → _____
yesterday → _____ , _____ / tomorrow → _____ , _____

GP 63 의문문의 간접화법 전환

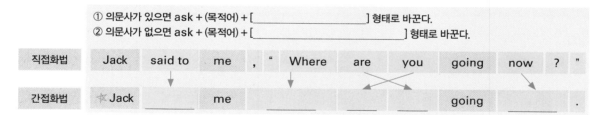

① 의문사가 있으면 ask + (목적어) + [_____] 형태로 바꾼다.
② 의문사가 없으면 ask + (목적어) + [_____] 형태로 바꾼다.

| 직접화법 | Jack | said to | me | , | " | Where | are | you | going | now | ? | " |

| 간접화법 | ☆ Jack | | me | | | | | | | going | | . |

Kate said to him, "Do you have any questions?"
→ ☆ Kate **asked** him **if (whether) he had** any questions.

GP 64 명령문의 간접화법 전환

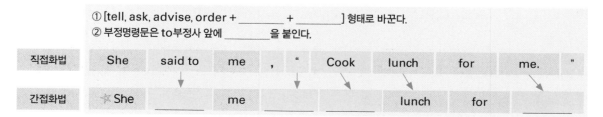

① [tell, ask, advise, order + _____ + _____] 형태로 바꾼다.
② 부정명령문은 to부정사 앞에 _____을 붙인다.

| 직접화법 | She | said to | me | , | " | Cook | lunch | for | me. | " |

| 간접화법 | ☆ She | | me | | | | lunch | for | | |

The teacher said to us, "Don't be late for school."
→ ☆ The teacher **ordered** us **not to be** late for school.

A ( ) 안에서 알맞은 것을 고르시오.

1 Each of the members (has, have) the right to vote.

2 He forgot that he (met, had met) her before.

3 I learned that Columbus (discovered, had discovered) the New World in 1492.

4 Five kilometers (is, are) a long distance to walk.

5 She said that time (is, was) money.

6 The number of car accidents yesterday (was, were) 29.

7 To visit foreign countries (sound, sounds) exciting.

B ( ) 안의 말을 현재시제로 고쳐 빈칸을 채우시오.

1 Nobody _____ safe from catching a cold. (be)

2 She believes that the rich _____ getting richer. (be)

3 Ten dollars _____ too expensive for this pencil. (be)

4 A number of people _____ watching the game on TV. (be)

5 Every seat _____ been taken. (have)

6 Physics _____ fun to learn. (be)

7 There _____ a number of shoppers in the mall. (be)

C ( ) 안의 말을 알맞은 시제로 고쳐 빈칸을 채우시오.

1 We learned that the moon _____ water from the Earth. (pull)

2 She knew that water _____ at zero degrees Celsius. (freeze)

3 Ellen said that she _____ going to the concert then. (be)

4 He said that Thomas Edison _____ the light bulb. (invent)

5 Do you know what Chris _____ yesterday? (buy)

6 I heard that he _____ to London already. (move)

7 Teddy said that he _____ go fishing the next day. (will)

D 우리말과 의미가 같도록 ( ) 안의 말을 배열하시오.

1 50권의 책을 읽는 것이 올해 나의 목표이다. (fifty books, to read, is)

→ _____ my goal this year.

2 집 청소하기에 두 시간은 너무 짧다. (too short, is, to clean, two hours)

→ _____ the house.

3 그 나라는 매년 많은 폭풍에 강타 당한다. (is hit, by, many storms, the country)

→ _____ every year.

4 나는 레오나르도 다빈치가 모나리자를 그렸다고 들었다. (heard, I, Leonardo da Vinci, that, painted)

→ _____ the *Mona Lisa*.

5 많은 위성들이 군사적 목적을 위해 사용된다. (satellites, are used, a, of, number, for)

→ _____ military purposes.

6 물은 산소와 수소로 이루어져 있다. (consists, oxygen, water, hydrogen, and, of)

→ _____ .

E 우리말과 의미가 같도록 ( ) 안의 말을 이용하여 문장을 완성하시오.

1 Adam은 그가 전날 그의 가방을 잃어버렸다고 말했다. (say, lose)

→ _____ _____ _____ _____ _____

_____ _____ the day before.

2 그 책은 피라미드가 파라오들의 무덤이라고 했다. (say, the pyramids)

→ _____ _____ _____ _____ _____

_____ the tombs of pharaohs.

3 부상을 입은 사람들은 인근 병원으로 실려 갔다. (the wounded, be taken to)

→ _____ _____ _____ _____ _____ a nearby hospital.

4 우리 엄마와 나 모두 일찍 일어난다. (both, be)

→ _____ _____ _____ _____ _____ _____ early birds.

5 우리는 1차 세계 대전이 1914년에 시작했다고 배웠다. (learn, the first World War, start)

→ _____ _____ _____ _____ _____ _____ _____

_____ in 1914.

6 그는 지구가 태양 주변을 도는 것을 알았다. (know, move)

→ _____ _____ _____ _____ _____ round the sun.

A 직접화법을 간접화법으로 바꿔 문장을 완성하시오.

1 They said, "We are waiting for a bus."

→ They _____.

2 She said to me, "Your advice was helpful."

→ She _____.

3 The nurse said to me, "How do you feel now?"

→ The nurse _____.

4 She said to me, "Have you ever been abroad?"

→ She asked me _____.

5 My mom said to me, "Use honey instead of sugar."

→ My mom _____.

6 Paul said to me, "Please set the table."

→ Paul _____.

7 The police said to them, "Don't move."

→ The police _____.

B 간접화법을 직접화법으로 바꿔 문장을 완성하시오.

1 Henry said that he had a toothache.

→ Henry _____.

2 Jessica told him that she had met his brother at the library.

→ Jessica _____.

3 She asked me how old I was.

→ She _____.

4 The girl asked her mom where her gloves were.

→ The _____.

5 Daniel asked her whether she liked the song.

→ Daniel _____.

6 He advised her to try to speak slowly.

→ He _____.

C 우리말과 의미가 같도록 ( ) 안의 말을 배열하시오.

1 Lily는 매일 조깅을 한다고 말했다. (she, said, goes running, that, every morning)

→ Lily _____.

2 그는 내게 낙타의 혹에 무엇이 있는지를 물어보았다. (what, asked, me, is, in)

→ He _____ a camel's humps.

3 의사는 그녀의 환자에게 걱정하지 말라고 말했다. (her, not, to, patient, worry, told)

→ The doctor _____.

4 나의 선생님은 나에게 교실로 들어가라고 하셨다. (me, to go into, told, the classroom)

→ My teacher _____.

5 그는 나에게 그 신발을 어디에서 샀는지 물어보았다. (where, me, I, asked, had bought)

→ He _____ the shoes.

6 나의 부모님은 우리에게 침대에서 먹지 말라고 하셨다. (told, not, to eat, the bed, us, on)

→ My parents _____.

7 Mr. Morgan은 메시지를 남겨도 되냐고 그녀에게 물어보았다. (whether, her, asked, leave, could, he, a message)

→ Mr. Morgan _____.

D 우리말과 의미가 같도록 ( ) 안의 말을 이용하여 문장을 완성하시오.

1 Aiden은 내게 그가 머그잔을 깼다고 말했다. (tell, break)

→ Aiden _____ _____ _____ _____ _____ a mug.

2 그녀는 그에게 시험결과에 만족하는지를 물어보았다. (ask, be satisfied)

→ She _____ _____ _____ _____ _____ _____

his test grade.

3 그는 영화감독이 될 것이라고 말했다. (say, movie director)

→ He _____ _____ _____ _____ _____ _____ _____.

4 그 소년은 내게 병을 열어달라고 부탁했다. (ask, open)

→ The boy _____ _____ _____ _____ _____ for him.

5 Mike는 축구공을 하나 살 예정이라고 말했다. (be going to)

→ Mike _____ _____ _____ _____ _____ _____

a soccer ball.

6 그는 우리에게 차에서 멀리 떨어지라고 말했다. (stay away from)

→ He _____ _____ _____ _____ _____ _____ _____ _____.

Error Correction

■ 밑줄 친 부분에 대한 설명을 체크하고 틀린 경우엔 바르게 고치시오. (맞으면 'O' 표시)

1	The Netherlands <u>are</u> famous for tulips and windmills. (→)	복수형 국가명은 (단수, 복수) 취급
2	Three dollars <u>are</u> enough to buy the milk. (→)	거리, 금액, 무게 등 단위명사는 (단수, 복수) 취급
3	The young <u>learns</u> things faster than the old. (→)	'the + 형용사는 (~한 사람, ~한 사람들) (단수, 복수) 취급
4	A number of people <u>is</u> resting on the beach. (→)	a number of는 (많은, ~의 수) 의미로 (단수, 복수) 취급
5	The number of visitors to the blog <u>are</u> increasing. (→)	the number of는 (많은, ~의 수) 의미로 (단수, 복수) 취급
6	I <u>knew</u> that my teacher trusts me. (→)	주절 + 종속절 (현재, 과거)시제 (현재시제)
7	The book said that children <u>had</u> more bones than adults. (→)	과학적 사실은 항상 (현재, 과거)시제
8	We learned that the Berlin Wall <u>had fallen</u> in 1989. (→)	역사적 사실은 항상 (현재, 과거)시제
9	He told me that he <u>wants</u> to meet me that day. (→)	주절 + 종속절 (과거시제) (현재, 과거)시제
10	Jack <u>told</u> me where I was going then. (→)	의문사 있는 의문문의 간접화법 (tell, ask) + 의문사 + 주어 + 동사
11	Kate asked him <u>that</u> he had any questions. (→)	의문사 없는 의문문의 간접화법 ask+ (if, that) + (주어 + 동사, 동사 + 주어)
12	She told me <u>cook</u> lunch for her. (→)	명령문의 간접화법 tell + 목적어 + (to부정사, 동사)
13	The teacher ordered us <u>don't</u> to be late for school. (→)	부정명령문의 간접화법 order + 목적어 + (not, don't) + to부정사

▪ 주어진 단어를 알맞게 이용하여 우리말과 의미가 같도록 영작하시오.

1	the Netherlands, windmills	네덜란드는 / ~로 유명하다 / 튤립과 풍차 →
2	enough to	3달러는 / 충분하다 / 그 우유를 사기에 →
3	learn things	젊은 사람들은 / 더 빨리 배운다 / 노인들보다 →
4	a number of, rest	많은 사람들이 / 쉬고 있다 / 해변에서 →
5	visitors to the blog	그 블로그 방문객 수가 / 증가하고 있다 →
6	trust	나는 안다 / 나의 선생님이 나를 신뢰하시는 것을 →
7	say, bones, adults	그 책은 말했다 / 아이들이 더 많은 뼈를 갖고 있다 / 성인들보다 →
8	the Berlin Wall, fall	우리는 배웠다 / 베를린 장벽이 무너졌던 것을 / 1989년에 →
9	tell, me, want	그는 내게 말했다 / 그가 나를 그날 만나고 싶었다고 →
10	be going, then	Jack은 내게 물어보았다 / 내가 그때 어디에 가는 중이냐고 →
11	have any questions	Kate는 그에게 물어보았다 / 그가 질문이 있는지를 →
12	cook	그녀는 내게 말했다 / 점심을 요리하라고 / 그녀를 위해 →
13	order	그 선생님은 우리에게 명령하셨다 / 학교에 지각하지 말라고 →

GP 65 강조

❶ **동사 강조**: [do / does / did + 동사원형] 형태로 동사의 의미를 강조 한다.

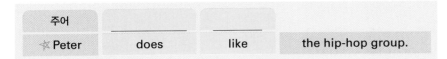

주어	_____	_____	
☆ Peter	does	like	the hip-hop group.

I **did** believe that she would fall in love with me.

❷ **[It is / was ~ that]에 의한 강조**: 강조 대상을 It is / was와 that 사이에 놓고 '～한 것은 바로 ～이다'로 해석한다.

	주어	동사	목적어	장소 부사(구)	시간 부사(구)
	Peter ❶	met	Alice ❷	in the park ❸	yesterday. ❹

	It	is (was)	_____	_____	나머지 문장
① 주어 강조	☆ It	was	Peter	that (who)	met Alice in the park yesterday.
② 목적어 강조	☆ It	was	Alice	that (whom)	Peter met in the park yesterday.
③ 장소 강조	☆ It	was	in the park	that (where)	Peter met Alice yesterday.
④ 시간 강조	It	was	yesterday	that (when)	Peter met Alice in the park.

Kelly will buy a new laptop tomorrow.

→ **It is** Kelly **that (who)** will buy a new laptop tomorrow.

→ **It is** a new laptop **that (which)** Kelly will buy tomorrow.

→ **It is** tomorrow **that (when)** Kelly will buy a new laptop.

> ○ Tip ○
> _____에 따라 _____
> 대신 who(m), which, when,
> where 등의 관계대명사나 관계
> 부사로 바꿔 쓸 수 있다.

GP 66 부정표현

❶ **전체부정**: no, none, neither, nothing 등이 문장에 쓰여 '_____'의 의미를 나타낸다.

☆ She had **nothing** to worry about.

(= She didn't have anything to worry about.)

None of my students likes English grammar.

(= All of my students don't like English grammar.)

> ○ Tip ○
> none: 셋 이상에 대한 부정어
> neither: 둘에 대한 부정어

❷ **부분부정**: 전체 중 일부만을 부정하는 것으로 '_____'의 의미를 나타낸다.

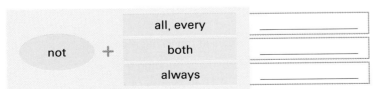

not	+	all, every	_____
		both	_____
		always	_____

Not all the students hate English grammar. (Not + all + _____명사)

☆ **Not every** man enjoys talking about soccer. (Not + every + _____명사)

☆ Rich people are **not always** happy.

❶ _____ : 장소나 운동의 방향을 나타내는 부사구가 강조되어 문장의 처음에 오면 [부사구 + 동사 + 주어]
의 어순이 된다.

On the bed slept a cute baby.
From the ceiling hung an enormous spider.

• Upgrade •

주어가 대명사이면 도치가 이루어지지 않고 [주어 + 동사] 어순 그대로 쓴다.
The bus comes here. → Here comes the bus.
She comes here. → ☆ Here she comes.

❷ _____ : not, never, little, seldom, hardly, only 등의 부정어가 강조되어 문장의 처음에 오면 [부정어 + 조동
사 + 주어]나 [부정어 + be동사 + 주어]의 어순이 된다.

Little did I dream of meeting the movie star.
Not a single word could he say.

❸ _____ : [so + 동사 + 주어]는 _____ 뒤에, [neither + 동사 + 주어]는 _____ 뒤에 쓰이고
'역시 ～하다 / 하지 않다'의 의미이다.

주어	일반동사 ~					☆ I am sick of fast food, and so is my friend.
주어	be동사 ~	+	so	be동사	주어	I didn't hear your complaints, and neither did John.
주어	조동사 ~		neither	조동사	주어	☆ She won't go to the party, and neither will I.
주어	have p.p. ~			have	주어	A: Susan has been to America. B: So have I.

명사, 대명사의 의미를 보충하거나 바꿔 말하기 위해 한 번 더 설명해 주는 말을 그 (대)명사의 동격이라고 한다.

(대)명사	,	(대)명사	☆ Mr. Morgan, a doctor, advised me to eat more fruit.
the 명사	of	명사(구)	Spain considered the possibility of building a canal.
the 명사	that	주어 + 동사	I agreed with the idea that the rule should be changed.

A ( ) 안에서 알맞은 것을 고르시오.

1 I don't like (any, none) of them.

2 She (do, does) look gorgeous today.

3 (All not, Not all) the passengers were rescued.

4 My baby did (walk, walked) by himself last night.

5 What (is it, it is) that you are talking about?

6 Not (all, every) person can be a great artist.

7 It was a romantic movie (what, that) we decided to see together.

8 It was John (who, whom) used my cell phone without my permission.

B 문장의 밑줄 친 부분을 강조하여 다시 쓸 때 빈칸에 알맞은 말을 쓰시오.

1 The ants save food for the winter.

→ The ants _____ for the winter.

2 They are complaining about the weather.

→ _____ they are complaining about.

3 She got to know my brother through me.

→ _____ she got to know my brother.

4 We found the information on the Internet.

→ _____ we found the information.

5 He didn't know the fact until yesterday.

→ _____ he knew the fact.

C 두 문장이 같은 의미를 갖도록 빈칸을 채우시오.

1 I don't have anything to be afraid of.

→ I have _____ to be afraid of.

2 All of them were not shocked by the car accident.

→ _____ of them were shocked by the car accident.

3 She doesn't like either of the two colors.

→ She likes _____ of the two colors.

4 The mystery has never been solved by anyone.

→ _____ has ever solved the mystery.

D 보기에서 알맞은 말을 골라 두 문장이 같은 의미를 갖도록 문장을 완성하시오.

| 보기 | all | every | always |

1 Most students gave up math, but others don't.

→ _____ student gave up math.

2 Most of the scientists agree with the theory, but others don't.

→ _____ of the scientists agree with the theory.

3 People are usually satisfied with the service, but sometimes they are not.

→ People are _____ satisfied with the service.

E 우리말과 의미가 같도록 ( ) 안의 말을 배열하시오.

1 양파는 정말로 치통을 줄여 준다. (do, pain, onions, tooth, reduce)

→ _____ .

2 네가 가장 필요한 것은 바로 충분한 휴식이야. (some, is, it, you, need, rest, most, good, that)

→ _____ .

3 모든 파일이 삭제되어야 하는 것은 아니다. (be, not, file, every, should, deleted)

→ _____ .

4 그가 컴퓨터를 발명한 곳은 바로 차고였어. (he, it, in, was, where, built, a computer, the garage)

→ _____ .

F 우리말과 의미가 같도록 ( ) 안의 말을 이용하여 문장을 완성하시오.

1 모든 가수들이 음악을 작곡하는 것은 아니다. (all)

→ _____ _____ _____ compose music.

2 그는 피자를 10분 안에 정말 배달했다. (deliver)

→ _____ _____ _____ the pizza within 10 minutes.

3 비닐봉지가 항상 재활용되는 것은 아니다. (recycled)

→ Plastic bags are _____ _____ _____ .

4 소녀들을 매력적으로 만드는 것은 다름 아닌 미소이다. (a smile)

→ _____ _____ _____ _____ _____ makes girls attractive.

5 내가 그녀와 영화를 본 것은 바로 지난 주말이었다. (when)

→ _____ _____ _____ _____ I watched a movie with her.

Unit 33 도치·동격

A ( ) 안에서 알맞은 것을 고르시오.

1 Away (the bird flew, flew the bird).

2 Under the parasol (she was, was she) lying.

3 Seldom (he does, does he) go out on Sundays.

4 My cousin has been to Europe, and so (do, have) I.

5 Only in the cafeteria (the students can, can the students) eat.

6 Below the bridge (passed a motorboat, a motorboat passed).

7 Not only (he was, was he) a teacher, but he was also a famous poet.

8 She didn't like the red dress, and neither (was, did) her mother.

9 I have a feeling (that, which) this winter will be freezing cold.

10 Mr. Kim, (was a good doctor, a good doctor), helped poor people a lot.

B 다음 문장을 주어진 말로 바꿔 쓸 때 빈칸에 알맞은 말을 쓰시오.

1 He could find his wallet nowhere.

→ Nowhere _____.

2 A lamppost is between the buildings.

→ Between the buildings _____.

3 I will never forget your kindness.

→ Never _____.

4 She came here with his family.

→ Here _____.

5 I little thought he would become a dancer.

→ Little _____.

6 A stranger stood in front of the door.

→ In front of the door _____.

7 He can go to an Internet café only twice a week.

→ Only twice a week _____.

8 My friend didn't say a word all day long.

→ Not a word _____.

9 I have rarely heard such a silly question.

→ Rarely _____.

10 A little rabbit hopped in the tall grass.

→ In the tall grass _____.

C 두 문장이 같은 의미를 갖도록 so 또는 neither를 이용하여 빈칸을 채우시오.

1 They came fast, and the ambulance did, too.

→ They came fast, and _____.

2 I haven't lied to my friend, and he hasn't either.

→ I haven't lied to my friend, and _____.

D ( ) 안의 말과 so 또는 neither를 이용하여 빈칸을 채우시오.

1 A: I don't feel well.   B: (I) _____.

2 A: I will keep my promise.   B: (she) _____.

3 A: I am proud of myself.   B: (he) _____.

4 A: I didn't learn how to drive.   B: (he) _____.

E 우리말과 의미가 같도록 ( ) 안의 말을 배열하시오.

1 한 아름다운 여인이 들어왔다. (a, came, woman, beautiful)

→ In _____.

2 그는 에너지드링크의 위험성을 거의 깨닫지 못했다. (he, the, did, realize, dangers)

→ Little _____ of energy drinks.

3 그 생선은 신선하지 않은데 야채도 그렇다. (the, are, and, neither, vegetables)

→ The fish isn't fresh, _____.

4 나는 우리 팀이 우승했다는 그 소식을 믿을 수 없다. (that, our, won, team, the news, the championship)

→ I can't believe _____.

F 우리말과 의미가 같도록 ( ) 안의 말을 이용하여 문장을 완성하시오.

1 테이블 위에 상자 하나가 놓여 있다. (lie)

→ On the table _____ _____ _____.

2 그녀는 절대로 청바지를 입지 않는다. (wear)

→ Never _____ _____ _____ blue jeans.

3 나는 그렇게 재미있는 경기를 TV에서 거의 본 적이 없다. (see)

→ Hardly _____ _____ _____ such an exciting game on TV.

Error Correction

■ 밑줄 친 부분에 대한 설명을 체크하고 틀린 경우엔 바르게 고치시오. (맞으면 'O' 표시)

1	Peter does <u>likes</u> the hip hop-group. (→)	동사 강조는 do / does / did + (동사, 동사원형)
2	It was Peter <u>what</u> met Alice in the park yesterday. (→)	주어를 강조할 때는 It is / was + 주어 + (that, what) + 동사
3	<u>This</u> was Alice that Peter met in the park yesterday. (→)	목적어를 강조할 때는 (This, It) is / was + 목적어 + that + 주어 + 동사
4	It was in the park <u>when</u> Peter met Alice yesterday. (→)	강조 대상이 (시간, 장소)일 때는 that 대신 (when, where) 사용 가능
5	She <u>didn't have</u> nothing to worry about. (→)	부정어 nothing과 not은 함께 쓸 수 (있다, 없다)
6	<u>No</u> every man enjoys talking about soccer. (→)	부분부정 '모두 ~인 것은 아니다'는 (No, Not) + every + (복수, 단수)명사
7	Rich people are <u>not always</u> happy. (→)	부분부정 '항상 ~인 것은 아니다'는 (not + always, always + not)
8	Under the table <u>a dog lies</u>. (→)	장소 부사구가 강조되어 문장의 처음에 오면 장소 부사구 + (주어 + 동사, 동사 + 주어)
9	Here <u>comes she</u>. (→)	장소 부사구 도치에서 주어가 대명사이면 장소 부사구 + (주어 + 동사, 동사 + 주어)
10	Seldom <u>Bob talks</u> to Janice. (→)	부정어가 강조되어 문장의 처음에 오면 부정어구 + (주어 + 현재동사, do(es) + 주어 + 동사원형)
11	I am sick of fast food, and <u>so my friend is</u>. (→)	주어 + 동사 (긍정문) and + (so, neither) + (주어 + 동사, 동사 + 주어)
12	She won't go to the party, and <u>so will I</u>. (→)	주어 + 동사 (부정문) and + (so, neither) + (주어 + 동사, 동사 + 주어)
13	Mr. Morgan, <u>is</u> a doctor, advised me to eat more fruit. (→)	동격을 나타낼 때 명사 + comma(,) + (명사, 동사 + 명사)

Sentence writing

Chapter 12
특수구문

■ 주어진 단어를 알맞게 이용하여 우리말과 의미가 같도록 영작하시오.

1	like, the hip-hop group	Peter는 / 정말 좋아한다 / 힙합 그룹을 →
2	it, that, meet, in the park	바로 Peter였다 / Alice를 만났던 사람은 / 공원에서 / 어제 →
3	it, that, meet, in the park	바로 Alice였다 / Peter가 만났던 사람은 / 공원에서 / 어제 →
4	it, that, meet, in the park	바로 공원이었다 / Peter가 Alice를 만났던 곳은 / 어제 →
5	nothing, worry about	그녀는 / 아무것도 갖고 있지 않았다 / 걱정할 →
6	every, enjoy, talk	모든 남자가 ~인 것은 아니다 / 말하는 것을 즐기는 / 축구에 대해 →
7	rich, people, always	부자들이 / 항상 ~인 것은 아니다 / 행복한 →
8	lie, under the table	테이블 아래에 / 누워 있다 / 개가 →
9	here, come	여기 / 그녀가 / 온다 →
10	seldom, talk to	거의 ~하지 않는다 / Bob이 말한다 / Janice에게 →
11	be sick of, fast food	나는 싫증이 난다 / 패스트푸드에, / 그리고 역시 그렇다 / 나의 친구도 →
12	will, go, not, the party	그녀는 / 가지 않을 거다 / 파티에, / 그리고 역시 그렇다 / 나도 →
13	advise, eat, more fruit	Morgan 씨는 / 의사인 / 충고했다 / 나에게 / 더 많은 야채를 먹으라고 →

도전! 필수구문 156

Chapter 01 시제 통문장 영작

001	그는 이미 그의 숙제를 끝마쳤다.	→
002	나는 그 도시를 세 번 방문한 적 있다.	→
003	그들은 서로를 5년 동안 알고 지내왔다.	→
004	그는 그의 결혼반지를 잃어버렸다. (지금 갖고 있지 않다.)	→
005	그는 그리스에 가 본 적이 있다.	→
006	그는 그리스로 가버렸다.	→
007	그녀는 그 책을 지금까지 한 시간 동안 읽어 오고 있는 중이다.	→
008	내가 극장에 들어갔을 때 연극은 이미 시작했었다.	→
009	그는 그가 20세가 될 때까지 해외에 가 본 적 없었다.	→
010	Judy는 의사가 왔을 때 이틀 동안 아파 왔었다.	→
011	나는 휴대폰을 잃어버려서, 네게 그때 전화 할 수 없었다.	→
012	그녀는 비가 오기 시작할 때 세차를 해 오고 있는 중이었다.	→
013	네가 이 영화를 다시 본다면, 너는 이것을 열 번째 보는 것이 될 것이다.	→

도전! 필수구문 156

Chapter 02 조동사 통문장 영작

014	그는 다섯 가지 외국어를 말할 수 있다.	→
015	그는 너의 아이디어를 좋아할지도 모른다.	→
016	당신은 박물관에서 사진을 찍으면 안 됩니다.	→
017	7세 이하 아동은 입장료를 지불할 필요가 없습니다.	→
018	너는 분명히 매우 열심히 연습했을 것이다.	→
019	우리는 우리 부모님을 존경해야 한다.	→
020	나는 내 숙제를 했어야만 했는데. (하지 못해서 유감이다.)	→
021	Mike는 외국 동전을 수집하곤 했었다.	→
022	그는 내 남자친구였지만, 지금은 아니다.	→
023	너는 창가 자리에 앉는 것이 좋겠다.	→
024	우리는 비 때문에 오늘밤에 나가지 않는 것이 좋겠다.	→
025	나는 집에서 TV를 보는 것보다 차라리 나가서 놀겠다.	→
026	더 이상 할 것이 없다면, 우리는 집에 가는 것이 낫겠다.	→

Chapter 03 수동태 통문장 영작

027	우주 엘리베이터가 그 회사에 의해 건설되어지고 있는 중이다.	→
028	그 길은 폭설 때문에 폐쇄되어져 왔다.	→
029	이 꽃들은 매일 물을 줘야 한다.	→
030	그 강아지는 그에 의해 보살펴졌다.	→
031	두 장의 콘서트 티켓이 그녀에 의해 그에게 주어졌다.	→
032	멋진 배낭이 나의 삼촌에 의해 나를 위해 구입되었다.	→
033	그녀는 걸어 다니는 사전이라고 불려졌다.	→
034	우리는 그에게 앉으라는 지시를 들었다.	→
035	나는 Jessica에 의해 방을 청소하게 되었다.	→
036	그 소년이 나무에 오르는 것이 보여졌다.	→
037	웃음이 행운을 가져온다고 이야기된다. (It으로 시작)	→
038	웃음은 행운을 가져온다고 이야기된다. (Laughter로 시작)	→
039	한국의 대중음악은 K-pop이라고 알려져 있다.	→

도전! 필수구문 156

Chapter 04 부정사 통문장 영작

040	이 앱은 날씨를 확인하는 것을 더 쉬운 상태로 만든다.	→	
041	우리는 어디에서 우리의 휴가를 보낼지를 결정했다.	→	
042	나는 가지고 쓸 연필이 필요하다.	→	
043	우리는 다음달에 멕시코를 방문할 예정이다.	→	
044	내 비밀번호는 기억하기에 쉬웠다.	→	
045	나는 네가 내 말을 주의깊게 듣기를 원한다.	→	
046	그의 재미있는 농담은 그녀를 웃게 만들었다.	→	
047	그녀는 새끼 고양이들이 공을 가지고 노는 것을 보았다.	→	
048	그가 할머니를 도와드렸던 것은 친절했다.	→	
049	그는 답을 알고 있는 것처럼 보인다.	→	
050	그는 답을 알고 있었던 것처럼 보인다.	→	
051	그는 당신 같은 여성과 결혼할 만큼 충분히 운이 좋았다.	→	
052	그 프로그램은 그가 시청하기엔 너무 폭력적이었다.	→	

도전! 필수구문 156

Chapter 05 동명사 통문장 영작

053	태양열을 이용하는 것은 지구에 좋다.	→
054	우리는 밤에 별을 보는 것을 즐겼다.	→
055	그녀는 이야기하는 것을 잘한다.	→
056	당신은 그녀가 문을 닫는 것을 꺼려하시나요?	→
057	그는 성우인 것을 자랑스러워한다.	→
058	그는 성우였던 것을 자랑스러워한다.	→
059	너는 크리스마스트리 장식하는 것을 끝냈니?	→
060	Judy는 마침내 그의 제안을 받아들이는 것을 동의했다.	→
061	Evan은 기타 연주하는 것을 시작했다.	→
062	그는 내게 그의 우산을 빌려주었던 것을 잊었다.	→
063	그는 내게 그의 우산을 빌려줄 것을 잊었다.	→
064	Tom은 내게 말하던 것을 멈췄다.	→
065	나는 결정하는 것을 어려워한다.	→

도전! 필수구문 156

Chapter 06 분사 통문장 영작

066	저 떠오르는 태양을 보아라.	→
067	동쪽에서 떠오르는 저 태양을 보아라.	→
068	그는 소녀가 기다리는 것을 계속하게 했다.	→
069	그는 그의 눈이 감긴 채로 계속 유지했다.	→
070	그는 그 남자가 그의 집을 페인트칠하는 것을 보았다.	→
071	그는 그의 집이 페인트칠된 것을 보았다.	→
072	나를 보자마자, 그녀는 기뻐서 소리질렀다.	→
073	어떻게 미안하다고 할지를 몰랐기 때문에, 소년은 그냥 울었다.	→
074	그녀를 이전에 보았었기 때문에, 나는 그녀의 얼굴을 안다.	→
075	그 소식에 충격을 받아서, 그는 한마디도 하지 않았다.	→
076	어제 비가 심하게 내려서, 그 콘서트가 취소되었다.	→
077	그는 잠을 자고 있었고 알람은 울리고 있었다.	→
078	비둘기 한 마리가 메시지가 다리에 묶여진 채로 내게 날아왔다.	→

도전! 필수구문 156

Chapter 07 비교표현 통문장 영작

079	나의 개는 치타만큼 빠르게 달릴 수 있다.	→
080	록 밴드는 걸 그룹만큼 유명하지 않다.	→
081	이 폰이 저 폰보다 더 싸다.	→
082	사하라 사막(The Sahara Desert)은 세계에서 가장 큰 사막이다.	→
083	이 자전거는 나의 오래된 자전거보다 세 배 더 가볍다.	→
084	너의 요점은 가능한 한 구체적이어야 한다.	→
085	철은 알루미늄보다 훨씬 더 무겁다.	→
086	우리의 세상은 점점 더 작아지고 있다.	→
087	날이 어두워질수록, 더 추워졌다.	→
088	Jennifer는 그녀의 반에서 가장 활동적인 소녀들 중 한 명이다.	→
089	그는 지금껏 내가 만난 가장 용감한 남자이다.	→
090	세계에서 다른 어떤 강도 나일 강(the Nile)보다 더 길지 않다.	→
091	나일 강(the Nile)은 세계에서 다른 어떤 강보다 더 길다.	→

Chapter 08 접속사 통문장 영작

092	그녀가 공부하고 있는 동안, 그녀는 음악을 들었다.	→	
093	법에 따르면, 네가 18세가 될 때까지 너는 아동이다.	→	
094	그가 초초함을 느낄 때, 그는 손톱을 물어뜯는다.	→	
095	그녀가 지금 떠나지 않으면, 그녀는 비행기를 놓칠 것이다.	→	
096	그는 이것이 너무 폭력적이어서 영화를 보는 것을 멈췄다.	→	
097	그가 티켓을 갖고 있었음에도 그는 뮤지컬을 보러 가지 않았다.	→	
098	내가 그녀를 다음번에 만나면, 나는 그녀에게 말을 걸 것이다.	→	
099	나는 그가 어디에 사는지를 모른다.	→	
100	나는 누가 창문을 깼었는지를 알아.	→	
101	너는 그의 진짜 직업이 무엇이라고 생각하니?	→	
102	나는 그녀가 콘테스트에서 이길지 아닐지를 모르겠다.	→	
103	Jack과 Jill 모두 대학교 학생들이다.	→	
104	그 아이들과 그들의 엄마 모두 고기를 좋아하지 않는다. (neither)	→	

도전! 필수구문 156

Chapter 09 관계사 통문장 영작

105	나는 우주에 관한 책을 샀다.	→	
106	그는 내가 가장 존경하는 남자다.	→	
107	나는 그의 딸이 유명한 여배우인 남자를 안다.	→	
108	너는 네가 하고 싶은 것을 할 수 있어.	→	
109	우리가 화성에 살 수 있는 날이 올 것이다.	→	
110	너는 로마가 멸망했던 이유를 아니?	→	
111	그 프로그램은 어떻게 사람들이 시간을 현명하게 관리하는지를 보여 준다.	→	
112	경찰은 공항에서 내가 잃어버렸던 가방을 찾았다.	→	
113	너는 내가 의지할 수 있는 사람이야.	→	
114	우리는 해산물 요리를 주문했는데, 그것은 정말로 맛이 없었다.	→	
115	성공하기를 원하는 누구든지 부지런해야만 한다.	→	
116	그 개는 그가 가는 곳은 어디든지 아빠를 따라간다.	→	
117	그가 아무리 똑똑하더라도, 그는 그녀의 눈물을 이해하지 못할 것이다.	→	

도전! 필수구문 156 135

Chapter 10 가정법 통문장 영작

118	만약 그가 공책이 있다면, 그는 나에게 빌려줄 텐데.	→		
119	네가 이 기회를 놓친다면, 너는 후회할 거야.	→		
120	이 차가 조금 더 쌌더라면, 나는 그것을 구입했을 텐데.	→		
121	만약 내가 나의 일을 어제 끝냈더라면, 나는 지금 더 많은 자유 시간을 가질 텐데.	→		
122	내가 좀 더 크면 좋을 텐데.	→		
123	내가 이 프로젝트를 더 일찍 끝냈었다면 좋을 텐데.	→		
124	그는 마치 나의 남자친구인 것처럼 행동한다.	→		
125	그는 마치 그 영화를 봤던 것처럼 말한다.	→		
126	이제 과거를 돌아봐야 할 시간이다.	→		
127	내가 너라면, 나는 일자리 제안을 받아들일 텐데.	→		
128	그녀가 그의 전화번호를 알았더라면, 그녀는 그에게 전화했을 텐데.	→		
129	불이 없으면, 우리는 정상적인 삶을 살 수 없을 텐데.	→		
130	만약 너의 도움이 없었더라면, 나는 나만의 블로그를 만들 수 없었을 텐데.	→		

도전! 필수구문 156

Chapter 11 일치와 화법 통문장 영작

131	네덜란드는 튤립과 풍차들로 유명하다.	→	
132	3달러는 그 우유를 사기에 충분하다.	→	
133	젊은 사람들은 노인들보다 빨리 배운다.	→	
134	많은 사람들이 해변에서 쉬고 있다.	→	
135	그 블로그 방문객 수가 증가하고 있다.	→	
136	나는 나의 선생님이 나를 신뢰하시는 것을 안다.	→	
137	그 책은 아이들이 성인들보다 더 많은 뼈를 갖고 있다고 했다.	→	
138	우리는 베를린 장벽이 1989년에 무너졌던 것을 배웠다.	→	
139	그는 내게 그가 나를 그날 만나고 싶었다고 말했다.	→	
140	Jack은 나에게 그때 내가 어디에 가는 중이었냐고 물어보았다.	→	
141	Kate는 그에게 그가 질문이 있는지를 물어보았다.	→	
142	그녀는 나에게 그녀를 위해 점심을 요리하라고 말했다.	→	
143	그 선생님은 우리에게 학교에 지각하지 말라고 명령하셨다.	→	

도전! 필수구문 156

Chapter 12 특수구문 통문장 영작

144	Peter는 힙합 그룹을 정말 좋아한다.	→	
145	어제 공원에서 Alice를 만났던 사람은 바로 Peter였다.	→	
146	어제 공원에서 Peter가 만났던 사람은 바로 Alice였다.	→	
147	Peter가 어제 Alice를 만났던 곳은 바로 공원이었다.	→	
148	그녀는 아무것도 걱정할 것이 없었다.	→	
149	모든 남자가 축구에 대해 말하는 것을 즐기는 것은 아니다.	→	
150	부자들이 항상 행복한 것은 아니다.	→	
151	테이블 아래에 개가 누워 있다.	→	
152	여기 그녀가 오네요.	→	
153	Bob은 Janice에게 거의 말 걸지 않는다.	→	
154	나는 패스트푸드에 싫증이 나는데, 나의 친구도 그래.	→	
155	그녀는 파티에 가지 않을 건데, 나도 그래.	→	
156	의사인 Morgan 씨는 나에게 더 많은 야채를 먹으라고 충고했다.	→	

138

문장 형식을 결정짓는 동사들, 다 모여!

❶ 완전 자동사 (1형식 동사)

주어	완전 자동사	수식어
	_____, _____, _____, _____, fall, happen, arrive...	

❷ 불완전 자동사 (2형식 동사)

주어	불완전 자동사		_____
	_____ 동사	_____ 동사, _____, stay, keep...	명사 / 형용사
	_____ 동사	_____, _____, _____, grow...	
	_____ 동사	_____, _____, smell, sound...	형용사

A 보기와 같이 문장에서 주어(S), 동사(V), 주격보어(S.C)를 표시하고 형식을 쓰시오.

보기	$\underset{\text{S}}{\text{Snow}}\ \underset{\text{V}}{\text{fell}}\ \text{heavily.}$ (1형식)	$\underset{\text{S}}{\text{The weather}}\ \underset{\text{V}}{\text{is getting}}\ \underset{\text{S.C}}{\text{hot.}}$ (2형식)

1 His uncle traveled around the world by ship. (_____형식)

2 The leaves turned red and yellow. (_____형식)

3 He looked young in his new shirt. (_____형식)

4 These trees grow only in the tropics. (_____형식)

5 Micky came to Korea with his family. (_____형식)

6 The baby bird fell from its nest. (_____형식)

7 The robot is useful for carrying heavy boxes. (_____형식)

B ( ) 안의 말을 이용하여 우리말과 같은 의미를 갖도록 영작하시오.

1 다크초콜릿은 쓴맛이 난다. (taste, bitter)

→ _____.

2 열기구가 하늘 높이 날아가고 있었다. (a hot air-balloon, fly)

→ _____ high in the sky.

3 우리는 그의 이야기에 점점 흥미를 느끼게 되었다. (become, interested)

→ _____ in his story.

4 내 강아지의 이름은 팅커벨이다. (Tinker Bell, the name of)

→ _____.

❸ 완전 타동사 (3형식 동사)

주어	완전 타동사	＿＿＿＿＿
	enter, reach, discuss, resemble...	명사 / 대명사
	want, ＿＿＿＿, ＿＿＿＿, ＿＿＿＿, ＿＿＿＿ ...	to부정사
	enjoy, ＿＿＿＿, ＿＿＿＿, ＿＿＿＿ ...	동명사
	say, ＿＿＿＿, ＿＿＿＿, ＿＿＿＿ ...	that절

C 보기와 같이 문장에서 주어(S), 동사(V), 목적어 (O)를 표시하시오.

보기	<u>I</u> <u>bought</u> <u>these nice shoes</u> at a flea market.
	S　　V　　　　　O

1 He built a new house for his parents.

2 William decided to plant apple trees next year.

3 She ordered two hamburgers and a soda.

4 I know that the park is closed on Sundays.

5 Do you mind changing seats with me?

6 We wash our hands to get rid of germs.

7 The moon keeps changing its shape.

8 She is planning to hold a party this Saturday.

D ( ) 안의 말을 이용하여 우리말과 같은 의미를 갖도록 영작하시오.

1 그는 미술관에서 그의 사진들을 전시했다. (display, photographs)

→ ＿＿＿＿＿＿＿＿＿＿＿＿＿＿＿＿＿ in the art museum.

2 Henry는 축구 동아리에 가입하는 것을 동의했다. (agree, join)

→ ＿＿＿＿＿＿＿＿＿＿＿＿＿＿＿＿＿ the soccer club.

3 그것의 나쁜 냄새는 해충으로부터 자신을 보호한다. (protect, itself)

→ ＿＿＿＿＿＿＿＿＿＿＿＿＿＿＿＿＿ from harmful insects.

4 너는 숙제하는 것을 언제 끝마쳤니? (finish, do)

→ ＿＿＿＿＿＿＿＿＿＿＿＿＿＿＿＿＿ your homework?

5 그 농구팀은 결승전을 이길 것을 기대했다. (expect, win)

→ ＿＿＿＿＿＿＿＿＿＿＿＿＿＿＿＿＿ the final game.

6 그녀는 여행 계획을 만드는 것을 즐겼다. (enjoy, make)

→ ＿＿＿＿＿＿＿＿＿＿＿＿＿＿＿＿＿ a travel plan.

❹ 수여동사 (4형식 동사)

주어	수여동사	_____목적어	_____목적어
	give, send, write, bring...		
	make, buy, cook, find...	명사 / 대명사	명사
	ask, inqure...		

* 4형식 문장의 3형식 문장으로의 전환

주어	수여동사	_____목적어	전치사	_____목적어
	_____, _____, _____, bring...		_____	
	_____, _____, _____, find...	명사 / 대명사	_____	명사 / 대명사
	_____, inqure...		_____	

E 보기와 같이 문장에서 주어(S), 동사(V), 간접목적어(I.O), 직접목적어(D.O)를 표시하고 형식을 쓰시오.

보기	Could you give me some advice about the contest? (4형식) 　　　　S　　V　I.O　　D.O

1 Andrew sent me the package by airmail.　　　　(_____형식)

2 May I ask you a personal question?　　　　(_____형식)

3 The waiter brought me some nice, warm soup.　　　　(_____형식)

4 The boy showed his new toys to his friends.　　　　(_____형식)

5 This new machine can make all of us coffee.　　　　(_____형식)

6 Could you show me your passport?　　　　(_____형식)

7 I bought a silk scarf for my mom.　　　　(_____형식)

F ( ) 안의 말을 이용하여 우리말과 같은 의미를 갖도록 영작하시오. (4형식으로 쓰기)

1 Sandra는 어제 내게 두 장의 영화 티켓을 주었다. (movie ticket)

→ _____ yesterday.

2 Mr. Kelly는 그 길고양이에게 새로운 집을 찾아주었다. (street cat, home)

→ _____ .

3 그 자원봉사자들은 가난한 아이들에게 새 책들을 가져다주었다. (the volunteers, bring)

→ _____ .

4 우리에게 점심으로 스파게티를 만들어주시겠어요? (some spaghetti)

→ Could _____ for lunch?

141

❺ 불완전 타동사 (5형식 동사)

주어	불완전 타동사	_____	_____
	call, name, elect...	명사 / 대명사	명사
	make, keep, find...		형용사
	_____, _____, _____, _____...		to부정사
	_____, _____, _____...		동사원형
	_____, _____, _____...		동사원형 / 현재분사

G 보기와 같이 문장에서 주어(S), 동사(V), 목적어(O), 목적격보어(O.C)를 표시하시오.

보기	<u>Miranda</u> <u>asked</u> <u>me</u> <u>to help her</u> last week.
	S V O OC

1 Hot baths always make me feel relaxed.

2 We all want other people to understand us.

3 I will let you know the reason soon.

4 The children call their dog Snoopy.

5 Simon found the weather in Korea very cold.

6 His hit song made him a star.

7 The doctor advised him to eat less fatty food.

8 He watched the airplane take off into the sky.

H 우리말과 같은 의미를 갖도록 ( ) 안의 말을 알맞게 배열하시오.

1 그들의 두꺼운 지방층은 그들의 몸을 따뜻하게 유지시킨다. (their bodies, warm, keeps)

   → Their thick layer of fat _____.

2 그녀는 바람이 그녀의 머리를 만지는 것을 느꼈다. (the wind, her hair, touching, felt)

   → She _____.

3 나는 네가 여기에 있을 것이라고 예상하지 않았어. (you, to, expect, be, here)

   → I didn't _____.

4 엄마는 내가 양치할 때 컵을 사용하도록 하셨어. (use, me, had, a cup)

   → My mom _____ when brushing my teeth.

5 우리는 세상을 더 나은 곳으로 만들 수 있어요. (the world, a better place, make)

   → We can _____.

❶ 같은 동사이지만 문장 형식에 따라 의미가 달라진다.

	주어	동사	간접목적어	직접목적어	목적격보어	
_____형식	He	made		a plan.		~를 _____
_____형식	Ken	made	me	a plane.		~에게 ~를 _____
_____형식	I	made		Tim	study.	~에게 ~하라고 _____

	주어	동사	간접목적어	직접목적어	목적격보어	
_____형식	They	found		a diamond.		~를 _____
_____형식	She	found	me	my lost pen.		~에게 ~를 _____
_____형식	We	found		Jessy	honest.	~가 ~임을 _____

A 밑줄 친 동사의 알맞은 해석을 고르시오.

1 Evan wanted you to say sorry first.   (~하기를 원하다, ~가 ~하기를 원하다)

2 Evan wanted to say sorry first.   (~하기를 원하다, ~가 ~하기를 원하다)

3 We keep vegetables in the refrigerator.   (~를 보관하다, ~를 ~상태로 유지하다)

4 The refrigerator keeps vegetables fresh.   (~를 보관하다, ~를 ~상태로 유지하다)

❷ 감각동사 (_____ 형식) VS. 지각동사 (_____ 형식)

❶ _____동사는 주어의 상태를 보충 설명해주는 주격보어와 쓰인다.

	주어	감각동사	_____	
시각	You	look	tired.	~ _____
청각	She	sounds	happy.	~ _____
후각	It	smells	delicious.	~ _____
촉각	The air	felt	fresh.	~ _____

❷ _____동사는 목적어의 상태나 동작을 보충 설명해 주는 목적격보어와 쓰인다.

	주어	지각동사	목적어	_____	
시각	I	saw	him	cook.	~ _____
청각	She	heard	us	singing.	~ _____
후각	We	smelled	something	burning.	~ _____
촉각	He	felt	someone	push him.	~ _____

B 다음 밑줄 친 동사가 감각동사인지 지각동사인지 고르시오.

1 He looked at his cat sleeping in a box.   (감각, 지각) 동사

2 His cat looked very peaceful in a box.   (감각, 지각) 동사

3 Her plan sounds interesting.   (감각, 지각) 동사

4 She heard birds singing in the early morning.   (감각, 지각) 동사

문장 형식을 결정짓는 동사들, 다 모여!

* 표의 빈칸은 본 교재 해당 내용 참조 (p.174 ~ p.176)

Unit 01 동사의 종류와 문장의 형식   p. 139

A

1 His uncle traveled around the world by ship. (1형식)
   S   V

2 The leaves turned red and yellow. (2형식)
    S   V   S.C

3 He looked young in his new shirt. (2형식)
  S   V   S.C

4 These trees grow only in the tropics. (1형식)
    S   V

5 Micky came to Korea with his family. (1형식)
  S   V

6 The baby bird fell from its nest. (1형식)
    S   V

7 The robot is useful for carrying heavy boxes. (2형식)
    S   V S.C

B

1 Dark chocolate tastes bitter
2 A hot air-balloon was flying
3 We became more interested
4 The name of my dog is Tinker Bell

C

1 He built a new house for his parents.
  S V   O

2 William decided to plant apple trees next year.
    S   V   O

3 She ordered two hamburgers and a soda.
  S   V   O

4 I know that the park is closed on Sundays.
 S V   O

5 Do you mind changing seats with me?
    S   V   O

6 We wash our hands to get rid of germs.
  S V   O

7 The moon keeps changing its shape.
    S   V   O

8 She is planning to hold a party this Saturday.
  S   V   O

D

1 He displayed his photographs
2 Henry agreed to join
3 Its bad smell protects itself
4 When did you finish doing
5 The basketball team expected to win
6 She enjoyed making

E

1 Andrew sent me the package by airmail. (4형식)
    S   V I.O   D.O

2 May I ask you a personal question? (4형식)
    S V I.O   D.O

3 The waiter brought me some nice, warm soup. (4형식)
    S   V   I.O   D.O

4 The boy showed his new toys to his friends. (3형식)
   S   V   O

5 This new machine can make all of us coffee. (4형식)
     S   V   I.O   D.O

6 Could you show me your passport? (4형식)
     S   V I.O   D.O

7 I bought a silk scarf for my mom. (3형식)
 S V   O

F

1 Sandra gave me two movie tickets
2 Mr. Kelly found the street cat a new home
3 The volunteers brought the poor children new books
4 you make us some spaghetti

G

1 Hot baths always make me feel relaxed.
    S   V O   O.C

2 We all want other people to understand us.
    S   V   O   O.C

3 I will let you know the reason soon.
 S   V O   O.C

4 The children call their dog Snoopy.
    S   V   O   O.C

5 Simon found the weather in Korea very cold.
  S   V   O   O.C

6 His hit song made him a star.
    S   V O O.C

7 The doctor advised him to eat less fatty food.
    S   V O   O.C

8 He watched the airplane take off into the sky.
  S   V   O   O.C

H

1 keeps their bodies warm
2 felt the wind touching her hair
3 expect you to be here
4 had me use a cup
5 make the world a better place

Unit 02 동사의 변신은 무죄!   p. 143

A

1 ~가 ~하기를 원하다   **2** ~하기를 원하다
3 ~를 보관하다   **4** ~를 ~상태로 유지하다

B

1 지각   **2** 감각
3 감각   **4** 지각

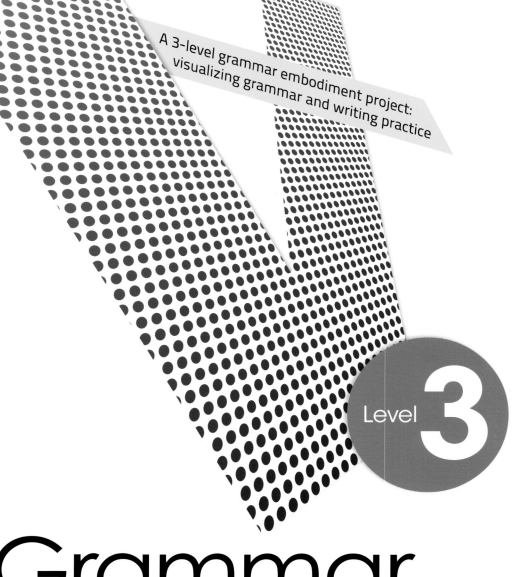

A 3-level grammar embodiment project:
visualizing grammar and writing practice

Level **3**

Grammar
ViSTA

정답과 해설

DARAKWON

Grammar ViSTA

Level 3

정답과 해설

● 본 교재　　　● workbook

GP Practice 01 현재완료
GP Practice 02 현재완료진행
p. 13

A 1 have　2 invented　3 since
4 been　5 has been

B 1 has been raining
2 has gone to　3 have left

C 1 Have we ever met
2 haven't decided
3 has been erupting for

D 1 has been running /
~해 오고 있는 중, has + been+ -ing
2 since / ~부터 계속, since, 과거 시점
3 been / ~ 가 본 적이 있다, been
4 have never seen / 경험, have + p.p.

GP Practice 03 과거완료
GP Practice 04 미래완료
p. 15

A 1 had driven　2 found
3 had　4 will have known
5 will have left

B 1 had been reading
2 had not eaten
3 will have arrived
4 had been swimming
5 had failed

C 1 had already started
2 had been watching
3 will have finished

D 1 had just left / had + p.p.
2 was / 과거
3 had been raining / had
4 will have become / will have + p.p.

Grammar & Writing
p. 16

A 1 has changed a lot since I left
2 have gained some weight
3 have been looking for
4 had been thinking about you
5 will have sponsored the African boy

6 I found I had gotten

B 1 have loved the song
2 has stopped raining
3 had been sleeping
4 had been flying
5 had washed all my socks
6 has been waiting for you

C 1 had learned
2 has learned
3 has been learning
4 will have learned

D 1 has lost
2 has gone to
3 have been cleaning
4 will have met

Actual Test
p. 18

1 ③　2 ⑤　3 ⑤　4 ②　5 ③　6 ②　7 ②　8 ④
9 ③　10 ③　11 ②　12 ①　13 has gone to
14 has been running　15 has forgotten
16 ③　17 ④　18 ⑤　19 ②　20 ③　21 has
taken pictures　22 had been chewing on
23 will have asked　24 ④　25 have lived in
this house since I was　26 had found the
error before　27 had been flying over the
Atlantic　28 has → had, 과거, had p.p.　29 are
→ have been, ~해 왔다, 현재완료　30 She had
never lost a game until then

1 '2002년 이래로 현재까지'처럼 과거부터 현재까지 계속되는
일은 현재완료를 씀.

2 과거 시점보다 이전의 일이므로 과거완료이다.

3 미래의 특정시점을 기준으로 그때까지 완료될 일이므로 미래
완료이다.

4 과거를 나타내는 부사(last year)는 과거시제와 함께 쓰임.

5 [has been to + 장소]: ~에 가 본 적 있다 (경험)

6 보기의 for a long time의 for는 '현재까지 ~동안 계속'이고
②의 since는 '~시점 이래로 현재까지 계속'을 의미함. ①, ④
는 완료, ③은 경험, ⑤는 결과이다.

7 보기와 ②는 경험, ①, ③은 완료, ④는 결과, ⑤는 계속이다.

8 과거 시점을 기준으로 그 이전의 일이므로 과거완료이다.

9 미래의 특정시점에 완료될 행동은 미래완료 [will have
won ~]을 씀.

10 ③은 현재 시점을 기준으로 그 이전에 펜을 잃어버려서 현재

없는 상태이므로 현재완료이다.

11 현재를 기준으로 각각 경험과 현재완료진행이며 3인칭 단수 주어이므로 [has p.p.], [has been + -ing]를 쓴다.

12 [since + 과거시점 / 주어 + 과거동사]: ~이래로

13 [have gone to]: ~로 가버리고 여기에 없다

14 과거 특정시점에 시작한 일이 현재에도 진행 중이면 현재완료진행형이다.

15 과거의 일이 현재까지 영향을 끼치면 현재완료이다.

16 과거 시점보다 이전의 일이므로 과거완료이다.

17 미래의 특정시점을 기준으로 그때까지 완료될 일이므로 미래완료이다.

18 과거부터 현재까지 얼마나 오래 해 왔는지를 묻는 질문이므로 현재완료로 대답함.

19 [has gone to]: ~로 가버리고 여기에 없다

20 ① has finished → will have finished ② have gone to → have been to ④ has repaired → had repaired ⑤ rained → raining

21 과거부터 현재까지 계속되는 일은 현재완료이다.

22 과거 특정시점보다 먼저 있었던 일이 그 과거 시점에도 진행되고 있는 일은 과거완료진행형이다.

23 미래의 특정시점을 기준으로 그때까지 완료될 일이므로 미래완료이다.

24 ⓓ는 그 이전부터 과거 시점까지 진행해 오던 일이므로 [had been cooking]이다.

25 [주절(현재완료) + since + 과거 시점]: ~이래로 ~해 왔다

26 과거 시점을 기준으로 그 전부터의 일이므로 과거완료이다.

27 그 이전부터 과거 시점까지 진행해 오던 일이므로 [had been + -ing]이다.

28 가수가 무대에 등장했던 과거를 기준시점으로 그 이전의 일은 [had + p.p.]이다.

29 since는 현재완료시제에 사용되므로 주절은 [주어 + 현재완료동사]이다.

30 과거 시점을 기준으로 그 전부터의 일이므로 과거완료이다.

Grammar Mapping

p. 22

① have / has + p.p.　② 현재　③ 완료　④ just
⑤ 경험　⑥ never　⑦ 계속 ~해 왔다　⑧ for
⑨ have / has + been + -ing　⑩ had + p.p.
⑪ 이전　⑫ 막 ~했었다　⑬ ~한 적이 있었다
⑭ 계속　⑮ ~해버렸다　⑯ will + have + p.p.
⑰ 미래

Chapter 02 조동사

GP Practice 05 can, may
GP Practice 06 must, should

p. 25

A	**1** Can	**2** can't	**3** be able to
	4 may	**5** must	
B	**1** may		**2** has to
	3 was able to		
C	**1** should have turned left		
	2 must have dialed		
	3 can't have read		
D	**1** cannot / ~일 리가 없다, cannot		
	2 be able to / 불가능, be able to		
	3 have cleaned / 과거, have p.p.		
	4 have come / 과거, have p.p.		

GP Practice 07 used to, would like to
GP Practice 08 had better, would rather, may as well

p. 27

A	**1** had better not	**2** would
	3 may as well	**4** would rather
	5 used to	
B	**1** used to	**2** would
	3 would rather	**4** had better
C	**1** would rather cook	
	2 had better not tell	
	3 used to be very energetic	
D	**1** used to / 상태, used to	
	2 had better not / 뒤, not	
	3 go / ~하는 것이 낫다, 동사원형	
	4 than / than, B, A	

Grammar & Writing

p. 28

A	**1** should not bother your pet
	2 May I have your attention
	3 used to carry me on her back
	4 cannot have been there
	5 had better not speak ill of others
	6 should have checked the schedule

B
1 must have eaten my chocolate
2 would like to introduce a new student
3 would rather go on foot
4 must be someone in the house
5 I may have met him before
6 had better take an umbrella

C
1 should be, should have been
2 cannot be, cannot have been
3 must be, must have been
4 may leave, may have left

D
1 used to have
2 would rather buy, fix
3 had better put on

Actual Test
p. 30

1 ③ 2 ④ 3 ④ 4 ③ 5 ③ 6 ③ 7 ② 8 ②
9 ① 10 ④ 11 would 12 must have known
13 don't have to 14 ⑤ 15 ④ 16 ② 17 ④
18 don't have to be responsible for 19 used
to be allergic 20 cannot have made that
foolish mistake 21 ② 22 ④ 23 ② 24 ③
25 has to feed 26 would rather take a walk
27 should have apologized 28 would → used
to, 상태, used to 29 had not better → had
better not, 뒤, not 30 must → have to, 동사
원형, have to 31 I should have brought my
swimsuit today

1 [cannot + 동사원형]: ~일 리가 없다
2 조동사 뒤에는 일반동사 원형을 사용한다.
3 [should have p.p.]는 '~했어야 했다'로 과거 일에 대한 유
   감이나 후회를 말함.
4 must는 과거형이 없으므로 과거의 의무를 나타낼 때는 had
   to를 씀.
5 현재를 기준으로 과거 사실에 관한 일은 [조동사(can, may,
   must, should) + have + p.p.] 형식을 씀.
6 파도가 높으므로 해변가에서 멀리 떨어져야 한다는 당위성 또
   는 의무가 문맥상 자연스럽다. can은 '능력, 허락, 추측'을 의
   미한다.
7 ② [would rather + 동사원형]: 차라리 ~하는 것이 낫겠다
8 ② [used to + 동사원형]: (예전에) ~했다
9 must는 의무(~해야 한다), 강한 추측(~임에 틀림없다) 의미
   를 가짐.
10 would는 '~하곤 했다'이고 [would like to]는 '~하고 싶다'
   이다.

11 [used to + 동사원형] = [would + 동사원형]: 과거에 ~하
   곤 했다
12 [must have p.p.]: ~했음이 분명하다
13 [don't have [need] to + 동사원형]: ~할 필요 없다
14 ① [조동사 + 동사원형] ② [may as well + 동사원형]:
   ~하는 것이 낫겠다 ③ [used to + 동사원형]: ~하곤 했다
   ④ [ought to + 동사원형]: ~해야 한다
15 [must have p.p.]는 현재를 기준으로 과거 사실에 대한 강
   한 추측을 나타냄.
16 [had better not + 동사원형]: ~하지 않는 것이 낫다
17 '열심히 했음이 분명하다'가 문맥상 자연스러우므로 [must
   have worked hard]를 써야 함.
18 [don't have to + 동사원형]: ~할 필요 없다
19 [used to + 동사원형]: (예전에) ~하곤 했다
20 [can't have p.p.]: ~했을 리가 없다
21 ② 그의 결정이 잘못될 리가 없다. (부정적 추측)
22 ④ [should have p.p.]는 '~했어야 했다'이고 [must have
   p.p.]는 '~했음이 분명하다'로 같은 의미가 아님.
23 ②는 '강한 추측'이고 나머지는 '의무'이다.
24 ⓐ [had better not + 동사원형]: ~하지 않는 편이 낫다
   ⓓ [would rather + A + than + B]: B하느니 A하겠다(A,
   B 모두 동사원형) ⓔ [should have p.p]: ~했어야 했다
25 [have to + 동사원형]은 '~해야 한다'이다. 주어가 3인칭 단
   수이며 현재시제이므로 has to를 씀.
26 [would rather + A(동사원형) + than + B(동사원형)]: B를
   하느니 차라리 A를 하겠다
27 [should have p.p.]: ~했어야 했는데
28 현재와 다른 과거 상태이면 [used to + 동사원형]이다.
29 had better는 일반동사이며 부정형은 바로 뒤에 not을 쓴다.
30 조동사 뒤에는 동사원형을 쓰므로 [will + have to]이다.
31 과거의 일에 대한 유감이나 후회는 [should have p.p.]를 씀.

Grammar Mapping
p. 34

① ~해도 된다 ② ~일 리가 없다 ③ cannot +
have + p.p. ④ ~일지도 모른다 ⑤ may + have
+ p.p. ⑥ ~임에 틀림없다 ⑦ must + have +
p.p. ⑧ ~해서는 안 된다 ⑨ ~할 필요가 없다
⑩ ~했어야 했는데 하지 못했다 ⑪ ~하곤 했다
⑫ ~이었다 ⑬ ~하는 것이 낫다 ⑭ had better
not ⑮ than

Chapter 03 수동태

A
1 being painted   2 be
3 been   4 were
5 contains

B
1 is being written
2 has been damaged
3 should be treated

C
1 is being carved
2 has been used
3 will be released

D
1 be obeyed / be + p.p.
2 have been won / been + p.p.
3 is being heated / being + p.p.
4 was carried out / carried out

A
1 to   2 was taught
3 to lay   4 to stand

B
1 was made to take out
2 were allowed to enter
3 was given a lot of attention
4 was given to olive oil

C
1 is not felt to move
2 is called poor man's food
3 was bought for Jack

D
1 to ride, riding / to부정사
2 to stand up / to부정사
3 for him / for
4 to me / to

A
1 for   2 to live
3 is expected   4 with

B
1 is believed that, is believed to bring
2 is thought that, is thought to be

C
1 is known to have
2 is made from
3 was reported to be

D
1 O / 동사원형
2 to have been / have p.p.
3 is believed / is believed
4 with / with

Grammar & Writing   p. 42

A
1 The package was delivered
2 He was advised to read
3 We were made to stay inside
4 are believed to have evolved
5 Sally was heard playing
6 was disappointed with her new bike

B
1 was given enough time
2 was kept secret by
3 Salt was passed to
4 My computer is being repaired
5 His artwork will be displayed
6 were laughed at by people

C
1 The next flight from Busan has been canceled
2 A video file was sent to Joshua
3 Your bed must be kept
4 Dogs have been trained
5 The tests were handed out
6 He was made to attend the meeting

D
1 was named Ace
2 was given a birthday gift
3 was given to
4 were cooked for

Actual Test   p. 44

1 ⑤   2 ③   3 ④   4 ⑤   5 ②   6 ②   7 ①
8 ②   9 ④   10 to sweep   11 to know
12 covered with   13 ④   14 ④   15 ②   16 ②
17 was believed that the tree protected the town, was believed to protect the town
18 was given to the visitors   19 was disappointed with her test grades   20 ①
21 Tim is expected to play the main role

22 was turned off during the movie 23 The recipe has been passed down 24 ② 25 has been translated 26 was seen climbing (to climb) 27 must be kept 28 ⑤ 29 wear → to wear, to부정사 30 be → being, being
31 The medicine should (must) be taken after breakfast

1 조동사 수동태 [조동사 + be + p.p.]
2 수동태 완료형 [have (has) + been + p.p.]
3 사역동사 make의 목적격보어인 원형부정사는 수동태 문장에서 to부정사로 바뀜.
4 수동태 진행형 [be동사 + being + p.p.]
5 수동태 진행형 [be동사 + being + p.p.]
6 지각동사의 목적격보어로 쓰인 현재분사 또는 동사원형은 수동태로 쓰일 때 현재분사 또는 to부정사로 바뀜.
7 지각동사의 목적격보어로 쓰인 동사원형과 5형식 동사의 목적격보어로 쓰인 to부정사는 수동태 문장으로 쓰일 때 to부정사로 씀.
8 [be tired of]: ~에 싫증내다, [be made of]: ~로 만들어지다
9 ④ 4형식 동사 make의 직접목적어가 수동태의 주어로 쓰이면 간접목적어 앞에 전치사 for를 씀.
10 사역동사 make의 목적격보어인 동사원형은 수동태 문장에서 to부정사로 바뀜.
11 that절이 목적어로 쓰인 문장을 수동태로 바꾸면 [that절의 주어 + be동사 + p.p. + to부정사]이고 의미는 '~한다고 생각되다'이다.
12 [be covered with]: ~로 덮여 있다
13 ① [run over]는 동사구로 한 단어로 취급하며 수동태로 쓰일 때는 [be동사 + run over]이다. ② with → from ③ 4형식 동사 buy는 직접목적어(a bag)를 주어로 하는 수동태만 만들 수 있다. ⑤ put은 [be동사 + put]으로 바꿔야 함.
14 that절이 목적어로 쓰인 문장을 수동태로 바꾸면 [that절의 주어 + be동사 + p.p. + to부정사]이고 의미는 '~한다고 알려지다'이다.
15 지각동사의 목적격보어로 쓰인 현재분사 또는 동사원형은 수동태로 쓰일 때 현재분사 또는 to부정사로 바뀜.
16 수동태 완료형 [have (has) + been + p.p.]
17 that절이 목적어로 쓰인 문장을 수동태 문장으로 바꿀 때 [It + be동사 + p.p. + that절]과 [that절의 주어 + be동사 + p.p. + to부정사] 두 가지 형태로 쓰임.
18 4형식 동사 give는 수동태로 바꿀 때 직접목적어가 주어로 쓰이면 간접목적어 앞에 전치사 to를 씀.
19 [be동사 disappointed with]: ~에 실망하다
20 ① 5형식 문장의 목적격보어는 목적어가 아니므로 수동태의 주어가 될 수 없음.

21 [be동사 expected to]: ~할 것으로 예상되다, 5형식 동사의 목적격보어로 쓰인 to부정사는 수동태 문장에서도 to부정사로 쓰임.
22 [turn off]는 '~을 끄다' 의미의 동사구로 하나의 단어로 취급함. 수동태는 [be동사 + turned off]이다.
23 수동태 완료형 [have (has) + been + p.p.]
24 ⓒ 4형식 동사 buy의 수동태 [직접목적어 주어 + be동사 bought + for + 간접목적어] ⓔ [be동사 allowed to]: ~하도록 허락받다
25 수동태 완료형 [have (has) + been + p.p.]
26 지각동사의 목적격보어로 쓰인 현재분사 또는 동사원형은 수동태로 쓰일 때 현재분사 또는 to부정사로 바뀜.
27 조동사 수동태 [조동사 + be + p.p.]
28 ⓐ for ⓑ for ⓒ with ⓓ after ⓔ to
29 사역동사 make의 수동태는 [be동사 + made + to부정사]이다.
30 '~되어지는 중' 의미의 진행형 수동태는 [be동사 + being + 과거분사]이다.
31 조동사 수동태 [조동사 + be + p.p.]

Grammar Mapping   p. 48

① be동사 ② be ③ being ④ been ⑤ 전치사 ⑥ She ⑦ for, of ⑧ to ⑨ 목적격보어 ⑩ I ⑪ 동사원형 ⑫ to부정사 ⑬ to carry ⑭ that절 ⑮ that절의 주어 ⑯ in, at, of, with

Chapter 04 부정사

GP Practice 16 to부정사의 명사적 쓰임   p. 51

A 1 to leave   2 it
   3 to say   4 to work
   5 how

B 1 It, to learn from mistakes
   2 It, to develop good habits
   3 what to do

C 1 Their mission, to search for
   2 it, exciting to travel   3 how to hang

D 1 It / 가주어, It
   2 not / not, 앞
   3 it / it, to부정사

4 should use / 어떻게, should + 동사원형

GP Practice 17 — to부정사의 형용사적 쓰임
GP Practice 18 — to부정사의 부사적 쓰임   p. 53

A
1 to learn   2 to show
3 to stay at   4 to hear

B
1 ③   2 ①   3 ②
4 ④   5 ⑤

C
1 are to stay
2 something to write about
3 to breed
4 difficult to spell

D
1 to sit on / 위에 앉을, on
2 are to follow / 의무, to부정사
3 convenient / 편리한, 형용사
4 to be / 결국 ~하다, to부정사

GP Practice 19 — 목적격보어로 쓰이는 부정사   p. 55

A
1 to take   2 look
3 to bring   4 sing
5 to reserve

B
1 knock / knocking   2 change
3 to put on   4 (to) remember

C
1 ordered him to pay
2 feel the mosquito bite / biting
3 let his cat sleep
4 had me recycle

D
1 follow, following / 원형부정사
2 feel / 원형부정사
3 O, to fix / 원형부정사, to부정사
4 to marry / to부정사

GP Practice 20 — to부정사의 의미상 주어
GP Practice 21 — to부정사의 시제   p. 57

A
1 of   2 to have
3 for   4 to have missed
5 to be treated

B
1 to share   2 to have left
3 to be loved

C
1 to be upgraded

2 for left-handed people to use
3 have sensed

D
1 of you / 있으면, of
2 O / 동사원형
3 to have lost / have p.p.
4 to be washed / 수동, be p.p.

GP Practice 22 — to부정사를 이용한 구문
GP Practice 23 — 독립부정사   p. 59

A
1 to say   2 too good
3 To make   4 to reach
5 fast enough

B
1 too young to open
2 too energetic to stay still
3 large enough to hold

C
1 smart enough to use
2 too foggy, to drive
3 To be frank with you

D
1 too / 너무 ~해서, too
2 hard enough / ~하기 충분히, 부사 + enough
3 To be sure / 확실히, be sure
4 so / so

Grammar & Writing   p. 60

A
1 thrilling to take pictures of
2 advised me not to watch
3 was too rare to eat
4 the file to be deleted
5 thoughtful of you to remember
6 seems to enjoy his busy life

B
1 want you to open
2 one millionth customer to visit
3 too young to travel
4 difficult to keep a secret
5 are to transfer
6 to have experienced many things
7 lets me eat his snacks

C
1 to enjoy her life
2 to wear to the party
3 to become an actor
4 to hold a summer sale soon
5 small to hold the big teddy bear
6 enough to appear in TV commercials

7

D   **1** made him set the table

       2 told him to wear sunscreen

       3 advised him to wear green pants

       4 helped him ride / to ride a bike

Actual Test

p. 62

1 ① **2** ③ **3** ④ **4** ④ **5** ④ **6** ④ **7** ⑤ **8** ⑤
9 ① **10** ③ **11** to arrive **12** for us to follow
13 not to buy **14** ③ **15** ④ **16** ① **17** ⑤
18 heard her whisper / whispering **19** how to
use **20** seems to have spent **21** ④ **22** fun
to learn magic tricks **23** is too bitter for me to
drink **24** seems to have found the evidence
25 ② **26** ① **27** seem to read **28** too small
to cover **29** to wash → wash, 목적격보어, 원형부
정사 **30** (to) changed → (to) be changed, 교체
되다, 수동태 **31** (to) travel → (to) have traveled,
다를 때, to + have p.p. **32** The curtain is thick
enough to block the sun

1 let은 목적격보어로 원형부정사를 가짐.

2 성품을 나타내는 형용사가 있을 때 to부정사의 의미상 주어는
[of + 목적격] 형태로 씀.

3 to부정사가 명사를 수식하는 형용사 용법임.

4 [to tell the truth]: 솔직히 말해서

5 tell은 목적격보어로 to부정사를 가짐.

6 성품 이외의 형용사가 앞에 오면 to부정사의 의미상 주어는
[for + 목적격] 형태로 씀.

7 [to be sure]: 확실히, [to make matters worse]: 설상가
상으로

8 [too + 형용사 + to 부정사]: ~하기에 너무 ~한

9 get은 목적격보어로 to부정사를 가짐.

10 ⓐ to부정사가 주절의 동사보다 이전 시제이므로 to부정사 완
료형 [to have forgotten] ⓑ 성품을 나타내는 형용사가 없
을 때 to부정사의 의미상 주어는 [for us] ⓒ allow는 목적격
보어로 to부정사를 쓰므로 [to sleep]이다.

11 expect는 목적격보어로 to부정사를 가짐.

12 성품 이외의 형용사 뒤에 to부정사의 의미상 주어는 [for + 목
적격 + to부정사]이다.

13 to부정사를 부정할 때는 not을 바로 앞에 씀.

14 보기와 ③은 명사적 용법이고 ①은 형용사 용법 ②는 감정의
원인(부사) ④는 결과(부사) ⑤는 목적(부사)이다.

15 [be + to부정사]인 보기와 ④는 의무이고 ①은 예정 ②는 가
능 ③은 예정 ⑤는 운명이다.

16 help는 목적격보어로 원형부정사 또는 to부정사를 쓰고 지각

동사 see는 목적격보어로 원형부정사 또는 현재분사를 씀.

17 가목적어 it 뒤에 진목적어 to부정사를 쓰고, 가주어 It 뒤에
진주어 to부정사를 쓴다.

18 지각동사는 목적격보어로 원형부정사 또는 현재분사를 씀.

19 [how + to부정사]: ~하는 방법

20 to부정사가 주절의 동사보다 이전 시제이므로 to부정사 완료
형 [seem to have p.p.] 형식을 씀.

21 '내가 읽기에'이므로 의미상 주어는 for me이다.

22 [주어 + 동사 + 가목적어 (it) + 목적격보어 + 진목적어 (to부
정사)]

23 [too + 형용사 + for + 목적격 + to부정사]: ~가 ~하기에 너
무 ~한

24 to부정사가 주절의 동사보다 이전 시제이므로 to부정사 완료
형 [seem to have p.p.] 형식을 씀.

25 [have + 목적어 + 목적격보어(원형부정사)]

26 [seems to have known → seems to know]: to부정사
가 주절의 동사와 같은 시제이므로 단순 부정사를 씀.

27 to부정사가 주절의 동사와 같은 시제이므로 단순 부정사
[seem to + 동사원형] 형태를 씀.

28 [too + 형용사 + to부정사]: ~하기에 너무 ~한

29 make는 목적격보어로 원형부정사를 갖는 동사이다.

30 '배터리가 교체되다'이므로 to부정사 수동태를 씀.

31 to부정사 시제가 주절의 시제보다 앞설 때 [to + have p.p.]
를 씀.

32 [형용사 / 부사 + enough + to부정사]: ~하기에 충분히 ~한

Grammar Mapping

p. 66

① 주어, 목적어, 보어   ② 가목적어 it   ③ 명사 수식
④ 부사   ⑤ to stay   ⑥ stay   ⑦ for   ⑧ of
⑨ to + have p.p.   ⑩ to + be p.p.   ⑪ enough
⑫ too   ⑬ ~은 말할 것도 없이   ⑭ 설상가상으로

Chapter 05 동명사

GP Practice 24 **동명사의 명사적 쓰임**
GP Practice 25 **동명사의 의미상 주어**
GP Practice 26 **동명사의 시제**   p. 69

A   **1** asking   **2** not having

       3 being kept   **4** knocking

       5 his

B   **1** our taking pictures
     2 having designed
     3 being watched

C   **1** Listening to others requires
     2 his shadow following
     3 having helped me

D   **1** Taking / 주어, 동명사
     2 his 또는 him / 소유격, 목적격
     3 having been / having p.p.
     4 being treated / 수동, being + p.p.

GP Practice 27   동명사와 to부정사
GP Practice 28   동명사의 관용적 쓰임   p. 71

A   **1** to look   **2** drinking
     3 to feel, feeling   **4** studying
     5 to eat

B   **1** complaining   **2** to get
     3 using   **4** adding

C   **1** remember meeting me
     2 stopped to drop off
     3 got used to living without

D   **1** catching / 동명사
     2 to show up / to부정사
     3 to rain, raining / to부정사, 동명사
     4 to call / ~할 것을, to부정사

Grammar & Writing   p. 72

A   **1** Try saving the file with a different name
     2 I couldn't help eating
     3 hated being treated like a child
     4 refused to wear a fur coat
     5 avoid talking to strangers
     6 is to search for life on Mars

B   **1** worth watching two times
     2 kept singing until late
     3 continued to fight for 30 years
     4 look forward to visiting you soon
     5 regret to tell you
     6 Eating food with your right hand

C   **1** being the leader of his team
     2 her working too hard these days
     3 not having invited you to the party

---

     4 visiting the tower
     5 not keeping his promise 또는 not having
         kept his promise

D   **1** to call   **2** not having called
     3 making   **4** making
     5 to make

Actual Test   p. 74

1 ④   **2** ②   **3** ④   **4** ③   **5** ④   **6** ⑤   **7** ④   **8** ⑤
9 ④   **10** ④   **11** ④   **12** ⑤   **13** ④   **14** ②   **15** ⑤
16 ④   **17** cleaning   **18** to tie   **19** planting
20 speaking   **21** reading   **22** ②   **23** He tried
folding colored paper into a ship   **24** Do you
mind my sitting next to you   **25** He denies
having spread the false rumor   **26** being late
for the meeting   **27** putting   **28** to work →
working, 동명사, ~하던 것을   **29** teaching →
having taught, 완료 동명사, having p.p.   **30** We
look forward to her coming back

1 avoid는 동명사를 목적어로 가짐.

2 동명사의 의미상 주어는 소유격이나 목적격 형태임.

3 agree는 to부정사를 목적어로 가짐.

4 [forget + to부정사]: ~할 것을 잊다

5 [can't help + 동명사]: ~하지 않을 수 없다

6 [look forward to + 동명사]는 '~할 것을 고대하다'이고,
like는 목적어로 to부정사나 동명사 모두를 가짐.

7 [forget + to부정사]: ~할 것을 잊다

8 [get used to + 동명사]: ~하는 것에 익숙해지다

9 [remember + 동명사]: ~했던 것을 기억하다, [remember
+ to부정사]: ~할 것을 기억하다

10 [give up]은 목적어로 동명사를, hate는 동명사나 to부정사
를 모두 가짐.

11 decide는 to부정사를 목적어로 가짐.

12 [be proud of + 동명사]는 '~하는 것을 자랑스러워하다'이
고, 동명사의 의미상 주어는 목적격 또는 소유격을 씀.

13 [try + to부정사]는 '~하기 위해 노력하다'이고, to부정사의
부정은 not을 바로 앞에 씀.

14 [be used to + 동명사]의 to는 전치사이고 나머지는 to부정
사이다.

15 ① had difficulty finding ② proud of not being
③ stop raining ④ is good at searching

16 ① hated doing / to do ② keep cheering ③ about
being ⑤ considered quitting

17 [How about -ing ~?]: ~하는 것이 어때?

18 [stop + to부정사]: ~하기 위해 멈추다

19 전치사는 목적어로 명사 또는 동명사를 가짐.

20 practice는 동명사를 목적어로 가짐.

21 [spend + 시간 + -ing]: ~하느라 시간을 보내다

22 ⓐ play → playing ⓔ 동명사 주어는 단수 취급 are → is이다.

23 [try + 동명사]: 시험 삼아 ~해 보다

24 [mind + 동명사]는 '~하는 것을 꺼려하다'이며 동명사 sitting의 의미상 주어는 my이다.

25 [deny + 완료 동명사(having p.p.)]: ~했던 것을 부인하다

26 전치사는 목적어로 명사 또는 동명사를 가짐.

27 [forget + 동명사]: ~했던 것을 잊어버리다

28 stop은 목적어로 동명사를 씀.

29 동명사 시제가 주절 시제보다 앞서면 완료 동명사를 씀.

30 [look forward to + 동명사]: ~하는 것을 고대하다

Grammar Mapping ○   p. 78

> ① 전치사   ② 소유격, 목적격   ③ having p.p.
> ④ being p.p.   ⑤ 동명사   ⑥ keep   ⑦ avoid
> ⑧ to부정사   ⑨ agree   ⑩ refuse   ⑪ 없는
> ⑫ 있는   ⑬ ~했던   ⑭ ~할   ⑮ ~해 보다   ⑯ 노력하다   ⑰ ~하는 데 익숙하다   ⑱ ~하지 않을 수 없다

Chapter 06 분사

GP Practice 29 ○ **현재분사와 과거분사**
GP Practice 30 ○ **분사의 형용사적 쓰임**   p. 81

A **1** sleeping   **2** recorded
   3 called   **4** made
   5 interesting

B **1** buried in the snow
   2 caught in a storm
   3 wearing a red tie

C **1** the five animals hidden
   2 a jellyfish floating
   3 amazing speed

D **1** used / 수동, 과거분사
   2 O / 진행, 현재분사
   3 boring / 느끼게 하는, 현재분사
   4 friend living in Brazil / 뒤

GP Practice 31 ○ **목적격보어로 쓰이는 분사**   p. 83

A **1** praising   **2** dyed
   3 frozen   **4** wrapped

B **1** her, walking
   2 her name, written
   3 the chair, broken
   4 my hamster, hiding

C **1** found her telling
   2 their heights measured
   3 hear the noise coming from
   4 had his left leg broken

D **1** O / 동사원형 + -ing, ~하는 것을
   2 playing / 동사원형 + -ing, ~하는 것을
   3 washed / p.p., 되도록
   4 done / p.p., ~되도록

GP Practice 32 ○ **분사구문**   p. 85

A **1** Having   **2** Walking
   3 Not being   **4** Considering

B **1** Having poor eyesight
   2 Taking this bus
   3 (Although) Not being tall

C **1** While I cleaned (was cleaning) my room
   2 Because he didn't feel well
   3 If you wear these jeans

D **1** Watching / 주어, 함
   2 Turning / 동사원형 + -ing
   3 Not being / not, 앞
   4 Judging from / ~로 판단하건대, Judging from

GP Practice 33 ○ **완료형 분사구문**
GP Practice 34 ○ **수동 분사구문**
GP Practice 35 ○ **주어가 있는 분사구문**
GP Practice 36 ○ **with + 명사 + 분사**   p. 87

A **1** coming   **2** following
   3 speaking   **4** Struck
   5 Having lived

B **1** Having slept through the winter
   2 Medusa looking at him
   3 (Being) Packed in a box

C
1 Kept in an airtight container
2 with my cat sitting
3 Having eaten salty soup

D
1 Seen / 수동, (Being) p.p.
2 Having worked / having p.p.
3 It being / 불가
4 turned / p.p., ~된 채로

Grammar & Writing

A
1 Having lost his key
2 The bank being closed
3 Eating less salt
4 with my cat sleeping next to me
5 looking for hidden treasure
6 Arriving early
7 heard someone whistling cheerfully

B
1 Proofreading his report
2 with tears running down
3 Compared with his peers
4 Turning right at the next corner
5 Although made in haste
6 Having been attacked by a dog

C
1 opened   2 downloaded
3 ringing   4 running

D
1 Surrounded by many people
2 Having read the books
3 Coming in first place
4 It being windy
5 Kept in the refrigerator
6 Having lived in Tokyo

Actual Test
p. 90

1 ③ **2** ③ **3** ⑤ **4** ② **5** ③ **6** ② **7** ③ **8** ④
9 ④ **10** ① **11** made **12** eating **13** watching
14 ⑤ **15** ③ **16** ④ **17** Wrapped **18** Looking
19 Judging **20** ⑤ **21** ③ **22** ④ **23** ③ **24**
Left **25** Having lived **26** with my eyes
closed **27** It being cold **28** exhausting →
exhausted, 수동, 과거 **29** spins → spinning, 진행,
현재 **30** Feeling tired, Max rested in his room

1 '그의 이름이 불려지는'은 수동 의미이므로 과거분사를 씀.

2 '놀라게 하는' 감정을 유발하는 형용사이므로 현재분사를 씀.

3 Although he lived near the school을 분사구문으로 바꿔서 접속사, 주절과 같은 주어 생략 후 [live + -ing] 형태를 씀.

4 '불이 타고 있는'은 진행 의미이므로 현재분사를 씀.

5 차를 잃어버린 시점이 경찰에 신고한 것보다 먼저 일어난 일이므로 완료분사 [Having + p.p.] 형태를 씀.

6 감정을 유발하는 형용사는 현재분사, 감정을 느끼는 형용사는 과거분사를 씀.

7 '칭찬을 받아서'는 수동이므로 과거분사, '손을 흔들며'는 능동이므로 현재분사를 씀.

8 ① Go → Going ② Being → It being 부사절의 주어(비인칭주어 It)가 주절의 주어와 다르면 생략 불가 ③ spoken → speaking '일반적으로 말해서' ⑤ Felt → Feeling으로 바꿔야 함..

9 부사절을 분사구문으로 고칠 때 접속사 생략, 주절과 같은 부사절 주어 생략, 부사절의 동사가 주절 시제와 같을 때 [동사원형 + -ing] 형태의 단순분사를 씀.

10 '의사이기 때문에'이므로 [이유 접속사 + 주어 + 동사] 형태를 씀.

11 시계가 '만들어진'이므로 수동 의미의 과거분사를 씀.

12 '먹고 있는'이므로 능동, 진행 의미의 현재분사를 씀.

13 [with + 명사 + 분사]에서 '친구들이 보고 있는 채로'이므로 현재분사를 씀.

14 '얼굴을 물감으로 칠해지도록 하다'는 목적어의 수동 상태를 의미하므로 과거분사를 써야 함.

15 '깨진'은 수동 의미이므로 과거분사를 써야 함.

16 부사절을 분사구문으로 고칠 때 접속사 생략, 주절과 같은 부사절 주어 생략, 부사절의 동사가 주절 시제와 같을 때 단순분사를 쓰므로 [Drives → Driving]이 되어야 함.

17 미라(mummy)가 '싸여진' 수동 상태이므로 과거분사를 씀.

18 '~하면서'는 능동 행동을 나타내므로 현재분사를 씀.

19 [Judging from]: ~로 판단하건대

20 수화를 배운 것은 과거, 의사소통이 가능한 것은 현재이므로 부사절과 주절 시제가 다를 경우 완료분사(having p.p.)를 써야 함.

21 ③ [Although she is rich, ~]로 '~임에도 불구하고'이며, 나머지는 '~할 때, ~하면서' 의미이다.

22 '손으로 만져지면'은 수동 의미의 과거분사를 씀.

23 ⓐ Don't feeling → Not feeling ⓒ spoken → speaking ⓔ crossing → crossed

24 분사구문 만들 때, 부사절의 접속사, 주절과 같은 주어 생략 후 동사 시제가 주절의 시제와 같을 때 [동사원형 + -ing] 형태로 고침. Being left에서 Being은 생략 가능함.

25 분사구문 만들 때, 부사절의 접속사, 주절과 같은 주어 생략 후 동사 시제가 주절보다 앞설 때 [having + p.p.] 형태를 씀.

26 '~가 ~된 채로'는 [with + 명사 + 과거분사] 형태임.

27 부사절 As it was cold를 분사구문으로 고칠 때, 주절과 다른 부사절 주어(It)는 생략 불가이다.

28 '매우 지쳤다'는 수동 상태이므로 exhaust의 과거분사를 씀.

29 거미가 '거미줄을 짜고 있는'은 목적어의 진행 상태이므로 spin의 현재분사를 씀.

30 '피로함을 느껴서'는 Feeling tired이다.

Grammar Mapping
p. 94

① 동사원형 + -ing　② 과거분사　③ 능동, 진행
④ 수동, 완료　⑤ ~하게 하는　⑥ ~당하는　⑦ 앞
⑧ 뒤　⑨ 주격　⑩ 목적격　⑪ 부사절　⑫ 접속사
⑬ 주어　⑭ having p.p.　⑮ p.p.　⑯ 분사

Chapter 07 비교표현

GP Practice 37 원급, 비교급, 최상급
GP Practice 38 원급을 이용한 표현
p. 97

A
1 clean　　2 nicer
3 most　　4 three times

B
1 as high
2 more exciting
3 they could

C
1 more important than
2 as big as
3 as often as I can
4 the coldest month in

D
1 better / 비교급 + than
2 O / as + 원급 + as
3 largest / 최상급
4 possible / possible

GP Practice 39 비교급을 이용한 표현
GP Practice 40 최상급을 이용한 표현
GP Practice 41 원급, 비교급을 이용한 최상급 의미 p. 99

A
1 more　　2 much
3 sports　　4 colder and colder

B
1 No (other) drink
2 three years older
3 The higher, the farther

C
1 much more thoughtful
2 The less, the more
3 one of the most popular
4 the most touching, ever watched

D
1 harder and harder / 비교급 + and + 비교급
2 much / 훨씬, much
3 boy / 단수
4 the easier / the + 비교급

Grammar & Writing
p. 100

A
1 is not as tall as her brother
2 is the happiest day of my life
3 the best cartoon I have ever read
4 save as much energy as possible
5 is much less expensive than
6 No insect, is more disgusting than

B
1 more helpful than
2 getting better and better
3 one of the greatest inventions
4 twice as fast as
5 The more often, the more confidence
6 more diligent than any other

C
1 as old as
2 the most popular
3 faster, other car
4 less expensive
5 (other) car, more expensive

D
1 as efficient as
2 three times bigger than
3 as clearly as they could
4 The more books, the more knowledge
5 No other, brighter than, No other, as bright as, brighter than any other planet

Actual Test
p. 102

1 ①　**2** ④　**3** ④　**4** ③　**5** ②　**6** ⑤　**7** ②　**8** ②
9 ①　**10** ③　**11** ①　**12** the most intelligent
13 not as expensive　**14** The more, the better
15 ④　**16** the most boring story I have ever heard　**17** The higher the prices are, the less
18 more　**19** possible　**20** ⑤　**21** ①　**22** ④
23 ②, ⑤　**24** a lot more effective than
25 one of the greatest figure skaters

26 more and more interested   **27** more

28 more beautiful → beautiful, 원급

29 students → student, 단수명사   **30** I left home as quietly as possible

1 [as + 원급 + as]: …만큼 ~한 (하게)

2 [the 비교급 ~ the 비교급 ~]: …하면 할수록 더 ~하다

3 [the + 최상급 + 명사 + (that) + 주어 + have p.p.]: 지금껏 한 것 중 가장 ~한

4 [비교급 + than]: …보다 ~한 (하게)

5 [부정 주어 + as + 원급 + as]: …만큼 ~한 것은 없다

6 [one + of + the + 최상급 + 복수명사]: 가장 ~한 것들 중 하나, [as + 원급 + as + possible = as + 원급 + as + 주어 can]: 가능한 한 ~한 (하게)

7 [as + 원급 + as]: …만큼 ~한 (하게), [the + 최상급 + 명사 + (that) + 주어 + have p.p.]: 지금껏 한 것 중 가장 ~한

8 very는 원급, much, even, far, a lot은 비교급을 강조함.

9 [one + of + the + 최상급 + 복수명사]: 가장 ~한 것들 중 하나

10 [the 비교급 ~ the 비교급 ~]: …하면 할수록 더 ~하다

11 most → more, [비교급 + than]: …보다 ~한 (하게)

12 [부정 주어 + 비교급 + than]: …만큼 ~한 것은 없다 = [the + 최상급]: 가장 ~한

13 [B 비교급 + than A] = [A not + as + 원급 + as B]

14 [the 비교급 ~ the 비교급 ~]: …하면 할수록 더 ~하다

15 [the 비교급 ~ the 비교급 ~]: …하면 할수록 더 ~하다

16 [the + 최상급 + 명사 + (that) + 주어 + have p.p.]: 지금껏 한 것 중 가장 ~한

17 [the 비교급 ~ the 비교급 ~]: …하면 할수록 더 ~하다

18 [A less + 원급 + than B] = [B 비교급 + than A]

19 [as + 원급 + as + possible] = [as + 원급 + as + 주어 can]: 가능한 한 ~한 (하게)

20 ① of → in ② than → to ③ very → much / ever / far / a lot / still ④ much → more

21 ①은 '가장 ~한 것들 중 하나'이고 나머지는 '가장 ~한'을 의미함.

22 ④는 원급 much이고 나머지는 비교급 more이다.

23 ② as twice old as → twice as old as ⑤ phones → phone

24 a lot + [비교급 + than]: …보다 훨씬 ~한 (하게)

25 [one + of + the + 최상급 + 복수명사]: 가장 ~한 것들 중 하나

26 [비교급 and 비교급]: 점점 더 ~한 (하게)

27 [비교급 and 비교급]: 점점 더 ~한 (하게), [비교급 + than]: …보다 ~한 (하게)

28 [as + 원급 + as]: …만큼 ~한 (하게)

29 [비교급 + than + any other] 다음에는 단수명사를 쓴다.

30 [as + 원급 + as + possible]: 가능한 한 ~한 (하게)

Grammar Mapping p. 106

① 배수사   ② possible   ③ 두 개   ④ than
⑤ much   ⑥ 비교급 and 비교급   ⑦ the 비교급
⑧ to   ⑨ 셋 이상   ⑩ in / of   ⑪ one   ⑫ have
(has) ever p.p.   ⑬ No (other)   ⑭ any other

Chapter 08 접속사

GP Practice 42 부사절을 이끄는 접속사 p. 109

A
1 while   **2** until   **3** have
4 lose   **5** Even if

B
1 since   **2** If
3 Even though   **4** Because

C
1 As soon as I unwrapped
2 unless it is an emergency
3 (Al)though penguins can't fly
4 until a huge wave comes

D
1 (Al)though / 비록 ~이지만, 양보
2 sees / 부사절, 현재
3 is / if ~ not, 사용 불가

GP Practice 43 간접의문문
GP Practice 44 상관접속사 p. 111

A
1 either   **2** she was   **3** if
4 not only   **5** When do you think

B
1 where the Statue of Liberty is
2 if (whether) he is telling the truth
3 When, we will have snow this year

C
1 both men and women
2 neither creative nor interesting
3 either busy or turned off

D
1 what my hobby was / S + V
2 if (whether) he liked / if (whether), S + V
3 Why do you think / 앞
4 am / B

A
1 because it lacks
2 If you sign up for six months
3 Do you know who planted
4 My dad as well as my mom has
5 Every time he washes his car
6 if you can attend the meeting

B
1 as / because / since the battery died
2 Both Jessica and I have curly hair
3 if / whether his dream will come true
4 What do you guess I have
5 Although / Though I usually use
6 until the computer is on sale

C
1 Neither, nor
2 as well as
3 Even though
4 as
5 Both, and

D
1 why I wanted to join
2 if (whether) I was good at dancing
3 when I had decided to become
4 who my role model was
5 if (whether) I could act the part

1 ⑤ 2 ① 3 ⑤ 4 ② 5 ③ 6 ③ 7 ② 8 ①
9 ⑤ 10 ③ 11 Unless 12 as well as 13 ④
14 ② 15 ③ 16 Since, since 17 while, While 18 what he is saying 19 Neither Jerome nor his brother 20 if (whether) the trophy is really made of 21 ② 22 ① 23 ④
24 Who do you guess the boy is 25 famous both in Korea and in Europe 26 (Al)Though / Even though she is a successful writer
27 Whenever I visited the bakery 28 while he lived in the White House 29 is the castle → the castle is, 간접, 주어 + 동사 30 will arrive → arrives, 미래, 현재 31 The nano-robot is smarter as well as smaller

1 의문사가 없는 간접의문문 [if (whether) + 주어 + 동사]: ∼인지 아닌지

2 unless: ∼하지 않는다면

3 부사절이 주절에 대해 상반된 내용이므로 '∼에도 불구하고'

를 씀.

4 주절에 생각동사(guess, think, imagine, believe) 등이 오면 간접의문문의 의문사는 문장 맨 앞에 온다.

5 [neither A nor B]: A와 B 둘 다 아닌

6 ① that → if ②와 ⑤는 간접의문문으로 [의문사 + 주어 + 동사] 어순 ④ 주절에 think 동사 있을 시 간접의문문의 의문사는 문장 맨 앞에 씀.

7 ①, ③, ④, ⑤는 시간 부사절로 '∼할 때'이고 ②는 명사절 [when + 주어 + 동사]로 '언제 ∼인지를' 의미함.

8 ①은 '∼인지 아닌지'이고 나머지는 '만약 ∼한다면'이다.

9 [both A and B]: A와 B 둘 다, [not only A but also B]: A뿐 아니라 B도

10 while: ∼하는 동안, if: ∼인지 아닌지를

11 [if ∼ not] = [unless]: 만약 ∼가 아니면

12 [not only A but also B] = [B as well as A]: A뿐 아니라 B도

13 간접의문문은 [의문사 + 주어 + 동사]이며, 주절에 think 동사가 있으면 의문사는 문장 맨 앞에 씀.

14 As → Although / Though, 주절과 부사절의 내용이 상반되므로 '∼에도 불구하고'를 씀.

15 시간 부사절에서는 미래시제 대신 현재시제를 씀.

16 since: ∼이기 때문에, ∼한 이래로

17 while: ∼하는 동안, ∼하는 반면

18 의문문이 문장의 일부가 되는 간접의문문은 [의문사 + 주어 + 동사]이다.

19 [neither A nor B]: A와 B 둘 다 아닌

20 의문사가 없는 간접의문문은 [if / whether + 주어 + 동사]이다.

21 since는 '∼ 때문에' 의미도 있지만 '∼한 이래로' 의미로도 사용됨.

22 ⓒ [B as well A]가 주어로 쓰이면 B에 동사 단복수 일치시키므로 am → is, ⓓ 의문사 when의 위치는 Do you know when he will ∼, ⓔ Unless → If이다.

23 ④ '글자가 작아서'로 이유를 나타내는 접속사이고 나머지는 '∼에도 불구하고'를 의미함.

24 간접의문문은 [의문사 + 주어 + 동사]이며, 주절에 동사 guess가 있으면 의문사는 문장 맨 앞에 씀.

25 [both in A and in B]: A와 B 안에서 모두

26 [(al)though / even though + 주어 + 동사]: ∼에도 불구하고

27 [whenever + 주어 + 동사]: ∼할 때마다

28 [while + 주어 + 동사]: ∼하는 동안

29 의문문이 문장의 일부가 되는 간접의문문의 어순은 [의문사 + 주어 + 동사]이다.

30 시간 부사절에서는 미래시제 대신 현재시제를 씀.

31 [B as well as A]: A뿐 아니라 B도

① 접속사 ② ~함에 따라 ③ ~한 이후로 ④ as soon as ⑤ since ⑥ unless ⑦ 비록 ~이지만 ⑧ 현재 ⑨ 미래 ⑩ 주어 + 동사 ⑪ where, Where ⑫ believe, guess ⑬ if / whether ⑭ both ⑮ either ⑯ nor ⑰ but also ⑱ as well as

Chapter 09 관계사

GP Practice 45 관계대명사 who, which, that, what
p. 121

A
1 whose　2 which
3 What　4 that

B
1 Most of the people who(m) / that we met were very friendly
2 The clothes which / that are made by famous designers cost more
3 The person whose job is studying animals is called a zoologist

C
1 what I am saying
2 who(m) / that she invited
3 whose hobby is
4 which / that leaves

D
1 O / 사람, 주격
2 삭제 / 목적격, 삭제
3 What / What
4 whose / 소유격

GP Practice 46 관계부사 when, where, why, how
p. 123

A
1 where　2 how
3 why　4 when

B
1 Australia is the country where my mom studied
2 The reason why dinosaurs disappeared is unknown
3 Tell us how you memorized English vocabulary so quickly

C
1 the day when
2 how the firefighter saved
3 the reason why
4 the place where

D
1 삭제 / 방법, 없음
2 O / 이유, why
3 where / 장소, where
4 when / 시간, when

GP Practice 47 관계대명사 생략
GP Practice 48 전치사 + 관계대명사
GP Practice 49 관계사의 계속적 용법
p. 125

A
1 written　2 to whom
3 who　4 where

B
1 who is one of my closest friends
2 when it was not crowded
3 which my brother broke the next day

C
1 the e-mail you sent
2 who practices
3 destroyed by the storm
4 which I am interested

D
1 which / which
2 O / 가능
3 which / which
4 O / 가능

GP Practice 50 복합관계대명사
GP Practice 51 복합관계부사
p. 127

A
1 Whatever　2 Whoever
3 However　4 Wherever

B
1 whenever　2 whoever
3 Whatever

C
1 Whoever visits him
2 Whenever we meet
3 Whatever has
4 However beautiful the flowers are

D
1 Whoever / whoever
2 that / 관계대명사
3 Wherever / Wherever
4 Whatever / Whatever

A
1 The lady who sat next to me
2 What you have to do
3 the reason why he didn't wait
4 Whichever way you choose
5 The house whose roof was painted red
6 the way in which clouds form

B
1 when you called
2 we bought yesterday
3 the only food that
4 which makes him happy
5 whomever I marry
6 where she spent

C
1 what Ally wants to eat
2 whose screen was broken
3 where they lay eggs
4 which King Sejong invented

D
1 that came into his head
2 whatever is on this table
3 what he told her
4 in which the team could finally win the game
5 Wherever you go

Actual Test   p. 130

1 ③ 2 ⑤ 3 ⑤ 4 ① 5 ② 6 ④ 7 ② 8 ④
9 ⑤ 10 ③ 11 ① 12 ⑤ 13 whoever
14 What 15 However 16 when 17 which
18 who 19 ③ 20 ②, ⑤ 21 whose
22 Whoever 23 Whatever 24 ④ 25 The
music she is listening to 26 However bright
he is 27 No matter where you hide 28 What,
what 29 he → 삭제, 주격, 삭제 30 where →
which, 불완전, which 31 The Internet has
changed how people live

1 선행사가 the man이고 '그 남자의 재킷'이라는 뜻이므로 소유격 관계대명사 whose를 씀.
2 선행사 앞에 the only가 있으면 관계대명사 that을 씀.
3 선행사가 시간(the time)을 나타낼 때 관계부사 when을 씀.
4 '~하는 누구든지'를 나타내는 복합관계대명사 whoever를 씀.
5 선행사가 the window이고 계속적 용법이므로 주격 관계대명사 which를 씀.

6 ④는 여가 시간을 보내는 방식을 의미하므로 관계부사 how를 쓰고, 나머지는 '~하는 것'의 의미인 관계대명사 what을 씀.
7 선행사가 a letter이고 계속적 용법이므로 관계대명사 which는 [접속사 + 대명사]로 나타낼 수 있다. 편지를 보냈는데 도착하지 않았으므로 but it이다.
8 why → for which, 관계부사는 [전치사 + 관계대명사]로 나타낼 수 있다.
9 ⑤ the way와 관계부사 how는 함께 쓰지 않는다.
10 ③ 선행사가 시간(the day)을 나타낼 때 관계부사 when을 씀.
11 선행사가 사람일 때 관계대명사는 who와 that, 선행사가 something일 때는 that을 씀.
12 ⑤ 전치사 뒤의 관계대명사는 생략 불가능하다. 목적격 관계대명사는 생략 가능하고 [주격 관계대명사 + be동사]도 생략 가능함.
13 [anyone who → whoever]: ~하는 누구든지
14 [the thing that → what]: ~하는 것
15 [no matter how → however]: 아무리 ~할지라도
16 선행사가 시간(school days)을 나타낼 때 관계부사 when을 씀.
17 선행사가 사물(the subject)이고 [전치사 + 관계대명사]이므로 which를 씀.
18 선행사가 사람(Mother Theresa)이고 계속적 용법이므로 주격 관계대명사 who를 씀.
19 ③ 전치사 뒤에 관계대명사 that은 쓸 수 없다.
20 두 개의 주어와 동사가 있으므로 접속사가 필요하고 [접속사 + 대명사]를 관계대명사로 바꿀 수 있다. (and it = which)
21 선행사가 the lady이고 '그 숙녀의 커피'라는 뜻이므로 소유격 관계대명사 whose를 씀.
22 '~하는 누구든지'를 나타내는 복합관계대명사 whoever를 씀.
23 '~하는 무엇이든'을 나타내는 복합관계대명사 whatever를 씀.
24 ⓑ that → what, ⓔ where → which / that
25 [선행사 + (목적격 관계대명사) + 주어 + 동사 + 전치사]
26 [however + 형용사 + 주어 + 동사]: 아무리 ~하더라도
27 [no matter where]: 어디에 ~하더라도
28 '~하는 것'을 나타내는 관계대명사 what을 씀.
29 주격 관계대명사 뒤에는 선행사를 가리키는 주어를 삭제함.
30 '울타리를 가지고 있지 않는'의 의미이고 관계사절이 불완전하므로 which를 씀.
31 방법을 나타내는 관계부사 how를 씀.

Grammar Mapping   p. 134

① 선행사 ② of which ③ 선행사 없음 ④ 사람 +
사물 ⑤ ~하는 것 ⑥ 목적격 ⑦ be동사 ⑧ 전치
사 ⑨ comma(,) ⑩ 보충 설명 ⑪ 시간 ⑫ 장소
⑬ 이유 ⑭ 방법 ⑮ 생략 ⑯ whichever
⑰ wherever

Chapter 10 가정법

GP Practice 52 ○ 가정법 과거
GP Practice 53 ○ 가정법 과거완료
GP Practice 54 ○ 혼합가정법   p. 137

A
1 would   2 will
3 have   4 hadn't turned

B
1 were not, could enjoy
2 had been, could have bought
3 hadn't helped, would be

C
1 is, will go
2 had taken, would have been
3 had, would hire
4 had practiced, would not be

D
1 were / 없는, 과거, would
2 O / 있는, 현재, will
3 have cut / 없는, have p.p.
4 be / R

GP Practice 55 ○ I wish + 가정법
GP Practice 56 ○ as if + 가정법
GP Practice 57 ○ it's time + 가정법   p. 139

A
1 had   2 took
3 had come   4 were

B
1 liked
2 had gone
3 my brother didn't play
4 Kelly had showed 또는 had shown

C
1 is time, bought
2 as if, were
3 I wish, had spent

D
1 had lent / had p.p.
2 were / 사실의 반대, 과거동사
3 O / 과거
4 went / 과거

GP Practice 58 ○ if 생략 가정법
GP Practice 59 ○ without, but for   p. 141

A
1 Were I   2 Without
3 Had he   4 see

B
1 he were a true friend
2 they had arrived
3 it had not been for

C
1 Were she my girlfriend
2 But for your help
3 Had she tried harder
4 Were it not for money

D
1 But for / ~이 없었다면, but for
2 Were I / Were + 주어
3 were not / were not
4 Had he heard / Had + 주어 + p.p.

Grammar & Writing   p. 142

A
1 I wish he would be more rational
2 as if he had had a hard time
3 Had they listened to me
4 Were I president for a day
5 To hear her speak Korean
6 Had it not been for his advice

B
1 But for, could not have won
2 went, would you do
3 It is time we started
4 had agreed, would have donated
5 Were it not for, could not imagine
6 had bought, would wear

C
1 become a fashion model
2 had practiced speaking English
3 knew her address
4 couldn't have gotten a discount

D
1 as if she were
2 wish I had read
3 had been, could have avoided
4 it not for
5 had finished, could go out

Actual Test   p. 144

1 ③ **2** ⑤ **3** ④ **4** ② **5** ④ **6** ⑤ **7** ③
8 ②, ⑤ **9** ① **10** ⑤ **11** ④ **12** ④ **13** would
/ could give **14** she taken **15** it were not for
16 ④ **17** ② **18** ④ **19** hadn't injured his
knee, could have played **20** were not feeling
21 I wish he had been elected **22** It is time

we got some rest　**23** Had he seen my report card　**24** I would not be hungry　**25** Were it not for lighthouses　**26** were not, could participate　**27** It is time you thought　**28** is → were, 사실의 반대, 과거　**29** have been → be, had + 과거분사, 동사원형　**30** I wish we traveled around Europe for a month

1 가정법 과거 [If + 주어 + 과거동사, 주어 + would / could / might + 동사원형]

2 가정법 과거완료 [If + 주어 + had + 과거분사, 주어 + would / could / might + have + 과거분사]

3 혼합가정법 [If + 주어 + had + 과거분사, 주어 + would / could / might + 동사원형]

4 as if + 가정법 과거완료 [as if + 주어 + had + 과거분사]

5 단순 조건문 [주어 + will / can / may + 동사원형 if + 주어 + 현재동사]

6 I wish + 가정법 과거완료 [I wish + 주어 + had + 과거분사]

7 단순 조건문 [If + 주어 + 현재동사, 주어 + will / can / may + 동사원형], as if + 가정법 과거 [as if + 주어 + 과거동사]

8 [without / but for]: ~이 없다면

9 I wish + 가정법 과거 [I wish + 주어 + 과거동사]

10 가정법 과거완료 [If + 주어 + had + 과거분사, 주어 + would / could / might + have + 과거분사]

11 I wish + 가정법 과거완료 [I wish + 주어 + had + 과거분사]

12 [without / but for / if it had not been for / had it not been for]: ~이 없었다면

13 가정법 과거 [If + 주어 + 과거동사, 주어 + would / could / might + 동사원형]

14 가정법 과거완료 [If + 주어 + had + 과거분사, 주어 + would / could / might + have + 과거분사], if 생략 [Had + 주어 + 과거분사]

15 [without / if it were not for]: ~이 없다면

16 ④ drank → had drunk, 가정법 과거완료 [If + 주어 + had + 과거분사, 주어 + would / could / might + have + 과거분사]

17 ② can → could, I wish 가정법 과거 [I wish + 주어 + 과거동사]

18 ⓑ am → were ⓔ took → had taken

19 가정법 과거완료 [If + 주어 + had + 과거분사, 주어 + would / could / might + have + 과거분사]

20 I wish + 가정법 과거 [I wish + 주어 + 과거동사]

21 I wish + 가정법 과거완료 [I wish + 주어 + had + 과거분사]

22 It's time + 가정법 [It's time (that) + 주어 + 과거동사]

23 가정법 과거완료 [If + 주어 + had + 과거분사, 주어 + would

24 혼합가정법 [If + 주어 + had + 과거분사, 주어 + would / could / might + 동사원형]

25 [were it not for]: ~이 없다면

26 가정법 과거 [If + 주어 + 과거동사, 주어 + could + 동사원형]

27 It's time + 가정법 [It's time (that) + 주어 + 과거동사]

28 현재 사실의 반대 '처럼'일 때 [as if + 주어 + 과거동사]이다.

29 '만약 ~했다면, ~할 텐데'의 혼합가정법은 [If + 주어 + had + 과거분사, 주어 + would + 동사원형]이다.

30 I wish + 가정법 과거 [I wish + 주어 + 과거동사]

Grammar Mapping　　　　　　　　　　p. 148

① 조동사 과거　② had + p.p.　③ have + p.p.
④ 동사원형　⑤ 현재　⑥ ~라면 좋을 텐데　⑦ 과거
⑧ ~했다면 좋을 텐데　⑨ ~인 것처럼 …하다　⑩ ~이었던 것처럼 …하다　⑪ 과거동사　⑫ ~해야 할 시간이다　⑬ 동사 + 주어　⑭ ~이 없다면　⑮ ~이 없었다면

Chapter 11　일치와 화법

GP Practice 60 수의 일치
GP Practice 61 시제 일치와 예외　　　　　　p. 151

A	1 has	2 is	3 love
	4 are	5 Does	
B	1 would	2 travels	3 sank
	4 was	5 get	
C	1 walls have		
	2 A number of people are		
	3 the dead were buried		
D	1 is / 단수		2 are / 복수, 많은
	3 O / 현재		4 invented / 과거

GP Practice 62 평서문의 간접화법 전환
GP Practice 63 의문문의 간접화법 전환
GP Practice 64 명령문의 간접화법 전환　　　p. 153

A	1 where I lived	2 told
	3 if	4 to put up

B
1 told me that she wouldn't forget my help
2 asked her why she had left
3 asked me if / whether I remembered
4 told Paula not to drive fast

C
1 told us that he would invite us
2 asked her what she wanted
3 advised me to wear

D
1 why he was / S + V
2 if I liked / if, S + V
3 to do / to부정사
4 not to say / not

Grammar & Writing
p. 154

A
1 Eating an apple a day keeps
2 said that the Earth moves
3 The number of jobless people is
4 told me that I looked very tired
5 asked us if we had enjoyed
6 said that practice makes perfect

B
1 Does anyone know
2 A number of students were late
3 asked me what my strengths are
4 learned that the sun is
5 told me to wear
6 asked me if / whether he could take a picture of

C
1 to try the traditional food
2 if / whether I had known the reason
3 to tell him the truth
4 (that) the first Olympic Games were held in 776 B.C.
5 (that) Athens is the capital of Greece

D
1 if / whether I liked cooking
2 what I wanted to cook
3 we would make cold noodles that day
4 to wash my hands first
5 not to boil the noodles too long

Actual Test
p. 156

1 ② **2** ② **3** ④ **4** ③ **5** ④ **6** ② **7** ③ **8** ④
9 ⑤ **10** ① **11** ②, ⑤ **12** has **13** can
14 would **15** ② **16** ④ **17** ② **18** ①

19 The deaf use sign language **20** I asked her whether she had **21** My mom told me not to skip **22** use their sweat **23** asked me if (whether) I had drawn **24** was donated
25 told him that she liked his present
26 asked her when her next concert was
27 me not to eat spicy food **28** was → is, 현재
29 is → are, 많은, 복수 **30** Mia learned that the Korean War ended in 1953

1 주절 시제와 상관없이 역사적 사실은 과거시제를 씀.

2 현재에도 지속되는 사실은 현재시제를 씀.

3 의문사가 없는 의문문을 간접화법으로 쓸 때 [ask + (목적어) + if (whether) + 주어 + 동사]이다.

4 명령문을 간접화법으로 쓸 때 [tell + 목적어 + to부정사]이다.

5 [ask (+ 목적어) + if + 주어 + 동사]: ～에게 ～인지를 묻다, [ask / advise / order / tell + 목적어 + to부정사]: ～에게 ～하라고 ～하다

6 주절이 과거시제이면 종속절은 과거 또는 과거완료시제를 쓰므로 breaks → broke가 되어야 함.

7 무게는 단수 취급하므로 were → was가 되어야 함.

8 부정대명사 each, 동명사는 단수 취급을 함.

9 a number of는 '많은' 의미이며 복수 취급, the number of는 '～의 수' 의미이며 단수 취급함.

10 주절이 과거이면 종속절은 과거, 과거완료 또는 현재까지 지속되는 일이면 현재시제, 일반적인 사실은 주절과 상관없이 현재시제를 씀.

11 주절이 과거시제이면 종속절은 과거, 과거완료시제를 씀.

12 국가명은 복수형이어도 단수 취급을 함.

13 일반적인 사실은 현재시제를 씀.

14 주절이 과거시제이면 종속절은 과거 또는 과거완료시제를 씀.

15 ② my → her, 간접화법으로 전환 시 전달자의 입장에 맞게 인칭, 시제, 부사 등을 바꿈.

16 평서문의 간접화법은 [tell + 목적어 + that 주어 + 동사]이다.

17 ① have → has ③ miss → missed ④ why was I → why I was ⑤ turn → to turn

18 ⓓ 시간은 단수 취급 are → is, ⓔ 일반적인 사실은 단수 취급하므로 was → is이다.

19 [the + 형용사]는 '～하는 사람들'로 복수동사와 씀.

20 의문사가 없는 의문문의 간접화법은 [ask + 목적어 + if (whether) + 주어 + 동사]이다.

21 부정 명령문을 간접화법으로 쓸 때 [tell / order / ask / advise + 목적어 + not + to부정사]이다.

22 일반적인 사실은 현재시제를 씀.

23 의문사가 없는 의문문의 간접화법 [if (whether) + 주어 + 동사], 질문 시점보다 이전의 시제를 씀.

24 액수는 단수 취급을 함.

25 평서문의 간접화법은 [say (tell + 목적어) + that 주어 + 동사]이다.

26 의문사가 있는 의문문의 간접화법은 [ask + 목적어 + 의문사 + 주어 + 동사]이다.

27 부정 명령문의 간접화법은 [advise + 목적어 + not + to부정사]이다.

28 일반적이나 과학적 사실은 항상 현재시제를 쓴다.

29 [a number of]는 '많은'을 의미하며 주어로 쓰일 때 복수 취급함.

30 역사적 사실은 과거시제를 씀.

Grammar Mapping

p. 160

① each   ② 동명사   ③ that절   ④ both   ⑤ a number of   ⑥ 현재시제   ⑦ 과거나 과거완료   ⑧ 현재의 습관   ⑨ 불변의 진리   ⑩ 과거시제   ① say   ② tell   ③ that   ④ ask   ⑤ if (whether)   ⑥ 의문사   ⑦ advise   ⑧ to부정사   ⑨ not

---

Chapter 12 특수구문

GP Practice 65 강조
GP Practice 66 부정표현

p. 163

A 　**1** does 　　　　**2** It
　　3 Neither 　　**4** Not

B 　**1** is at 9 o'clock that (when)
　　2 do know
　　3 was a live concert that (which)

C 　**1** We do believe
　　2 Not every student
　　3 None of the players
　　4 It was his hair that

D 　**1** understand / 동사원형
　　2 that, which / that
　　3 삭제 / 없다
　　4 O / Not + all

GP Practice 67 도치
GP Practice 68 동격

p. 165

A 　**1** sat a gentleman 　**2** is his tie
　　3 has 　　　　　　　**4** of

B 　**1** flew the drone
　　2 he fell
　　3 do teenagers write letters on paper

C 　**1** lives a starfish
　　2 the news that
　　3 Little did he
　　4 so does she

D 　**1** hid the kids / V + S
　　2 O / S + V
　　3 could I / 조동사 + S
　　4 so did I / so, V + S

Grammar & Writing

p. 166

A 　**1** and so did I
　　2 is the house where he lived
　　3 Not all animals are fierce
　　4 The child did tie his shoelaces
　　5 did I dream of meeting you
　　6 It was fireworks that we watched yesterday

B 　**1** None of them supported
　　2 did suffer from
　　3 has she left home
　　4 It was my father that (who)
　　5 denied the fact that
　　6 neither could my friend

C 　**1** the cloud appeared the sun
　　2 a single error did the teacher find
　　3 did I imagine winning the lottery

D 　**1** it is her friends that she will meet at the school gate
　　2 it is at 1 p.m. that she will go to science class
　　3 it is dancing that she will practice for the school festival
　　4 it is at a Mexican restaurant that she will have dinner with her family

1 ⑤ 2 ② 3 ① 4 ③ 5 ④ 6 ① 7 ③, ⑤
8 ④ 9 ③ 10 ④ 11 ③ 12 of 13 nothing
14 don't always 15 Not all 16 ⑤ 17 ③
18 hung a big portrait 19 did I notice that he was angry 20 None of my students cheated
21 ④ 22 did I dream 23 were his letter and present 24 was child safety that / which
25 do know 26 ③ 27 No → Not, not + every
28 So → Neither, neither 29 the king has → has the king, have + 주어 + p.p. 30 It was last month that I started to learn Chinese

1 [It is / was ~ that]에 의한 강조: 강조 대상이 see의 목적어인 Mr. White이다.

2 현재동사 강조는 [do / does + 동사원형]이다.

3 [주어 + 일반동사 ~ (긍정문), so + do / does / did + 주어]: 역시 ~하다

4 부분부정 [not + every + 단수명사]: 모두 ~인 것은 아니다

5 부정어 도치는 [부정어 + have + 주어 + p.p.]이다.

6 동격 표현은 [명사, + 명사], [명사 + of + 명사구], [명사 + that + 주어 + 동사]이다.

7 [It is / was ~ that]에 의한 강조에서 강조 대상이 시간을 나타내므로 that / when을 씀.

8 부정어 도치 [부정어 + do / does / did + 주어 + 동사원형], ④ knew I → did I know로 바꿔야 함.

9 [It is / was ~ that]에 의한 강조, ③ what → that으로 바꿔야 함.

10 ④는 가주어 it과 접속사 that, 나머지는 [It is / was ~ that]에 의한 강조이다.

11 ③은 일반동사 do, 나머지는 동사 강조 do이다.

12 동격 표현은 [명사 + of + 명사구]이다.

13 전체부정 [not + anything → nothing]: 아무것도 ~않다

14 부분부정 [not + always]: 항상 ~인 것은 아니다

15 부분부정 [not + all + 복수명사]: 모두 ~인 것은 아니다

16 부분부정 [not + both]: 둘 다 ~인 것은 아니다

17 [주어 + be동사 ~ (긍정문), so + am / are / is + 주어]: 역시 ~하다

18 장소 부사구 도치는 [장소 부사구 + 동사 + 주어]이다.

19 부정어 도치는 [부정어 + do / does / did + 주어 + 동사원형]이다.

20 전체부정 [none of 명사 + 동사]: 아무도 ~않다

21 ④ so was her sister → so does her sister

22 부정어 도치는 [부정어 + do / does / did + 주어 + 동사원형]이다.

23 장소 부사구 도치는 [장소 부사구 + 동사 + 주어]이다.

24 [It is / was ~ that]에 의한 강조이다.

25 현재동사 강조는 [do / does + 동사원형]이다.

26 ⓐ he could → could he ⓔ did → was

27 부분부정 '모두 ~인 것은 아니다'는 [not + every + 단수명사]이다.

28 [부정문 + neither + 동사 + 주어]의 어순에 주의한다.

29 [부정어구 + have + 주어 + p.p.]에서 have와 주어의 어순에 주의한다.

30 [It is / was ~ that]에 의한 강조로 강조 대상은 last month이다.

Grammar Mapping ○ p. 172

① do / does / did ② 강조 대상 ③ any / either / anything ④ all / every / both / always ⑤ 주어 + 동사 ⑥ 동사 + 주어 ⑦ not, never, little, seldom, hardly ⑧ be동사 + 주어 ⑨ 조동사 + 주어 ⑩ 동사원형 ⑪ have / has / had ⑫ 동의 ⑬ 긍정문 ⑭ 부정문 ⑮ 동격 ⑯ that

Grammar
ViSTA

Level 3

정답과 해설

- 본 교재   • workbook

Unit 01
p. 6

현재완료·현재완료진행

A
1 has been ringing   2 have
3 hasn't checked   4 been working
5 was   6 has grown
7 for   8 been to
9 have been waiting   10 since

B
1 has been sick since
2 haven't eaten anything
3 has been eating dinner
4 has been snowing
5 has been on a diet
6 has bought

C
1 has been building his house for
2 How long have you been playing
3 has never traveled
4 has not arrived yet
5 Have you ever wondered
6 has gone to his home country

D
1 have been to the restaurant twice
2 hasn't tried
3 has been driving for
4 has been reading this book since
5 Have you ever seen
6 has been the team's captain for

Unit 02
p. 8

과거완료·미래완료

A
1 had   2 missed
3 will have   4 dating
5 had   6 will have failed
7 known   8 had broken down
9 worked   10 teach

B
1 had not eaten
2 had drunk
3 will have built
4 had already closed
5 had already seen
6 had not rained
7 will have run

8 had worked
9 will have grown up
10 had never seen

C
1 had been crying
2 had never been to Busan
3 will have become a new person
4 will have been living
5 will have visited the museum ten times
6 had been taking a shower

D
1 will have left
2 had shared
3 had been living
4 will have arrived
5 will have been sailing
6 had put on her seatbelt

Error Correction
p. 10

1	has already finished	완료, has + p.p.
2	have visited	경험, have + p.p.
3	for	~동안 계속, for, 기간
4	O	현재완료, has lost
5	has been to	~ 가 본 적 있다, been
6	has gone to	~ 가버렸다, gone
7	has been reading	~해 오고 있는 중, has + been + -ing
8	went	과거
9	had never been	had + p.p.
10	had been	had + p.p.
11	had lost	had + p.p.
12	had been washing	had + been + -ing
13	will have watched	will have p.p.

Sentence Writing
p. 11

도전! 필수구문 156 p. 127

1 001	He has already finished his homework.
2 002	I have visited the city three times.
3 003	They have known each other for five years.

4
004
He has lost his wedding ring.

5
005
He has been to Greece.

6
006
He has gone to Greece.

7
007
She has been reading the book for an hour.

8
008
The play had already started when I went into the theater.

9
009
He had never been abroad until he turned 20.

10
010
Judy had been sick for two days when the doctor came.

11
011
I had lost my cell phone, so I couldn't call you then.

12
012
She had been washing her car when it began to rain.

13
013
If you watch this movie again, you will have watched it ten times.

Chapter 02 | 조동사

Unit 03   p. 14

can, may·must, should

A	**1** must	**2** should
	3 be able to	**4** can
	5 should	**6** had to
	7 May	**8** must
B	**1** have to	**2** was able to
	3 cannot	**4** don't have to
	5 must	**6** should have seen
C	**1** must be, must have been	
	2 should call, should have called	
	3 cannot be, cannot have been	
	4 may know, may have known	
D	**1** I cannot thank you	
	2 should not judge a book by its cover	
	3 The movie must be good	
	4 may not have locked the door	

E	**1** don't have to get a visa
	2 can't have said such a thing
	3 must not miss this big summer sale
	4 I will have to pull the tooth

Unit 04   p. 16

used to, would like to
had better, would rather, may as well

A	**1** had better	**2** may as well
	3 used to	**4** would like
	5 used to	**6** than
	7 had better not	
B	**1** used to	**2** would rather
	3 would like to	**4** had better not
	5 may as well	
C	**1** would like to	**2** had better not
	3 used to	**4** would rather
	5 may as well	
D	**1** you may as well do it alone	
	2 would rather call her than	
	3 had better charge your cell phone	
	4 used to use signal fires	
	5 would bring their own lunch	
	6 had better not eat snacks	
E	**1** had better not put these plants	
	2 would like to check out these two books	
	3 you may as well quit	
	4 would like to thank everyone	
	5 used to be a housewife	
	6 would rather work alone	

Error Correction   p. 18

1	be able to	불가능, be able to
2	may like	약한 추측, 동사원형
3	O	뒤, not
4	don't have to	~할 필요 없다, don't,
5	must have practiced	과거, have p.p.
6	to respect	충고, to + 동사원형
7	should have done	과거, have p.p.

8	O / used to	습관, would, used to
9	used to	상태, used to
10	had better	~하는 것이 낫다, had
11	had better not	뒤, not
12	than	than, B, A
13	go	~하는 것이 낫다, 동사원형

1 014	He can (= is able to) speak five foreign languages.
2 015	He may like your idea.
3 016	You must not take pictures in the museum.
4 017	Children under seven don't have to pay an entrance fee.
5 018	You must have practiced very hard.
6 019	We ought to (= should) respect our parents.
7 020	I should have done my homework.
8 021	Mike used to (would) collect foreign coins.
9 022	He used to be my boyfriend, but he isn't now.
10 023	You had better take a window seat.
11 024	We had better not go out tonight because of the rain.
12 025	I would rather play outside than watch TV at home.
13 026	If there's nothing more to do, we may as well go home.

Chapter 03 | 수동태

수동태의 의미와 기본 및 다양한 형태·동사구 수동태

A	1 forget	2 turned on
	3 being washed	4 was introduced
	5 be remembered	6 been
	7 looked after	

B	1 was discussed at the meeting by them
	2 are being made by robots
	3 has been spread by word of mouth
	4 were taken care of by the mother eagle
	5 should be saved by us
	6 was put off by Henry
	7 must be washed by hand (by you)
	8 were handed out to homeless people by her

C	1 A report will be written by
	2 A report is being written by
	3 A report has been written by
	4 A report must be written by

D	1 My brother was named after
	2 The keyboard is being pressed
	3 His writing style has been influenced by
	4 The story has been loved by
	5 The survey was carried out

E	1 His bag was discovered at the park
	2 The new bridge will be built
	3 Your hamburger cannot be delivered
	4 He is looked up to by
	5 Cookies are being baked

4형식·5형식 문장의 수동태

| A | 1 to | 2 for |
| | 3 of | 4 to |

B	1 to use	2 is kept
	3 to feed	4 to pick up
	5 to change	6 to

| C | 1 was taught some tricks by me, were taught to my dog by me |

2 was given a piece of advice by him, was given to me by him

3 A box of pizza was handed to

4 A difficult question was asked of

5 A kid's meal was brought to

D **1** were made to read the book again by her

2 was called a soccer genius

3 was heard shouting for help by the police

4 was advised to rest for two weeks by the doctor

E **1** The handmade bag was bought

2 They were made to serve

3 Pepper was considered valuable

4 He was heard to whistle

F **1** was asked to introduce

2 was cooked for the guests

3 Bangkok is often called

4 was made curious

Unit 07   p. 27

목적어가 that절인 문장의 수동태 by 이외의 전치사를 쓰는 수동태

A **1** is said   **2** in

3 for   **4** to be

5 is said   **6** with

7 that

B **1** was reported that the singer was missing, was reported to be missing

2 is believed that elephants have good memories, are believed to have good memories

3 was believed that the wizard had magical powers, was believed to have magical powers

4 is said that the city is safe and clean, is said to be safe and clean

5 is thought that Paula has a sense of humor, is thought to have a sense of humor

C **1** are known to be very smart

2 Life is filled with

3 It is said that stress causes

4 is expected to use

5 The mountaintop is covered with

6 are required to pray

D **1** is said that global warming

2 is known to be useful

3 I am pleased with

4 is expected to be successful

5 His fans are disappointed with

6 is made of pure gold

Error Correction   p. 29

1	are being built	being + p.p.
2	has been closed	been + p.p.
3	be watered	be + p.p.
4	looked after	looked after
5	to	to
6	for	for
7	called	called
8	to sit	to + V
9	to clean	to + V
10	to climb / climbing	to + V, V + -ing
11	is said	is said
12	to bring	to + V
13	as	~라고 알려지다, as

Sentence Writing   p. 30

도전! 필수구문 156   p. 129

1 027	Space elevators are being built by the company.
2 028	The road has been closed because of heavy snow.
3 029	These flowers should be watered every day.
4 030	The puppy was looked after by him.
5 031	Two concert tickets were given to him by her.
6 032	A nice backpack was bought for me by my uncle.

7 033	She was called a Walking Dictionary.	
8 034	We were told to sit down by him.	
9 035	I was made to clean the room by Jessica.	
10 036	The boy was seen to climb (climbing) the tree.	
11 037	It is said that laughter brings good luck.	
12 038	Laughter is said to bring good luck.	
13 039	Korean popular music is known as K-pop.	

Chapter 04 | 부정사

Unit 08　　p. 36

to부정사의 명사적 쓰임

A
1 to become
2 how
3 to say
4 to order
5 it
6 It
7 To prepare
8 to walk
9 to see
10 not

B
1 It takes only 10 seconds to download
2 It is a great idea to deliver pizza
3 It is dangerous to swim across
4 when to stop talking
5 whom to ask
6 when to turn off

C
1 how to walk
2 where to go
3 what to cook
4 when to get up

D
1 was to feed penguins
2 how to use sign language
3 it is necessary to say no
4 not to wake up the baby

E
1 easy to understand Korean history
2 to walk on fallen leaves
3 The project is to build
4 planning to rent

Unit 09　　p. 38

to부정사의 형용사적·부사적 쓰임

A
1 도착한
2 같이 살 룸메이트
3 듣게 되어서 기쁜
4 찾아서 신난 / 흥분한
5 떠나야 한다
6 성공할 방법
7 사용하기에 쉬운

B
1 to see you again
2 to trust Paula
3 to become the president of the country
4 to get a discount

C
1 You are to wear a helmet
2 The volcano is to erupt
3 No water is to be found
4 you are to meet

D
1 to do freelance work
2 in order to attract insects
3 was to be heard
4 very cozy to sleep in
5 many friends to play with
6 are not to ask personal questions

E
1 the best time to visit
2 a lot of food to stay
3 is very easy to imitate
4 the only person to know the truth
5 are to talk with
6 is to hold a fire drill

Unit 10　　p. 40

목적격보어로 쓰이는 부정사

A
1 to make
2 to accept
3 eat
4 look
5 to babysit
6 sing
7 take

B
1 shake / shaking
2 to complete
3 where to get off
4 not to talk
5 not to drop
6 happen
7 to come

C
1 (to) paint
2 to brush
3 to keep
4 do
5 drive
6 wash / washing
7 to stop
8 to listen to

D
1 ask any child to choose
2 I heard my sister talking

3 had Betty think again

4 told us not to break our promise

5 want me to tell the truth

6 Let the sleeping dog lie

E **1** helped the firefighters put out

2 felt sweat run / running

3 saw someone walking along

4 made us repeat after

5 told him to get in

6 encourage people to borrow money

7 allow me to skip breakfast

Unit 11   p. 42

to부정사의 의미상 주어·to부정사의 시제

A **1** of

2 for her

3 to be disturbed

4 to like

5 for him

6 for you

7 to have visited

8 to be called

B **1** for the reporter   **2** O

3 for you   **4** for him

5 to be built   **6** to have found

C **1** seems to like

2 seems to enjoy

3 seems to be very good at

4 seem to have heard about the scientist

5 seems to have been a baseball player

D **1** careless of me to leave

2 needs to be wrapped

3 seems to enjoy his job

4 generous of him to sponsor

5 the only player to have won the prize

6 seems to have been created

E **1** thoughtful of him to warm up

2 hard for me to do two things

3 seems to have

4 sorry to have broken

5 seems to have changed

6 useless for me to try

7 thrilled to be invited

Unit 12   p. 44

to부정사를 이용한 구문·독립부정사

A **1** To begin   **2** To be sure

3 kind enough   **4** to park

5 too late   **6** so

7 to speak   **8** To tell

B **1** too foggy for him to drive

2 popular enough to become a bestseller

3 too fat to pass through the hole

4 small enough to be toured in three hours

5 too beautiful for me to eat

6 too old fashioned, to wear

7 smart enough to solve the quiz

C **1** small enough to fit

2 smart enough to have an alibi

3 too small for him to wear

4 loud enough to wake me up

5 too big for me to finish

6 too small for six people to ride in

D **1** Strange to say, the funny song became

2 salty enough for me to float

3 To be frank with you, he is not

4 Not to mention, she is cute

5 ripe enough to be picked

6 To make matters worse, it began

7 too simple to catch the eyes

Error Correction   p. 46

1	it	it, to부정사
2	to spend	어디서, to부정사
3	to write with	가지고 쓸, with
4	to visit	예정, to부정사
5	easy	쉬운, 형용사
6	to listen	to부정사
7	laugh	원형부정사
8	play / playing	원형부정사
9	O	있으면, of
10	to know	동사원형
11	to have known	have p.p.
12	lucky enough	～하기 충분한, 형용사 + enough

13 too violent   너무 ~해서, too + 형용사

Sentence Writing   p. 47

도전! 필수구문 156   p. 130

1
040
This app makes it easier to check the weather.

2
041
We decided where to spend our holiday.

3
042
I need a pencil to write with.

4
043
We are to visit Mexico next month.

5
044
My password was easy to remember.

6
045
I want you to listen to me carefully.

7
046
His funny joke made her laugh.

8
047
She watched the kittens play (playing) with a ball.

9
048
It was kind of him to help the old woman.

10
049
He seems to know the answer.

11
050
He seems to have known the answer.

12
051
He was lucky enough to marry a woman like you.

13
052
The program was too violent for him to watch.

Chapter 05 | 동명사

Unit 13   p. 50

동명사의 명사적 쓰임·의미상 주어·시제

A			
1 Studying		**2** her	
3 taking		**4** being	
5 asking		**6** not remembering	
7 having been		**8** picking	

B	
1 taking a picture	
2 my taking a picture	

---

3 becoming the school president

4 her becoming the school president

5 being late for the meeting

6 having been late for the meeting

7 being interested in

8 having been interested in

C			
1 being touched		**2** him / his	
3 winning		**4** becoming	
5 her			

D	
1 making money is easier
2 was afraid of being forgotten by people
3 imagine riding in a flying car
4 apologized for having lied
5 anyone teaching them

E	
1 not having stopped
2 instead of staying at home
3 cooking or eating
4 the advantage of getting up early
5 keep stirring it for five minutes

Unit 14   p. 52

동명사와 to부정사·동명사의 관용적 쓰임

A			
1 to eat, eating		**2** fighting	
3 being		**4** to help	
5 to bring		**6** opening	
7 posing		**8** riding	
9 to hold		**10** crying	

B			
1 to change		**2** making	
3 talking		**4** shopping / to shop	
5 thinking		**6** wearing	
7 to win		**8** to say	
9 asking		**10** wagging	

C	
1 remembers to turn off
2 remember telling me the secret
3 forget to return the book
4 regret eating a heavy dinner

D	
1 Why don't you try counting sheep
2 suggested adopting a dog
3 forgot ordering pizza
4 feel like discussing the issue

E	
1 stopped to check the tires
2 is worth watching again
3 regrets not buying the cute doll
4 has difficulty hearing

Error Correction   p. 54

1	Using	동명사
2	watching	동명사
3	telling	동명사
4	her	소유격, 목적격
5	being	동사원형 + -ing
6	having been	having p.p.
7	decorating	동명사
8	to accept	to부정사
9	to play / playing	to부정사, 동명사
10	O	동명사
11	to lend	to부정사
12	O	동명사
13	making	동명사

Sentence Writing   p. 55

도전! 필수구문 156   p. 131

1 053	Using solar energy is good for the Earth.
2 054	We enjoyed watching the stars at night.
3 055	She is good at telling stories.
4 056	Do you mind her closing the door?
5 057	He is proud of being a voice actor.
6 058	He is proud of having been a voice actor.
7 059	Did you finish decorating the Christmas tree?
8 060	Judy finally agreed to accept his offer.
9 061	Evan began playing (to play) the guitar.
10 062	He forgot lending me his umbrella.
11 063	He forgot to lend me his umbrella.
12 064	Tom stopped talking to me.
13 065	I have difficulty making decisions.

Chapter 06 | 분사

Unit 15   p. 60

현재분사와 과거분사·분사의 형용사적 쓰임

A	**1** sliced	**2** talking	
	3 frozen	**4** locked	
	5 knocking	**6** amazing	
	7 broken		

B	**1** disappointing, disappointed
	2 surprising, surprised
	3 amazing, amazed
	4 frightening, frightened
	5 interesting, interested

C	**1** used	**2** left
	3 waiting	**4** fried
	5 married	**6** passing by
	7 oncoming	

D	**1** living in Canada
	2 flying up into the sky
	3 riding a scooter
	4 knitted by my mom

E	**1** the pillows filled with feathers
	2 The speaker felt embarrassed
	3 two messages left for you
	4 laying its eggs in the other bird's nest

F	**1** caught in a trap
	2 got their food frozen
	3 surprised at the sound
	4 handing on the wall

Unit 16   p. 62

목적격보어로 쓰이는 분사

A	**1** ~하고 있는	**2** ~하고 있는	
	3 ~하고 있는	**4** ~하고 있는	
	5 ~하고 있는	**6** ~된	
	7 ~된	**8** ~된	
	9 ~된	**10** ~된	

B	**1** melting	**2** done
	3 pulled out	**4** checked
	5 knocking	**6** burning
	7 interesting	

C	1	taken	2	boring
	3	delivered	4	boiling
	5	playing		

D	1	my heart beating
	2	got his ears pierced
	3	his shoes polished
	4	her kids playing
	5	her novel made

E	1	your group project done
	2	the door locked
	3	the movie exciting
	4	Jason hitting / hit
	5	his dog running after

Unit 17 p. 64

분사구문

A	1	Feeling cold
	2	Making a decision
	3	Using my phone
	4	Not knowing English
	5	Taking notes
	6	Being almost 80 years old

B	1	Because Jennifer loves animals
	2	Although it is a used TV
	3	When the kids crossed the street
	4	If you take this shortcut
	5	Because he felt hungry
	6	While the campers ate lunch

C	1	Eating enough fruit
	2	Not being careful
	3	Coming out from behind the cloud
	4	clapping and cheering
	5	Saying, "Yes,"
	6	Getting on the bus

D	1	Opening the box
	2	Being lazy
	3	Having light bones
	4	Entering the house
	5	Feeling embarrassed
	6	Not wanting to make mistakes

Unit 18 p. 66

완료형·수동·주어가 있는 분사구문
[with + 명사 + 분사]

A	1	Saved	2	Having gained
	3	folded	4	Decorated
	5	speaking	6	speaking
	7	Asked	8	being

B	1	It being daytime
	2	Having watched the movie
	3	The button being touched
	4	Having reserved a seat
	5	Having slept enough
	6	Loved by its owner
	7	Written in a hurry

C	1	with its leg hurt
	2	with the sun setting
	3	with his eyes closed
	4	with spectators cheering

D	1	Having slept enough
	2	Having been trained
	3	Having been educated
	4	Considering his long working hours

E	1	Having been stung
	2	Having lost her memory
	3	Not having checked
	4	Compared to my cat

Error Correction p. 68

1	rising	진행, 현재분사
2	the sun rising in the east	뒤
3	waiting	V + -ing, ~하는 것을
4	closed	p.p., ~된 것을
5	painting	V + -ing, ~하는 것을
6	O	p.p., ~된 것을
7	Seeing	V + -ing
8	Not knowing	not, 앞
9	Having seen	Having p.p.
10	(Being) Shocked	수동, (Being) p.p.
11	It raining	불가

| 12 | ringing | V + -ing, ~하면서 |
| 13 | O | p.p., ~된 채로 |

| Sentence Writing | p. 69 |
| 도전! 필수구문 156 | p. 132 |

1 066	Look at the rising sun.
2 067	Look at the sun rising in the east.
3 068	He kept the girl waiting.
4 069	He kept his eyes closed.
5 070	He saw the man painting his house.
6 071	He saw his house painted.
7 072	Seeing me, she shouted with joy.
8 073	Not knowing how to say sorry, the boy just cried.
9 074	Having seen her before, I know her face.
10 075	(Being) Shocked by the news, he didn't say a word.
11 076	It raining heavily yesterday, the concert was canceled.
12 077	He was sleeping with the alarm ringing.
13 078	A pigeon flew to me with a message tied to its leg.

Chapter 07 | 비교표현

| Unit 19 | p. 72 |

원급, 비교급, 최상급·원급을 이용한 표현

A
1 brave
2 heavier
3 hard
4 in
5 not as rich as
6 than
7 possible
8 twice as thick as

B
1 best
2 little

3 dirtier
4 the most crowded
5 more practical
6 the thinnest
7 busy
8 the shortest

C
1 as quietly as
2 less fierce
3 more coffee

D
1 as soon as possible
2 more convenient than cash
3 not as quiet as the country
4 twice as much money as he did
5 less warm than that of Jeju Island
6 the most adventurous person of all my friends

E
1 the busiest person in
2 as often as you can
3 twice as many T-shirts
4 more important than
5 the most convenient of
6 three times longer than

| Unit 20 | p. 74 |

비교급·최상급을 이용한 표현
원급, 비교급을 이용한 최상급 의미

A
1 much
2 more
3 smaller and smaller
4 strangest
5 to
6 faster
7 runner
8 disasters

B
1 the stronger
2 taller and taller
3 the most humorous
4 the best pitchers
5 even more dangerous

C
1 older than
2 The more, the healthier
3 I have ever studied
4 as curious as, more curious than, more curious, any other girl

D
1 much more quickly than ice
2 one of the wisest people
3 better service than any other resort
4 the most delicious food I have ever eaten
5 No other teacher at my school is as friendly as
6 the more ideas you will get

E
1 louder and louder
2 far more logical
3 I have ever watched
4 The closer, the longer
5 bigger than any other
6 one of the most famous scientists

Error Correction   p. 76

1	fast	as + 원급 + as
2	O	not as
3	cheaper	비교급 + than
4	biggest	최상급
5	three times as	배수사 + as
6	possible	possible
7	much	훨씬, much
8	smaller and smaller	비교급 + and + 비교급
9	the colder	the + 비교급
10	O	복수명사
11	have ever met	have ever p.p.
12	No	No
13	river	단수명사

Sentence Writing   p. 77
도전! 필수구문 156   p. 133

1
079 My dog can run as fast as a cheetah.

2
080 The rock band is not as popular as the girl group.

3
081 This cell phone is cheaper than that one.

4
082 The Sahara Desert is the biggest desert in the world.

5
083 This bike is three times as light as my old one.

6
084 Your point has to be as specific as possible.

7
085 Iron is much heavier than aluminum.

8
086 Our world is becoming smaller and smaller.

9
087 The darker it grew, the colder it became.

10
088 Jennifer is one of the most energetic girls in her class.

11
089 He is the bravest man (that) I have ever met.

12
090 No (other) river in the world is longer than the Nile.

13
091 The Nile is longer than any other river in the world.

Chapter 08 | 접속사

Unit 21   p. 80

부사절을 이끄는 접속사

A
1 as soon as	2 while
3 Since	4 meet
5 goes	6 since
7 even though	

B
1 If	2 even though
3 until	4 While
5 As soon as	6 since
7 Although	8 because
9 when	10 If
11 until	12 Unless

C
1 If you go for a hike
2 Every time Patrick takes an umbrella
3 If you cannot stand the heat
4 since my summer vacation started
5 When she looks at me
6 as soon as it was released

D
1 As / Because / Since the ice cream was hard
2 Unless you take off the monster costume
3 while he tries to study
4 when you get off the bus
5 since I graduated from middle school
6 Although the diamond is fake
7 until they turned dark

간접의문문·상관접속사

A　　**1** where we are　　**2** were
　　　3 seems　　　　　**4** the actor is
　　　5 if
　　　6 how tall the Eiffel Tower is
　　　7 think

B　　**1** how big the moon is
　　　2 How big do you think the moon is
　　　3 if she likes my suggestion
　　　4 if you are coming to the party
　　　5 what my cat wants to say
　　　6 What do you believe caused
　　　7 who cooked the delicious pasta
　　　8 when Mom proposed to you

C　　**1** both public schools and private schools
　　　2 Not only Max but also I am ready
　　　3 neither better nor worse
　　　4 either cook or do the dishes

D　　**1** I learned what the symbol meant
　　　2 My uncle neither drinks nor smokes
　　　3 We not only love but also respect
　　　4 Who do you believe is telling the truth

E　　**1** either you or I will be the winner
　　　2 invite you as well as Emily
　　　3 who designed the glass house
　　　4 if (whether) he will keep his promise

Error Correction　　　　　　　　p. 84

1	O	~하는 동안, 시간
2	O	~할 때까지, until
3	When	~할 때, 시간
4	leaves	if ~ not, 사용 불가
5	as / because / since	~때문에, 이유
6	although / even though	비록 ~이지만, 양보
7	meet	부사절, 현재
8	he lives	주어 + 동사
9	O	동사
10	What do you think	앞
11	if / whether	if, whether
12	are	복수
13	likes	B

Sentence Writing　　　　　　　p. 85
도전! 필수구문 156　　　　　　　p. 134

1 092	While she was studying, she listened to music.
2 093	By law, you are a child until you are 18 years old.
3 094	When he feels nervous, he bites his nails.
4 095	Unless she leaves now, she will miss her flight.
5 096	He stopped watching the movie because it was too violent.
6 097	He didn't go to see the musical although he had a ticket.
7 098	I will speak to her when I meet her the next time.
8 099	I don't know where he lives.
9 100	I know who broke this window.
10 101	What do you think his real job is?
11 102	I don't know if (whether) she will win the contest.
12 103	Both Jack and Jill are college students.
13 104	Neither the kids nor their mom likes meat.

Chapter 09 | 관계사

관계대명사 who, which, that, what

A　　**1** that　　**2** whose　　**3** which
　　　4 who　　**5** what

B
1 what I expected
2 that live next door
3 whose design is unique
4 who stole my cell phone

C
1 The woman who is singing on the stage is my mother
2 I lost the sneakers which I bought at a flea market
3 There are many people whose opinions are different from yours
4 The data which you gathered on the Internet might be inaccurate
5 The team is looking for the pilot and the plane that crashed into the sea

D
1 that, 있음   2 What, 없음
3 that, 있음   4 what, 없음
5 that, 있음   6 What, 없음

E
1 any medicine which works well
2 What we know, what we do
3 a robot that is programmed
4 the classmate whose notes I borrowed

F
1 which / that has more memory
2 What you need most
3 that I can tell
4 whose price is reasonable

관계부사 when, where, why, how

A
1 where   2 how
3 why   4 when

B
1 when she left me alone, on which she left me alone
2 where your family stayed, at which your family stayed
3 why he became popular, for which he became popular
4 how people reduce stress, the way in which people reduce stress

C
1 when, 완전   2 which, 불완전
3 how, 완전   4 which, 불완전

D
1 how she looks to people
2 the time when we make a new start
3 the reason why he broke up with her

---

4 The library where I usually study
5 the way he had treated his brother
6 The box where she keeps her jewelry

E
1 why he called you
2 when people play tricks
3 where they were born
4 how she survived
5 which I grew up
6 why you refused to go

관계대명사 생략 · [전치사 + 관계대명사] 관계사의 계속적 용법

A
1 whom   2 which
3 at which   4 painted
5 to which   6 who

B
1 that, ①   2 X
3 who are, ②   4 who, ①
5 X

C
1 which were only two years old
2 when it was very cold
3 which made them very tired
4 where I ran into my childhood friend
5 who overcame her physical difficulties

D
1 The man taking a photo
2 The new bed I slept in
3 The chair on which he is
4 when he was sixteen years old
5 who did not tell her the answer
6 which often gets me into trouble

E
1 who was poor
2 in which he is
3 I wanted
4 which has
5 who(m) / that you can work
6 where she lived

복합관계대명사 · 복합관계부사

A
1 However   2 Whoever
3 Whatever   4 Whenever
5 whichever   6 Wherever
7 Whomever   8 However

B	**1** Whatever	**2** Whichever
	3 wherever	**4** Whenever
	5 whomever	**6** However

C	**1** no matter what may happen
	2 Whichever team wins tonight
	3 However expensive the car is
	4 Whoever finds a solution to the problem
	5 Whatever you do for others
	6 whenever she has some free time

D	**1** whichever she needs
	2 whenever you feel thirsty
	3 whomever he recommends
	4 However rich he is
	5 whatever you cook
	6 Wherever you are

Error Correction　　　　　　　　　p. 98

1	which / that	사물, 주격
2	삭제	목적격, 삭제
3	whose	소유격
4	what	what
5	when	시간, when
6	for	이유, for
7	삭제	방법, 없음
8	O	가능
9	whom	whom
10	which	which
11	Whoever	Whoever
12	wherever	wherever
13	However	However

Sentence Writing　　　　　　　　　p. 99
도전! 필수구문 156　　　　　　　　　p. 135

1
105　I bought a book which (that) is about space.

2
106　He is the man who(m) (that) I respect the most.

3
107　I know a man whose daughter is a popular actress.

4
108　You can do what you'd like to do.

5
109　The day when we can live on Mars will come.

6
110　Do you know the reason why Rome collapsed?

7
111　The program shows a way (how) people manage time wisely.

8
112　The police found the bag I had lost at the airport.

9
113　You are the person on whom I can rely.

10
114　We ordered some seafood dishes, which tasted really awful.

11
115　Whoever wants to succeed should be diligent.

12
116　The dog follows my dad wherever he goes.

13
117　However smart he is, he won't understand her tears.

Chapter 10 | 가정법

Unit 27　　　　　　　　　　　　p. 103

가정법 과거·과거완료·혼합가정법

A	**1** were	**2** will have
	3 have led	**4** were
	5 missed	**6** be

B	**1** would be	**2** had
	3 would visit	**4** would have fixed
	5 behave	**6** had entered

C	**1** were, cheat
	2 had not rained, could have gone
	3 lived, could meet
	4 had caught, would not have walked
	5 had made, would not have

D	**1** If he were not, he would be
	2 If she had, she could play dolls

3 You would be, if I told you

4 If I had accepted, I would be

5 If he had not worked, he could not have gotten

6 If she had listened, she would not have made

E **1** were, would buy

2 come, will hold

3 didn't ignore, would not get

4 had snowed, could have made

5 had seen, would not be worse

6 had not lost, could have opened

Unit 28   p. 105

[I wish + 가정법]·[as if + 가정법]
[it's time + 가정법]

A **1** didn't   **2** left

3 had taken   **4** were

5 said   **6** had seen

B **1** were   **2** had not lost

3 finished   **4** had stopped

5 were   **6** had known

C **1** I wish she had gone

2 they liked spicy food

3 you told me

4 I wish he paid attention

5 she had not found out about my poor grades

D **1** as if I were flying in the sky

2 It's time I decided my career path

3 She wishes her house had a swimming pool

4 as if he had been a millionaire

5 I wish I had said nothing to him

6 I wish you could make all the decisions

E **1** as if he were a singer

2 Olivia were my new English teacher

3 It is time we found

4 I wish I had learned

5 I wish more people used

6 as if he had not gotten

Unit 29   p. 107

if 생략 가정법·without, but for

A **1** Were I   **2** Without

3 to win   **4** With

5 Were   **6** Had

B **1** If it had not been

2 If you tasted

3 If it were not for

4 If it had not rained

C **1** Were I president

2 Had he gotten up

3 Were it not for

4 Had it not been for

D **1** Were I in your shoes

2 Without my cell phone, I would

3 Were it not for the KTX

4 Had it stormed yesterday

5 But for the Internet, we would

6 Had it not been for the director

E **1** would use

2 Were you, would, do

3 Without laws, would be

4 Were I you, would plan

5 Had he eaten, would not have gotten

6 Had it not been, could not have caught

Error Correction   p. 109

1	had	없는, 과거, could
2	O	있는, 현재, will
3	have bought	없는, have p.p.
4	have	R
5	O	과거
6	had finished	had p.p.
7	were	사실의 반대, 과거동사
8	had seen	사실의 반대, had p.p.
9	looked	과거
10	Were I	동사 + 주어
11	Had she	Had + 주어 + p.p.
12	But for	~이 없다면, But for
13	had not been	had not been

37

1
118 If he had a notebook, he could lend it to me.

2
119 If you miss this chance, you will regret it.

3
120 If the car had been a little cheaper, I could have bought it.

4
121 If I had finished my work yesterday, I would have more free time now.

5
122 I wish I were a bit taller.

6
123 I wish I had finished the project earlier.

7
124 He acts as if he were my boyfriend.

8
125 He talks as if he had seen the movie.

9
126 It's time we looked back over the past.

10
127 Were I you, I would accept the job offer.

11
128 Had she known his phone number, she would have called him.

12
129 But for fire, we couldn't live normal lives.

13
130 If it had not been for your help, I couldn't have made my own blog.

● ● ● ● ● ● ● ● ● ● ● ● ● ●
Chapter 11 | 일치와 화법

수의 일치·시제 일치와 예외

A **1** has   **2** had met
   3 discovered   **4** is
   5 is   **6** was
   7 sounds

B **1** is   **2** are
   3 is   **4** are
   5 has   **6** is
   7 are

C **1** pulls   **2** freezes
   3 was   **4** invented
   5 bought   **6** had moved
   7 would

D **1** To read fifty books is
   2 Two hours is too short to clean
   3 The country is hit by many storms
   4 I heard that Leonardo da Vinci painted
   5 A number of satellites are used for
   6 Water consists of oxygen and hydrogen

E **1** Adam said that he had lost his bag
   2 The book said that the pyramids are
   3 The wounded were taken to
   4 Both my mom and I are
   5 We learned that the first World War started
   6 He knew that the Earth moves

평서문·의문문·명령문의 간접화법 전환

A **1** said that they were waiting for a bus
   2 told me that my advice had been helpful
   3 asked me how I felt then
   4 if / whether I had ever been abroad
   5 told me to use honey instead of sugar
   6 asked me to set the table
   7 ordered / told them not to move

B **1** said, "I have a toothache."
   2 said to him, "I met your brother at the library."
   3 said to me, "How old are you?"
   4 girl said to her mom, "Where are my gloves?"
   5 said to her, "Do you like the song?"
   6 said to her, "Try to speak slowly."

C **1** said that she goes running every morning
   2 asked me what is in
   3 told her patient not to worry
   4 told me to go into the classroom
   5 asked me where I had bought
   6 told us not to eat on the bed
   7 asked her whether he could leave a message

D
1 told me that he had broken
2 asked him if he was satisfied with
3 said that he would become a movie director
4 asked me to open the bottle
5 said that he was going to buy
6 told us to stay away from the cars

Error Correction		p. 117
1	is	단수
2	is	단수
3	learn	~한 사람들, 복수
4	are	많은, 복수
5	is	~의 수, 단수
6	know	현재
7	have	현재
8	fell	과거
9	wanted	과거
10	ask	ask
11	if / whether	if, 주어 + 동사
12	to cook	to부정사
13	not	not

Sentence Writing	p. 118
도전! 필수구문 156	p. 137

1
131 The Netherlands is famous for tulips and windmills.

2
132 Three dollars is enough to buy the milk.

3
133 The young learn things faster than the old.

4
134 A number of people are resting on the beach.

5
135 The number of visitors to the blog is increasing.

6
136 I know that my teacher trusts me.

7
137 The book said that children have more bones than adults.

8
138 We learned that the Berlin Wall fell in 1989.

9
139 He told me that he wanted to meet me that day.

10
140 Jack asked me where I was going then.

11
141 Kate asked him if (whether) he had any questions.

12
142 She told me to cook lunch for her.

13
143 The teacher ordered us not to be late for school.

Chapter 12 | 특수구문

Unit 32	p. 121

강조·부정표현

A
1 any	**2** does
3 Not all	**4** walk
5 is it	**6** every
7 that	**8** who

B
1 do save food
2 It is the weather that
3 It was through me that
4 It was on the Internet that
5 It wasn't until yesterday that

C
1 nothing	**2** None
3 neither	**4** No one

D
1 Not every	**2** Not all
3 not always	

E
1 Onions do reduce tooth pain
2 It is some good rest that you need most
3 Not every file should be deleted
4 It was in the garage where he built a computer

F
1 Not all singers
2 He did deliver
3 not always recycled
4 It is a smile that / which
5 It was last weekend when

도치·동격

A
1 flew the bird
2 she was
3 does he
4 have
5 can the students
6 passed a motorboat
7 was he
8 did
9 that
10 a good doctor

B
1 could he find his wallet
2 is a lamppost
3 will I forget your kindness
4 she came with his family
5 did I think he would become a dancer
6 stood a stranger
7 can he go to an Internet cafe
8 did my friend say all day long
9 have I heard such a silly question
10 hopped a little rabbit

C
1 so did the ambulance
2 neither has he

D
1 Neither do I   2 So will she
3 So is he   4 Neither did he

E
1 came a beautiful woman
2 did he realize the dangers
3 and neither are the vegetables
4 the news that our team won the championship

F
1 lies a box
2 does she wear
3 have I seen

1	like	동사원형
2	that	that
3	It	It
4	where	장소, where
5	had	없다
6	Not	Not, 단수

7	O	not + always
8	lies a dog	동사 + 주어
9	she comes	주어 + 동사
10	does Bob talk	do(es) + 주어 + 동사원형
11	so is my friend	so, 동사 + 주어
12	neither will I	neither, 동사 + 주어
13	삭제	명사

1 144	Peter does like the hip-hop group.
2 145	It was Peter that met Alice in the park yesterday.
3 146	It was Alice that Peter met in the park yesterday.
4 147	It was in the park that Peter met Alice yesterday.
5 148	She had nothing to worry about.
6 149	Not every man enjoys talking about soccer.
7 150	Rich people are not always happy.
8 151	Under the table lies a dog.
9 152	Here she comes.
10 153	Seldom does Bob talk to Janice.
11 154	I am sick of fast food, and so is my friend.
12 155	She won't go to the party, and neither will I.
13 156	Mr. Morgan, a doctor, advised me to eat more fruit.

Grammar ViSTA Level 3

학교 내신시험 대비하기
Practice Tests for School

그래머 맵핑 완성하기
Grammar Mapping

영작 연습하기
Writing Exercises

문법 노트 작성하기
Grammar Note-Taking

문법 개념
스스로 체크하기
Self-Diagnosis Guide

오답 바로잡기
Error Correction

눈에 보이는 문법!
능동적인 자기주도 학습!

많은 문법 문제를 풀어 보고 알고 있다고 생각해도 비슷한 문제를 틀리고 실수하는 것은 정확한 문법 체계를 이해하고 있지 못하기 때문입니다. Grammar Vista Series는 문법 개념의 이해를 돕기 위해 체계적인 문법도식을 고안하여 시각적으로 학습할 수 있게 하였습니다. 또한 문법 개념을 명확하게 이해했는지를 학생 스스로 반복 확인할 수 있게 기획하여 자기주도 학습능력을 향상시킬 수 있도록 하였습니다.

문법 문제 풀어보기
Tests for Grammar

영작 연습하기
Sentence Writing

문법도식 학습하기
Visualization of Grammar

도전! 필수구문 156!
Challenge 156!